PEDALING
ON
PURPOSE

By Ken Rogers

With additional thoughts by Steve Anderson

Cheryl,
I hope you enjoy
our story as much as
we enjoyed living it.

Steve Anderson

Published by INSPIRIT Publishing, 201 SW 5th Street, Pine Island, Minnesota 55963.

Cover design by Michael Roth

Printed in the USA
ISBN 978-1-60461-634-7

First edition Revised and Updated December 2016

Visit Ken Rogers on line at www.pedalingonpurpose.com

To mom and dad,
Dorothy and Stan Rogers

You not only gave me needed roots and wings,
Your unconditional love and prayers
Continue to give me the courage to reach for the stars.

I will always love you with all my heart.

CONTENTS

ACKNOWLEDGEMENTS

This part of a book is the author's opportunity to publicly thank the people who have helped and encouraged him along the way to the completion of the book. It sometimes reads like a long acceptance speech at the academy awards. One of the reasons why people get bored reading this section or hearing those speeches is because it's not about them! It's simply a chance for me this time to "acknowledge" with humble appreciation those who helped me on this project.

First and foremost, I would like to thank my wife Robin. She has stood by me, believed in me and defended my "path" through many winding and confounding roads during our eighteen years of marriage. In my darkest and most confusing days she loved me and encouraged me to do whatever it was that I needed to do that satisfied my talents and made me joyful. Thank you for standing side-by-side with me even when you were afraid and not sure where we were heading.

I would also like to thank my three children, David, Amanda and Andrew. To varying age specific degrees, you have all had to put up with my grumpy moods when I wasn't doing what I should have been doing (writing this book!) and for trying to understand that I primarily work in my office. How many times have I heard when you asked me a question and I said, "Go find your mom, I'm not here!" and one of you innocently said, "Yes you are daddy, I see you right there." It's not been easy but I thank you for listening and giving me room to work when you wanted to play. I know that's still hard.

I want to credit the first person that really tried to get this book moving again after a decade of gathering dust. Jo Ellen Nelson was my right hand assistant when I was the National Accounts Manager at Hazelden Publishing back in 1993-94. On her own time she took my handwritten journal and deciphered and typed up my first real rough draft of 150 pages. She encouraged me to keep moving forward with the book. I did not heed her words, but when I finally got serious, her typed pages built my momentum.

I would like to thank everybody who helped me with even a single word improvement with my manuscript. My most important editor was Steve. I might have spelled "Denny's Restaurant" perfectly, but after reading an early draft, only Steve could tell me, "That is wrong. We ate at a Dairy Queen in Aberdeen, buddy. Don't you remember?" He read every word and kept me honest, exaggeration-free and green-lighted me on some pretty personal conversations and feelings shared on the road together. Even more importantly, his many insightful thoughts and unique perspectives shared throughout these pages made it a much stronger and better book than only my words could have ever conveyed.

I would like to thank Judy Hallgren, whose incisive editing during the first and final chapters of my book opened my eyes to the power of a fresh perspective and a great linguist. She really got my book off to a great start. Along with my dad, Judy also allowed me to email my book with each revision as a backup safety. Thanks for the peace of mind and your encouragement!

Finally in the writing process, I want to profoundly thank Wendy Rogalinski, my "East Coast editor" as I affectionately called her. She tackled editing the majority of my work as a labor of love and also stated she was "honored and proud to be a part of it." I reworked several pages many times over to my perfectionist personal approval and then Wendy would take those very same pages and still find ten words or phrases that she then rewrote, reorganized or cleaned up, to make a much better passage. She was tough, tender and thorough, my miracle worker whom I deeply appreciated. This is now a much, much better book because of her insights, perspectives and skills.

Helping me edit this second edition and finding my missed mistakes the first time through were the always meticulous Bruce Furu, who was indispensable, Carol Smith, Shawn Evenson, the precious Vivian Allen and an idea from Ken Venner that made for an even more valuable book.

I want to thank Father Jack Frerker, my friend and author mentor who helped me navigate through the muddled waters of self-publishing my first book. Your experience as a successful published author that you readily shared with me was immeasurably helpful and encouraging.

Michael Roth, my phenomenal graphic designer, living right in my own backyard as my friend and cheerleader, your cover design front and back was awesome. Thank you for your inspiration, creativity and hard work under strict time pressures several times. Your requested fee for your production services on the first cover design and then your sole request for only a fat tire the second time around will always humble me. Your campfire in my backyard will always await you.

I also deeply appreciated the first advanced purchases of my book back during the fall of 2006, especially Kerry Schad, who bought my very first copy and started this whole writing thing rolling again by personally booking me to speak at Mesabi Junior College. I will forever be in your debt. Thank you too, mom and dad, Godmom Joanie, Bill and Ruthie Brown and Shari Oldenburg, for your early belief in my book and your purchases, as well as "the gang," notably precious Val, Martha, Barry, Jen, Chris, Kendel, Jeff, Doc, Gale, Katie and many others who always asked, "How's the book coming?" and "Get it done so I can buy one!" David you especially never let up on me and I greatly appreciated and needed that. You all kept me accountable and inspired.

Thank you too my "founding members" who bought my book in advance in the fall of 2007. Your belief in me and your decision to buy my book and reserve your copy early, allowed me financially to get this to press and complete my dream 25 years in the making. May God bless each and every one of you.

And speaking of God, who better to close out in thanks! Thank you for my life, my family and friends, my gifts and for helping me get this book out of my heart, onto paper and into print. I only hope that it blesses and encourages your people.

May I serve you better and more efficiently with each breath I have left.

kcr

PREFACE

"As Willie and I wound up our conversation for the night, she reminded me that we had an 'obligation' to write a book someday about our exploits on the road. She had seen my little tape recorder and heard some of our stories.

'It sounds as if you have inspired a few people already on this trip. But if you write a book about what happened out here and even one person reads your story and decides to pursue their dreams, or take their own adventure for a cause or even seek the Lord because they were inspired by your exploits, they could change the world. Always remember that you now have an obligation. And also know that I want to read it when it comes out.'

She smiled and hugged me goodnight." - **Excerpt from <u>Pedaling on Purpose</u>, page 228**

Steve and I bicycled into Roselawn, Indiana on Tuesday evening, November 2, 1982 and later that same night at the home of our hosts Pastor John and his wife Willie, I dictated the above words into my audiotape recorder. I heard them for the very first time in December 2006, **over 24 years later!**

Ouch. I cringed back in December five years ago and the words today still cut my heart to shreds.

The reason that Willie's insightful, encouraging and *forgotten* words hurt me so much is because I knew 28 years ago after we bicycled back into Minnesota that we had "lived a good book" and that we would share our thoughts and our experiences. Steve and I both intended to write a book that entertained and hopefully inspired others to consider pursuing their own dreams and adventures. In fact we each started writing 10 pages a week for months, keeping each other accountable and moving forward deciphering our scribbled journals from the road. Then one day, a few weeks before Christmas 1984, Steve suggested that we take a writing break. I readily agreed. The holidays were such a hectic and demanding time that it just made sense to both of us.

For the next 22 years neither one of us wrote another word.

Our scribbled journals, handwritten partial first drafts, trip logs, audiocassette logs, radio transcripts, trip memorabilia and letters sent to us on the road all gathered more and more dust. In fairness to us, we did put together a 45-minute slide show that we have given many, many times over the years. But "the book" seemed like such a monumental task and an overwhelming project that we gave up on it. We both moved on to other careers, other projects and even other adventures. I thought about the book a lot and even had an assistant at work put some of my handwritten pages into a clean word-processed document back in 1994. But I never wrote or added another single word. As the years turned into decades, the weight of this unfinished project never, ever ceased to lighten.

"Nothing is so fatiguing as the eternal hanging on of an uncompleted task."
~**William James**

Inspired by an incredibly positive response to a **Pedaling on Purpose** multi-media presentation that I gave to Mesabi Junior College in northern Minnesota in late 2006, I finally realized that I had to immediately finish this book. On May 11, 2007 I was able to tearfully type the words, "The End." Although I was still over a year from being actually finished with my first edition, it was a life-changing moment and monumental relief.

This is a timeless story and one that has never been fully told. All the behind-the-scenes-drama and the experiences of almost seven months pedaling across America could never be shared in any compelling detail with 45 minutes of slides.

So enjoy the book that you finally have in your hands. It is the story of two very regular guys about 30-years-old who one day realized that they were leading lives that were a little too comfortable and not achieving what I like to call "significance." Over a casual conversation the seeds of a dream were born. What then ensue are the historic origins and first five wishes of Make-A-Wish of Minnesota and a journey of faith, courage, drama, humor and the adventure and friendship of a lifetime.

Finally, if you are inspired to take action on any of your dreams, adventures or goals *do it sooner than later.* I've often said that as great as it is to learn from your own mistakes, life is too short. It is much more efficient to learn from others' mistakes. It took me 25 years to write this book. Now that it is written and before the first copy was sold, I guarantee you that this was the best gift that I could have ever given myself. My world now has clarity, joy, and unbridled excitement at the possibilities, ideas for another 20 books and that huge weight of a gorilla or better yet, *King Kong* has been lifted. It's as if my best stuff inside of me stayed stuck until I finished this and so now look out world!

Finish your stuff. How's that for personal development coaching jargon! For now, sit back and enjoy. Let's chat again at the end of the book.

Be strong and of good courage,

Ken Rogers

COILED. READY TO STRIKE. I WAS ONLY TWENTY YARDS AWAY AND CLOSING FAST.

I *hated* snakes and this one looked black, huge and right in my way. With cars zooming over my left shoulder passing me at 60 MPH literally two feet away, and this repulsive creature now only ten feet dead ahead, I took my only option.

I headed for the ditch.

My 18-speed TREK bicycle loaded down with 50 pounds of gear, swerved and shook as I hit loose gravel and tall weeds. I desperately worked the brakes and handlebars, barely avoiding a painful and dangerous wipe out. Slowly crunching to a stop a safe five feet to the right of my coiled friend, I stared in disbelief.

I heard the howls of laughter from my buddy Steve, who had witnessed the entire episode. He coasted to a stop behind me. My slithering black, phobia-producing monster was nothing more than…*an old broken fan belt!*

My sheepish grin turned to a bellowing laugh as I imagined Steve watching his 6 foot 2 inch, 227-pound buddy almost wreck his bike in an effort to avoid a fan belt.

"Ken, Ken, Ken."

He could still hardly catch his breath as the roaring traffic tried to drown out his laughter.

"It's going to be a long, *long* year!"

We climbed back on our bicycles and kept heading west on highway 55, slowly leaving Minneapolis, Minnesota behind. We were free, free, free! This was going to be an adventure of a lifetime.

We had really quit our jobs, bought tents and bicycles, put our belongings in storage and had gone on radio and TV to tell the world why we were about to live on bicycle seats for a year.

Having said our goodbyes less than an hour ago, we were finally on our way.

CHAPTER ONE
IN THE BEGINNING

"Nothing is so powerful as an idea whose time has come." ~ **Victor Hugo**

"CAN I HELP YOU?"

"Yes, thank you. My name is Ken Rogers from Starr Office Services. I'd like to briefly speak to whoever is in charge of ordering office supplies."

The receptionist carefully studied my business card as I stood smiling in my three-piece dark brown suit, holding my leather folder and Starr Office Services product catalog. She seemed annoyed that I was in her presence and taking up her precious time. I thought how misleading the word "receptionist" was for this particular blue-eyed young woman.

"Well, I do all of the ordering and I'm really happy with our supplier, and so I'm not interested."

She was terse as she spoke, avoiding direct eye contact and hoping that her response would get me to do a 180 out the door. But I was trained in sales over the years and I knew that this was only an objection to be overcome, a small obstacle in my quest for at least a chance to make a presentation. It was late in the afternoon. I was tired and wearing down but the words instinctively flowed out of my mouth.

"What if I could show you how by ordering through Starr I could offer you a better discount with quicker service, would you be interested in a two-minute presentation?"

Her icy blue eyes dipped about 18 more degrees.

"No, I would not. We are very happy at this time. Thank you, Mr. Rogers."

She handed me back my card. Not a good sign.

My smile was weak and shoulders hunched as I headed for the door. Back in the parking lot, I slipped behind the wheel of my car. I felt defeated.

"I *hate* this!" I yelled to my car's interior.

"I GOTTA GET OUT OF HERE. THIS IS MAKING ME NUTS."

"I understand how you feel, Ken, but you know it's not a forever thing. Just make some bucks and have some fun with it while you're here."

"Two more, Tommy!"

My weary day as a salesman was finally over. Steve and I had promised each other when we were loading office supplies into our cars to deliver to our customers that we would meet at Victoria Station, a local watering hole between our two territories for a couple of cold ones when we were done. Tom McNally was Steve's roommate, another Starr Office employee and our good friend. He bartended on the side. Tom could always be counted on for both moral support and an infectious laugh that always brightened our day.

As Steve headed to the restroom, I thought about our selling and delivery operation at Starr. Most sales people sell all day and then go home. Not us. We sell most of the day and then throw on a pair of white overalls over our three-piece suits and deliver our own office supplies out of the trunks of our cars. As unusual as that was, I had to admit I enjoyed the change of pace, white collar to blue collar in minutes. Plus there was no more rejection in my day. Customers receiving their needed office supplies were always happy to see us.

Steve rejoined me and listened as I continued to vent.

"I'm really tired of spending the majority of my Monday through Friday hours doing something that makes absolutely no sense to me. I mean, in the overall scheme of life, who really cares if I sell somebody file folders and paper clips? If I don't sell them to my customers, somebody else will. Big deal. Honestly, what is it, the middle of September? If a truck flattened me like a pancake tomorrow, Fred would run another ad in the Sunday paper and have a three-piece-suited clone in my territory before the leaves turned colors. What a sickening thought. I want to make a difference. I want to stand for something that makes a lot more sense. For me anyway."

Steve started to smile with a faraway look in his eyes.

"You know my brother and I pulled off something kind of neat about ten years ago." Steve paused slowly…and then the words charged out of his mouth.

"We bicycled from Minneapolis to Florida on ten-speeds. Took about three weeks. We camped out along the way. We wanted to quit after one day but we hung in there and loved it!"

"You have got to be kidding me!" You did this on ten speeds?" Now my blood was really pumping.

"Beat-up Schwinn Continentals," Steve replied proudly. "I always had a dream to bicycle all 48 states after that."

"Wow! All 48 states!"

My mind was racing, adrenalin flowing and competitive juices kicking in.

"Has anybody ever done that before, you think?" I asked incredulously.

"No idea."

"Did you ever read about a guy named Peter Jenkins walking across America?"

"No, why?" Steve wondered.

"Well, it's just a great story about a guy out of college who takes off with his dog to walk across the country to see what's all going on out there. My buddy, Bill, in Carbondale, Illinois mailed me the story in a National Geographic magazine a couple of years ago and I never forgot it. Walking is too slow but now biking makes some sense." My mind started to pick up speed.

"Wouldn't it be awesome to just quit Starr and bike all 48? What a great physical challenge. What an adventure that…"

I caught myself in mid-sentence. I was talking and thinking like a little kid. Even the words were coming out of my mouth at warp speed! Something was igniting inside of me, deep inside, that made me feel *alive* and incredibly energized. I looked Steve in the eyes and slowed down my words.

"Steve, I am serious. I would really be up for something like this. My debts will be completely paid off by June. We could give notice at work, take about a year and really make this happen!"

Steve seemed excited too but ideas were pouring out too quickly. He was psyched but realistic. Fifteen minutes of sharing a dream with your buddy doesn't automatically force you to commit to a decision that will turn your life on its side. This was big stuff! Quitting jobs, probably selling or at least storing possessions, living on a bike seat for a year…

"I'm not saying no but I'm not ready to commit to anything tonight. I want to think this through. It seriously sounds tremendous. And I can't think of a single person in the world who I would even consider spending a year of my life with on a bicycle except for you."

We warmly shook hands on that thought.

"Me either, buddy," I quietly returned, "and that's a promise."

"But I have to feel that I'm not running from anything here but that I'm running to something else. That's a big difference."

"That makes a lot of sense; for both of us, really."

Steve appeared a little more relaxed after slowing us both down a little. I was the impulsive dreamer and he the practical pragmatist. We were a good fit. The problem was this was his dream and I was the one red hot to jump all over it!

"I really *am* pumped," Steve continued. "I mean…all 48 states!"

Tommy our bartender buddy had overheard enough bits and pieces of our conversation to understand the gist. He strolled over to give us some fatherly advice and counsel.

"You guys are totally, absolutely nuts! A motorcycle, maybe. But pedaling all 48 states on bicycles? Why?"

OCTOBER IN MINNESOTA WAS MY FAVORITE MONTH IN MY favorite state. I enjoyed the short ride to work and the crispness in the morning air. It was a golden day.

I slowly and carefully pulled my '73 Chevy Impala alongside Steve's parked Olds Cutlass. I got my passenger car door literally within one inch of his driver's door without taking off the paint and then turned off my engine. No way could he move unless I moved. I giggled as I hit the steps of Starr Office Services.

"Morning Don!"

"Hey Ken."

Don was the buyer for Starr since the first day they opened their doors. He was short, stocky, and a great guy after about noon. But my watch read 8:45 AM and Don bristled by me in a surly mood. Maybe he needed a better breakfast and more coffee before heading out of the house in the morning.

"Kenny! Good morning! You're looking rather dapper this morning. Even your socks match." My buddy Tom McNally was giving me guff within the very first minute of the day.

"I love you too, Tommy. Cold calls today. Need some biz. They may tell me 'No,' but they'll remember that they said no to a great-looking stud. How you doing?"

I loved Friday mornings at Starr. Everybody was always wound up and in great spirits after a long week hitting the pavement. Plus we knew that the weekend started in about seven hours.

"Ken Rogers, customer on line three. If Ken Rogers is in the building, customer on line three."

Our brand new PA system was wasting no time in getting my day jump-started.

"Ken Rogers."

"Yes, Ken. Glad I caught you in this morning. Jim Ferguson here from

Rosewood Industries. I need a quote on 172 solid oak desks. If it's possible and the numbers work, I would like them to be delivered to our loading dock first thing Monday morning."

Stephen Jay Anderson. I'd recognize that demented voice anywhere. He must have been in the front office behind closed doors. As usual, I didn't miss a beat.

"I'll make the numbers work for you, Jim. You've been very loyal to me over the years. As for delivery, however, we have some issues with the manufacturer of our wooden desks. They're made in Indonesia and the recent typhoons over there have us really back-ordered. Would delivery the day after Christmas three years from now be a problem? I'll drive them over myself in one of our larger trucks."

Steve broke character first.

"How'd you know it was me?" he asked laughingly. "I've been working on that accent in front of my mirror all week."

"You really need to get out more. Get back here with the men and leave Donna and the rest of the women alone. It's Friday and I want to be done with deliveries by 3 PM."

I hung up and watched him swing through the doors of the front office and join us, an assortment of true characters, officially referred to as the sales guys, checking our orders of office supplies on the shelves of the huge back warehouse before heading into our territories.

He walked towards me with a huge grin.

"Morning buddy! That was a fun start to my day."

"You're a dog. You need to find a friend that I don't know to call me if you really want to pull off your shenanigans."

"Hey, you got a second, Ken? Can you join me on the loading dock? I want to show you something."

Now, what was he up to? My radar was always up when he had that twinkle in his eyes, especially on Fridays.

"Sure."

As I followed him out the back door of the warehouse and onto the loading dock, Steve suddenly turned around and looked very serious.

"I've made a decision."

My heart started racing. I had not brought up the possibility of bicycling all 48 states for days. I knew that first night at Victoria Station that I was a "go" if I had a partner. I prayed that Steve would make the same decision without my prodding him. This was way too big of a challenge to not decide entirely on ones own. There were too many consequences. I also knew that he would struggle more with this than me. He had recently left the real estate field to take some of the pressure out of his life. He had actually been hired at Starr Office Services as a truck driver. He was simply too personable and a natural salesperson for Fred Ryan, our boss, to keep him "down in the minor leagues" for too long. And Fred was right, as Steve was having an exceptional first year in sales.

I tried to read Steve's face. I just knew he was about to tell me something profound that would affect my life in a huge way, regardless of his answer.

I finally realized that he was going to make me ask him. I played dumb.

"What are you talking about?" I held my breath.

"I'm in." A huge grin crossed his face.

"Are you serious?" In one unexpected moment a huge surge of adrenaline, fear and excitement swept over my entire being.

Steve extended his hand. Together we shook firmly and a little longer than normal. We both knew ourselves well enough and realized that this handshake meant the point of no return.

"That's it then." I smiled tensely. Oh, my God! I thought. Our worlds were about to spiral into a direction that neither of us had ever before experienced.

All of a sudden Steve started to laugh hysterically. Everybody handles a pressure moment differently. I understood the significance of the handshake but I didn't see the humor. I then realized that out of the corner of his eyes he saw my car practically glued alongside his. I had forgotten my little prank to start the day. My objective was always the same: at a minimum it was to make Steve smile. Mission accomplished. He was laughing so hard I saw tears.

"Well, we know one thing for sure," Steve laughed. "If we don't die somewhere out in the middle of nowhere on our bicycles, we'll probably have some funny stories to share in a book."

CHAPTER 2
DISCOVERING OUR CAUSE: MAKE-A-WISH OF MINNESOTA

"It is one of the most beautiful compensations of this life that no man can sincerely try to help another without helping himself." ~ **Ralph Waldo Emerson**

I HEADED BACK TO MY CAR WITH A THREE-PAGE ORDER IN MY hand. Nothing feels better or more uplifting to a salesman. I have often believed that nobody really hated selling as I had heard many people complain over the years. What they meant is that they hated sales when they were trying to sell and they were *not selling!*

I slid behind the wheel, started the car and switched on a local alternative rock station and started to boogie with 97.1 FM. When the song ended I switched to the AM dial.

"Sergeant Schmidt, I thank you very much for coming on the program and frankly I'm happy privately that we have made contact in this way."

"Well, thank you very much, Dick, and I certainly hope that somebody in your community will jump in and get something going there because it's a need and I don't know of any other way it's fulfilled in our country. It's a great thing to do and brings great rewards. We found out, as I think you represent, that all over the country people have seen this and said, 'Gee, what a good thing to do!' And when you can spread that kind of positiveness around the country, then we all kind of feel better about things."

"I appreciate you taking the call."

"Sure thing."

"Take care."

SHOOT! Why didn't I turn this on earlier instead of listening to music? I loved listening to KSTP's talk show host Dick Pomerantz in the morning. In the fourteen months that he had been on the air, he had developed almost a cult following because of his controversial, challenging style of interviewing. Whether you loved him or disliked him, he was certainly stimulating and fun to listen to. Barbara Walters had once been interviewed by Dick and called him the very in the business. But what had he and his guest just finished talking about?

I swear at that very moment he actually heard my thoughts.

"If you just tuned in I'll explain to you briefly what they have done. This is in Phoenix, Arizona. It began approximately a year, year and a half ago. A seven-year-old boy was dying. He had a terminal illness. He had leukemia. He wanted to have one wish fulfilled. He knew he was dying. His wish was to become a policeman; a highway patrolman. That wish was granted. Ultimately that led to the establishment of a foundation. And they've done everything from having children have their wishes fulfilled by formally joining the fire department to being flown to visit uncles in California or even going to Disneyland."

"I'm going to ask the audience, and I'll put it to you the following way because if it has to be done privately so be it. But maybe we can get it started right now. No funds right now and it's going to take a lot of work. We can say it will go nowhere very quickly but if there is any commitment out there from mothers and fathers and business people and if you happened to just tune in and you're driving in your limousine and you happen to be a very wealthy individual and you're saying, 'Look, that's something I'd like to put something behind, some effort, time and obviously some money, would you please give me a shout right now! Is it a worthwhile effort? One would think it would be but perhaps I tend to be the idealist. We've had a number of people call in off the air I guess saying that they would like to help. I need more people. What do you think? Should we try to do it? Because if we say, 'Yes,' then we go ahead with it. We have to put our work and our money where our mouth is. Are you willing, ladies and gentlemen? I'd like to hear from you, first-time callers, those who are not. Forget this is a talk show. Is it not worth it to all of us, as adults in our own small and/or large way to do something, to make a wish come true for children who are dying to terminal illnesses? Can you think of anything more fulfilling?"

"We'll be back."

WOW. I sat in my car, motor still running in the parking lot, my every sense overwhelmed. The clarity and passion in Dick's voice still resonated somewhere in my heart. This was it! This was our cause; the underlying and powerful driving force of our 48 states bicycle adventure.

I had been looking for a cause ever since Steve and I had shaken hands two months ago. Although our decision was primarily based on a mutual desire for adventure and a challenge, I also needed more meaning and significance in my life. I knew deep down that this would be an often physically painful experience and I knew that someone or something worthwhile should benefit from our 11,000-mile trip and assuredly sore legs and butts. A cause or fundraiser would also add purpose and meaning to the trip. It just made sense.

Three weeks earlier I had read about a guy in our local newspaper, the Star and Tribune, who had been involved in fundraising for world hunger. He had recently cross-country-skied across two states in an effort to raise money for the starving overseas. After reading this I had been unable to shake the image of a famished little child huddled in an alley. This had sounded promising. I called him up and told him about my possible interest of doing a bicycle trip fundraiser for him. He was pumped and asked me to meet him and a few other volunteers to stuff some flyers at his house one evening. I told him I would love to do that.

After three hours of stuffing envelopes and listening to these well-meaning individuals excitedly share news that the Second Coming of Christ that had already happened and that *Jesus was now living in a suburb in Pittsburg*, I could not get out of that house fast enough.

But Dick Pomerantz's plea a moment ago was different. I pulled out a legal pad and started to write, the motor still running in the parking lot.

"Dear Dick,

I heard your show today on the Make-A-Wish organization in Phoenix. Count me in as one who supports the idea and would be more than willing to help. In fact I have a proposition. I am planning to bicycle all 48 states next July and would like to raise money for YOUR organization with this trip. Please contact me at the enclosed phone number and we will discuss this further.

I hope that you are experiencing a tremendous response to today's show.

Enthusiastically,

Ken Rogers

Now *that* should entice them! Wait until I tell Steve. I hope that he's psyched too. I purposely did not mention Steve's name in my letter because Steve was no longer convinced that he was going to bicycle *all* 48 states. We had shook hands two months ago but he had since met Lori, a beautiful blonde and he was not quite as pumped anymore. I didn't blame him or resent her. I just wished that it hadn't happened now.

In Steve's own words:

I met Lori on August 17, the day Fred Ryan, the owner of Starr Office Services acquired Suburban Stationers, another office supplies company. A couple of days earlier Fred demanded that all of us salesmen get to Suburban at 8 AM, "And don't be late!" I was late. Everybody else was on time. Fred was pairing the Starr people with the Suburban people so that we could take inventory of everything in the store. Lori was the only Suburban employee left unpaired. It was my lucky day. I was smitten by Ms. Lori Marie Peetsch from the moment I laid eyes on her. She was 5' tall, had beautiful blonde hair, big green-grey pretty eyes and was as cute as a bug. I extended my

hand and said, "Hi, I'm Steve." She reached for my hand and said in a voice that I could hardly hear, "I'm Lori." It was very obvious that she was far from awestruck with me.

Ken got paired up with a 19-year-old boy that the other Suburban employees called, "Lips." Around 10:30 AM Ken came up to me and whispered, "Anderson, I hate you." I laughed loudly and went back to watching Lori and counting pencils.

In late November our relationship really started and it wasn't long after that I started thinking about telling her about my plans of leaving for a year.

Lori handled it very well. I don't think that she thought I was actually going to do it.

In fact her reaction was about the same as anybody else that I told. I would always picture them saying to themselves, "Well, that sounds real nice. But you're just all talk and no action. You'll never do it. You'll never give up your job. Why would you even WANT to do it?"

It really didn't make it any easier for me after I told Lori my plans. I kept falling deeper in love and my burning desire for going for "all 48" was slowly being snuffed. I was going through what I think anyone in my position would have gone through. I was wondering if this lady that I loved could wait a year for me or...would she find a more stable person to fall in love with and was this trip worth taking the risk of losing Lori.

Ken was beginning to see the predicament I was in and was starting to think he might be making the trip alone. He was very understanding with my situation and did not try to sway me one way or another but it was very apparent to both of us that there was a growing major kink in our plans.

CHAPTER 3
PREPARATION, BROADCASTING PLANS AND, AH…TRAINING?

"Two are better than one, because they have a good reward for their labor. For if they fail, one will lift up his companion." ~ **Ecclesiastes 4: 9-10**

"JOHN, I HAVE TO TELL YOU SOMETHING. I WON'T BE BIKING all 48 states alone."

"What are you talking about?" John Rubel, Chairman of the Board of Make-A-Wish of Minnesota, always calm and reassuring, looked clearly uneasy with my announcement.

"John, I'm bicycling the country with a friend, a very special buddy named Steve Anderson. He's been involved since the beginning. It was actually his original dream. But he couldn't commit to all 48 states so I never told you and obligated him to the challenge. But now he and I settled the issue and he is going to bike all the way with me."

John's cheeks flushed. He looked like a man whose organized game plan had just been shattered. I knew that my news was unsettling but his grave concern was really starting to bother me.

Bob Oakes did not look too happy either. John and I were sitting in his office at KSTP as I told them both that I needed to talk to them. Bob was the station manager of KSTP. I did not know him very well but I knew that he was someone that I needed in my corner. Pensive and carefully weighing his words, Bob finally spoke.

"I liked the idea of one man against the world. Traveling, making his dream come true, helping kids, painting houses to pay his own way. It's adventure, romantic. But now…*two* guys!"

He paused.

"People are going to think you guys are gay!"

"WHAT?" The word exploded out of my mouth. I never felt the meaning of this word before but for once in my 29-year-old life I was literally *"aghast!"*

"You gotta be kidding me, Bob! To the average person, picturing two guys together on the road should not equal *homosexual!* We are buddies, comrades, I Spy Bill Cosby and Robert Culp, Butch and Sundance. I just cannot believe that this is a negative thing. Sure, it's different than 'one man against the elements,' but it's not necessarily worse. Just market it differently!"

Nobody said anything. You could have cut the tension in the room with the proverbial knife. I felt very alone and very frustrated. My heart and gut told me that I was on the money and had nothing to be defensive about. But I sure felt it was me on one side and the world on the other in that small 10' x 12' office. I looked to John for some encouragement. He had been such a warm, fatherly supportive friend since I had met him three weeks ago. But now, I couldn't get a read on him. He was quiet, thinking it all through.

I broke the tense silence first.

"John, do you really automatically think 'gay' when I say 'two guys on the road?'"

"Well, to be perfectly honest, the whole idea actually makes more sense to me now the more that I think about it. I'd feel a hell of a lot better knowing there were two of you out there on the road watching out for each other."

"See what I mean, Bob?"

I finally had Make-A-Wish on my side, and now I was looking for the corporate sponsor on my side. Bob Oakes still looked ill at ease and unconvinced. His PR dream was all shook up. His eyes shot over my shoulder and out the door.

"Hey Dick! Come in here for a second."

Dick Pomerantz casually strolled into Bob's office. He had just finished his morning talk show and was on his way to lunch.

"Ah...Dick". Bob started slowly, "Ken Rogers, the guy planning to bike the 48 states for Make-A-Wish has just informed us that he's not going to do it alone. He's got a male friend going to do it with him. Now my concern is that the general public is going to have a problem with this and might perceive these two guys as gay. That would obviously hurt our image here. What do you think? Should we not let anyone know that Ken's friend...is it 'Steve Anderson'?"

Bob stared at me.

"That's right." I replied tersely.

"…is going along with him?"

Dick glanced and looked directly at me. He didn't smile, didn't seem appalled like I did that a "gay" theory existed simply because two men were going on an adventure. But I intuitively knew that whatever Dick was about to announce would be the final say.

"No, I don't see any problem." As usual for Dick, he was matter of fact in tone and demeanor.

"Can we get your buddy to go on the radio with you?" Dick asked me.

"I don't see any problem. I can't say yes for him of course, but I'll ask and I'm sure he'll be there."

I felt like the tide had turned. Dick looked at Bob.

"No, Bob, just as long as we get Steve on the air *with* Ken, I mean nobody knows anything yet, it should work well. I gotta run. See you on the 1st, Ken. Debbie, my producer, will call you and set up the time."

I looked at John and Bob. The atmosphere in the room seemed suddenly relaxed and confident. In one short minute Dick had turned it all around. Bob even had a slight smile.

"Well that's it. Steve's in. We'll see you on the 1st."

IT WASN'T UNTIL MAY THAT I REALLY KNEW IN MY HEART what I was going to do about our upcoming adventure. I guess all along the number one reason I knew I would go with Ken is because months before, we had shaken hands on it. I knew too that if I didn't go, from the day that Ken would have left without me I would have regretted not having stuck to my commitment. I knew that I would have ended up resenting Lori. It seems that no major decisions in one's life come easily and this was no different. But having finally made the decision to go, I felt much better and I knew that my life would be changed in ways I couldn't imagine because of it.

IT WAS A BEAUTIFUL, LAZY, SUNNY SPRING AFTERNOON IN Minnesota. Once you have endured a winter that can last almost a good five months in the upper Midwest, you really appreciate the warmth, colors and smells of spring. As I drove back to Starr Office Services to load up my office supplies for delivery, I thrust my arm out of the open window and took in the incredible fresh aroma of a huge row of lilac bushes near our warehouse. I was relaxed and carefree with the sun beaming down, relieved that another day of sales was over. Now I was able to return to my "boys," my fun co-workers at Starr, and simply load up my pens, paper and ink and deliver them to my customers before heading home.

But, when I allowed my mind to really think, I got very anxious.

I knew that I had to tell Fred, the owner of the company, that I was going to quit. My heart started to beat just a little faster as I thought about the scene in his office. I had already played it out in my mind at least a hundred times. I don't quit well. My bosses have never taken it well and I just had to do it. Soon. Tomorrow. First thing tomorrow morning. My heartbeat kicked up another notch.

As I rolled into the back door of the warehouse and headed to my shelf, I almost yelped out loud. I must have been doing a great job of selling the past few days because my shelves were full and there were a pile of computer paper boxes, a two-drawer file in its box and simply a ton of stuff overflowing out into the aisle.

Fred the owner ambled by. He was in a good mood. I was nervous because I thought that he could read my mind about quitting. That was impossible and stupid.

"You'll never get that all in your car, Ken." He laughed.

I sized it all up. Now my competitive juices were starting to flow.

"Let me get it all out on the dock in one pile and then I'll make the call, Fred."

"Won't make a difference. No way. But come get me when it's on the dock and then let's make a bet."

About 30 minutes later every one of my deliveries for the day was in a pile on the cement dock. My 1973 Chevy Impala was nearby. Big car. Big trunk. Big back seat. It was going to be close. No other salesman had a car as large as mine that had even a remote shot at this improbable packing challenge. I was about to run down Fred when he saved me a trip by stepping outside and looked at my huge pile of supplies and a two-door file.

"No way!" he simultaneously beamed and laughed that infamous Irish laugh of his. "You're pretty good but not that good. Supper will be on me next week if you can get it all in one trip. Vise versa if you can't. Do we have a bet?"

A small crowd of salesmen were starting to gather and some wanted in on the action. Deep down I was still bumming that I had planned to give notice the very next day. But I also wanted to win the bet.

"You're on."

Fred walked into the warehouse to get back to business. I slowly and methodically started to load the trunk. I started with the two drawer boxed filing cabinet in my trunk. It fit like a glove. Box by box, I slowly used every available square inch of space. Minute by minute my supplies got stacked, piled and crammed into my car. I filled my trunk so full that I had to bungee cord it open. Next, I filled the back seat. Finally, after several minutes, it was increasingly clear that I was going to make it. Steve watched from the dock with amazement.

"Looks like Fred is going to owe you a good meal!"

"I watched my dad load up the old station wagon for family vacations. I swear to this day that he actually made some items disappear. It's in the blood, baby."

I looked around at what I had left. It was over. Then…I had an idea out of nowhere.

"Steve, you got a few minutes before you need to take care of your orders?"

"I'm light today. I'm a go for whatever. What in the heck are you thinking and why are you smiling like that?"

Ten minutes later I asked Tom McNally to get Fred. When Fred finally opened the door, he saw a sight that I am betting stayed with him for a lifetime.

The dock where all of my deliveries once were stacked was empty. My car was running, trunk, back seat *and the front seat* were filled with boxes. I was lying on the roof of my car, with my left hand in the window holding the steering wheel. Steve was crunched down on the floor on the passenger front seat out of sight with his hands on the gas and brake pedal. Before the bewildered Fred could utter a sound, I shouted out.

"I made it Fred! It got close but I made it. I'll take a steak at Eddy Websters on the 494 strip."

With that I quietly knocked on the windshield and Steve slowly moved the gas pedal with his hand and away we went out of the one-way covered dock area. I could barely hear Fred's howling laughter over the giggles of Steve and me. As "we" turned for the street I had tears rolling down my cheeks from laughing so hard as I imagined what it must have looked like to Fred. I was glad that on my last official day of full-time employment I made the boss laugh.

Nothing would be too funny tomorrow. Even my steak was probably in jeopardy.

ON JUNE 12TH KEN WENT INTO FRED'S OFFICE AT 8:15 AM AND shut the door behind him. I had no idea what he was up to. Salesmen were always going in there to discuss discounts, commissions, or just to shoot the breeze, but very seldom did a salesman close the door behind him. Ken came out about 20 minutes later and I happened to still be in the lobby giving the women up front a hard time. He grabbed my arm and nodded his head towards the front door. When we stepped outside, he whispered.

"I did it."

"Did what?"

"I gave Fred my notice!"

I was shocked. I never expected Ken to give his notice this long before we left.

"I didn't tell him anything about you leaving, Steve, but he does know that I am going on an extended bike trip. He wished me luck but he looked hurt and I know that he thinks I'm nuts."

It seemed like such a long time since we had committed ourselves to this adventure by shaking hands, and of course by now we really knew that we were going through with it. But with Ken giving his notice, the reality of what we were about to do hit me like a ton of bricks. I saw this day as the beginning of the end of the good, comfortable, normal life as I had known it.

I had been in sales for the past eight years, since I was 21-years-old. I found sales the easiest way to make a good living, have lots of freedom and not be stuck behind a desk.

In sales you have every opportunity to work as hard as you want and experience as much success as you want. When I looked back, selling was the easy way out for me. I was getting a little too comfortable with my life. So comfortable, in fact, that everything seemed to be coming too easily. Even setting yearly financial goals and achieving them seem to hold no reward for me.

It really makes life more enjoyable when you have to suffer now and then and I needed to find a way to do just that.

As a seemingly relieved Ken walked away towards his car with an easy smile on his face, I thought to myself that I was about to get my chance to do that suffering very soon.

JULY 1ST. AS I HIT MY ALARM BUTTON, I IMMEDIATELY KNEW that today was different. I felt the tension as soon as the memories of my dreams faded. They were replaced by the realization that today Steve and I were driving to a 50,000-watt radio station to tell the world of our plans.

Riding together to the KSTP studios was truly a strange experience. The usual barrage of jokes and put downs weren't there and if a joke was cracked it didn't seem all that funny. Ken and I had never been in a radio station before much less guests on the Dick Pomerantz Show with our voices going out to thousands of listeners. Ken made me aware of this by pointing out the KSTP radio tower to me as soon as it was in sight.

"Just imagine Steve, in a matter of minutes your voice will be traveling up and up and up that tower and going out in all directions for miles and miles to thousands and thousands of listeners. Now don't get nervous buddy!"

His sinister laugh was amusing but still didn't calm my nerves as I continued to stare at a towering antenna that looked like it belonged to Jack and the Beanstalk.

As we were escorted to the recording studio, I was like a wide-eyed little kid taking in every sight and sound that I saw. I had majored in Radio and Television in college but had never pursued a career in the field, and certainly had never been in a major market television or radio studio. I was more fascinated by my surroundings than I was nervous about our impending interview.

We finally arrived just outside of the studio where Dick was finishing up a telephone interview with the mom of a young boy who had his first wish granted in Arizona about two years earlier. This family's story was the impetus as to why Steve and I were standing in the studio about to bicycle 48 states within three weeks. Dick's telephone conversation was being broadcast through speakers in the hallway where we were asked to wait until the break.

"I want you to forget about everything. I want you to have a totally clear mind when I ask you this question. When you think of Chris, what picture comes to mind? Give me the picture in words."

"The picture in words is Chris standing there when he first walked out of the bedroom with his uniform on and all the guys were standing around and he just gleamed. The smile on his face, he just was so proud. The smile on the officers' faces, they just brought tears to my eyes. And that's a very happy memory for me. I do not think of him in the hospital the last few days because Chris did pass away two days after they gave him the uniform."

"Therefore his final wish has become one of your fondest memories?"

"Yes it has. It helped me tremendously through the two years since he has been gone."

"Lynn Bergendahl I thank you very much. This is a very special day for us here as well."

"I thank you and for all that you are doing back there."

"We'll be back."

Dick motioned for Steve and me to come on. Dick and I had met earlier, but this was the first meeting for them. I knew how much Steve admired Dick, as a regular listener of his show, and I also knew that Dick was proud of what Steve was endeavoring to do. It was a great moment for me to see them shake hands.

We quickly got on our headsets and were seated next to our own microphones.

"…Make-A-Wish Foundation, Make-A-Wish Memorial, to allow a child who is terminally-ill to have his or her wish, ultimately their final wish come true. To help those children, I have two guests in the studio, Ken Rogers and Steve Anderson and gentlemen you are going to be trying something totally different. I want you to explain it briefly and then we will tell the people how they can help. For either one of you, Ken?"

"Well, what we have decided to do Dick, is we both made a personal challenge to bicycle all 48 states. So we have quit our full-time jobs and what we are planning to do as far as Make-A-Wish is that people would pledge for each state line that we do cross. We think this trip will take approximately ten months."

"Steve, why would you do it? Why, one, would you want to go to 48 states, only a nut would want to do that, and secondly, why link it up with Make-A-Wish?"

"Originally it started as just a personal challenge for myself and I found someone, Ken, who looked at it as just as much a personal challenge. Ken was the one who first introduced me to Make-A-Wish and it sounded like about as good a cause as you could possibly get to make a trip like this."

"Do you see your traveling to the 48 states as an impossible act?"

"Not at all!" Dick usually looked directly at the person who he wanted to answer his question. That way only one person usually talks at a time. This time, however, Steve and I both answered his question at exactly the same time with exactly the same words. Then Dick looked at me.

"How many miles are we talking about? Ballpark?"

"Ballpark, 10,000 miles."

"10,000 miles by bike over ten months?"

"Correct."

"What kind of training are you doing to do that?"

I thought that he was asking Steve as I had answered the last two questions, but we both paused. Neither of us wanted to answer this one. Thousands of people were about to be asked to pledge hopefully thousands of dollars for each state line that we crossed to grant special wishes to children with life-threatening illnesses. Everything was on the line. I knew that the real answer was, "We are not doing one single thing to train for this trip. Who has the time? Heck, Dick, I don't even *own* a bicycle yet!" Dick and his audience were not about to hear it today. After an uncomfortably long pause, I finally spoke up.

"We've both been working out, bicycling every day, just basically getting ourselves into shape." Although not perceptible to the human eye, I believe that my nose grew a couple of millimeters.

"How many miles a day do you plan to cover?"

"Hopefully, a hundred," Steve laughed nervously.

"To the best of your knowledge, will you be going through mountainous terrain?"

"Oh, yes!" Steve replied more confidently this time.

"I'm assuming that you can't do 100 miles a day in mountainous terrain?"

"No."

"We also better explain that any money that would be raised by those who would call the program and off the air, and we'll give those numbers out in a few minutes, for the Make-A-Wish Foundation, even though you are going to all 48 states and that will cost you X dollars, there will be not be a single penny from the Make-A-Wish Foundation which will go to help to defray your costs. Correct?"

"That is correct. There is not one penny that will be going to us. We are leaving with a set amount of money that will get us down the road apiece. When we do run out of money we will stop, paint a barn, paint a house, see what needs to be done in a given town. Basically we are funding our own trip." I felt great clearly stating that answer.

"So theoretically, if I called the number that I am going to give out after the eleven o'clock hour and said, 'I want to contribute let's say ten cents for every state, a quarter, ten dollars for every state that you guys touch on all 48 states,' I'm not paying for your costs. I'm not paying for your trip. Every dollar will go into the Make-A-Wish Foundation."

"That's right. Every single penny will be going towards granting a wish for that child."

"When I say a child who is terminally-ill, speak to me as a friend now, man to man, what's your reaction? What does your gut tell you? What do you picture?"

"My gut says it just stinks." The words jumped out of my mouth. Not very eloquently stated but they were from my heart and were part of the motivating factors of this trip now. I tried to expand my thoughts.

"When I think of a child I think of someone who has a lot of dreams. I believe we all think of tomorrow, tomorrow, tomorrow and to think of a young little girl, little boy who doesn't have the opportunity to have that very first date, to make that first prom or to play that first football game just disturbs me really deeply. It hurts."

"Ken you were very modest in the meeting that we had a couple of days ago, I'm saying this with respect to you. You don't want to be perceived, along with Steve, as being heroes in this?"

"No, we do not at all."

"OK, what role do you see yourself playing there? Because some will say, 'Hey, that's a hell of a thing you're doing.'"

"Steve and I are in a position where, both being single men, both in between careers, we have a desire to help Make-A-Wish. Some people will be able to do that by pledging money. We are in a situation that we can do it this way. This is just our way of kicking in."

"You become the impetus around which I can motivate myself and say, 'Well, I need an incentive, you're the guinea pigs, you go to the 48 states and I'll give X dollars per state." Dick's analogy confused me in the moment but he was right.

"Your biggest concern was, 'Well Dick, I just don't want to feel like I let people down if I don't do it within a certain period of time.' Do you feel that there is undue pressure on you?"

"I feel there's pressure. I think it helps. I think the fact that when we're climbing uphill all day long and I realize that there are people back in Minnesota and children that are going to be helped and people that are pledging and saying 'Hey, they're going to do it,' is going to fire us up."

"Steve Anderson, did your friend scare the hell out of you when he said, 'Hey, listen I want to try this and we know that we want to touch all 48 states anyways but now we got to do it because every state we touch, we cross, we're going to be able to generate x thousands of dollars?' "

Steve laughed and pounced on this question with all of his heart. You could hear it in each and every word he gave Dick and our audience.

"No, that's exactly what I needed to hear!"

"Tell me why? Why did you need to hear it?" Dick was really getting into Steve's answer.

"Well, when you commit yourself to something like this there's absolutely no way you cannot do it. I'd been on a trip before and I know that you feel like turning back once in awhile."

"I have to stop both of you here. Gentlemen, good luck with it. Your formal take off will be July 20th. Ladies and gentlemen when we return we will continue our discussion about Make-A-Wish. I will tell you more about how to make a donation right after the news."

Dick Pomerantz at the controls

Done. Dick shook our hands and thanked us for the interview. You could tell that he was really passionate about this cause and about our trip. This had not been just another interview for him. That was actually fun for all of us; or so I thought.

Steve and I walked down the hallway heading for the door leading back outside.

"I need to find a bathroom. Think I need to throw away my underwear. I don't believe that I have ever been that nervous in my entire life." Steve groaned and smiled weakly.

I laughed so hard I thought that I might wet my own pants! After our emotional interview had finished and a burden lifted, Steve took relief to a new level.

As Dick came back after the news, I could hear even more sustained fervor in his voice as he concluded our interview and reemphasized the Make-A-Wish cause, broadcasted again in speakers located throughout the hallway.

"…and for every mother and every father and every grandmother, and uncle and everyone of us who has ever been a child, and there is no one living today who has not been a child, the Minnesota Make-A-Wish Memorial Foundation is a very, very crucial, and perhaps one of the most gratifying organizations that you will ever find. The reason for it is because, 'We cannot stop', as Camu said, 'children from dying.' However, maybe what we can do is just to some extent, reduce the degree of the suffering they go through. What Minnesota-Make-A-Wish is doing, and will do, with your help, is make a wish come true."

"We have two gentlemen, Steve Anderson and Ken Rogers who are going to be bicycling around the United States, within 48 states, they will literally touch every single one of those 48 states, and we need your help. For every state they cross, if you care about children, do it in the name of your own children or your grandchildren. There but for the grace of God go they. If you could contribute a dime, a nickel, a dollar, ten dollars, a hundred dollars, whatever, for every state that Steve and Ken touch, so that we can make a wish come true for the children who have a terminal illness, it is something that we will all come away that much more rewarded by."

Steve and I hit the front door and the sunlight of the day. No words needed to be spoken, as was so often the case with both of us. We knew.

We were officially and humbly a part of something that was much bigger than either of us could have ever anticipated.

Now…a big part of the rest was going to be up to us.

KEN SOLD HIS CAR EXACTLY TWO WEEKS BEFORE THE DAY
we were to bicycle out of town. I decided to keep my car so I would have some motorized transportation when the trip was finished. I called Ken on the Friday after he sold his car to ask if he wanted to come over to my place on Saturday for a barbeque with some of our friends.

"Sounds like a lot of fun and I would definitely be there, but I have already made plans to spend one last weekend with Brad and Kari and the kids."

"How are you getting there?"

Brad and Kari are real close friends of Ken's from college who live in Elk River, about 40 miles northwest of Minneapolis.

"I'm going to ride my bike."

Yikes. I immediately started thinking that if he were to ride his bike 40 miles there and 40 miles back, he might get too good of a taste what riding a bike nearly non-stop for the better part of a year would be like…Not much fun! I can't say that I had trained for this trip as I had only bicycled around my neighborhood a few times. However, Ken hadn't ridden his new 18-speed TREK bicycle at all yet, and so I decided to make him an offer that I hoped he would take.

"Hey Ken, why don't you just use my car? I won't really need it this weekend anyway."

Without a second thought he said, "I was hoping that you would say that. You've got a deal!"

Realizing that once again we were on the same wavelength, preferring to remain ignorant of the physical demands of the trip, I had to laugh.

"Ken, do you realize that on July 20th when we leave St. Paul we won't have a firm muscle in our four legs? They will be like four strands of overcooked spaghetti, ready to fall apart at any minute. We won't have biker legs until we hit the west coast!"

Ken was laughing by now and shouted back in the phone,

"I know! Won't it be great?"

IT WAS TEN DAYS TO GO BEFORE WE WOULD TACKLE ALL 48 states with our bicycles. I felt ready. I had given notice and quit my job, sold my car and bought a bicycle the week before. I was a little concerned that I had not ridden it yet but there would be tons of time for that over the next year on the road.

I had also sold all of my furniture at my own yard sale, moved out of my apartment and into my good friend Mike Newman's house. I was spending three weeks with Mike until he walked the aisle and decided on a new roommate, his wife-to-be Deb. Since I was in the wedding as a groomsman, Steve and I decided to leave on our yearlong journey three days after the wedding on July 20. But on this day I felt psyched and ready. As I sat there fielding questions from friends at Mike Newman's bachelor party, one new question caught me by surprise.

"You do have this thing all mapped out, right?"

It was a great question, and one that no one had ever asked me before. Unlike previous inquiries about our training, I was finally confident of my answer.

"Oh, sure, we got it all mapped out. I've got the plans in my bedroom. I'll show you guys what I got figured out and how we did it."

As I headed downstairs to my sleeping quarters for two more weeks, I realized how pumped I got when I talked about this trip. I had no real idea what we were actually getting ourselves into but I was sure proud to be a part of it all. I grabbed my Rand McNally road atlas and bound back upstairs to share our strategy with my eager audience.

"Here we go. Let's see...yeah...this is the map. You see where the pencil line..."

"You gotta be kidding!"

The entire room was in an uproar. Eight grown men were huddled around me in utter disbelief. Bill Heiman, Mike's ex-roommate was the only one who could get words out of his mouth.

"That's your map?" He incredulously repeated. "I pictured these poster size Trip-tics from AAA hanging over an entire wall of a room. This is *all* you two have got?"

Everyone kept laughing and I smiled sheepishly but as my cheeks warmed with a slight red glow, I felt suddenly unsure of myself again. I had thought that my placemat-sized map route of the USA was pretty ingenious. I had spent a good hour or so getting a pencil line to continuously hit all 48 state borders with minimal backtracking. My big squiggly circle hit every single state border except Hawaii and Alaska, leaving Minneapolis heading West and eventually leading back in from Wisconsin on the east side. I was pretty impressed with the game plan. I had even measured the circumference of a quarter, found the scale on my map of the US and rolled the quarter all across the map on my penciled "route." I came up with approximately 10,000 miles. But now, as the very first observers gazed and continued to laugh, I felt uneasy.

"Where the heck are the roads? Your pencil line doesn't hit any roads according to this map!" That really got them laughing.

"There are lots of roads out there guys. I am sure there's plenty near our line. It'll all work out."

Newmie handed my map back to me.

"You are crazy, Rogers. I used to think so but now I know so. But I also know that somehow, someway, you will do it. Your butt may be raw meat a year from now but you'll bicycle all 48 states." He smiled with a confidence that I definitely did not have. But I did feel better with his endorsement after enduring a room full of snickering.

"Let's go burn some love letters in the fire pit," somebody shouted. "This is a bachelor's party, remember?"

CHAPTER 4
D-DAY AS KEN PRAYS TO NOT FALL OFF HIS BIKE ON TV

"The journey of a thousand miles begins with a single step." -Lao-tzu

I GLANCED AT THE CLOCK. 4:15 AM. I STARED AT THE MESS IN front of me. It was now obvious that there was more to do than time to do it before our 9 AM departure at KSTP with the media. Any sleep for me would have to wait until tomorrow night. I had to tend to the matters at hand.

I was trying to sort through and organize all the stuff I was leaving behind and box everything that I had not thrown out. I had sold everything I owned bigger than a bread box three weeks ago at my own garage sale, but I still had all of my photos, memorabilia, dishes, clothes, fishing gear, and tons of little miscellaneous. I had to keep at it because the sun would be coming up in an hour and the day would move on with or without me. Time was running out.

July 20th had arrived and I was about as prepared to spend a year bicycling 10,000 miles, as I was to fly Air Force One for the President!

The next three hours or so simply dissolved in a chaotic, unsettling fog.

"Come on in, Tommy!"

Tom McNally looked around dumbfounded.

"You all set?"

"Almost."

It was obvious that Tom could not believe the sight of me still in the middle of the floor sorting papers. His laugh filled the room.

"Ken, Ken. How long have you been doing this?"

"7:30 AM. *Yesterday*. Would you give me a hand with these boxes?"

"Sure. Your bike all packed up?"

"No time. I'm just going to stuff the saddlebags or panniers or whatever you call them full of dirty clothes and pack it the right way tonight. We're staying in Buffalo this evening at Steve's brother's and Lori's coming up too. I'm too tired to think. We better get moving. We're supposed to be at the studio by 9 AM."

Tom and I pulled into the studio parking lot as Steve and Lori were just getting out of their car. It was a beautiful, sunny and slowly-warming summer morning. Steve quickly got his bike out of the trunk and started putting his panniers on the frame of his bike, as Tom gave me a hand with mine. I felt rushed, massively disorganized, excited, nervous and numb beyond words. Although Steve was feverishly working only four feet way from me, he wasn't saying anything. He looked tense. I finally broke the ice.

"Well buddy, this is it!"

Steve glanced back over his shoulder at me as he finished strapping his sleeping bag to his beautiful blue FUJI AMERICA 18-speed touring bicycle. Wearing a bright yellow t-shirt with "Make-A-Wish" printed on the front, black bicycling shorts, tennis shoes and a six-week-old beard, he looked literally ready to roll.

"You set?"

"You bet."

He glanced at my bicycle all loaded to roll on down the highway. Looking puzzled, he took a step closer and pinched my tires.

"My God, Ken, you don't have any air in them!"

He sounded stressed and definitely irritated.

"They're all right Steve. Let's go."

"Ken I'm serious! You need 90 pounds of pressure in both tires. I bet you don't have 30!"

He pulled the air pump off of his bike and knelt over my front tire and started pumping like a madman. It was exactly one minute until 9 AM.

"Hey, you guys! Dick needs you on the air like NOW!"

The station manager, Bob Oakes, briskly walked up to us in his three-piece suit. He had that business-as-usual look about him.

"Morning, Bob. What are you talking about? On the air *now*?"

"Didn't Debbie contact you?"

Deborah Sturges was Dick's effervescent and bubbly producer.

"You and Steve are kicking off today's show from the studio. We have to fly. We start with you right after the news."

Steve put the air pump back on his bike and we quickly followed Bob with our bikes from the parking lot to the KSTP front door. You could have cut even the outside air with the proverbial knife as the pressure kept mounting.

"Here they come!"

As we neared the front of the building we saw several friends and family members waiting for us to wish us a safe, yearlong journey.

"Hey Pack! Great to see you!" Rick Palmer, "Pack," my old roommate and buddy from college was all dressed up before heading to work. Although Pack and I were the same age, he was always like a big brother to me, a stabilizing force and an encourager too. Boy did I need that today!

"Pack, stick around. I guess we start off inside with Dick for a few minutes but we'll be back."

Steve and I were quickly ushered into the building by a security guard. Another man with a television camera followed us into the building.

"Who is that guy?" I asked the security guy.

"He's taping you for the magazine television show, **Good Company**."

This was total insanity.

It suddenly started to hit me. One month ago that was *me* in the three-piece suit like Bob Oakes or the dress shirt, tie and slacks like Pack. Now dressed in a T-shirt, shorts and a biking helmet I realized to some vague extent that my life was about to change dramatically. Adrenaline was flowing.

"Morning Dick."

"Kenneth, Stephen, good morning. Thought maybe you guys changed your minds."

Dick was cheerful and relaxed. He was actually the first happy and calm person I had run into this morning. He was soothing my nerves without having any idea that he was.

"Put on your headsets. As soon as the news wraps, I'm going to…"

"Thirty seconds, Dick."

Man, we'd cut this morning close already.

"I'm going to introduce you guys and then take some callers wishing you guys farewell. After ten minutes or so we'll break for a commercial and then go outside and say goodbye out front as you leave."

"Five seconds, Dick. Three, two…"

I tucked my shirt in as the television camera in the booth moved in for a close up.

Our radio interview indoor segment was over quickly. Now we were finishing up our television taping. Everything was blurring.

"In closing, you two men are attempting an incredible feat and the hearts of Minnesotans everywhere will be going with you. From all of us at *Good Company*, good luck, God speed and safe traveling."

"Okay, thanks you guys. That's it."

The media blitz was almost over. Kermath Ward, one of the main coordinators and founding board members for Make-A-Wish grabbed my arm as we wrapped up the interview.

"The Star Tribune is sending a guy out to take some shots of you both at the Golden Valley Shopping Center on Highway 55. We'll figure on you being there in about 45 minutes or so. I'll see you there too. Good luck!"

"Thanks Kerm."

Steve and I headed back outside to the front of KSTP studios where a growing throng of friends and family were continuing to gather. More media were getting into position and Dick was outside now getting set up with microphones.

It was time for our final goodbyes. Steve was hugging his sister as I got in my final goodbyes with friends.

The clock had run out of time.

I felt numb, tired from no sleep, excited that our long-awaited departure had finally arrived and disoriented because this was such a new and explosive experience.

"Bye Deb. You take care of yourself while I'm gone."

Tears welled up in her eyes. I had known Deb and her husband Jeff for years.

"Me take care? You two take care and take care of each other."

This was not easy. I gave her a big bear hug. My eyes were clouding up now.

"We'll be fine. But pray for us."

I took one more look around. Pack came over and gave me a final hug and warm handshake. No words were spoken. I had to get going before I lost it.

Dick Pomerantz finally got our attention and we walked our bikes over to his sound guys with microphones and headsets.

My emotions were raw and the scene was surreal. I don't remember anything that he asked me or how I answered his questions.

After a few final questions from Dick and his live audience and a commitment to call in every Friday that we were bicycling to update his audience on how we were doing, Dick, Steve and I warmly shook hands.

"Ready?" I glanced at Steve. He gripped his handlebars and put on his sunglasses. He had a small rearview mirror wired to his sunglasses to see the traffic behind him as he biked. He gave me the big thumbs up.

"Ready. Let's do this!"

We waved as the small crowd waved and cheered. We turned right and bicycled onto the sidewalk as our bicycles now pointed towards California. I had only one thought; one simple prayer:

"Please, God, don't let me fall down on my bicycle in front of all of these people and cameras!"

I had never ridden a bicycle with all the bags on before. I *looked* like a professional bicyclist and yet I had no idea what to do or how to do it. For now, it was hit the streets and follow Steve. The sun was warmly beating down as we bicycled west into downtown Minneapolis traffic. I felt so fragile as cars and trucks flew by me only a few feet away. My butt was already becoming sore and I hadn't bicycled 100 yards yet.

"HEY! YOU GUYS ARE GREAT! GOOD LUCK!" THE YOUNG MAN in the dark blue Dodge Omni rolled up his window, waving once more and honked as he slowly drove away.

I felt like some kind of celebrity and yet awkward about all of this early attention. As Steve and I continued our trek westward out of Minneapolis, I thought about how the people who usually get radio and television exposure, fanfare and cars honking at them are people who have accomplished things of magnitude. All Steve and I had done so far was to tell people what we were *planning* to do! I felt deserving of nothing. I just hoped that we would not let anybody down and that we would be able to do what we had set out to do. But this was no time for doubts. Traffic was flying by and I was bicycling about 20 feet in back of Steve as we slowly were leaving the city limits.

"How you doing, Ken?" Steve was still facing straight ahead, but glancing into his rear view mirror attached to his sunglasses.

I flashed a big thumbs up.

We were on our way.

The reality of what we were doing was almost literally numbing. Ken managed to divert my attention momentarily from the chilling thought that I still had 9,995 miles left to ride. Less than five miles into our trip

with Ken momentarily leading the way, he suddenly swerved off of the road and into a six-foot ditch. I thought that he was trying to make me laugh like he did so often. It worked.

"What are you doing down there?"

As he sheepishly pointed to a large broken fan belt, I realized that he must have thought that it was a snake. He is deathly afraid of snakes and I just knew what he had been thinking. Forget about the wild grizzly bears and rattlesnakes out west. Broken fan belts still in the city limits of Minneapolis had one of us shook up already!

Our first break off of our bikes occurred about five miles west of Minneapolis at a Dairy Queen where we quietly sipped on chocolate shakes under the shade of a tree. All of the media and fanfare hadn't lasted even four miles.

Ken slowly turned to me and said, "This does not compute." I knew right away what he meant by that and in my mind I could not have stated it more clearly. I was also only fifteen minutes from home by car but I was already feeling scared, vulnerable and alone. If I had taken this trip without Ken I don't know if I could have made it even through the first day.

I PEERED DOWN THROUGH THE SPOKES OF MY FRONT WHEEL …"41.6." My little black bicycle odometer had just put in its first day on the job.

"41.6 miles, Steve. I hope that you realize I just shattered my old record for non-stop bicycling miles. My previous best day was about 12 miles.

The sun was setting on Mike and Kris's little house in Buffalo, Minnesota. We were spending the night at Steve's brother and wife's home, complete with home cooking, warm beds and even Lori. Tomorrow would be our final, real goodbye. Today was sort of a practice run and getting through all of the media hoopla.

Steve and I were both physically and emotionally exhausted. I hadn't slept in almost two days. I still had to properly pack for the trip, as my packs were full of dirty laundry. Beautiful little Lori drove up soon after we arrived with boxes for Steve and all of my "leftovers" from my morning packing job.

"Anybody else taking this trip would have worked out the details of what they were taking months ago. But not you," Steve yawned.

With both of our bikes in the middle of Mike's and Kris's living room, clothes, equipment and miscellaneous things everywhere, Steve, Lori and I went to work. The smell of some sort of roast drifted wonderfully from the kitchen. I felt like a man about to eat his last real meal for a long, long time.

As I was packing up my bike in the living room of all places, I laughed to myself thinking back to the day Ken bought his bike. He asked me to come over and take a look at his "girl." He said that it was in his living room, all packed and ready to go. I was impressed. When I stepped into his little apartment, however, I just broke up laughing. There was his brand-new, beautiful, blue, 18-speed TREK bicycle with four paper grocery bags hanging from the frame, two on each side of his front wheel and two on each side of his back wheels. They were attached to the bike with gobs of duct tape and jammed full of overflowing clothes. On his front handlebars he had tied a portable TV and on the rear rack he had tied on his stereo, two speakers and an electric frying pan. He also had two playing cards clamped on to his rear wheel with clothespins, a trick we had all done as kids. He lifted his back wheel and spun it for me.

"Sort of sounds like a Harley, doesn't it?"

Ken always went out of his way to creatively do things like this just to make me laugh. I did then and I did now in my exhaustion of packing up for real in preparation for the next year.

I was starving but almost packed up. Our bikes were looking very similar, and it looked like Steve and I would each have about 50 pounds of gear apiece. My front two panniers or saddlebags were hung on low rider Blackbourn racks, about six inches off the ground. Full of my socks, underwear, bicycle repair kit, spare inner tubes and toiletries, this low-riding balance would really help stabilize the bike when semis blew by us at 70 miles per hour. Over the rear wheel I had two larger panniers strapped on, full of T-shirts, two pairs of chamois-lined biking shorts, sweat pants, a coat, maps, our journals, pens and some cheap rain gear. On top of the back rack we both had our own sleeping bag and one-man tents attached with bungee cords.

I stared at both bicycles now fully loaded correctly with a glowing confidence.

"Time to wash up! Supper, guys!"

For possibly the first time in my twenty-nine years, I felt like I might be too tired to eat.

CHAPTER 5
PEDALING WEST THROUGH EXHILARATION, PAIN & DOUBT

"Do the thing and you will have the power." - Emerson

AS I WHEELED MY BIKE OUTSIDE INTO THE MORNING sunshine, I painfully realized that the time for me to say goodbye to Lori had finally arrived.

It was one of the saddest moments of my life.

She was fine until she went to hug Ken goodbye. Without warning she started to cry and barely got her words out.

"Goodbye, Ken. Be careful."

My eyes were starting to leak and I was getting a lump in my throat. I was feeling like a jerk for doing this to Lori.

We walked out to her car and hugged each other, not wanting to let go.

"I love you Steve, and I AM proud of you."

"I love you too, honey, and I'll be back before you know it. I'll call or write as often as I can. Make sure you listen to the radio every Friday too."

With tears in our eyes we hugged and kissed one last time. I waved until she had driven out of sight. I thought to myself how she must be wondering how she ever got involved with someone as strange as me. I also knew that it was not going to be a very fun day at work for her.

I turned to go back into the house and a neighbor across the street stuck her head out the front door and yelled, "Hey, aren't you one of the Make-A-Wish guys?" I was a little surprised.

"Yeah, I guess I am. How did you know?"

"There's an article in the Tribune this morning about you and your friend."

That quickly snapped me out of my blue mood and reminded me that Ken and I had a job to do.

I SAW STEVE SLOWLY COAST TO A STOP IN FRONT OF ME.

"What do we have?" He asked.

"73.4."

"This is home for the night."

"Home" was the side of the road. Some grass behind a clump of trees. Last night's memories of a warm soft bed, a great home-cooked meal and a little Hill Street Blues television were all behind us. This was our new world. We were both exhausted and no words needed to be said about "quittin' time." It had been a glorious day, bicycling through small Minnesota rural towns on a warm sunny day. Riding free and easy, getting the feel of bicycling together, growing more confident with every mile. This was a new frontier and new rules of conduct.

We'd already decided earlier in the day on our first guiding principle of the trip. Steve had rolled to a stop a good 100 yards ahead of me. As I glided up next to him, I casually asked, "What's up?"

"I'm starving. You hungry?"

"I'm really not, Steve, but the hungry man has the priority; the same thing with stopping to rest. The tired man has the priority. In fact, the hungry man and the tired man *always* have the priority. Let's make that our rule of the trip."

"Perfect. Let's just find a place to chow. But I like that rule!" Steve was smiling from ear to ear.

But now, our bicycling was done for the day. The once bright yellow sun was glowing in a deep orange and gently, ever so gently dropping towards the horizon. We rolled our bicycles off the highway and behind the trees.

SWAT!

I felt one, then three, and then several mosquitoes swarm my exposed calves near the tall grass.

SLAP! SLAP! SLAP!!

"Man, they are thick!"

We both unloaded our tents off our bike frames and quickly tried to figure out how to put them together and get in and away from these bloodthirsty critters, infamously referred to at times as the Minnesota State Bird.

We were exhausted, sunburned, sweaty, smelly, hungry and sore. Steve started to laugh almost deliriously.

"So this is living on the road, born free and all that! I want Lori! I want to go home! How in God's name did I ever let you talk me into this? I quit!"

I smiled but I didn't laugh, as I was too busy trying to fight mosquitoes and figuring out how to set my dang tent up.

I finally mockingly grumbled, "Why didn't I at least set this up once in my own backyard in the daylight before we left?"

"Makes sense, that's why!"

SLAP. SLAP.

The mosquitoes were literally tearing at our exposed flesh, as the sun was now completely down. I finally got the stakes down in the swampy ground and dove inside my tent and zipped it up. The poles to keep the nylon top and sides up and off my body would have to come later. For now I simply enjoyed my freedom. I took the can of mosquito repellant that I had stashed in my pocket and doused my entire body in the juice. Laying in my sweat and repellant-drenched body with my tent literally in my face, I gradually became very aware of my body and my breathing. I was exhausted. All I could hear was the sound of mosquitoes, crickets and Steve humming and bungling around in the dusk with his tent. A smile crept on my face as I lay there.

I had bicycled over 73 miles that day and I kept up with Steve all day. I could have bicycled even further tonight if the sun had stayed in the sky longer. It was not going to be an easy bicycle trip but I now knew for sure that I would make it. We were two days into the trip, a mere 112 miles from Minneapolis. But I felt like a little child whose dad just let go of my two-wheeler and I had kept bicycling all on my own down the block. All the doubts and anxiety drained from my body as the sun dropped from the sky. I felt a comfortable peace.

"What the heck are you doing in there? Your tent looks like a big blob of manure in a cow pasture."

So much for my thoughtful introspection.

"I'm giving the mosquitoes a chance to ravage your chicken legs and fly away before I join you. By the way, what's for supper?"

"Dinty Moore Beef Stew."

I disliked my own mom's homemade beef stew growing up. Tonight, the idea of canned meat sounded like a broiled medium rare steak.

"HEY, THERE IT IS!"

Steve was pointing excitedly and I pedaled quickly to make up the 60 yards between us. I pulled up alongside of him.

"YAHOO!" It was now only 50 more yards and closing fast.

"WELCOME TO NORTH DAKOTA." The huge border sign loomed ahead. We bicycled side-by-side on the shoulder of the road.

With only several feet to go, I glanced over to Steve on my right who spontaneously and without a word reached over with his left hand. I grabbed it with my right hand and held it high above our bicycles as together we shouted…

"Number one! 47 to go!"

We shot into foreign soil and then let go of our still clutched hands and glided to a full stop. We wheeled our bicycles back around 180 degrees and headed for the sign. It was time for our first photograph of one of us standing in front of the sign holding up a piece of cardboard with the words, "NO DAK #1."

"I feel like a little kid at Christmas!" I exclaimed. "This is great!"

We'd put on 72 miles already on a beautiful sunny day. It was 5:45 PM.

"I'll get a shot of you, Steve, with the…"

"No, no, this is your baby. You've been bicycling like an animal, keeping up and amazing the heck out of me so far. You deserve the first one. We'll take turns every other state line after this one."

I slipped a blank page out of my daily logbook. With a big felt-tip magic marker I etched out "NORTH DAKOTA STATE #1."

With the triumphant look of an explorer discovering a new and exotic land on my face, Steve hit the shutter and our first moments in North Dakota via a three-day bicycling trip were captured forever on film.

THE COOL, REINVIGORATING WATER PELTED ON MY HEAD AND down my face and body. A shower! It was the most refreshing sensation that I could ever remember. Taken for granted and often disdained for the first twelve years of my life before discovering the opposite sex, 48 hours on the road without one had been pure and living hell! Steve and I had bicycled 85 miles to Fairmont, North Dakota and had immediately discovered a city park where we could camp *and* take a cool, soapy shower. Our sweat, grime, mosquito spray and road dust all washed off of us and down the shower drain. It was heaven on earth. As I slid into my sleeping bag, the refreshing clean and cool marked a significant high after sleeping in my sweaty grime of last night.

I KNEW BY THE LIGHT VISIBLE THROUGH THE WALLS OF MY tent that the sun had risen and it was time to get up. Steve was already moving around outside. He was an early riser and I was one of those people who set an alarm to go off twice; once to break my sound sleeping and a second buzzer to give me about thirty more minutes to ever so slowly wake up and even drift in and out of sleep. Without alarm clocks, I had to adjust to simply getting up in one swift movement. I was already having a hard time trying to match Steve's immediate waking up routine.

"Holy Hannah!" I started to unwrap myself from my sleeping bag like I had done for the first two mornings on the road, but today something was very, very different.

"Steve!"

"Yeah."

"How are you feeling?"

There was a long pause.

"I have muscles hurting me today that I never knew that I had. It has taken me almost 30 minutes to simply uncoil my body. I just started standing about ten minutes ago. I can't even imagine getting on a bike much less riding it!"

"This is our third morning out here. After a painless first two days, I thought our training regimen was just about perfect. Now…OUCH…I'm not so sure!"

Steve laughed weakly.

We both already knew that today was going to be a very long day.

THE FIRST HOUR OF BICYCLING IN THE COOL MORNING sunshine was nothing less than excruciating. My legs were cramping, my shoulders, neck and forearms were sore, my back was sunburned and the insides of my inner thighs felt like raw meat. My butt was in a world of hurt like I had never known. The confidence and even cockiness of painlessly negotiating the first 200 miles or so of this trip was over. HOLY COW! Thankfully, with each revolution of my wheels I felt just a little bit looser and a little bit more pain free in my muscles at least.

As the morning wore on, the heat picked up and the wind now ripped through the golden stalks of wheat and slashed dust across my face. It was **brutal.** My legs ached again. Bicycling into the face of a 22-mile-per-hour headwind was painfully slow and frustrating. We had been bicycling for over four hours now and were averaging a mere seven miles per hour. With a temperature of 94 degrees and a glaring sun beating down on us, I felt some of the 226 pounds on my bones melting away.

But, in a strange way, it did feel good.

After two years of playing salesman and cozily living in the middle class suburbs of Minneapolis, I realized how comfortable and how controlled my environment had become. Daily and taken for granted were shelter, hot food, cold drinks, running water, keys to an automobile and even toilets. I took so much of life for granted. It was pretty easy to do. But now after only a few days I was already experiencing exhilarating highs and today…painful lows. Today I was feeling muscles in my body that I was unaware were even connected to my bones, tissue and skin.

At times I felt pain, a famishing hunger, parched thirst and hot, grimy skin from the burning sun and kicked up dust and dirt around me. But I was also feeling and smelling and seeing and experiencing wondrous things from my head to my toes. I felt so alive! Life wasn't blasting by me anymore. I was *in* it!

Broken glass shimmered in the sun right in my path on the shoulder. I swerved hard to the left and listened quietly for a possible hiss. No sound.

I bore down on my pedals and started to really fly. The paved concrete stretched flat and straight as far as the eye could see. Feeling like a powerful machine I charged forward.

I was finally aware of Steve about 100 yards behind me. He saw me pedaling hard and so he too started to pour it on. It was quickly obvious that he was trying to catch up with me. Determined that he would never catch me on this stretch of road, I put every muscle I could to work. Fields of wheat and cows were blowing by. I looked over my shoulders as Satchel Paige had warned me not to do. I saw a gritty, smiling Steve close to within ten yards of me and coming on strong. My adrenaline pumped.

"No way buddy!" I screamed into the wind. I was exhausted from our spontaneous burst and laughing from the pressure of physically keeping him behind my 18-speed bike. Ten more minutes passed of maniacal racing with nobody giving or getting more than one or two feet. Suddenly, I heard Steve scream behind me.

"Ken! Hold it! I've got trouble!"

He sounded scared. I stopped pedaling and slowly pumped my hand brakes. As I turned to check on Steve, he suddenly accelerated and raced by me.

"You jerk, Anderson!"

I heard laughter and watched him really pull away.

Our day was winding down. Four days on the road. We belonged out here.

KEN AND I HAD DEVLEOPED A CERTAIN FONDNESS FOR OUR bicycles. In our eyes they were incredible machines. With our 18-speed range, we were able to reduce a great many steep hills we encountered into molehills by simply switching to a lower gear. I was cleaning the dirt and grease out of my Fuji's chain, gears and derailleur when Ken asked me a question.

"When are you going to name your bike?"

Before we had ever left Minneapolis, Ken had named his bicycle, 'Acabar.' He had gotten the name out of an inspirational book he had read several years earlier called, <u>The Gift of Acabar</u>, by Og Mandino. It obviously had some heartfelt significance for Ken.

I had never thought of naming my bike before this, but as soon as Ken asked me this, the name "Betty" instantly flashed into my mind, and I have no explanation as to why.

"I just christened her 'Betty,' I answered.

"Betty? How did you ever come up with a name like that?" Ken replied in an insulting tone of voice.

With no better explanation in mind I told Ken, "From a book I read a few years ago, <u>The Gift of Betty</u>, by Og Mandino."

"Oh," Ken laughed, "I must have missed that book of Og's. I guess her name is now 'Betty.'" My humor seemed to soothe Ken's initial irritated response.

After our last break of the day, we hopped on Betty and Acabar and headed west towards Aberdeen, South Dakota and a fiery sunset. I joyfully yelled, "Hi Ho Betty...AWAY!"

As strange and thoughtless as my name for my bike sounded, we found out later that "Betty," (although spelled "Bette"), was the name of Og Mandino's wife of 39 years!

I SLOWED TO A STOP ALONGSIDE BETTY AND STEVE.

"Hungry?"

"Famished. You read my mind. This traffic is nuts too. Let's hit that Dairy Queen up ahead. I saw a sign."

It was 3 PM on another hot, scorching summer day. We were over heating. At a minimum we needed to get out of the sun for a while. We rolled into the outskirts of Aberdeen, South Dakota. I'd been humming a Chuck Berry tune, "Oh Aberdeen, won't you be true," but Steve had been quick to point out that "Abilene" is about 800 miles due south in the state of Texas and to therefore shut my mouth.

We parked our bicycles next to the window at DQ as we customarily did now. It was a safe place to keep our eyes on everything that we owned as we energized our bodies.

Slipping into a booth, I took out a map of the United States. It had been a long, grinding day and our spirits, for the first time since we left KSTP studios in St. Paul five days ago, were collectively down. The initial feeling of freedom and excitement had worn off and we weren't quite sure what to replace them with. I quickly found Minneapolis/St. Paul on the map and traced our path with my index finger to Aberdeen. Then I glanced towards the West Coast and scanned back to Maine. A very ominous and sick feeling hit my gut.

"Steve, look at this garbage. Look how far we have come. We have bicycled about two and a half inches on a three-foot-wide map of the good ol' USA! We have not even dented this dang country!"

As he studied the map, he too looked ill. A new realization was rolling over us.

Our adventure was overwhelming.

What had been so easy to say to everyone back home, what had been so free, easy and fun to do for about a week was now looming as an almost impossible task. We felt insignificant as we stared at the size of the country and the desolation of the mountains and desert to our west.

Our first feelings of doubt, fear and loneliness were bowling us both over.

"I feel like nuclear waste."

Steve never minced his words. I loved that about him. He was so honest that I always felt safe with Steve. I may not have liked what he had to say but I always knew that he would be direct with me, good and bad, and that I never had to guess or wonder what he might be thinking behind my back.

I tried to put on a positive spin on our current situation. I felt about one degree more optimistic than Steve.

"Let's just take this baby one day at a time and eventually we will get back home." Deep in my heart I was as devastated as he was. Today, one of us had to be just a little bit stronger.

Steve smiled weakly and told me in no uncertain terms to get the map folded up and put away so that he could finish his milkshake in peace.

He sat in a state of quiet. Finally he spoke.

"We don't have too many other choices do we? Let's put some more miles on before dark and before I get sick." Steve looked as unsure of himself as I had ever seen him. It was my turn to be strong for him. I knew that his time would come for me many times before this was over.

"We can do this buddy. Let's get out of here, put on a few miles and find a patch of land to call home. I promise you that we will be okay."

CHAPTER 6
O'NEILL, NE - THE AMERICA THAT RARELY MAKES THE NEWS

"To read the papers and to listen to the news...one would think the country is in terrible trouble. You do not get that impression when you travel the back roads and the small towns do care about their country and wish it well."
~ Charles Kuralt

I BLINKED TWICE. MY HEAD WAS THICK. I HAD NO IDEA where I was. A semi rolled by and the sun kept beating her heat on my head. I very groggily woke up. Wow. It was one of those hard, drooling mid-day naps. I finally figured it all out as I saw the big "Welcome to Nebraska" sign a few feet away. Steve and I had triumphantly bicycled into state #3, took our photos and promptly fell asleep in the shade of a huge oak tree just off the road. Steve had obviously taken a nap as well. He groggily awoke and stirred about.

"I feel like warmed-up-nine-day-old liver!" I quietly said.

"I'm feeling pretty good too," Steve mumbled.

We were both definitely beat out and sore from our cumulative miles. But we couldn't call it a day yet at 50 miles because we were in the middle of nowhere. In Nebraska, when I say nowhere, I mean nowhere as in cornfields, an empty highway, more cornfields and a relentless sun.

"How far to home?" Steve yawned and quietly asked.

I studied the atlas strapped to my bike.

"Looks like O'Neill is the next town of any size. I figure about 30 more miles."

"30 miles?"

Steve wasn't too happy *before* this conversation. This new info wasn't helping to change things at all.

"Tell you what. I'll lead and break every ten miles."

Only I had an odometer on my bike, something I really enjoyed. It was a small 2" x 1" box connected to my front wheel axle. It helped me to set little mileage goals to keep my sanity. Today was one of those times when it was a perfect tool to keep us both focused.

"Let's roll, buddy. There's gotta be a cold one waiting for us at the end of the line." Encouragement can come in many forms.

As my sore legs straddled my bike frame and I eased down the road, a quick glance ahead dampened my already exhausted spirits. The flat lands of western Minnesota and North and South Dakota were indeed history. The road ahead was winding uphill at a steep grade and my legs were really feeling the tension.

I shifted into my smallest gear and charged the hill with all the adrenaline I had. With burning legs and heavy breathing I edged to the crest and down the backside. More hills greeted my short-lived victory over my savage hill.

A solid hour later, I rolled to a stop at 60.0 miles, ten grueling miles from our previous nap site under a tree. Steve rolled in less than a minute behind me.

"Wow", Steve wearily exclaimed. "What are we going to do when we hit the Rockies?"

"Hopefully our legs will look like tree stumps by then."

All I knew about Nebraska was that it grew a lot of corn, Johnny Carson was born there and to drive across it in a car would nearly kill you with boredom. In my first ever hour in the state myself, I learned that it had some steep hills on the north side.

I had strained my left knee two days ago trying to keep up with a truck so that I could take advantage of its draft. These hills were not helping one bit. I tried to take some pressure off my knee by pushing harder with my right leg. This helped a little but now my right Achilles tendon was hurting from the added pressure. I was in a no win situation. Either I strain my left knee or my right tendon.

I was in constant pain and running out of gas.

I slammed down a good half quart of water before I slipped my water bottle back into its metal bracket attached to my bike frame. I always did my water breaks as I coasted down the back of a hill. I leaned forward and stared down at my odometer. It read 69.2. It was now less than .8 of a mile until our last break before the final ten miles into O'Neill. I glanced back. No Steve. I had seen him a few miles back and so I knew that he was still with me.

The last seven miles had been the most grueling seven miles of the trip so far. I was sunburnt, windburnt, muscle burnt and totally drained.

The hills had taken the guts out of me. Bicycling 50 pounds of equipment and myself almost straight up had left me groping for gears that weren't on my bike. My smallest gear had not been enough to ease the pain in my burning legs. 69.8. Almost there. Keep moving my legs, I silently commanded. 69.9. I bore down with all that I had left. Wheat fields and farmhouses ever so slowly crept by. 70.0

I stopped immediately. Leaning my bike against a mailbox two feet away, I slumped to the roadside gravel on the shoulder as I finished off my water. Waiting for Steve, I closed my eyes; the only sound was the distant bellowing of cows.

After several minutes I finally heard a familiar voice down the road creeping slowly closer.

"Please tell me, *please* tell me that we have gone more than ten miles. Fifteen? Twenty? "

"Ten."

"Ten?"

"Ten."

"I wanna die. I'm going home."

All conversation ceased. Steve joined me on the shoulder of the road; our bare, sweaty backs sprawled in the dirt and gravel. There was no traffic as the sun dropped towards the horizon, softening her glow but none of her heat.

I took a drink from my water bottle and poured the rest over my head. Ken, looking as bad as I felt, turned his head towards me so that his cheek was in the dirt and gravel too.

"You have any water? I just ran out."

I could feel the last of my water dripping from my hair on the back of my head. I said apologetically, "Oh, I'm sorry. I just poured it over my head."

"That's okay. I think O'Neill is only about nine miles down the road."

Ken would have normally said something like, "That's alright. I ran out of water 40 miles back, but I can just lick up the water that you poured in the dirt. Don't worry. I'll be alright."

He would go on and on like this, trying to make me feel guilty, but at this moment we were both too tired to joke around.

Ten minutes passed.

"Hey! What are you guys doing?' An eleven-or-so-year-old boy on an old Schwinn bike had come up the long driveway in front of the house and the mailbox that we had leaned our bikes. He was so happy, so curious, so friendly. His enthusiasm made me sick. I was in no mood.

"We're resting," I weakly replied without opening my eyes.

"Where are you guys going? Where you from? What's all that stuff on your bike?"

I turned towards Steve, my eyes pleading for help. We always tried to be friendly and courteous when people of all ages would ask us questions. And sometimes they were insistent, inconsiderate and dumb questions. But between the two of us, one would invariably take the lead and handle our curious friend while the other one relaxed or finished his meal. But today Steve's glance in the dirt responding to my pleading stare told me he too didn't have the strength or patience to be very kind.

Neither one of us answered his questions, hoping our silence and closed eyes would discourage him to bicycle back home. No such luck.

"Hey, you guys want something cold to drink?"

My empty water bottle lay in the gravel.

"We got some iced tea back at the house."

I hated iced tea. I mean I *really* hated iced tea. But Steve and I had a major rule we collaborated on during the first few days of the trip.

NEVER SAY NO TO A REASONABLE OFFER. A yes to any offer could be an opportunity in disguise.

"Thanks. We'll take you up on that."

Steve and I grabbed our bikes and slowly walked them down the long driveway to the house. We introduced ourselves to our new little friend, 12-year-old Leo. I think we both felt bad about being short with him. Steve and I thoroughly enjoyed kids, I guess in part because as Steve often said, we were so much like them. Leo seemed to be a very nice boy, with the manners of a young gentleman. He looked like a typical American farm boy, skinny with a well-tanned freckled face, T-shirt and blue jeans.

The kitchen was a disaster area. Dirty dishes were piled high. Everything that had a place seemed at best to be only near where it was supposed to be.

"Dad, these are two guys I found up on the road." I don't believe that I had ever been introduced to someone exactly that way but it was true.

"Pete Matthews."

The burly man shook our hands and smiled a smile that filled the kitchen.

"Iced tea and donuts?"

"Sounds great. I'm Ken Rogers and…"

"Steve Anderson."

"Please to meet you both. You look like hell. Please sit down." I loved his heavy twang.

"Hey honey. Guys this is my wife, Gladys, and my daughters Brenda and Cindy. Leo found these guys up on the road."

Dirty, flushed with overheated bodies and dying for a cool anything, Steve and I had found our first family and hospitality on the trip. It felt wonderful.

Quick with a joke and even quicker with a laugh, Pete Matthews was just a fun guy to be around. After filling us with iced tea, water and doughnuts, he offered us everything that he had to eat in his house. Ken and I would have eaten everything he had inside, plus the hogs, cows and chickens out back, but we politely declined.

Pete saw right through us.

He grilled us big, fat juicy steaks on the grill. While Pete was grilling, Gladys washed all of our clothes and the kids introduced us to all of their farm animals and let us bottle-feed some of their young calves.

After a delicious dinner, Ken and I took baths and then we all retired to the living room where we simply all shared story after story. While we chatted, ten and eight-year-old Brenda and Cindy massaged our tired feet with lotion.

It was wonderful to be a part of this special family, if for only one night. They had taken us in with open arms, no questions asked and had trusted us completely. A bond had grown very quickly between all of us.

A long, brutal day was serendipitously ending at exactly mile 70.0 and with the exceptional gift of the Pete Matthews family hospitality.

I HEARD THE ROOSTER SCREAMING "GOOD MORNING"ABOUT ten feet from my left ear. It was too early for a wake up call. Still in a fog from a delightful dream about an old girlfriend, I slowly cleared my head and checked my surroundings. I was wrapped in a blanket on a big, brown couch in the Matthews' living room. It was squishy in all the right places. The sun wasn't quite up yet but I could see the huddled outline of Steve across the room on a cot. The rooster belted his "Cock a Doodle" once again.

Steve stirred slightly.

"Happy Birthday, buddy!"

"Thanks. Goodnight."

"Come on! Rise and shine! Big day. July 28. You only turn 30 for one day in a lifetime! The early bird catches the worm! Let's get one for the Gipper! Carpe Diem! Blah, blah, blah!"

"Would you shut up already? I'm up. I'm up!"

This sure was a switch. I did feel wide-awake and ready for the day. Normally, Steve was Mr. Sunshine at the crack and I was in the deep fog. But the tables were turned today for some reason and I was loving it.

After last night's incredible hospitality, I felt like a new man; renewed and ready for the road!

"Happy Birthday Steve!" I tipped off our hosts last night and so Steve was greeted with a chorus of greetings as we walked into the kitchen.

During a scrumptious farm breakfast of sausage, eggs and fried potatoes, Leo, Brenda and Cindy took turns desperately trying to talk Steve and me into staying just one more day. It was a tempting idea. These kids were also way too cute and kind to us for Steve and I to say "No way" in any sort of a harsh way. Gladys finally came to our rescue.

"That's enough kids. I'm sure that Steve and Ken would love to stay another day but they have a long way to go and I know they want to put on as many miles as they can while the weather's good. Now, eat your breakfast and let Ken and Steve eat theirs."

What an insightful and greatly appreciated response. She really cut to the quick and actually explained our position perfectly. As much as we already loved this family, the road was beckoning and if the wind stayed calm it could be another 80 or 90-mile day.

We all got in our hugs after breakfast and heading the five miles into little O'Neill, a town of about 3,000 people.

"I'M SORRY. I DON'T HAVE ANY CAKES LEFT TODAY."

A bakery with no cakes left at noon. This was weird. I realize that I could be considered a "city boy" coming from Minneapolis but I had also lived in small towns at different times in my young life and a bakery with no cakes made no sense.

"How about pies?"

Ten minutes later I snuck back to my bicycle with a chocolate cream pie and a banana cream pie to help celebrate Steve's birthday. This should be interesting on a bicycle in 90-degree heat. Somehow, someway I was determined that today would be special for Steve. I am a big birthday guy. I think of it as your own personal New Year. It should be celebrated and a special memory created. Steve had no Lori, no family and no friends but me. If we were back in Minneapolis, Steve would be having a huge surprise bash of some sort. I promised myself that I would do my best to make up for the lack of buddies celebrating with Steve. Being his 30th, I felt a little extra pressure.

At a minimum we would have a pie together, a cold brew, I would sing him "Happy Birthday," we might see a movie and we would *not* bicycle 90 miles and hurt ourselves today. We would get in some miles and work our way down the road but it would be at a relaxed pace. Although today was only Wednesday, with the sunshine, a special birthday and last evening's relaxing, it felt like a Friday. Today would be a good day. I would make it a good day.

Steve was still cleaning his bicycle chain in some oil at the corner gas station where I had left him. He had no idea that I was birthday cake shopping.

"Hey, there goes Pete's car!"

Although we had already said goodbye to Pete, just seeing his station wagon turn down an alley made me feel giddy and happy. We had never hit a town yet where we had a friend and today, there was Pete turning a corner. I don't know exactly what I was thinking but I impulsively jumped on my bike and tried to catch up with Pete.

After about six turns through streets and alleys, I found him on his way into a house that he was painting. Pete was a professional housepainter by trade and he supplemented his income by buying, raising and selling hogs.

He was happily shocked to see me.

"What are you guys doing?" he excitedly asked.

"Cleaning bikes. We're over at that little gas station on Main Street trying to get all of the sand and junk out of our chains and derailleur. After last night's clean clothes and clean bodies we are on a roll! I bought Steve a birthday pie that I'm hiding in my saddlebags. Not exactly sure what the plan for the day is."

"Well if you are both still in town and no place you have to be yet, can I at least buy you guys a birthday beer before you leave town?"

It wasn't even 1 PM and Steve and I had only five miles under our belts so far. But this big man with a smile and a mischievous twinkle in his eye had me already second-guessing my tentative plans to see a movie and get some more miles on. I also knew that all that easy living last night had taken off my edge as a "road warrior." I felt clean, fresh and comfortable and more up for play than pain.

I caught myself smiling back at Pete's suggestion.

"Let's get back to Steve and figure this out. I'm leaning, Pete. I'm leaning."

Pete laughed heartily. I could already see where this was going.

From the moment we got into Pete's car, he was determined to make my 30th birthday a day I wouldn't forget. We drove all over O'Neill seeing Pete's buddies. Wherever we went, someone knew Pete. Although we certainly had no idea who he was when we pulled up to his house last night, it was quickly becoming apparent that he was one of if not the most popular person in town! We were introduced to many of Pete's good friends, Joe Cavanaugh, a rodeo announcer and pig farmer, Joe's old farm hand Frank and Larry Wanser, an auctioneer at the livestock sale barn. This was a whole new world full of people with occupations that we had never really known existed.

We eventually sat at a local pub and shared our story with everybody, including the fact that it was my birthday. The day just kept gaining momentum and energy. We eventually headed out to Joe's ranch for a chicken barbeque, corn on the cob and lots of laughter with a ton of people. Ken surprised me with a chocolate cream pie and a banana cream pie in lieu of a birthday cake and had arranged for Lori and many of my friends to call me at Joe's house. That was a totally unexpected surprise. I had not talked to anyone since we had left St. Paul eight days ago.

It was and I'm sure will remain the best birthday that I ever had. These Nebraska folks certainly showed us city boys what country hospitality was all about!

"WHO'LL GIVE ME 30, 30, 30, HEY, 35, 35, 35, 35, 35, GIVE ME 40, 40, 40, 40, Hey, Hey, Hey, Hey, Hey, 60, 60, 60, 60…"

I had seen furniture and miscellaneous stuff get auctioned before but never had I seen horses, cattle, sheep and pigs sold to the highest bidder. Our new buddy, Larry Wanser, was center stage, microphone in hand. We had promised him at last night's impromptu birthday bash for Steve that we would see him at his job before we finally climbed back on *our* "horses," Acabar and Betty.

We sat next to Pete and his son Leo on long wooden benches in the small but crowded auction barn. About 200 people were watching and bidding as livestock were slowly herded group by group to the center of the dirt floor barn to be viewed, bid on and sold. All the smells of country animals filled the enclosed arena.

I watched in admiration and disbelief as Larry barked out his auctioneer lingo at what seemed to be 1,000 words per minute. He was good. I marveled at how he could talk so fast and how he could pick up the subtlest signals from the farmers sitting around him, indicating that they were bidding on a particular pig, cow or horse.

I would follow Larry's eyes to see which farmer he was getting signals from. After awhile I could see one farmer touch his ear lobe and Larry would call out the number he had pinned to his shirt, letting that farmer know that he had acknowledged his bid. Another would just brush his nose, another nod his head. I was afraid to move for fear that Larry would call out my name for some inadvertent body signal and I would end up buying a pig that I would now have to haul around the country on my bicycle.

"Hey Pete, you got some chew?"

A beautiful little blonde girl about eight years old, pigtails and pleading brown eyes asked a question that I thought was reserved for 40-year-old truck drivers and professional baseball players. I knew that Pete would be flabbergasted by her innocent little request.

"You bet, Melissa."

He reached for his pocket.

I stared in total disbelief as precious little Melissa took a pinch from Pete's can of Skoal and placed it in her mouth. Sitting on the wooden bench next to Pete she calmly chewed, watched the bidding on a Holstein steer and then spit onto the cement floor.

I glanced at Steve. It was obvious that he too could not believe his eyes. We chuckled under our breath.

"Hey Pete, we really have to head on down the road."

"Taking off, huh?" Pete slid out of his seat and escorted us slowly towards the parking lot, stopping in the boiler room where our loaded bicycles were safely locked away.

Larry joined Pete and Joe, who had happily sold three of his own pigs, in the parking lot. We all warmly shook hands and said our farewells. After so much incredible hospitality, warm beds, excellent food and friendship, Highway 281 heading south out of town looked awfully cruel and frightening. But I felt like David Janssen in The Fugitive, that we had made some special friends.

Now the road beckoned us.

"There will be another time," one of the guys said as we slowly bicycled away.

You bet there will, I hoped and prayed to myself.

CHAPTER 7
EQUIPMENT FAILURE - KEN'S WHEEL & STEVE'S "WHEEL"

"I have always depended on the kindness of strangers." ~ **Tennessee Williams**

MY BACK WHEEL TORE TO THE RIGHT. SOMETHING WAS seriously wrong. The whole bicycle wobbled and shook. Rubber scraped metal.

"Steve!"

He had bicycled out of sight. Dang it. I couldn't even turn the pedal. The pressure of the tire against the frame was too intense. I jumped off of my bike and took a long, hard look at the damage. What in the heck had happened? The whole back tire had just snapped as I roared over a bridge entering Grand Island, Nebraska during rush hour traffic.

It was Friday evening. It was time to find a home for the night and a cold brew to quench our thirst of bicycling a sweltering 70 miles. But instead I had a twisted and unridable bike in heavy traffic and a bicycling partner who had no idea that I was in trouble.

I slowly walked my disabled machine down the edge of the highway towards the direction where Steve had to be. Cars and trucks continued to blow by me heading home for the week. I was bummed. I knew so little about fixing a bicycle. Steve still helped me fix my flat tires. It was a very insecure feeling knowing that I could not handle myself when mechanical problems arose. Emotionally, mentally and physically I felt so confident since the second day on the road. But now...I was tired and scared.

"What happened?" Steve was only about 100 yards ahead of the bridge where my wheel had broken, sitting on a curb near the closed Grand Island Post Office. I felt a little less alone just seeing his face in a totally unfamiliar town.

"I don't know. The wheel snapped and is now so bent up and twisted that I can't even ride it."

"Wow!" He knelt down and inspected the damage.

"It snapped crossing that bridge back there. I don't think I hit anything but it sure is messed up. What do you think?"

Steve had bicycled from Minneapolis to Florida on a ten-speed eight years or so earlier with his brother. I figured him for some learned answers.

"I don't know what could have done that. Something's wrong, though."

"Thanks a million, doc. I thought that you knew all about this stuff. You're my guru, man. I'm the big Polish kid who doesn't know anything about bike repair and felt secure being in your able, experienced hands."

"You dream too much. I can fix flats but this obviously isn't a flat tire. See, I can tell because when you try to pinch the rubber here I still feel a lot of air pressure, meaning that the problem isn't..."

"Enough, flat-tire-only-expert-guy! I get the picture. I have to get this to a bicycle repair shop. Let's find a phone book."

THE OWNER OF WAYNE CYCLERY GENTLY ROTATED MY WHEEL and felt each set of spokes with his fingers.

"See your spokes are too tight. They're strung like a drum and with your 220 pounds and gear you're asking for trouble."

John Wayne, movie legend hero to the world, was now my personal hero tonight as the only open bike repair shop in Grand Island featured owner, "John Wayne." He was about 25-years-old, a good-looking guy who seemed to really know his stuff and was very friendly. He asked me as many questions about our trip as I asked him about fixing bikes.

I watched as he quickly diagnosed my problem as a broken spoke, then repaired it, trued up my entire wheel of spokes and finally loosened every single spoke a quarter of a turn to put the perfect amount of pressure on the wheel.

"I'm going to sell you a free-wheel remover in case this ever happens again and you're not so fortunate to be within a mile of an open bicycle repair shop. Figuring that you guys have over 9,000 miles to go, I think that the $2.80 investment will be worth it."

He eased my wheel off of his bench.

"That should do it sir. You're back on the road."

"Well, thanks again, John, for taking care of me so quickly and just for being open on a Friday night. What do I owe you?"

"Let's see...uh...$2.50."

"$2.50? You replaced my spoke, trued my wheel, redid my spokes and sold me a $2.80 tool...for $2.50?" I again asked incredulously.

"$2.50."

He smiled but was definitely firm and sure of his figuring.

"My way of helping some of those kids back in Minnesota. You guys just have a safe trip around this country. A lot of us wish that we were in your shoes. Gentle winds to you."

He smiled, shook my hand as I walked my bike out the door and turned his, "Open for Business" sign over to "Closed" and turned off the lights.

I found Steve in a prearranged small tavern surrounded by an entire girl's softball team. Two hours had passed since we parted ways. It was obvious that he had not missed me for a moment.

"Hey Ken, you're back! You road ready?"

"Road ready."

"Great. What happened?"

"Long story for later but I do feel pretty good about Grand Island, Nebraska."

"Ken, I'd like you to meet Linda, Michelle, is it Katy? Katy, and...."

Major mistake. It was now 9:30 PM. The sun had set. We had no home. I followed Steve's bicycle down the pitch-black road as a sports car screamed by honking angrily at us. We had no lights on our bikes.

"Buddy, next time we find a home and then we relax and socialize. Make sense?"

"I'm with you."

Steve had a $3.98 KMART flashlight in his hand showing a weak way for both of us. We were slowly leaving the lights of the town behind.

"Glass!" Steve shouted.

Bicycling 20 feet ahead, Steve flashed his light towards the broken pop bottle on the shoulder. Avoiding glass and metal debris at 20 miles an hour during the day was a challenge. On a moonless, starless night it put new meaning to the word "adventure."

"How much further to that campground Linda told us about?" I was tired and ready for bed. Any piece of dry grass to pitch my tent was all I needed right now.

Steve slowed to a stop. I pulled up alongside. The sound of crickets and a few bullfrogs were the only sounds of the night.

"We should have been there by now. I don't see anything up ahead."

I didn't think that it was possible, but Steve's flashlight was growing even dimmer.

"Our beacon in the night is worthless. Let's walk our bikes."

We slowly trudged down the pitch-black road, saying nothing and looking for a light of any kind to welcome our weary bodies home.

"Hey, there's something!" Finally, about 100 yards on the left side of the road were the lights of a campground. Our day was just about over. We walked up to the gate and welcome sign.

"Dang it. It's all locked up. And there's a $5.00 fee. Yuck." I was mad.

A ten-foot steel fence surrounded the small, enclosed camping area. Steve and I looked at each other, hoping for an answer. I spoke first.

"Well, I'm not paying $5.00 to pitch a tent for eight hours. Let's just find a field."

Steve nodded and pointed across the street. Five feet of barbed wire now separated us from home.

Five minutes later I hoisted Acabar up over my shoulders.

"You got it? You got it?!"

"I got it. Drop it!" I let go of my grip on Acabar as Steve's grip tightened on her and slipped her to the ground. Now I was the only thing left on the wrong side of the fence. It was dark but I could dimly see the sharp barbs and carefully hauled myself up and over.

"Home."

"Home."

I looked around. We were on the edge of a grass-grazing field. Dirt, grass, more dirt, more grass. Too dark to see enough to pitch my tent, I realized our only option.

"Jellyfish time."

"Jellyfish? What in the heck…"

I cut him off in mid sentence because I was really, really tired.

"My brother Tom and I originated this unique camping method in southern Florida one night. Since it's too dark to find and pound stakes in the tents, just open and spread your tent on the ground, put you and your sleeping bag inside and then zip up the tent with the screen door over your face. You breathe, sleep wonderfully and keep the bugs and snakes out. It's great. Good night."

Steve was still mumbling and fumbling with zippers as I tucked myself away, staring at a blackened, starless night through the tent door as I drifted off to sleep.

"HAKOWEE!"

I abruptly awoke from a soft, soothing dream.

"Where the hakowee?"

Steve had often told a bad Indian joke about the HAKOWEE Indians. I had purposefully forgotten it but I believe that the punch line would have worked perfectly this morning.

My head was in a fog, like most mornings, but I looked through my screened ceiling and saw Steve sitting up in his one man "casket tent" as I affectionately called it. He was smiling and looking around for bearings. This was our first glimpse of our home under the morning sun.

"O...My...God!" Steve sounded genuinely terrified and done joking. I ripped open my tent and stared in the direction he was staring. Thirty yards away from our bodies were two one-ton bulls looking directly at us, their overnight intruders.

"You gotta be kidding me!" I was wide-awake and my brain raced for options.

"Do those things charge like on TV?"

"I'm not sure, " Steve nervously answered, "but I'm going to take about 60 seconds or so to pack up, break camp and get Betty and me on the other side of that barbed fence."

One bull took two menacing steps towards us.

"Sounds like a pretty good plan, Steve!"

Hearts pounding, adrenaline racing and eyes glancing at but not staring down both bulls, we silently and quickly threw our unpacked tents, mattresses and sleeping bags over the fence. We then reached for our bikes. The second bull snorted. In panic attack mode, knowing that a snorting bull cannot possibly be a good thing, we ran for the fence and got out of there safely before either bull took another step in our direction.

"If we ever stupidly decide to climb over a barbed wire fence in complete darkness and then smell manure like we did last night, let's remember that it's not a great camping plan!" I laughed at my insight. It was easy to laugh when a fence *separated* us from two ornery bulls!

IT WAS A BEAUTIFUL SUN-KISSED SATURDAY BICYCLING IN THE country. I still had not gotten tired of all the country smells like fresh damp hay, the flowers or even the assorted animal manures. It all smelled wonderful to a man too long cooped up in the city.

I glanced over my shoulder to make a check on Steve's whereabouts. I saw him about 400 yards behind me, a little too much distance apart for us, and he was slowing to a stop on the shoulder. I waited.

Minutes later, I finally heard his breathing behind me. I turned to greet him.

"How ya doing there, buddy? You sure are pretty worthless as far as…"

One look at his contorted face shut me up. He was in obvious pain.

"My knee is tearing me up. I am so sick of this!"

About five or six days earlier Steve had strained his knee while trying to keep up with a 40-mile-per-hour truck. I laughed hysterically at the time but it was increasingly obvious that Steve had damaged something in his knee. With approximately 9,600 miles to go before we hit Minnesota, this was an untimely injury.

"Sick of what?" I queried.

"I am sick of my body keeping me from doing the things that I want to do in life. My back has constantly kept me from…"

He looked anguished and afraid.

"I'm just concerned that this knee is jeopardizing this trip. I need a rest or something."

It was sadly ironic that Steve was having knee problems. I had major surgery on my knee three times in the past twelve years and Steve and I had both been concerned whether my ligament-repaired knee would hold up on this trip. But my legs and knees were fine. Steve had a chronic arthritic back that gave him problems but his back was fine.

"Tell you what, Steve. The sign back there said nine miles to Hastings. Let's find a place to camp near town and hole up there until you feel better.

"PARDON ME, BUT ARE YOU THE FELLAS THAT BELONG TO those loaded-down bikes out there?"

I was sitting in McDonalds with a large bag of ice on my left knee, which was swollen to twice its normal size. I looked up to the source of this booming voice and answered, "That's us."

"Looks like you've got yourself a knee problem. How far ya come?"

"We left St. Paul, Minnesota a couple of weeks ago."

"I'm sorry to interrupt you during your lunch," the big man drawled, "but my son's really into bike racing and he just bought himself a TREK and I was noticing that one of you fellas has a TREK."

"Yeah, that's me," Ken almost grudgingly volunteered. He was already starting to grow weary of people asking questions while we were eating.

"I'm Ken Rogers and this is my friend Steve Anderson."

The big man extended his hand and introduced himself as John Tjaden. I invited him to sit down with us while we finished our Big Macs, quarter pounders, fries and malts.

"I don't think that I've ever seen any two people pack in that much food in one sitting!" John chuckled in his deep voice when we were finally finished.

Just the way he said it made us both laugh. He also had a real comforting and fatherly presence.

A comforting presence is exactly what I needed. My knee was hurting so badly today that I finally could not pedal at all with it. My right leg was doing all of the work and even an inexperienced bike rider like me knew that I couldn't go 10,000 miles with my left leg hanging off to the side.

Ken and I poked fun at any situation involving each other and this predicament was no different. We both agreed that we would probably get more press if I only used one leg the whole way. We also speculated that I would have to invest in some new jeans at the end of the trip since my right leg would be the size of a tree stump and my left leg would resemble that of a flamingo's.

I was scared though.

I had never had a knee problem in my life but that's not what I was scared about. I was afraid that if my knee didn't get better I wouldn't be able to finish our trip. Ken, as he did so often, made me feel better by telling me that he was not going to finish the trip without me and we would take as many days off as it took for my knee to heal.

John gave us directions to a public park in the middle of Hastings where we could pitch our tents and get showers at the municipal pool. He said that he would probably stop by later with his son and see how we were doing.

I PEACEFULLY STIRRED AND OPENED MY EYES. I COULDN'T actually see the sun but I felt its warmth through my earth brown tent wall. Sunday morning. No place to get to. No miles to ride. What a tremendous feeling. I rolled on my back and felt almost giddy. The Lord did say the seventh day was to be a day of rest and Steve and I could not agree more.

Last night we decided that to make this beautiful friendly park our home for another day. This would be our first day since leaving St. Paul that we were purposely going to relax and recharge our worn-down bodies.

We started our day by going to church. After hearing our story after Mass, Father Bob gave us five dollars and wanted us to have a good lunch on him. Then I went swimming and sunning while Steve relaxed in the park. Steve had barely moved a muscle all day and his knee seemed to be responding.

"How's it feeling, buddy?"

Steve was sitting at the picnic table writing Lori a letter.

"Better. Not great but better. I've got an idea, though." He dropped his pen and stared at me as I toweled off after my late afternoon swim.

"I'd like to pray about it together. We've never done this before but I know the power is there and I want my health 100% more than anything."

I smiled. My insides felt warm and good about this.

"Sure. Let's do it."

We sat across from each other at the picnic table and then Steve bowed his head.

"God, I'm thankful for so many things; my family, friends and especially Lori and Ken. They've been such a blessing to me. But right now I need help. My body is hurting again and this time it is really messing up my life. I need to finish this bicycle trip and my knee is hurting so bad right now that I'm not sure I can make it. Please make my knee better."

He stopped and closed his eyes. After about ten seconds, I quietly spoke.

"Dear Lord, keep my friend Steve healthy. I asked you months ago what you wanted me to do this year and everything added up to this trip. Steve and I have committed to each other, to our friends and family and to the people who pledged money for the eventual kids of Make-A-Wish to complete this endeavor together. We need your help to keep us both healthy and safe. Make Steve well, heal and strengthen his knee. We'll do the rest. Thank you for taking some time to hear us out. We appreciate all of our blessings, especially our families and the friendship Steve and I share. Amen."

I looked up at Steve. He smiled.

"Let's go get us some 30,000-foot mountains with sheer cliffs and wild grizzly bears running around looking for human food to snack on…"

Steve rambled on, but in a gentle, warm tone. He was being silly, however he looked more confident and at peace.

If nothing else, the power of shared prayer sure felt good.

"This is my son, Brian," John Tjaden said. "Just thought we'd stop by and harass you for awhile. I brought some tape and an ace bandage for you, Steve. Thought I'd show you how to wrap that knee and bring down the swelling. As a former amateur athlete, I unfortunately know from experience that this technique works."

John went on to tell me that the fluid in my knee was my body's way of protecting me from myself, an indication that something is wrong. He showed me how to wrap the knee, forcing the fluid up my leg. He then showed me how to give my knee enough support to take the strain of pedaling by crisscrossing strips of adhesive tape just below the kneecap.

He was a wealth of information and shared it in a very humble way. He really boosted our spirits and convinced me that my knee problem was just temporary. He did that not by simply telling me so, but by his confidence that his taping and bandaging trick could actually work.

John stopped over every day we were there to make sure that we were okay. After three days in the park resting, writing letters, eating, sleeping and swimming, my knee returned to its normal size and we were itching to put miles behind us once again.

I GLANCED AT THE BLUE HILL SOUTH CENTRAL STATE BANK. "1:37 PM. 101 degrees." Wow! No wonder I felt whipped and continued to guzzle water. It was a grueling Tuesday in intense heat for a couple of Minnesota boys where 80 degrees is a sweltering hot day in the summer sun. We also had a serious wind in our face all morning making for very slow miles.

But most importantly, today was Test Day. We had left our park campground this morning with the new "Tjaden knee wrap." We bicycled south with high hopes of healthy bicycling. And Steve was doing great! He was in almost no pain and leading us most of the day. I kept singing Willie's, "On the Road Again."

It felt great. Border number four, the great state of Kansas would be tomorrow.

"WHERE ARE YOU GUYS GOING?"

I slowed ACABAR to a stop as a pretty 24-year-old or so woman with long, curly brown locks, dressed in a robe with sandals, slowly put down her four-foot-long sign, **Remember Hiroshima."**

The temperature was pushing 106 degrees and any excuse to stop was welcome.

"You first. Where are *you* all going?" I asked her.

"We're walking from Seattle, Washington to Bethlehem."

"*The* Bethlehem, as in "little town of?" I asked incredulously.

She smiled.

Wow. She was in Kansas heading east. My overheated mind didn't take long to figure that she and her seventeen compatriots had one heck of a stretch of road ahead. Our 10,000 plus bicycle trip suddenly seemed like an air-conditioned Cadillac cruise across town.

"How long time-wise do you figure?"

73

"Well we left in April (today was August 4) and we hope to hit Bethlehem not this Christmas but next Christmas."

I closed my eyes. The sun was bearing down. I knew that Steve and I bordered on bona fide crazy but the idea of a two-year walk blew me away. I felt nothing but tremendous respect and awe for these people who were making a stand on something that they obviously deeply believed in. She continued with her story.

"Our group of 18 is being led by Father Jim, the man in the yellow shorts up there. He was the chaplain on the plane that dropped the bomb on Hiroshima."

She paused as she watched her own words sink in with me.

"That day left an understandable life-long impact on him and he's been involved in the anti-nuclear movement ever since. Our pilgrimage to the birthplace of Jesus will hopefully bring attention to what we all deeply feel is a serious threat to our future."

She smiled again and I sensed that she had to catch up with the others.

"Before I go, please tell me what you guys are doing on your bicycles?"

After quickly and ever-so-humbly relating our quest and cause for the kids, we hugged goodbye. Strangers only minutes before and never to see each other again, we felt a bond of friendship. I watched, no name to attach to her, as she walked east.

I sat there for one final moment as I remembered her answer to my final question. I had asked her how many rattlesnakes they had "encountered" since leaving Seattle. "Only three or four," I unhappily muttered to myself.

I pounded my pedals downward and turned it on to catch up to an out-of-sight Steve.

Kansas seemed to be mile after mile of blowing dirt and suffocating heat. I never realized that is what they must have meant when they referred to the state as the "Land of Oz." I was feeling like an overcooked noodle when I spotted life outside near a farmhouse. Sure

enough Ken and I found the owner and his wife peeling potatoes in the shade of a huge tree.

"Excuse us, but can we use a garden hose or an outside spigot to refill our water bottles?"

"No problem. There is a garden hose on the other side of the house. Help yourselves."

I reached the hose first. I have never picked up a garden hose when there are people within shooting distance when I haven't been at least tempted to be a brat and get them wet. Today was no different; in fact I didn't even give temptation a chance. Ken was still fifteen feet away when I turned around and proceeded to soak him from head to foot. One drop in a million was going into his open water bottle when I said,

"Let me know when it is filled!"

As usual, Ken retaliated and ended up soaking me too. We thanked Mr. and Mrs. Potato Farmer and once more headed west. It didn't take long for our clothes and bodies to dry in 100-degree-plus-heat and be replaced again with sweat and grime.

But, our brief encounter with that garden hose was one of the most refreshing memories of my life and the way that I will always remember our very short time in Kansas.

It was time to soon leave the relative comfort of the Midwest with all of its charm, small towns, friendly people, characteristic water towers and grain elevators rising out of the plains and cross over to Colorado.

CHAPTER 8
THE MIRACLES OF TWO EXTRA STEAKS AND QUITTIN' EARLY

"A coincidence is a small miracle where God chose to remain anonymous."
~ Heidi Quade

"KEN, I DON'T THINK THAT PICTURE WILL WIN YOU ANY awards in any category or be published in any magazine!"

I looked through the eye of the camera, set the f-stop, focused and shot. I moved in a little closer. "Click." I put the camera down.

"Looks pretty unbelievable to me, Steve. I think they call it a 'Kodak moment.'"

There, on the paved highway near the shoulder, were two strips of adhesive tape that normally held Steve's knee together forming a huge "X."

It was mile 1,000.

We had bicycled into Colorado a mere mile ago. Although our border photo at state #5 was a big deal, bicycling 1,000 miles was an even bigger milestone. When I made the big "X" on the road with the tape, Steve was laughing but I knew that he loved it and was proud of both of us...and his knees!

Time to keep moving. The sun was setting and we had our eyes on a town still about fifteen miles away.

"WELCOME TO WRAY, COLORADO, POPULATION 1,872"

Ah, a comforting welcome sign signaling that we were almost home, wherever that would be. The sun had set 30 minutes ago and darkness was quickly approaching. A real chill was in the air for the first time since we'd left home.

I hadn't seen Steve in awhile, but I knew that he was safely behind me. I always bicycled hard as the days drew to a close. The temperature was cooler and with 70 to 90 miles on our bikes, I felt strong and confident during evening and dusk hours.

Bicycle touring in the elements demands one to constantly be conserving energy for later, but with only a couple of hours left in the day it was exhilarating for me to hold nothing back and charge towards a final destination.

A Honda 750 roared up behind me and broke up my thoughts.

"Hey, you wanna join us for a cold brew?" he turned off his engine so that he could hear my reply.

A young 18-year-old man, with a big warm smile had a tremendous offer after a long dusty day. However, I didn't know him from Adam and I didn't have a bicycling buddy or a home for the night in sight.

"Thanks a lot, man, but I've got to find my friend."

"Steve's back down the road at 'The Pitts' with my buddy and he told me to come and get you. The name's James." He reached out to shake my hand.

How quickly plans change on the road.

"THIS IS TREMENDOUS, RUTH! I CAN'T BELIEVE THAT I'M sitting at your dinner table with a hot shower behind me and a hot charcoal-broiled steak in front of me."

I passed the butter to Steve and checked to see how impatient James looked. He still wanted in on that cold brew that he had offered us an hour and a half ago. I had followed him back to a lounge called The Pitts where Steve was waiting. We both explained to James that before we could relax we had to find a home for the night first. We had made that mistake before and almost got gored by two ornery bulls that didn't appreciate us sleeping in their field. James made a quick call to his mom and she said, "Bring them home."

I was already impressed with her. How many moms in the world would take a 29-year-old and 30-year-old bearded and filthy man on bikes into their home, sight unseen, simply because their teenage son asked them nicely?"

Ruth was indeed an incredible woman. An attractive, petite brunette in her 40's, she had a glow about her and a vivacious sparkle in every move she made and in every word she spoke. We had not only been welcomed with open arms, but Ruth had made us feel very special in only a matter of minutes.

"My husband asked me why we were grilling six steaks when there were only four of us. I honestly did not have an answer. I'd pulled six from the freezer to thaw and I just figured there must be a reason. Now I obviously know why!"

She giggled and then continued.

"The Lord always has His reasons for everything He leads us to do."

I glanced at Steve. We considered ourselves to be Christian men, but this "six steaks stuff" seemed eerie. But Ruth radiated such a warm smile while we continued to plunge food into our mouths, that I figured she was just really close to God and He used her more often than I had experienced in the past.

"Well, I'm sure glad James pulled us over and invited us to come home with him. This is my first day ever in Colorado and I'm impressed so far. Is this going to happen like this every night, Ken?"

We all laughed at Steve.

After eating everything that wasn't nailed down - our ravenous appetites always startled new friends on the road - we relaxed in the living room and Ruth quietly spoke of the Bible, her faith and her growing relationship with the Lord. Her stories were humbly shared and full of life and vitality. Steve and I both listened intently.

She wasn't preachy or heavy about it. She laughed often and freely quoted from the Bible interesting verses and related them to her and to us. James talked about a miracle healing of his broken leg during last year's football season. I couldn't comprehend it all, but I peacefully dropped off to sleep on the sofa and I knew that I felt secure, safe and loved.

I thanked God for that.

"NO DISASTER CAN OVERTAKE YOU, NO PLAGUE COME NEAR your tent. He will put you in his angels' charge to guard you wherever you go." - Psalm 91

Ruth stopped reading aloud and closed her Bible. The sun was already bearing down in the early hours of a beautiful Colorado morning.

It was Friday, August 6, our 18th day on the road.

"Thank you guys so much for everything." I gave her a big hug as Steve shook James's hand.

"You both will now be on my daily prayer list. I'll be praying for Steve's knee to heal and that you both get back to Minneapolis safe and sound."

"We hit mile 1,000 yesterday, and so with about 9,000 miles yet to go, we deeply appreciate all of your much needed prayers."

I headed out of the driveway as Steve got in his hug. Turning our bicycles into the street, we slowly pedaled west.

"HOW MANY MILES WE GOT, KEN?"

"We're at 54.3."

"What do you think?"

"It's 23 miles to the next town. I figure we've got about two hours of sunlight left. Twelve miles per hour would be cutting it a little close but that tailwind sure is sweet. You know my answer, buddy."

"Okay then, it's a go."

I flashed Steve a huge smile. I loved riding hard until the sun went down. A normally hesitant Steve at this late hour was up for it too because of a nice tailwind pushing us down the road. It had been a pretty uneventful day of riding since leaving Ruth and James 54.3 miles ago. Two more hours would feel good to both of us.

Steve grabbed a half loaf of raisin bread from his back pannier and we both slammed down these "carbos" and followed them with slugs of cold water from our bottles. It was our little energy boost to help us fly towards our home to be.

I hopped on Acabar, Steve flashed a raised clenched fist and we were off.

With virtually no highway traffic, a perfect 63-degree temperature and a refreshing breeze behind us, conditions were ideal. We were effortlessly bicycling westward into what looked to be another spectacular sunset.

Sixty yards of building speed and suddenly…I slammed down on my brakes. Steve flew by me as he tried to stop.

"What's up?" he yelled back to me.

"Forget it."

"Forget what?"

"We're done for the day."

Steve smiled incredulously.

"What are you talking about? We just decided to charge down the road. You *always* want to keep riding!"

"That's right. 'Always.' Maybe I'm getting too predictable. I don't know. I just feel like we should relax, grab a café supper and call it.

It was obvious Steve was delighted with the news. He still looked a little confused but I loved keeping him off guard. He kept asking me why I changed my mind so suddenly. I didn't really know. It just felt like the thing to do.

Our new plan made us both giddy. We were like two little kids who unexpectedly found themselves let out of school early. Even life on the road can build routine habits and it was fun to break them up.

After a great little supper back in town, we walked our bicycles over to the city park across the street where we decided to pitch our tents. It seemed to be getting dark a little early. Then I glanced directly west.

"Would you look at that?" Steve checked the heavens with me. The sky was pitch black and lightning was slowly starting to flash. The temperature seemed to be literally dropping as we stood there in our bicycling shorts and T-shirts.

"That is unbelievable. We're talking 45 minutes ago it was beautiful." Big wet drops slowly dropped on us.

CRACK! CRACK…A…BOOM! Close. The tree that we were standing under holding onto our metal bikes suddenly looked like a real bad place to take "refuge." The rain started to pour down. It was all happening so fast that we were confused as to our next move. I looked at Steve.

"This is not the answer. Let's head back to the café until the weather breaks."

Steve's quick thinking made healthy sense.

"Hey!"

Across the street near the café a young man was motioning us to come over. We ran our bikes through the now-drenching-rain towards him and the cafés' awning.

"You guys look lost! My name's Don."

He extended his hand. I guessed him to be about 36-years-old, tall, slender, blond, athletic, a good-looking guy with a warm smile.

"How ya doin? I'm Ken."

"Steve."

"You guys have a place to stay? That park looks awfully wet and dangerous with all this lightning."

"Well we haven't thought about a plan B just yet."

"Listen guys. My family and I are moving back to Ohio on Tuesday next week and we've got a basement all cleared out. It's not much but it is warm, dry and best of all, less than two blocks from where we're standing."

"You're on, Don. Thanks a lot. The timing of your offer couldn't be much better!"

Steve and I were drenched and chuckling. The sky was now pouring and the thunder and lightning cracked all around us. It was a dangerous and scary block and a half "run" to his house holding onto our metal bicycles, as the thought of jumping back on them in this lightning storm sounded even more dangerous.

Our new friend, Don, turned out to be "Pastor Don," a warm, down-to-earth Lutheran minister. We were introduced to his wife and two children and then Steve and I changed out of our soaked clothes and into dry ones. Thankfully our saddlebags really were waterproof.

While sipping hot chocolate and sharing stories around the kitchen table, we heard the loud pattering of golf-ball-size hail on the roof. I was feeling very blessed and protected.

Steve and I should have been cowering in some ditch on the side of a road, being pelted with ice balls from the skies in a wet, windy, cold, dark and very dangerous electrical storm. We were so close to riding on. Why had we changed our minds? I knew one thing. The Lord was protecting us in a very real and practical way.

I sipped on my cocoa and Don shared a neat story about spreading the word of God among some Eskimo trappers years ago while he was a bush pilot in Alaska. Thunder cracked and the hail continued to storm down. I thought of Ruth's prayer and Bible reading this very morning in her driveway.

"No disaster can overtake you, no plague come near your tent: He will put you in his angels' charge to guard you wherever you go." - **Psalm 91**

For the second night in a row I closed my eyes and in my heart said a peaceful and simple prayer, "Thank you Lord." I honestly did not understand it all, but God and life were indeed good.

CHAPTER 9
UP, UP AND (ARGH) UP 10,276 FEET AND OVER THE ROCKIES

"You gain strength, courage and confidence by every experience in which you really stop to look fear in the face...You must do the thing you think you cannot do." ~Eleanor Roosevelt

"THAT IS UNBELIEVABLY INCREDIBLE!"

There was awe and uneasiness in Steve's voice. This was his first ever look. They seemed to rise right up through the clouds and into the heavens: the Rocky Mountains. They were still about 50 miles away but they loomed ominously near, snow-capped and gargantuan in size. Awesome to gaze at, soon they would be our ultimate physical and mental challenge to bicycle up, over and through.

I continued to watch Steve, straddling his bicycle on the shoulder of the road, eyes intently staring at the "purple mountain majesty," the once meaningless phrase to a beautiful song in grade school that was our inspiring reality today.

On every hill we crested since Fort Morgan, Colorado, I would scan the horizon for my first glimpse of the Rocky Mountains. I was finally rewarded about 20 miles out of Fort Morgan on I-76. As I pedaled to the top of a hill, I saw what I thought were clouds on the horizon. They looked almost ghostly at about 50 miles away. I couldn't help but wonder what the pioneers must have thought when they got their first glimpse of the mountains on their way west. They were probably awestruck as I was today.

Ken, having seen the Rockies several times before, asked me, "What do you think?"

"They're beautiful. It's hard to believe that they are still so far away."

Almost like he had read my thoughts earlier, he asked, "Can you imagine how long it must have taken the pioneers to cross the mountains in covered wagons?"

"No, I can't. I cannot even imagine how long it will take you and me to cross them. I've got to admit, Ken, seeing them stand out there in front of us as far North and South as I can see, and knowing that's the only way of getting to the West Coast, is kind of scary."

"There does seem to be a little something standing between us and the ocean. Yeah, I'm a little nervous myself."

We sat there on the shoulder of I-76, feeling pretty insignificant in the majesty of what lay ahead of us.

My mind wandered back to a sales seminar I had attended about five years ago. The speaker was trying to teach us to be a big frog in a small pond rather than a small frog in a big pond. I had pretty much adopted that philosophy in my sales career, picking one small geographic area and trying to be the best and most well known salesman in that area.

Now I felt like the small frog in the big pond, but it felt wonderful. Knowing that you're such a teeny, tiny part of God's creation kind of takes the pressure off. You realize that all of your mistakes, problems and even achievements don't matter a whole lot in God's master plan. But the realization that maybe God didn't watch me as closely as I may have thought didn't make me feel farther from God. I had never felt so close to Him in my life.

IT WAS LATE, AND THE NIGHT COMPLETELY ENGULFED US AS we tried to set up our tents near the river in Poudre Canyon. There were no stars or moon to give us light. Ken and I took turns holding a flashlight as we each set up our tents.

I went to sleep to the gurgling of the Poudre River and the sound of light raindrops on my tent. Although the formidable Rocky Mountains loomed directly in front of us, a tremendous calm penetrated my entire body as I laid there in total awe of my surroundings. For the first time of this incredible journey, I slept the whole night without waking up once.

I woke up at daybreak. While Ken snored away in his tent, I sat on a rock next to the river and wrote a long overdue letter to Lori. Having pulled into camp so late last night, I never got a good look at my surroundings. I now knew that we were in a canyon with rock cliffs rising on both sides of us.

I heard a little "clip clop" sound behind me and turned to see a small buck deer cross the road and scurry up a steep embankment on the other side. He stopped and turned to look at me. We watched each other for a long time. I marveled at how beautiful he was. With my stubbly beard, hair sticking up on one side and plastered down on the side I slept on, my filthy clothes, I wondered if this incredible looking animal thought the same of me.

"I'LL HAVE THE BUTTERMILK STACK, THREE EGGS OVER EASY, sausage, wheat toast, a large orange juice and one of your famous cinnamon raisin rolls. Oh, and one order of hash browns. Thanks."

She had her head down feverishly writing and then looked up to see if I was finally done ordering. I just smiled. She gave me one of those patented weak, glued-on smiles and walked towards the kitchen. Apparently she had never bicycled 500 miles in six days. This was simply our typical energy boost to start our day. It normally would be burned off by noon.

This was also one of the true joys of long distance bicycling. I had been fighting my weight ever since I retired from college football almost a decade ago. Now on this trip I could pig out on anything and still watch the pounds melt away.

"Our TWINS won last night. They're now only 18 ½ games out of first. Let's see, if we win our next 32 games and Kansas City loses its next 37 straight, that would put…"

"Steve put down the newspaper and read your placemat."

He smiled and then looked out the window and stared at tomorrow's riding. His grin faded into an apprehensive frown. This was going to be our first major physical challenge. We would find out quickly after three weeks of riding what we were really made of. Tomorrow the two city dudes from the flatlands of Minnesota would have to bicycle up and over the Rocky Mountains. Steve finally spoke.

"What do you think?"

"I think the TWINS stink. Until our owner starts paying people..."

"About tomorrow!"

"I don't want to."

"I'm serious. I'm scared. I'm nervous already."

"Well, I'm getting there, but I checked the map last night and believe me, if we intend to hit all 48 states, we don't have any other options. Those babies are directly in our way. We'll be fine. Exhausted, bloody, dehydrated, torn knees maybe, but we'll be fine."

Steve went back to his paper now looking like a man on death row. I hadn't been much of a comfort. Deep down I shared his anxiety and concern. I honestly wondered if physically we would be able to do it. Between my knees and Steve's back and knee...

"Hey! John!" Steve had spotted a familiar face.

"How ya doin' guys?" Our new already dear friend, big John Tjaden was strolling through. We had met him and his son, Brian, back in Hastings, Nebraska and he told us then of his Colorado vacation plans. We thought and hoped that we'd see him here, but there were so many variables. But here he was! What a great and reassuring sight.

"How long have you been in?" He sat down with his piping hot cup of coffee.

"Last night. We slept in Poudre Canyon, right next to the river. It was gorgeous. I even saw a deer about 30 yards from our tents."

"Are you planning to tackle the crest tomorrow?"

"Yup. We need today to just rest, wash some clothes and psych up."

"Oh, you'll do it. It will be a long day but a good day. It's about 62 miles to the top of Cameron Pass, elevation about 10,276. It's a pretty graded climb in most spots."

"Sixty-two miles up hill?"

"Up mountain," John corrected.

Ouch.

I AWOKE WITH A START. I OPENED UP MY EYES AND SAW JESUS. I blinked twice. It was not a dream. It was not a vision. I had not died during the night. We had spent a very warm and peaceful night sleeping on the altar of a small LaPorte, Colorado church, where the evening before the pastor had given us permission to stay. The eight-foot-statue of Christ nailed to the cross seemed to look down at me as if to say, "Get up and on those bikes. Now it's your turn." It was still dark but I could hear Steve wrestling around.

"You up?"

"Been."

"You ready?"

I could hear him take a slow, deep breath.

"Yup. Let's get 'em."

"MORNING JOHN. MORNING BRIAN. HOW ARE YOU DOING, MRS. TJADEN?"

We were back at Vern's, home of the best breakfast outside of mom's. The sun was just creeping up but well hidden by mountain ridges.

"You guys finished eatin'?" John asked.

"We forced down a cinnamon roll and hot chocolate. I have never been unable to eat before but this morning I honestly can't. I even went to the bathroom three times! Feel like I'm dressed for the big game and I'm in the locker room waiting for the ref to come in and quietly say, 'Coach, it's time.'" I was deadly serious.

Everyone laughed. The nervous tension, however, was not subsiding.

"Well, it is time then. You and Steve throw your saddlebags in the back of our truck. We're going to eat now. Brian's a racer and so he'll catch up with you and we'll drive up and eventually meet you at Cameron Pass."

I looked to Steve. Throwing our saddlebags in the back of John's pickup seemed like cheating. I really wanted to see if we could bicycle 62 miles uphill with 50 pounds of gear.

"We'll have plenty, plenty of times to bicycle up and through the mountains with full packs. Let's take John up on his offer. This will never present itself again."

Steve had a great point. I now readily agreed. We left on our front panniers and threw our pack panniers, sleeping bags and tents in the truck.

"See you at the top!" Zig Ziglar would have been proud of the reference.

The next seven hours were seven of the most glorious hours of my life. It was a sunny, crisp, beautiful day in the mountains. Steve and I gained confidence with every mile. The grade of the road was a gradual incline, and except for a few stretches of steep climbing, it was just a day of ever-so-slowly bicycling uphill. Brooks of snow-melted rushing water, Douglas fir pine trees, majestic snow-capped ridges and deep blue sky surrounded us. The smell of the air was indescribable. It was so fresh, so sweet, so invigorating.

Steve and I were childlike in our joy to be where we were. We constantly got off our bicycles and snapped photos and just enjoyed the moments.

Finally, nine and a half hours later, still exuberant, but with burning legs, we spotted John and his family sitting on top of Cameron Pass, the top of the mountain, 200 steep yards away. My odometer read 59.6 miles in the thin air, now November-like in its temperature.

"There she is, Steve!" I was pumped. I checked back at Steve who was struggling with his bicycle, 30 yards away, virtually standing on his bicycle pedals and hardly moving with each rotation of his wheel. We were both in the smallest gear of our 18 speed bikes, challenging our exhausted legs to finish this final stretch of mountain. The road was so steep that it was almost impossible simply to stop and hold your bike without feeling gravity pulling you back down toward the base of the mountain. It was now about 42 degrees but we were both sweating profusely. Steve stopped next to me.

We would bicycle the final yards together.

"You all right, buddy?" Steve's knee had pretty much healed the past week, but it had been bothering him off and on today during the steeper grades of climbing. His FUJI did not have quite as small a gear as my TREK did and it was a painful, painful difference today.

"Yeah, I'm okay." He was breathing hard. But his eyes were on fire as he saw Big John so close, signaling the end of our monumental struggle to bicycle over our first mountain.

Excruciatingly slowly we bicycled the final yards side by side. As we closed in on the crest, we reached out and held our hands together over our heads and let out a whoop of joy as we hit the top. We laid down our bikes and gave each other a bear hug, soon joined by John and Brian and his mom.

"I feel like we just biked to the top of the Himalayas. YAAHOOOO!"

It was a moment of triumph to be relished and then tucked away inside. I felt so strong, so confident and so grateful for the miracle of a spectacular day.

Our joy had to quickly subside, as it was growing darker and colder by the minute. It was now time to say goodbye to the Tjaden family. They had truly been our family today, sharing, helping, encouraging and celebrating with us. John had been so gentle and reassuring like a loving dad to both of us. He had formed a special bond with Steve, and I had to turn my head as I saw Steve's eyes tear up as they hugged goodbye.

As they climbed into the truck, I hollered back, "Hey John, how do we bicycle down the other side of this mountain?"

"Just hang on and remember where your brakes are!" He laughed and slowly drove away. Steve and I stood next to our bikes on a now very quiet mountaintop. It was quickly getting darker and colder and lonelier.

"I'll see you at the bottom!" and in a second Steve was gone.

We were flying. I mean we were *flying!* My bike with its 50 pounds of gear and 215-pound rider was charging down the mountain like an out-of-control freight train. After nearly ten hours of creeping and crawling up 10,276 feet, our descent felt like reckless abandon. My body was rigid as I gripped my handlebars and constantly applied pressure to the brakes. It didn't seem to be doing much good, but Steve was rocketing down ahead of me even faster, so maybe my brakes were doing something besides screeching and smoking. We were at speeds in excess of 45-50 miles per hour and the bugs at dusk were smashing on and off my face like BB gun pellets.

It was exhilarating. It was nuts. It was scarier than heck!

The miles were blowing off: 62, 64, 70, 76. "Please God don't let me hit a rock or a pothole or I'm done!"

Finally at mile 81, I pulled to a stop. Steve was already waiting next to a grocery store in the tiny town of Gould. This was to be our home, the first civilization we had seen since leaving the town of LaPorte eleven hours ago.

"Some kind of ridin', huh?" Steve was laughing like a wild man.

"Did you ever use your brakes? I lost you miles ago!"

"What for? Brakes are for sissies. It was time to do some serious riding."

I laughed, but I was also convinced that Steve was crazy. My brakes still smelled like burning rubber. It had been a 20-mile thrill ride, exhilarating and dangerous. My adrenaline was calming down now and I was starting to realize how tired I really was. It had been a very long day full of a lot of emotions that had demanded a lot of us physically, emotionally and mentally.

"This place looks all closed up. There's nothing here." Steve was buried in our trusted map scoping out where home should be.

"Well its eleven more miles to Walden, the next town. Population is 734. Another church would be great. Unless you feel like camping here."

"No, let's just go. It's been a long day and I'd love some food and then a warm place to lay my sleeping bag. I'm starting to freeze again," I said.

We saddled up and headed west. The road had flattened out and we bicycled over gently rolling hills until we hit Walden. We grabbed two convenience store submarine sandwiches, two cold Coors brews and found our church.

Sitting on the back porch of the small country church, stars and moon overhead, we quietly talked about the past day. It had been a spectacular and yet brutal 92 miles and 13 hours. But something had happened to us far more significantly than distance bicycled and a mountain crested. We had changed inside. We had overcome fear and the unknown. We had quietly been filled with a belief in our God-given abilities that we could complete this challenge. Inspirational and motivational words can only take you so far. This morning we had put it all on the line. We did what we set out to do. It took everything that we had.

We both prayed aloud. "Thank you God for giving us the strength and courage to do what we had to do today. Thanks for crossing our paths with the Tjaden's who helped us tremendously. And thanks for our growing friendship."

I closed my eyes and drifted away. Not a muscle of mine moved for the next nine hours.

CHAPTER 10
FRIDAY THE 13th THAT LASTED THREE BRUTAL DAYS

"Inches make the champion." ~ **Vince Lombardi**

"GO AHEAD! PULL IT OVER MORON!" STEVE WAS SCREAMING and gesturing wildly.

The burly cowboy in the busted-up, blue two-ton Ford pickup truck motioned Steve to pull around the corner and get ready to use his fists. I pulled up behind Steve. The trucker, now seeing both of us, drove away.

"What was *that* all about?"

"Ah, the jerk face almost ran me off the road and then flipped me off. I told him to pull over and then…I don't know what I figured I'd do."

Steve was really fuming.

It had been a gut-wrenching morning, lots of traffic, narrow roads with no shoulders and unruly drivers. Rain was coming down and we were both ornery and unimpressed with Colorado people today. But a fight with a redneck cowboy would have really spoiled all the fun.

"Steve, we don't have much going for us if we lip off and get somebody mad at us. Man, he can shoot or run us over in his truck if he's drunk, on drugs, is crazy or is simply in a sour mood."

"You're right, you're right, you're right." Steve was finally calming down.

"How far is it to the next town?" I asked.

"Fifteen miles. I checked the atlas first thing this morning."

"Well let's get out of beautiful, friendly Craig and make our call to Dick from there. Is it my week?"

"Yup."

Steve checked his watch. There was plenty of time to make our 11 AM phone call connection. The drenching rain continued as we left the city limits deep in our own thoughts.

All of a sudden it hit me that today was *Friday the 13th*. I'm not superstitious, but not much had gone right so far. Thankfully it was Friday, though, our favorite day of the week. Unlike a normal workweek, Friday did not signal the end of working and the beginning of two days of play and relaxation. We normally bicycled hard all seven days. But Fridays were the days that we called our local radio station back in St. Paul, KSTP-AM 1500, and spent ten minutes or so talking to talk show host Dick Pomerantz. Steve and I were in the process of building a special relationship with Dick as our collective hearts shared the Make-A-Wish cause. We had been making this call every Friday morning since we had left in July in an effort to let people know how the trip was progressing and to hopefully inspire people to continue pledging money for the eventual kids of Make-A-Wish. Personally, it was great fun for Steve and me to call "home," where many of our friends and families were listening on their radios at home, at work and in their cars. The call made us feel close to Minnesota again and filled some of the void of missing the people that we cared most about.

It was a hilly ride and we were consequently making lousy time. Finally, with my odometer showing me that we had bicycled exactly 15 miles, I stopped.

There were no towns, signs for a nearby town or even a house or farm in sight. Steve bicycled to a stop alongside of me as I scanned the road ahead. He started digging for our road atlas.

"I thought you said there was a town about here. I don't see a man made anything much less a dang town."

"It says we should be in a town called, Lay. There's no population listed here in the atlas. Must be one of those tiny unincorporated jobs."

"How far to the next town?"

"Nine miles."

"Time?"

"11:40 AM our time, 10:40 AM Minnesota time."

We always called in at 11 AM sharp during Dick's nine-to-noon show. For the first time, in the wide-open stretches of the west, there was going to be no way that we would make it on time.

"Let's bicycle hard. First guy that finds a phone makes the call."

Off we flew, determined to make our connection. It was such an uplifting time for us that we looked forward to each week. I suddenly realized just how much that ten-minute call meant to our week of riding.

The road in front of me curved up towards the sky. Then it started to rain. I pedaled and pedaled and pedaled. Five miles. I lost Steve in the hills. Six miles. I didn't have a watch on, something that I'd regretted since I left Minnesota, but I knew that it was late. The constant hills were grueling and unforgiving in my efforts to make miles fly by. Eight miles. I coasted down a small hill, a mile from the next town. I now angrily stared up at the worst climb of the day. I charged down the remaining yards of the small hill and gained steam to tackle the big one. I was flying at about 30 MPH when I hit the base of the incline and quickly dropped into the smallest gear, now wrenching out about 1.8 MPH. It was a draining climb, rain was now pouring down, I was running out of time and my legs were burning in pain. Finally, at the crest, I saw a small diner at the bottom of the hill. It was now 11:51 AM in Minnesota.

"Ken?"

"Yes sir!"

How you doing?"

"Hey Dick."

"You sound tired."

"Almost didn't make it today."

"Where are you?"

"We're in Elk Springs, Colorado. It's about 40 miles from the Utah border which we should hit this afternoon."

"Is it mountainous?"

I imagined Dick comfortably sitting in his radio studio, slacks, shirt, tie and a few minutes from a hot lunch.

I was cold, starving, soaked to the bone, shivering, hadn't bathed in three days and my legs were still shaking from the pace I had put them through charging the mountainous terrain to get to a pay phone. There was no real way to convey to Dick and his listeners that it was in fact, "mountainous" every painful and yet exhilarating inch the past eight days.

"It's been and is mountainous."

"Are you enjoying it?"

"Ah, we would never do it again!"

Dick roared with laughter.

"It's honestly been a phenomenal experience. The scenery, the people have been outstanding; it's been what we're supposed to be doing. But, I guess Dick, it's just been one of the most physically demanding things that I have ever experienced, and Steve concurs wholeheartedly. We had no idea. Before you do something like this, you can only think in your mind that it's going to be tough. But until you're out here battling everything...it's been...brutal."

"Just think about this Ken, for Make-A-Wish you only have 43 more states to go!"

I laughed. I'm not sure why.

"Listen my friend, give my regards and our affection and love to Steve as well, safe traveling and we'll talk to you next week."

"Okay, Dick. Thanks so much."

"Take care."

After Ken's call with Dick, a steady rain literally engulfed us mile after mile. It was a hopeless cause to try to stay dry today and so we simply made the best of our situation like always and proceeded to get thoroughly soaked. At one point we got off our bikes and just walked for several miles together. We rarely ever biked side-by-side and virtually never walked our bikes, no matter how steep the climb, (our competitive nature) and so we took advantage of this rare moment in time. As we sloshed along, we talked about everything. I wish someone had taken a picture of us walking down the road in this steady downpour surrounded by the red rock cliffs. I felt like I was born for the sole purpose of experiencing this moment.

Only a few months ago we were trying to get people we didn't even know to buy pencils, paper and desks from us, fighting heavy traffic every day while chasing sales quotas. Raising money for the kids of Make-A-Wish, forcing our bodies to go above and beyond the call of

duty every day and attempting to get closer to God seemed much more important than the work-a-day world of sales.

My last thoughts of the day were of how proud I was of Ken. Of the two of us, our friends had the most doubts of Ken not finishing this trip. I was somewhat more experienced at bike touring before this trip and I hadn't had three major operations on my knee like Ken had. Quite frankly Ken had his doubts too before the trip. After what we had been through so far, I had absolutely no doubt about Ken. He would finish. He was in his element!

I FINISHED MY THIRD BIG MAC. I WASN'T HUNGRY. I WAS stalling. It was 6 PM on a Saturday night. Back home I would be showering, throwing on some cologne and getting psyched to pick up my date for dinner and a night on the town. But tonight in Vernal, Utah, I was slamming down hamburgers and getting ready to bicycle up a mountain with Steve.

"I'm going to go outside and ask around to make sure Highway 191 is the best way to go."

Steve was still fidgeting with his fish fillet. He was not the inspirational George Patton figure that I needed tonight.

I eased out the doors and into the sun-filled parking lot. There were campers, Winnebagos and boat trailers everywhere. Tourists. Not what I needed. I finally found a couple climbing into their pickup truck with Utah license plates.

"Excuse me. I'm from out of town and just wondering if Highway 191 is our best bet heading north into Wyoming."

"That's your only bet. It's steep, but you shouldn't have problems if your load isn't too heavy. What kind of a rig are you pulling?"

I quickly realized that our bicycles were parked on the other side of the building, safely out of view.

"Well actually my "rig" is a bicycle. My buddy and I are bicycling America and we…"

"Bicycling! You gotta be kidding!" They were both laughing. I wasn't in the mood.

"Then your best bet is to bicycle west on highway 40 towards Provo." They kept laughing as if it was their own private joke.

"Provo?" I asked

"Yeah, that's where the state mental hospital is." A small group of local people were gathering and the word was spreading.

"Thanks." I walked back inside.

A stand up comic. Great. I needed a little compassion, support, and some good advice on roads. No. I get ridicule.

Again I imagined my date's warm hug and sweet fragrance as I met her at the door.

I STOOD ON MY PEDALS, INCHING ACABAR UP ANOTHER EIGHT inches. This was beyond brutal. A Winnebago passed by at about 12 mph, billowing smoke and sounding as if its transmission was about to drop on the road. The spiraling road ahead looked like a sheer cliff heading to the heavens. I was grunting and groaning in pain. I finally jumped off my bike and waited for Steve. He could have been 40 yards behind me but the road was winding so tightly around the mountain that my field of vision only covered 30 yards. He quickly caught up to me.

"We could crawl on our hands and knees faster than this. This is the worst. This is nuts. I quit!"

"Steve, we've been through this several times already. You can't quit. You've got all the maps."

"Then I'll give them all to you."

"I don't have the room for them."

"Oh."

This was like a Smothers Brothers stand-up comic routine between Steve and me. We were always only joking but if you inadvertently overheard us, you would think that we were dead serious.

"Let's walk the bikes a little. Maybe that will help."

It still hurt.

The sun had set thirty minutes ago at about 8 PM. But we were finally, finally at the top. It had been fourteen of the most grueling miles that we had encountered since pedaling out of St. Paul. However, we still had ten miles to go before hitting our destination; a National Forest Campground on the map. I sure hoped that it was really there.

We bicycled hard through a winding but relatively flat stretch of road. I silently glided around a bend in the road and then held my breath. There, less than 30 yards ahead, on the side of the road, stood a majestic doe, 180-plus-pounds of breathtaking beauty. Her huge brown eyes turned towards me, as I'm sure that she picked up my scent. She immediately bounded for the safety and cover of the forest. For a brief moment, I appreciated my motorless bicycle on this punishing mountain. My bike's silence allowed me to see this beautiful creature more closely than if I had been in the grinding Winnebago billowing by me earlier.

Steve passed me without a word. We were both exhausted and concerned about the ever-increasing darkness. We'd never bought bike lights and we were too tired to dig through our bags for a flashlight. We strained our eyes on the blacktop, carefully watching for the glass that could blow a tire or a pothole that could wreck a bike. Eight miles and 40 minutes later we were in complete blackness.

"Hey Steve!"

"Yeah."

I heard his voice about 20 yards ahead of me.

"I can't see a thing anymore. I just don't want to hit you."

"Do you want me to sing a song or something?" Steve finally asked.

"Just find us that campground. Soon."

There was no traffic. There was no moon, only stars to guide our way. We were going right down the middle of the road. Suddenly I felt my bicycle picking up speed. We were steeply heading downward. I was really uncomfortable.

This was scary, stupid and dangerous.

"Steve!"

No response.

"You up there?"

He must have not been using his brakes again. I couldn't believe him! I was clamping down on mine but the cool mountain breeze was whistling by my face. I could only hope and pray that there was nothing on the road. I could have hit a deer or elk head-on before either one of us would have known what had happened. My palms were sweaty and my eyes straining to find the white center of the line.

I started to inhale the wonderful smell of burning wood. I finally saw the light of a campfire to my right!

"YAHOOOOO!" I slowed to a stop and saw Steve resting near the campground entrance twenty yards off the road. We were home.

"STEVE, HOW MUCH DID YOU SPEND ON THIS SLEEPING BAG?"

"Uh...about $19.95 I think. You got a problem with that?"

I carefully stuffed the bag into my nylon bag cover and strapped it on the back of my bike. It was another glorious mountain morning, but I was still thawing out and moving slow.

"No problem, buddy. It's just great sleeping out at 9,000 feet above sea level and 40 degrees in a bag guaranteed to keep you warm at 70 degrees or above."

"Then use your own, Mr. Road Load."

"I get the message, something about beggars and choosers. Just next time I borrow a bag from you, I'll make darn sure that you put it through a more severe testing than sleeping overnight on your buddy's living room floor."

I didn't own a sleeping bag. Steve had a goose down bag and had loaned me his "other" one before leaving Minneapolis. It seemed like a great way to save a little money. But since camping in the mountains this past week, I knew that something had to change. I was too cold to sleep through the night and it was getting harder and harder for me to physically put in a tough day of bicycling in the mountains.

We started our day bicycling downhill into a canyon-like place called Flaming Gorge. With every foot we descended, we knew that we would have to climb back up out of the gorge. It was beautiful once we got to the bottom; a fortress of rock and stone. We then struggled with our gears and our bikes as we climbed up and out and into state #7, WYOMING. There was no "Welcome to Wyoming" sign to take our traditional border photo shot. Instead, we were greeted with a sign that tersely stated,

"NO SERVICES NEXT 66 MILES."

"Now that's a scary sign!" I shouted in Steve's direction.

The hot, piercing August sun beat down on my bare back. A threatening and insecure feeling was swelling up inside. Thirst, 90-plus-degrees and 66 miles of nothing was an unsettling combination.

"Well, there's our last fuel and water for the day." Steve looked over at the truck stop down the hill from the sign. "Let's go and dump out all of our clothes and fill the bags up with water and submarine sandwiches."

It seriously sounded like a great idea. We both had about a half-gallon water carrying capacity and room for a loaf of bread and some candy bars.

We knew that it was going to be a brutal day ahead.

The warning sign pulled no punches. As we bicycled north through the desert-like mountains of Wyoming, we saw no people, no ranches, no animals, no anything. The miles were agonizingly slowly rolling over on my odometer. Every turn of the wheel seemed like a battle with gravity. The sun scorched down on us. There was absolutely no place to take refuge from the sun, the heat or the pain. We kept plodding forward. I briefly closed my eyes and thought of wonderful times and laughter shared with girlfriends of the past. First love Debbie Jo, vivacious Nancy Lou, stunning Gail Lisa. I was smiling through the pain and sweat rolling off my face and the sting of salt in my eyes. It was helping.

My throat was parched. I reached for my water bottle on my bike frame. Empty. I pulled off to the shoulder and reached for my quart bottle hidden from the sun in my back pannier. I had filled it with half water and half ice cubes. Now, two and a half hours and 28-miles later, it was as warm as bath water. I rationed two good sips. It was heavenly. Refreshed and with water-moistened lips, I felt a little surge again. Lord, help me make it through this day.

Halfway through our tortuous run, my water supply was almost depleted. I bicycled up to Steve who was relaxing on the side of the road and munching on some raisins. He lay on his back looking exhausted. His water was holding out much better than mine, but I refused his generous offer to share.

As Steve appeared to drift off to sleep, I left the road and headed down into a small field where our first signs of life in hours were lazily grazing. It was a herd of cows drinking from a small trickle of water in the ground! I had my empty water bottle in hand and walked upstream where hopefully the animals hadn't pooped in the water. The cows, confused and frightened by my boldness, quickly moved away. I finally found a clear spot and cupped my hand into the stream for a sample. Cold and pure tasting! I drank like a man lost in the desert for a week. I filled up my bottle and headed back to my bike. I felt powerful and confident again.

Hours later the sun was setting. There were still miles and miles to go before "civilization." We were prepared to spend the night in the mountains. I slowly inched up another long incline. Steve was right behind me as I hit the top, expecting a flat road for a few hundred yards and then more gradual climbing as we'd done all day.

I was shocked to see the road heading down, down and more down.

The air was quickly cooling as I shot down the mountain. All right! This was fun bicycling again! We were both charging, averaging 20 – 30 miles per hour.

Miles were blowing by. We were now either bicycling a flat road with a wind at our backs or we were bicycling downhill. Adrenaline filled our bodies with exhilaration and surging strength as we muscled through the remaining miles. We flew around a curve in the road. Dusk was settling in. City lights! Lots and lots of city lights. We had made it!

"WELCOME TO ROCK SPRINGS Population 17,646"

Steve was yipping and hollering in back of me. He rode alongside and stopped as we both stared at the wonderful lights of a city and its people. We hugged each other. It was a triumphant moment.

"We are animals. ANIMALS! I never would have believed that we'd see people tonight or a hot meal. Yahoooooo! I am proud of you, Steve. This was a Herculean effort!"

"Me? You! Great job buddy."

"Let's find a church."

"Forget the church. Did I get you anything for your birthday yet?"

"Birthday? It's August. My birthday isn't until next March."

"Well, that's what I mean. Did I get you anything yet?"

I laughed at Steve and the tremendous smile on his face. "No you haven't."

"Well, Happy Birthday! We're staying in a motel tonight. We'll get some chicken, a few cold brews to celebrate our border crossing today, a bed, TV…"

"Oh, man. That sounds like heaven on earth. Saddle up pilgrim! Let's ride!"

CHAPTER 11
CHRONIC ULCERATIVE COLITIS UNLEASHED!

"Illness is the doctor to whom we pay the most heed; to kindness, to knowledge, we make promise only. Pain we obey." ~ Marcel Proust

WHEN I WOKE UP ON AUGUST 15th IN OUR LITTLE MOTEL room in Rock Springs, Wyoming, it didn't take long for me to realize that an old nemesis of mine was back to haunt me again; chronic ulcerative colitis.

I was first struck with it when I was 21-years-old. It manifests itself in several ways. Sometime it is with severe stomach cramps, blood with your bowel movements or diarrhea, or in my case all three at the same time. To this day it's still not known exactly what causes colitis. It is widely thought that that it is caused by stress or an improper diet. With me it was probably both. After 27 days on the road it would have been hard to count on one hand the good, healthy meals that we had eaten. I couldn't blame my colitis on any mental stress this time because I just wasn't feeling any. I hadn't felt so good about my life and what I was doing for years. But the stress that I was putting on my body was incredible. About the only time that I got a good night's sleep was on those very rare times that we stayed in a motel.

The biggest strain on our bodies had been the last three days and I believed that was directly responsible for this colitis attack. On Friday it was the biking and walking all day in the rain and on Saturday it was climbing out of Vernal, Utah on the toughest climb of the trip so far. Finally, yesterday in Wyoming was an even more physically grueling day with our 66 miles of no service and very little water and food. On top of all of that I got one of the major scares of my life yesterday. A truck almost hit me when it skidded to avoid a dumb cow that walked onto the road just as the truck was flying by. Now I could understand why there were so many dead cows lying in the ditches in this part of the country.

I'm not a good sick person. I'm sort of like a dog when they are sick or injured. We just want to crawl in a corner until we get better and we don't want sympathy or to be bothered by anyone. Even though he'd only known me for two years, Ken thought that he knew me pretty well. Although I kept my initial colitis attacks to myself, nothing could have prepared him for the rotten side of me when I was sick. He was unfortunately about to slowly find out.

A COYOTE HOWLED IN THE STILL OF THE NIGHT. I THREW another log on our now roaring campfire. We were a long way from Minneapolis, Minnesota. The night air was crisp and a few degrees below cool.

Steve looked depressed.

When there are only two of you, you cannot help but to be affected by each other's moods. Steve had been sullen and unusually quiet the past few days. I didn't know why. I was enjoying every moment of our adventure so far. I even loved the painful and grueling days. After years of sedentary and unfulfilling work, I felt alive and meaningful. I was proud of who I was and what we were doing. I believed in taking risks, going against the norm when it made sense to, doing something for people less fortunate, being outdoors surrounded by nature and the elements. All of my values seemed to finally be expressed in this one present endeavor. I knew for a fact now, because I was living it, that when what you believe in doing and what you actually *are* doing are the same, your self-esteem and self-worth head towards the heavens. I felt strong, at peace with God and excited about every day with its new challenges and experiences.

But I truly loved Steve too and he didn't seem happy lately. Was it me? Was he tired of all the time that he spent with only me? I had admitted to a few close friends and family members before we left that I had only one major fear about this yearlong trip. It was not my phobia of snakes, or whether my thrice-operated knee could handle the physical challenge.

My main fear was could I survive one year of 24-hour days with Steve Anderson.

I was a very independent man, with many different circles of friends. Always having been a somewhat complex person with many interests, I enjoyed being around different kinds of people fulfilling different needs and desires in my personality. Could I spend 24 hours a day with anybody for months and months of time? I was convinced before I left that if I could do it, it could only be with Steve. I hadn't known him that long, but we thought alike in so many important ways - about God, dreams, goals, women, how to treat people - and we also seemed to personally mesh so incredibly well. We had an almost innate ability to wear very gently on each other. We rarely if ever rubbed each other the wrong way. We had our moments like any friends, brothers, or even a husband and wife do, but they were so seldom and short-lived. And so the reality of my fear of not getting along with Steve had not yet come to pass.

But what about Steve? Was he homesick? Bummed with me? Missing Lori? Wishing we had never shaken hands months ago? It was eating at me. I had to know.

"Missing Lori?"

Steve was warming and rubbing his hands while gazing into the glowing embers and dancing, mesmerizing flames of the fire. His eyes shot to my face.

"Where did *that* come from?"

"Just been wondering. You've seemed bummed the last few days."

Steve continued staring at our hypnotic fire. "Yeah, I miss her, and being home sometimes."

He wasn't sharing much. After another long moment of silence, I redirected my question.

"Do you wish that we'd never committed to a year on the road?"

I held my breath, fearing his answer.

"No way!" He looked up with an intensity that I hadn't seen in a long time.

"Hey, I have *never* regretted our decision. Don't ever think that. Sure, sometimes I wish that maybe I hadn't met Lori when I did, but that never changed my desire to be with you on the road. I'd be going crazy back home if I knew you were out here by yourself."

Silence. Another coyote howled at the moon in the distance.

"Well, I feel better. I just figured maybe you wished you were back home with Lori."

"Ken, we'll both have our days. I haven't been feeling too well the past couple of days and that has me on edge too. Don't you ever miss home?"

I had to think for a few seconds.

"No, not really. It's only been a month, but I love this too much to wish that I was back in Minnesota. My family is spread out all over the country so I don't see them anyway. I'm sure not being involved with any special female right now helps. I wasn't too happy with how I was spending my time back there, Starr Office and everything, to miss it yet."

The air was getting downright nippy on my backside away from the flames. My body was tired, but my mind and heart felt at peace after hearing Steve's thinking. I finally said,

"It's about time for me to hit it. I'll be up shaking half the night so I better at least get an early start."

"You're going to have to do something about getting a better bag, buddy. These mountains aren't going to go away in the next few days."

The fire felt too good to leave just yet.

"I know, I know. I'll figure out something. Hey, thanks for sharing some of your guts. I feel a lot better and charged for some miles tomorrow."

"If you ever think I don't want to be a part of this thing again, I promise I'll find some 12-foot rattlesnakes and stuff 'em in your sleeping bag when you're not around. They'll keep you warm!"

I stripped to my underwear and eased into my sleeping bag, checking carefully with both hands for anything that slithered.

CHAPTER 12
THE 85-MILE-DAY THAT FOREVER CHANGED OUR LIVES

"There is as much opportunity in change as there is danger." ~ **Earl Nightengale**

I FINISHED THE LAST BITE OF MY BREAKFAST, A CHARBROILED hamburger. Burger and fries were not my normal breakfast food, but last night a camper recommended them and so I thought I would try it.

"How was everything?"

"It was pretty good, Allison." Our waitress was a neat, 29-year-old young woman who had spent three and a half years on a wagon train traveling across country with delinquent teenagers. She had spotted our bicycles and asked all about us. She was the *only* person that we had met so far that truly understood what we were doing and what we were going through. Allison described our adventure as "going to war." What a phrase! But it conveyed perfectly the physical, emotional and mental "battle" one goes through when tackling monumental goals and demanding the max from your body, heart and soul.

"Anything else guys?"

"No thanks. Just our checks. The road's calling."

Steve dropped his head under the table.

"Oh Kenny! Oh Stevie! Let's go! Time to put your buns back on those rock hard seats and start moving or you will never see home again!"

I guess he was doing his impression of the road calling. It was easy to be an idiot when you're the only ones in the restaurant. Allison thought that he was cute and giggled.

"Don't laugh, Allison. You will only encourage him. Just be thankful that you'll never see him again. I've got to spend the next eleven months with him. Day in, day out, day after day after day..."

Now we were all laughing. It felt good. It had been a great morning already.

"Well here are your checks. But the owner, Mrs. Benson, told me to tell you that breakfast is on us today."

I flashed Steve a huge smile.

"She lost her little six-year-old son to heart disease 26 years ago. I told her what you guys are doing for Make-A-Wish and she thinks that's great. Just autograph your checks for her and travel safe."

We were deeply moved and humbled. Out of our sleeping bags for less than a few hours and two very special women had already touched us. Steve and I gave Allison a goodbye hug and waved a thank you to Mrs. Benson who was shyly standing back in the kitchen. Allison slipped me a leather band with hand-stitched beads as I headed for my bike.

"I made them in New Mexico while on the wagon train. Keep them for good luck. Fair winds to you both."

I gave her a final hug. My heart was filling up my whole chest.

"KEN! OVER THERE!" STEVE POINTED TO A FARM ON THE LEFT. Wow! Buffalo. Real live buffalo just like on the westerns on television.

"Oh, give me a home, where the buffalo roam, and the deer and the antelope play!" I was singing at the top of my lungs. The sun was shining and ever so slowly warming the crisp mountain air. It was a glorious morning. Mountains surrounded us and the fragrance of evergreen and mountain floral filled our senses. We were "smelling the roses" today and taking in the breathtaking beauty of Wyoming.

We were extra psyched today because today was MAIL DAY! This event was one of our most celebrated rituals of the road. Although not an exact science, our ritual consisted of making a couple of strategic phone calls to friends and family members telling them to spread the word to write to us and mail to a particular town's general delivery down the road.

Timing had to be perfect.

This was a challenge to do for two reasons. First, we were never positive when we awoke in the morning how many miles we would be able to make that specific day. Wind in particular but also uphill grades that rarely showed on a map, weather in general, our health, who we met, all combined for complex conditions that affected how far we could bicycle. And secondly, our route had the potential to change each and every day. Some days we stayed on the roads that we had anticipated, other days we received new information from locals or from our own experiences and plans changed. So to get mail or clothing sent to us was a challenge. But we usually pulled it off by picking a town way down the road and we didn't do it that often, making "mail day" something I imagined was like getting a package from home in a war zone overseas. It was a rare treat.

A leisurely morning pace of pedaling in the mountains eventually got us to Jackson, Wyoming, a bustling tourist town in the height of its busy season. Traffic was horrendous as we bicycled to the post office.

"Damn!"

Steve looked really disgusted.

"Don't tell me."

"Nothing. Nothing at all."

"I can't believe it. We're too early. I cannot believe that we could possibly be *early*!" I was angry and heartsick. "Now what do we do?"

We both checked the map. North Bend, Oregon was the compromised next stop. That's the best Steve and I could figure out on the spot; on the Oregon coast, probably a couple of weeks away. We would have to tell this post office that when our mail did finally come to forward it there. It was a small consolation. Our spirits had dropped to gutter level. We had been so psyched for this. Steve was really taking a beating as beautiful little Lori had promised a long letter.

Our Kentucky Fried lunch went down without a word.

RISING 13,770 FEET TO THE WEST OF US WAS THE LEGENDARY Grand Teton. After seeing several majestic mountains since pedaling into Colorado, I was a little disappointed at this highly touted tourist attraction. They were right about one thing, though. Although controversy still surrounds the meaning behind the name, we were told that "Grand Teton" loosely translates into "Big Boobs," named by some French Canadian explorer back in the 19th century. They did sort of look like…hmmm…if this is a true translation, he and his fellow explorers must have been without female companionship for a long while!

The road was now flat and we were putting in some good miles.

BOOM! Like a bolt of lightning, a life-altering thought slammed into my brain. Wow. It was a tremendous idea. I knew it immediately.

Steve and I had planned a one-year bicycle trip. Leaving as we did in late July, our goal was to get through the mountain passes of the Northwest during the summer months before the deep snow came that closed roads, and then bicycle down the west coast and across the southern half of the country en route to Florida. We would hit the "Sunshine State" around Christmas, spending the winter months there until spring thawed the northern states, enabling us to bicycle to Maine and then west to Minnesota. But all of a sudden I thought…

WHY NOT BICYCLE STRAIGHT THROUGH TO MINNESOTA WITHOUT STOPPING!

We were making great time anyway. We could possibly be home for Christmas, spend less money, Steve could be back with Lori sooner and most importantly, I realized that Steve and I were not happy when we were not moving. Our original plan was to take a year off and bicycle all 48 states. But now being so involved with Make-A-Wish of Minnesota and calling KSTP every Friday morning to report in on our progress, our "adventure" had evolved into a very committed and intense "cause-driven challenge." We were trying to get people back in Minnesota enthusiastically involved in our cause of pledging money for children with life-threatening illnesses. I could just imagine us spending two to three months in Florida and calling up Dick on a Friday.

"Hey Dick. Steve and I are picking oranges this month and getting some sun at the beach as we gaze at lots of bikini-clad women. I understand that it's 47 degrees below zero in Minneapolis and St. Paul today. Please tell everybody to keep pledging their hard earned dollars on our behalf for the Make-A-Wish children. We'll talk to you next week and update your listeners on how our tans are progressing."

That didn't make any sense to me anymore.

My idea really got me pumped. I charged my bike to catch Steve who was a couple of hundred yards ahead of me. I shared my idea as we bicycled side by side.

He thought I was nuts.

I dropped back several yards and let him think about it. I knew that Steve needed time to process things. My mind was still racing. Finally, about a half an hour later he pulled off the shoulder for a cookie and a water break. I pulled over and just stared at him with a huge grin on my face.

"Well?" I kept smiling at him waiting for any response.

"Well what?"

"What do you think of my idea?"

"You really are serious!"

"You bet I am! Think about it. We won't tell anybody. We'll just keep right on charging, pedaling mile after mile, November, December, January, blasting through blizzards, freezing temperatures and icy roads. What a challenge!"

My eyes and voice were on fire. Steve listened intently and finally understood how serious and enthusiastic I was. It was outrageous.

We shook hands. We would go for it and blast home by Christmas.

Our 80-mile day ended in a drenching rain. Cold, wet, hungry and in pitch-blackness again, we rolled into a campground. As we walked our bikes to a site, the awful sound of hissing pierced the quiet. Steve had rolled over a thorn and flattened his bike tire. He cussed up a storm in tired, wet frustration. A mere twelve hours earlier we had been served a special breakfast by Allison on the house on a glorious, sunny morning.

Unlike a sometimes routine or even monotonous day back home, these long days on the road were full of exhilarating highs and despairing lows, all within a single sunup to sundown.

CHAPTER 13
GRIZZLIES, DETERIORATING STEVE & HUNTING HARMON

"We must accept finite disappointment, but never lose infinite hope."
~ Martin Luther King, Jr.

"YOU GUYS HAVE ONLY ONE OPTION. TALK TO THE RANGERS and see if they'll put you up somewhere. Two years ago a couple of bicyclists passed through and didn't stop at a designated area. The next morning they found pieces of those guys over an acre area. Grizzlies are not animals to screw around with." The elderly, weather-beaten cook at the Old Faithful Inn turned and ambled back inside.

"Now *that's* what I call good, sound advice!" I looked over at Mr. Anderson. It was obvious that we didn't need to discuss this any further. It was off to the ranger station.

We were in the middle of Yellowstone National Park at dusk. It had been a historic day of firsts. We had seen our first elk, moose, hot spring and geyser. We felt that it was in our best interests not to add "grizzly bear" to that list.

The ranger station was easy to locate, about 200 yards from Old Faithful herself, the most famous geyser in the world. It was a large log cabin that blended perfectly with its rustic and wilderness setting.

They told us to sleep in our bags only, no tents, and to please hang all of our food high up in a tree. Promising to follow those instructions, they allowed us to sleep right in back of the ranger station.

I slipped into my bag about five yards from Steve. The sky was aglow with millions of stars.

"Sleep well tonight, buddy." I thought that I detected a slightly mischievous tone to Steve's voice.

"I will. You too."

"Oh. I won't have any problems. You just be careful."

"Careful?"

"Of those big, bad grizzly guys."

"I'm too ugly and smelly. And you don't have enough meat on your scrawny body to make it worth their while to even rip into your bag. Good night."

"Just make sure that you say your prayers before you drift off to sleep."

I hadn't bitten yet but now it was obvious he was setting me up for something.

"What are you getting at?"

"Well, I really shouldn't tell you this but tonight when you're sleeping, I intend to take some needle and thread and sew six strips of bacon onto your sleeping bag." Steve was giggling now. "So, sleep well."

I snapped. I started to laugh so hard that I could barely breathe. Through my tears I managed a weak and pathetic sounding reply.

"Thanks buddy. Just please clean up all of my bones in the morning so the ranger doesn't get mad at us." We giggled off to sleep.

As I rolled out of my sleeping bag, I already knew that I was in for a nightmare of a day. Last night had been fun, but already this morning I was cramping up and my day was only a few minutes old. Ken was getting a real crash course on the effects of colitis on both of us. My diarrhea was so bad now that I was running for the bathroom, or more accurately the woods, every half hour or so.

We had opted for taking the desert part of Idaho instead of the mountains so that I wouldn't have to exert myself so much. This brought another problem that added to my frustration. Finding a private place in the desert can be very difficult, especially when there's a lot of traffic going by. In the past five days it had gotten so bad that I was passing mostly blood. When you see that much blood coming out of yourself it gets pretty scary.

I called my doctor back in Minnesota, Dr. Ron Pizinger. He was quite surprised to hear where I was calling from and even more surprised to hear how I had gotten there. He had been my doctor for several years ever since I got colitis. Through regular usage of a medicine called, agulfidine, we had kept my colitis in check. When I had an occasional flair up we treated it with cortenemas and that would usually take care of it. He told me on the telephone that none of these treatments would work if I didn't get some rest. After 37 days on the road, I was so used to the everyday grind of biking, that I confidently and calmly told him,

"Well, we're riding through the desert now instead of the mountains and we're only riding about 70 miles a day."

He almost came through the phone.

"Are you nuts? Are you trying to kill yourself? That's a hell of a lot of work even for a healthy person. You are sick. If you don't get some rest NOW you will never get better!"

I realized after his outburst, that suggesting riding through the desert instead of over the mountains was getting rest, was merely rationalization on my part.

"Well, do you think that it will help if I stop riding for a few days and start taking cortenemas a couple times a day?"

I was looking for a positive answer from Dr. Pizinger. I did not want to cut this trip short for any reason. I was totally consumed with our venture and it meant more to me than anything had previously in my life. The answer that I got was not want I wanted.

"I want you to come home so I can take a look at you and then we'll determine if you can continue or not."

The shock of this statement left me almost speechless. Almost in tears, I pleaded with him for a different solution to my problem.

"Completing this trip means everything to me. I'm doing this for Make-A-Wish of Minnesota. There are a lot of people back home depending on me. I just have to finish this. It's not like I'm desperately ill. I haven't lost too much weight and I'm feeling fine. It's just that this diarrhea is just so inconvenient. If I can just get rid of it, I'll be fine."

I was really understating my case. I could already tell I had lost a lot of weight and I didn't feel fine a lot of the time. I was feeling very run down, I suppose because of all of the blood that I was losing.

In a tone of resignation, Dr. Pizinger answered,

"Okay, Steve, we'll see what we can do for you so you can continue this craziness. Call me with the number of the next drug store you get to and I'll get a prescription for some cortenemas. Good luck, kid."

After I hung up I wondered if Dr. Pizinger would use my case as a testimonial to other patients that you can still live an active life even if you have colitis. Probably not. He knew that I was doing my body no good by continuing to ride but he also knew that he couldn't stop me.

I was hoping for a miracle. I knew that my condition was bad and I was so afraid. I was scared to death that this was just one more thing in my life that I would not complete.

IDAHO, STATE NUMBER NINE, WAS QUICKLY BECOMING ONE OF my favorite states. Home of awesome scenery, great potatoes and friendly people, it was also the home of my boyhood idol, Harmon Killebrew.

This was wilderness country. A gas station owner, Big Bill of Mack's Inn, Idaho, had told quite a story to us earlier in the day. Last winter, a little four-and-a-half-foot 65-year-old lady was sleeping on the second floor of her house. She awoke suddenly hearing loud knocks on her front door. When she went to the window, she looked down to see an eight-foot grizzly bear standing at her door! She calmly went to her closet, pulled out and loaded her 12-gauge shotgun, returned to the window and shot the eyes right out of that grizzly bear and then went back to bed! Now, true or false or somewhere in between, that's a story!

I had enjoyed an exhilarating day of bicycling, but Steve was progressively deteriorating. His colitis was not getting better. The drugs that he had gotten earlier from a drug store didn't seem to be working. He was often listless, quiet and unsure of himself.

As we pulled into the campground, I found a beautiful site near a stream.

"Not there!" Steve gruffly shot at me. "Over here." It was a much smaller area, with only a few barren trees. But I immediately saw why it was Steve's choice. There, ten feet way from the site, was an outhouse. He needed to have a place nearby where he could go to the bathroom quickly and privately. I wasn't going to argue.

We set up camp for the night. I then milled around and started asking people where I could find Harmon Killebrew. It was a long shot for sure, but I wanted to phone him and tell him what we were up to and to say how much that I had respected him all of my life. Nobody knew where he was currently living. Finally, a warm, friendly camper named Wayne asked around for me.

"Found him!"

"Seriously?" I asked.

"You bet; asked my son-in-law, Kenny. Killer built a new place over in Fruitland, just over the Oregon border." I knew that Fruitland was on the road west that we would be taking.

"That's tremendous, Wayne. You're a good man."

"Glad to help. Hope you find him."

As I lay down in my tent for the night, I heard the distant sounds of a band playing at a nearby club. It was 9 PM on a Friday night. I imagined the place to be full of pretty women dancing and people happily chatting and relaxing after a long week of work. I would love to have been there. But, Steve and I didn't have weekend breaks. Our trip was relentless that way. There were always more miles to put on, especially when the weather was accommodating.

Tomorrow was hopefully going to be a day of good riding. Forecast was good and we needed an 80-plus-mile-day under our belts to lift our spirits. We had been averaging 60 miles the past two days because of mountains, wind and rain. 80 miles seemed to be our magic number, the break point to let us know that we had a successful day. So there'd be no playing tonight like folks were doing all across the country. But as quickly as I felt sorry for myself, I shook it off.

We were different. We were probably the only two people in the entire world doing exactly what we were doing. I would dance when I got back home.

"HONK! HONK!" IT WAS THE UNMISTAKABLE SOUND OF A SEMI horn blasting me his message. In plain English it translated to, "Get your damn bicycle off *my* road now and onto the shoulder because here I come, wimpy bike boy!" I had learned the hard way weeks ago that a truck horn behind me meant more than, "be careful because I'm coming." I made the mistake of simply hugging the outermost part of the road to give a driver ample road, when he suddenly roared by me and then drove the cab of his truck onto the shoulder. This brought his entire rig onto the shoulder forcing me into the ditch and blowing one of my tires. I never argued with a semi horn again. I simply had no leverage when these 20-ton bullies kicked sand in my face.

It was another tremendous day of bicycling in sunny, gorgeous Idaho. The wind was at our back and Steve and I were putting on some miles. By 1:30 PM we had 34 miles under our belts and needed a break to cool off from a dry, 86-degree sun. I spotted a little country store on the side of the road.

"I'm buying. What will work for you?"

My parched throat greatly appreciated Mr. Anderson's offer.

"V8."

"I'm going to grab a Popsicle for myself."

"I'll refill the water bottles." I headed for the men's washroom to reload our four water bottles with the coldest water that I could find. At 86 degrees they wouldn't stay cold for too long.

"Nice bikes!" She was a pretty 18-year-old woman sitting on her ten-speed. I loaded our water on the bicycles.

"Where in the heck are you guys from?" It was a question that we answered a dozen times a day.

"Minnesota."

"You are kidding me!" She seemed even more incredulous than most. The fact that she was on her own bicycle probably helped her to appreciate just how far we had come on our machines.

"What are you guys trying to do?"

Steve arrived with my V8. We made introductions and briefly told our story. Our new friend, Susan, seemed genuinely impressed with our adventure. Finally it was time to roll, time to get those good miles that were out there for us today. I went to shake Susan's hand.

"Hey, how about you guys coming back to the house for a little bit. I live with a bunch of young people who are really into bicycling and would love to meet you and see these bikes. Our place is right on your way out of town."

Steve gave me "the look." We really were in the mood to bicycle and not to chat. The wind was at our back and we had another six hours of daylight. However, our now legendary rule, **"Never say no to any reasonable offer"** was always in effect.

"That would be fun, Susan. But we have to make it a quick visit," I added.

Susan's "house" was a seminary! Susan's gang of bicycling enthusiasts was several fellow seminarians studying to be ministers. Steve and I were both surprised by this revelation.

"Steve, Ken, I want you to meet Reverend Bill Bibbens, our leader and advisor here at the Seminary."

Bill, a big burly man with a full beard extended his hand and gave us both a huge smile. He was about 35-years-old and looked a lot like the legendary trumpet player, Al Hirt. Just by being in his presence for a few quick introductory moments, I could feel something very special about him. He sort of glowed. We then met the gang of ten students, including "Bear," a Doberman pinscher that sent chills up my spine. He didn't like strangers and I accepted that and kept a good distance away.

Everybody had questions, questions and more questions. I took Steve aside and whispered to him, "It's 2:30. Let's be on the road by 3:15."

"Sounds good."

We left 19 hours later.

Our minutes at the seminary turned into hours. When their questions wound down, we took our turn. Bill Bibbens was one of the most fascinating men I had ever met. We talked politics, communism, cult worship, Mormonism, radio programming, miracle healing, favorite country music artists and on and on. One thing led to another; supper, a trip to a country radio station where Bill worked a three hour afternoon DJ shift, discussions around the fire during the evening and finally to overnight sleeping. The next day, with a great Sunday morning breakfast literally under our belts, it was time to bid farewell to our new friends.

Bill, who had had a healing ministry over the years, laid hands on Steve, anointed him with oils and prayed that his colitis would heal.

As we prepared to leave, Bill told me not to worry about my health problems. He believed with all his heart that God had caused Ken's and my paths to cross for the sole purpose of this adventure. He could not believe that God wouldn't let us complete our goal since we were doing it for Make-A-Wish and there were lots of people back home and people we had already met across the country who were biking vicariously through what we were doing.

For good measure, Bill anointed me with oil and laid his hands on my head and asked God to heal me. Tears came to my eyes as I felt a warmth surge through every fiber of my body. For a second I thought maybe that this was the miracle I was looking for. All I knew for sure was that I was feeling a lot of love from the Reverend Bill Bibbens and his students standing around me.

We waved our final goodbye to Bill and the others standing there in front of a backdrop of the majestic Grand Teton. I felt better than I had in weeks. I wondered if Bill really did have healing hands. As good as I felt right now I had a feeling it was very temporary.

Unfortunately, I was right.

Ten miles west of Rexburg on Route 33, I could feel the burning sensation in my stomach. I jumped off my bike and scrambled for the ditch just in time to pass a lot of blood. Ken had learned quickly in the early stages of my affliction that when he saw my shoulders hunch up, I was experiencing some pain and I would be searching for a place to relieve myself as quickly as I possibly could. If he was riding behind me, he would hang way back in order to give me a little privacy.

When I came out of the ditch, Ken was slowly rolling by. With a look of genuine compassion and sadness he asked, "Are you okay buddy?"

I found it very hard to look into his eyes as I simply nodded my head up and down.

We rode a good distance from each other for the rest of that day.

My colitis had come back with a fury. I knew that Ken was as let down as I was. My dream of covering America on a bicycle was turning into a nightmare and it was for Ken too. Ken's natural instincts were to help someone in need. Again, like a wounded dog I just wanted to be left alone. This left Ken very frustrated and forced him to spend most of his day in silence, because he never knew when it was safe to talk to me.

Despite my problem, we headed west. What a strange and beautiful country, I thought to myself, as we eventually rolled 77 miles closer to Oregon.

The second highlight of my draining day was that a cute blonde girl in a little red Toyota just outside of, ironically, Butte City mooned me. Surprises on the road took all kinds of forms!

"YOU GUYS NEED SOME ICE-COLD WATER?"

Steve and I were in the middle of the sagebrush desert of Idaho. It was 44 miles between towns and water. The old man in the pickup on the shoulder of the road had made an irresistible offer as we slowly tried to bicycle by him.

"You sure you got enough for yourself?" I asked politely.

"Heck, if a guy can't offer some water to his neighbor, this world of ours has no chance."

The water was ice cold and a real uplift on a 90-degree-plus-day. We shared some of our story and he proceeded to give us ten dollars for the kids of Make-A-Wish. He was down the road before we had even exchanged names.

The screwballs and troublemakers of the world always make the newspapers and somehow they seem to be everywhere. But as Steve and I continued to run into people, one on one, on the back roads of America, most of them reached out and tried to help us. When times were the most brutal, lonely or painful, somebody seemed to pop up somewhere and gently reinforce us.

The wind soon shifted and started to blow right in our faces. Halfway through our 44-mile-stretch to the next town, we found a building at a very strange roadside rest area, called Craters of the Moon. Other than a couple of buildings devoted to restrooms, it was a desolate area very appropriately named.

We slowly walked our bicycles over to a building that appeared to have no function. It did, however, provide us with our one desperate need; shade.

The sun was tormenting.

We leaned our bicycles against the building in the hopes that the wind would die down even a few miles per hour. Both of us promptly fell asleep.

"Ken, Ken!" I lazily rolled over in the cool shade. "It's 6 PM." As my mind slowly shifted from dreamland to reality, the first thing that I realized was that the wind was still blowing hard out of the southwest. I glanced at Steve. He looked really troubled.

"What do you want to do?"

"I can't make it."

I had never seen Steve like this. In recent days he'd become much more quiet, irritable and listless because of the medication he was taking for his colitis. But now for the first time in my life as I stared at him and tried to get a game plan together, I noticed something new. I saw fear in his eyes.

"Steve, we easily have three hours of daylight left and only 24 miles to go to the next town. We can make it, wind or no wind."

"We can't make it. I need more medication. I don't think that I can bicycle another mile."

I was shook up. We were in the middle of the desert, stuck in a little oasis that literally looked like craters on a moon. It was downright eerie. There was a place to camp, because of tourists who drive by, but there was no food. Steve finally decided to hitchhike, bike and all, the next 130 miles to a good-sized-city called, Mountain Home, where he could get some serious prescription drugs to combat this colitis hell.

There was virtually no traffic. The few that sped by took one look at a bearded biker *and* his bike and decided to keep speeding by. Eventually we made the decision to spend the night where we were. Steve was in his sleeping bag before the sun went down. This colitis thing was becoming very scary.

We awoke at 6:30 AM and took advantage of the still air to put on miles. Desert riding was at least flat; dry, dusty, scorching hot...but flat as a proverbial pancake. By 3:30 PM we had 80 miles under our belts. Steve was miserable and ornery but he was riding the whole day at a great clip. 93.5 miles later we set up camp for the night.

The following day we rolled into Mountain Home and checked into the cheapest motel that we could find. It was $20 a night for a room with a kitchenette. It was time to rest, regroup, wash clothes, get more medicine and get Steve healthy.

"Hey Steve, I'm going to find a Laundromat and wash my clothes. Do you want me to wash yours too?"

"I can do it."

"Hey, I'm heading over there to do mine anyway. You stay off your feet and I'll get it. It's really no big deal."

"Ken, I said I'll do it. Damn it! Don't baby me! It's not like I'm sick, sick."

"All right! I'm gone."

I grabbed my clothes and headed out the door without saying another word. I was burning. My anger was swelling and exploding inside so much that my head hurt. That son-of-a-gun better get better soon!

I walked down the street with my dirty clothes in my sleeping bag, slung over my shoulder like a sailor. The sidewalks were full of people, but I was too deep in thought to see anybody. Steve was miserable and that made me sad. But, I was also having a really rough time dealing with his lows and my inability to do anything for him. He doesn't want me to baby him. Humph! My nature is to take care of somebody when they're hurting. And damn it, he is "sick, sick!" The doctor told him that he would only get better if he was off of his feet.

This was getting maddening.

"DEAR PRODUCER OF THE TONIGHT SHOW:

Three months ago my friend Steve Anderson and I, Ken Rogers, took off on a 10,000-mile, 48-state bicycle trip. We are raising money for terminally-ill children. We didn't plan, physically train or know anything about bicycling the day that we left. We will be in the Los Angeles area in about two weeks."

"Steve, you're going to love this! I've written to Bicycling Magazine, National Geographic and now to The Tonight Show. Think big, right?"

"The Tonight Show?" Steve was lying flat on his back and watching some tube. In only two days of being off the bicycle he seemed to be a lot better.

"Sure! Do you ever see some of the idiots those guys put on late in the show? We're interesting stuff. We could bicycle out from behind the curtain, tell him how it took me 2,000 miles to learn how to fix a flat tire, about the blonde that mooned you last week; they'll love it! Sure beats some guy who comes out with a 20-pound potato he grew in his basement. We'll be major Hollywood stars!"

I could tell Steve was coming around. He wasn't paying any attention to my exaggerated hyperbole. We would be back on the road soon.

"INFORMATION PLEASE. YES, I WOULD LIKE THE NUMBER FOR Harmon Clayton Killebrew in Fruitland, Oregon please?"

"Just a moment sir."

Pause. My heart was pounding. I felt like a teenager trying to get his first date for the prom.

"I'm sorry sir. That number is unlisted."

"You're kidding!"

"No sir. I am sorry." Click.

I felt drained. I had been so pumped, so psyched and nervous for that call. Now I felt like a big bowl of Jell-O. I walked out of the small Amoco station.

"Well?" Steve peered quizzically at my depressed face.

"Unpublished number."

"Well, you tried."

"Gol darn it!" My loss now was turning to anger.

"I really wanted to see that guy. This will probably be my only chance to ever meet him on even terms. I mean, you know, we're doing something pretty unusual and kind of special and after spending all of those years in Minnesota he might have been interested to see us."

"Who are you looking for?" The old guy pumping gas had overheard my strange conversation with Steve.

"Harmon Killebrew."

"Not in town."

I angrily thought to myself, what are you, his buddy or what? How did he know where in the heck Harmon was?

"He's in Sun Valley, Idaho, at a celebrity golf tournament; does it every year."

Back on the road, the day was far from a total loss. We were blowing off the miles. It felt tremendous to be moving again and pounding out a great day. Steve was really encouraging and in great spirits.

"How many miles?" Steve knew that it was going to be a good number.

"Believe it or not, we not only got state number ten today, Oregon, but we nailed 104.5 miles!"

"Yahoo! Our first 100-mile day! Boy did we need that. We still have to do more serious digging to get back on track after our little 'vacation' in Mountain Home. But what a great day it's been. We are animals!"

That's what happens when we bicycle hard from 8 AM to 8 PM. I missed the comfort of my soft, cozy, warm motel bed. But I wouldn't trade my sleeping bag on my little air mattress in the middle of desolation somewhere in Oregon for anything!

"I'd rather wake up in the middle of nowhere than in any city on earth."
~ Steve McQueen

CHAPTER 14
FOGGY MOUNTAIN BREAKDOWN

THE CRUNCHING SOUND WAS GETTING WORSE. SOMETHING was really wrong. After 2,500 miles on my Acabar, I knew every rattle and clink sound that she made.

This was new. This was scary.

I shifted to my lowest gear and I continued to climb a pretty steep grade. Much better, I thought. The pressure was lighter as I pedaled. The "crunch," although still there, had really quieted down. We were a good 15 miles from Unity, Oregon, the next town down the road. Steve was bicycling ahead of me, miles ahead I guessed since I had not seen him for a good twenty minutes. I hated bicycling behind and out of eyesight. Steve had our only set of tools to fix a flat or repair any minor breakdowns. I should really get my own set of tools and be a little more independent of Steve in case anything...

CRUNCH, CRUNCH...KACHOOM! My pedal shot straight to the ground. I lost all mechanical tension and stopped moving completely. I looked to my back wheel. There on the pavement was my entire freewheel! One of *the* most important mechanisms on any bicycle was on the ground. Now what?

I bent down and then saw little ball bearings strewn all over the place. I felt totally helpless. They had been impacted in my free wheel and now with the free wheel off they were all over the highway. There was no traffic. There was no Steve. I carried my bike to the shoulder and gently laid her down. Dropping to my hands and knees, I crawled onto the highway and started to slowly pick up my ball bearings...one at a time...1...2...3...8...17...27...

"What's going on?"

Steve had realized that I had been gone for too long out of sight and had circled back to check on me. Seeing him quieted my fears a little.

"Lost my free wheel and now my bearings...36...37...38...have to find them all so I can put them all back in." I must have looked like a crazed and desperate man.

"Ken, no way are you going to find them all. You need every last one of them or it won't work."

There...46...47...I couldn't see any more. I scanned down the road. Six feet back I saw two more bearings glistening in the sun...48...49. I looked long and hard at #49. It was all torn up, about one third of its original size. My heart dropped into my gut. It hit me. The crunching noise. I had been tearing up my ball bearings for miles. They could have been grinding up and spitting from my bike for who knows how far back down the mountain I had been climbing.

I was sunk.

"Do you understand what I am trying to say? With even one bearing missing, they are packed so that…"

"Forget it. I'm dead meat. I'm not even close to having them all." I suddenly felt very tired. I was worn out, a beaten man. We were in the middle of nowhere and I couldn't bicycle a single foot. I lay down by my bicycle and closed my eyes in the blistering sun.

It didn't take long for Steve and me to figure out that I had no other options except to hitchhike the next 15 miles. It was a very disappointing decision. I was a purist. Steve and I had committed to the people of Minnesota that we would bicycle all 48 states.

The possibility of not bicycling even one mile had never entered either of our minds. Steve had gently, but firmly told me that we were a **team.** Part of the team would be bicycling the miles. I didn't have a choice. I wasn't, nor were we, cheating in any way. It had to be this way.

The driver kept his eyes straight ahead, as if he never saw me. That would have been impossible. There I stood, 6'2", 210 pounds, beard, stripped to the waist, thumb out and a bicycle next to me, upside down and its wheel off, signifying serious trouble. Another car zoomed by. Ten minutes later a car finally pulled over. I sadly loaded my broken Acabar into the trunk.

For the first time in 3,000 miles I was about to be a passenger. I felt sick.

"I CAN'T HELP YOU SON. NOTHIN'S BROKEN, BUT YOU'RE missing about 100 ball bearings. I can't even get close to that size for you."

Dang it. What else can go wrong? I walked out the door of the only mechanic in Unity, Oregon. I headed for the phone book. After 30 minutes of calling towns and explaining my predicament, I found somebody who could help me. Randy at Oregon Sound and Cycle would fix me tomorrow at 9 AM. The only problem was that his bike shop was in John Day, 51 miles further down the road.

Steve eventually bicycled into town and I told him what I was up to. It was back to the thumb. Steve would bicycle as far as he could until the sun went down and then camp out. I would hitch into John Day and find a place to sleep there until 9 AM tomorrow.

"It is very weird saying goodbye to you, Steve." I was back on the side of the road next to my upside down bicycle. I wouldn't see Steve again for about 16 – 18 hours. We had not spent a night apart since our last night in Minneapolis before we left town.

"You gonna be okay, buddy? No grizzlies are going to gnaw on your legs tonight or anything will they?" I had my lower lip as low as it could go in a mock pouting look. I was trying to be funny but I really did feel sad, and I was concerned about Steve being all alone with no backup.

A car pulled over, interrupting my gloom.

"Looks like you got a problem." A young man named Kevin put Acabar into his trunk and off we flew as Steve waved goodbye. Kevin had a million questions and I just wanted to be alone in my thoughts. It was around 5:30 PM and the evening drive through the Oregon Mountains and forests was beautiful. Everything seemed so surreal at 60 MPH. Every hill I imagined what gears I'd be using on my bike. Every mile that flew by was a mile I would never bicycle nor be able to go back to. The further we drove, the more depressed I became.

It took me three rides to get my 51 miles. We slowed to 30 mph as we hit the city limits of John Day.

"Well, Kenny, where do you think that you are going to spend the night?" Tena was a vivacious, shapely brunette who had been my most enjoyable company of the three drivers. Her large dog, Zan, was in the back of the pickup truck. I didn't normally accept rides from women whenever I hitchhiked in the past. Hitchhiking is risky enough for both rider and driver and I wouldn't want my girlfriend, sister or daughter picking up a strange man. But Zan looked like he could take my head off with one swing of his meaty paw if I made the wrong move, so I knew that Tena's risks in picking somebody up were minimal.

"I don't know, Tena. I'll probably find a little motel in town. I haven't slept in a bed for quite a while."

"No way. You're coming home with Zan and me. My husband David is waiting and we're going to get pizza and relax tonight. You've got the couch on the porch."

Tena never asked. She just took the reins. I smiled. I was really beat up on the inside and so I appreciated her taking any decisions right out of my hands. It would also be comforting and invigorating to spend the evening with new friends.

MY BIKE WAS BACK IN ONE PIECE. ACABAR LOOKED GOOD. "Dr. Randy" at Oregon Cycle had not only fixed the problem, he had given her a full tune-up. I was now road ready.

"Well, Tena, you have been a little angel with skin on for me. Thank you for your home, scrumptious breakfast and just sort of taking care of me." Her husband, Dave, was at work and she had driven me to the bike shop earlier in the morning. Steve had blown into town a few minutes ago and we were both ready to team up again.

I hugged Tena. She smiled.

"I'll drop a line when we get back to Minnesota."

"Let's go get Washington," Steve excitedly exclaimed. Off we flew together again. He seemed to be feeling a little better despite freezing his butt off camping in the mountains last night.

"And I was worrying about you! Pizza, beer, a hot bath, soft couch, rough livin'! I had a Milky Way for supper, coyotes for friends, about 28 degrees and a rock hard ground to sleep on."

"Yeah, and you wouldn't have traded places with me for the world."

We both knew that he never would have. Steve had bicycled 64 miles that I had not. His bicycle tires had never left the ground for even an inch since we left St. Paul.

I would just have to live with that.

CHAPTER 15
TO COAST OR NOT TO COAST, THAT IS THE QUESTION

"Quarrel with a friend, and you are both wrong." ~ **Lao-tzu**

IT HAD BEEN A TOUGH CLIMB. I INCHED PAST STEVE AND flashed him a grimacing smile.

"I sure am making some compromises," he growled at me with a somber, pained look.

What in the heck was *that* all about, I wondered? My legs hurt too badly to worry about his ornery remark.

It was high noon. It was time for fuel.

As I dug into my double cheese bacon burger and fries, I watched curiously as Steve kept scratching figures with a pen on a piece of paper next to his Western United States map. I didn't even ask. He finally laid down his pen.

"The great debate will soon begin." It was a stern, ominous announcement.

"What are you talking about?"

"I'm talking about our route. I've given this a lot of thought lately. I do not want to bicycle to the coast. It doesn't make sense."

My French fry choked up in the back of my throat. I was stunned. My eyes started to water. They only do that when I get ferociously angry. I tried to measure my words.

"You don't want to bicycle to the Oregon coast? That's been our plan since way before we left Minnesota! This isn't anything we even need to talk about or compromise on. What is the problem?"

"Look…" There was a fire in Steve's eyes that I had never, ever seen before.

132

"If we bicycle to the Oregon coast, down California and back to Nevada, we'll be going 352 miles out of our way, we'll have to bicycle over three mountain passes that we don't need to, there will be more time, more rain…"

"I don't give a damn! Bicycling down the Oregon/California coast on Highway 101 and Highway 1 has always been my dream! The ocean! Hell, my dream? It was *our* dream!"

"We simply don't need to bicycle that far to get our states. We'll think this through later."

I was enraged. I pushed the rest of my burger aside and paid my check.

My mind started to cloud with bitterness and resentful thoughts. I pounded off the miles. Steve must be in a footrace to get back to Lori. I wanted to scream.

I wanted to see the Pacific Ocean from my bicycle seat!

I had heard stories about the awesomeness of that coastline for years and years. Now we had bicycled from St. Paul, Minnesota to the state of Oregon and we were still heading west. I mean, I could almost taste it and today Steve says to forget it. "We don't need to bicycle that far to get our states." His stunning words continued to sting in my ears and in my soul. My heart felt like a rock.

I had never had a serious disagreement with Steve since I had known him in two years. But now I was in a quiet rage. And, to make it worse, I could not get away from it! We were stuck together. There wasn't even another friend that I could turn and talk to like I would normally back home. I just kept bicycling ahead of Steve. I did not even want to see him.

We bicycled in silence for over three hours. At occasional breaks, Steve was friendly and asked me questions regarding other things. I was stoic. I could not look him in the eyes or speak beyond a needed "yes" or "no."

I felt betrayed and very alone.

After thousands of miles on the road together, Ken and I had learned the fine art of compromise. Our only three decisions that we had to make almost daily were which route to take, where should we eat and where should we stay for the night. With one of our original rules of the road stating, "The tired man and hungry man calls the shots," we experienced almost no tension because it would have seemed so petty to both of us to ever have any disagreement on our three daily variables. We got along so well and gave each other almost too much room to make decisions that we finally came up with a guiding principle that stayed with us throughout the trip.

"Any decision is a good decision."

Needless to say, I NEVER thought that Ken and I would ever have a major disagreement. Well, on our 44th day we finally did.

That day during lunch I really dropped a bomb on Ken. I proposed a major route change. Since the planning stages of the trip, we had not only envisioned covering all 48 states, but also of seeing the Pacific and Atlantic Oceans.

My colitis was not getting any better; in fact it was getting worse and I consequently wanted to more directly cover the western states by avoiding lots of mountain climbing and close to 400 miles while still touching all of the states needed to reach our goal. My new route did all of that. It also meant not being able to see some breathtaking scenery and not being able to bicycle down the legendary Pacific Coast Highway.

This left Ken noticeably stunned and upset. He barely said ten words to me the rest of the day. Ken was concerned for my well being and wanted me to get well, but this was one solution to the problem that he was not expecting.

As the sun was dropped lower in the sky around dusk, I pulled my bicycle over and stretched out on the shoulder. I was way ahead of Steve, having not even seen a glimpse of him for over an hour.

I could not continue to bicycle in bitterness.

I did not have to feel so alone. I gave it all to God. A favorite Bible verse heard over the years shot through my consciousness. "The Lord is my shepherd. I shall not want." I believed that salvation was mine and He was in control. With eternity in perspective, what difference does a silly coast make?

"Take it all, God. Give me back my peace. This anger and bitterness feels awful. And, by the way, let's do this *tomorrow*. I'll be happy again tomorrow. I'm still sort of grinded by the whole deal today and I want to sulk for a few more hours yet."

It was a very real and honest prayer. I felt better. Not great, but better. I got on my bike and continued down the road.

I OPENED MY SLEEPING BAG. NO NEED FOR A TENT TONIGHT. The air was dry and balmy, the bugs seemed to be somewhere else and it was a clear, starry night. It was a beautiful place to camp, as we were right on the sandy beach of the John Day River.

"Ken?"

Yeah?"

"Ah...I need some feedback from you. I've never seen you like this."

Steve was sitting up on his sleeping bag about six feet away. He seemed unsettled. I knew that I had been a jerk since lunch, hardly saying a word to him at all. I simply did not want to say anything more today. I could have gotten away with it back home. There were other places to go, other people to be with. But on the road Steve and I only had each other. And we were committed to a 10,000-mile cause, 24 hours a day. If there were any problems between us, we had no choice but to somehow work them out. But tonight I just wanted to go to sleep.

"Steve, I don't really want to talk about it tonight. We're not going to see eye-to-eye on this one."

"Yeah, but I've never seen you this mad at me. If I thought that this decision was going to threaten our friendship then I never would have brought it up."

He looked really sad.

My heart softened a little. I reached for words.

"Steve, it's just that we were both so darn excited about the West Coast. That was going to be the highlight of our whole trip! The ocean, the little coastal towns, southern California beaches; it's been my dream ever since college. Now, we're so close. And I always thought that it was a given. There are a thousand decisions and compromises I knew that you and I would have to make in order to get back home, but *this* was never to be one of them! Until today. I honestly feel like you're just chopping off miles to get back to Lori. Maybe I'd feel the same way if I were you. But, I'm not and I don't. I want the ocean. And you're trying to take that away. I have been as angry today as I can get."

I paused. The words were pouring out of my mouth. My thoughts had been accumulating with every bitter mile I bicycled today. I felt a relief just getting them out of my chest and heart.

"Look Ken, it's not a Lori thing. I promise. I'm just tired, tired of climbing mountains, tired of being wet all of the time. My colitis scares the hell out of me. Maybe if I were healthy I'd feel differently. You don't know what I'm going through. You can't. I just don't want to put on hundreds of miles that we don't have to."

The pragmatist and the romantic. We were both looking at this dilemma from our own perspectives. It was impossible not to. Up to this point I had no idea that Steve's colitis was affecting him so deeply. But at least now we understood each other a little better. Our brutal honesty with each other greatly helped us.

It wasn't over. But I knew our friendship was going to survive its biggest challenge so far.

After much cajoling, I finally got Ken to talk to me. We ended up going to sleep friends once again. I was glad about this, but I also had an overwhelming feeling of guilt. I felt terrible that Ken would have to change his plans so drastically because of me. I knew that if the roles were reversed, I would do the same, but that didn't help much.

MY LEGS SURGED WITH POWER. I STOMPED DOWN ON MY bicycle pedal like a lap swimmer pushing off the side of the pool on the turn. State #11, Washington, was in back of us! Straddling our bikes in the northwest corner of the United States, we had pedaled as far as we would go in this direction.

Our bicycles now pointed south!

The Washington State sign had been our turning point. The state line happened to be halfway across the Sam Hill Memorial Bridge, 2,567-feet-long over the Columbia River. We then bicycled over the bridge to dance on Washington soil and then headed back, feeling exuberant.

We were also excited about not having to battle the prevailing west winds any more. We had faced the often demoralizing westerlies almost daily since the start of the trip. We figured that since we would now be heading south, at worst the wind would be at our side.

In Kent, Oregon at Carl's Mobil gas station, Steve made our Friday call to KSTP back in Minnesota. It had been a rough week for Steve and me and so it was even more revitalizing than usual to be calling home. After Dick got done with Steve, Joe Coppersmith came on the line and talked to Steve off the air. He was on the Board of Make-A-Wish, a warm, friendly man whom we met and knew only briefly before we left town.

"How you guys doing out there?"

"All right, I guess. Feeling a little lonely at times and we sure miss everybody back home."

"Well, don't you guys ever feel lonely. You guys are *kings* back here. Everybody is always talking about you both, wondering how you're doing and blown away by the miles that you are putting on. You're really smoking!"

We eased down the road bicycling side-by-side. We rarely bicycled together, but Steve was sharing everything of his conversation with Dick and Joe. I held on to every word, starving for news from home.

"Joe says we're not forgotten back home and everybody's shocked by our mileage so far."

Man did that feel good to hear! We were both encouraged and pumped up. Those few words of concern and encouragement would propel us for miles and miles. It had been so desolate out west. It was easy to think that people back home were busy with their lives and were slowly forgetting about us. We knew that wasn't true, but still, it sure was great to hear that people cared about us.

We needed the love from home today. The day was quickly deteriorating into miserable hill after miserable hill, a strong wind directly in our face and occasional rain. So much for finally heading south and getting our first break with the wind!

We took a short break from our grueling day in a town called Antelope, Oregon. It was quite the experience for two city boys from the Midwest as the entire "town" was actually a commune. An internationally known guru named Bhagwan Shree Rajneesh and his 4,000 orange-robed followers inhabited the whole community. I thought that I time-warped back to the "peace, love, dove" days of the 60's. Our few minutes in town were bizarre and almost unsettling. We kept pedaling south.

The wind was growing stronger. It swirled around us, as our winding road seemed to cut right through the mountains. I heard Steve bicycling in back of me, laughing deliriously. I began singing in the rain with my deepest bass voice bellowing, "Swing low, sweet chariot, coming fo' to carry me home!" We were getting slaphappy crazy. Steve's delirium finally passed.

"I have the plan." Steve was smiling. That was a good thing.

"What do you mean, 'the plan?'"

"I'm buying you your wedding present tonight."

"My wedding present?" There was no special woman in my life. What in the world…?

"A motel room for the night. My gift to you and your bride somewhere down the line. If you ever meet her and walk her down the aisle, remind her that I gave already."

Boy did that sound wonderful. I left Minneapolis with every penny that I owned, approximately $500 in travelers checks. I was stretching it as best I could. Steve still had a little in his savings account back home. It was a precious emergency fund for him, and so I really appreciated his generous spirit. He always loved to surprise me with treats. What a buddy!

We stopped for a snack break at a small café in Willow Springs, Oregon. Steve and I finally figured out a compromise to the "Coast or no Coast" decision. We had rerouted our missed mail in Wyoming to the Oregon coastal town of North Bend. Steve suggested that we bicycle south to a town called Klamath Falls and there we could rent a car and drive to the coast! We would pick up our anxiously awaited mail, see the ocean, the Oregon coast, spend a day or two in the area and then drive back to Klamath Falls and resume bicycling.

This sounded terrific! We had hammered out a fantastic compromise that had satisfied both parties. Maybe Steve and I had a life in politics to look forward to after a year on the road.

SUNDAY, SEPTEMBER 5, TWO DAYS LATER. DECISION TIME.
There were two routes out of Oregon and into northwestern California. One took us down HWY 97 and into Klamath Falls, a good-sized town that had two car rental places. The other route took us down HWY 31 through smaller towns with no car rental agencies and into California. Steve had already committed to Klamath Falls and a car. No problem. He still felt badly that he had somewhat forced the issue and that I had conceded to forgo my dream of bicycling the coast.

But now we were at the literal fork in the road. The signs up ahead read HWY 97 South and HWY 31 East. I walked into the Standard gas station.

"Excuse me, sir. What's the best way to get to California from here, HWY 97 or 31?"

I laid out my map to the owner sitting at the register. I already knew the answer that I wanted to hear.

"My friend and I are on bicycles and we're trying to take the least painful route."

He smiled. "Well son, I'll tell ya. Your best bet would be HWY 31. There would be a lot less traffic and much better terrain than south to Klamath Falls."

I suddenly deflated.

"Yeah, lookie here. You see this 97?" His greasy index finger ran up and down a three-inch stretch on our map. "That baby is four-lane and full of Sunday drivers headed over to the coast today. There's some tough climbin' too. Now HWY 31 is really a pretty drive. Not many people heading in that direction, no sir. That'd be my bet."

I smiled weakly. "Thanks. You've been a big help."

Kicking myself I questioned why I had I felt the need to go in there and ask anything. Steve had already said, "Yes." Now I went and got all of the wrong answers from someone who really knew the area.

"Well?" Steve was sitting next to his bicycle in the early morning sun, peeling an orange.

"The son-of-a-gun told us that unless we loved climbing mountains and having traffic running us off the road all day, our route better be HWY 31." I was depressed. "Let's just do it, Steve. It's the sensible answer."

Steve looked sad. He knew how much I wanted the coast. He grabbed the map from me as I filled up my water bottle.

"Look, here's an airport near Lakeview, in northern California. We can rent a car there. It ain't over 'till it's over!"

I looked up and took a deep breath. Every time that Steve made a concession and gave me a green light on the coast, it seemed to be taken away from a logical perspective. Yes, no, yes, almost yes, no…this was getting old and it was getting emotionally draining.

I stared at Steve.

"Forget the coast. History. Let's move on."

Suddenly I was relieved.

"Are you sure? Look, I mean when we get to..."

"I'm sure. Maybe we're simply not supposed to be there. There are always obstacles popping up. I really want to forget it. I deeply appreciate you trying to make it happen. You've come more than half way in your efforts and attitude. We have learned a lot about a lot on this one."

I started to smile. I could feel a gentle breeze picking up on my back.

"Let's go get #12!"

Steve loved my thinking. We mounted our bikes. "HWY 31, next right." I glanced west over my shoulder. I will be back some day.

CHAPTER 16
AMBUSHED BY CREATURES...SIZE BOTH GREAT AND SMALL!

"The single most powerful tool for winning a negotiation is the ability to get up and walk away from the table without a deal." ~ **Anonymous**

AMBUSHED! CREATURES OF TERROR! THEY MUST HAVE smelled human blood. Their collective attack was ferocious. I threw my bicycle against the tree and ripped open my saddlebag. Where in the heck was my weapon?

"Steve! Steve, you alright?"

"NO! They are savage!"

I then heard cuss words. I didn't have time to worry about him.

Finally! Found it! In one motion I grabbed, aimed and fired!

SWHISSSSSSSSHHH! The air filled with spray. The onslaught of thousands of killer mosquitoes was temporarily delayed.

I ripped open another bag on my bike. Furiously I pulled on overalls and a sweatshirt.

Only minutes before, Steve and I had been winding down an 80-mile-day in the setting sun of scenic northern California. We saw a very welcomed, "CAMPGROUND AHEAD 1,000 FEET" sign and descended down a hill into the shade of a peaceful little valley. The air quickly cooled as we sped downhill and suddenly felt the pings of hundreds and hundreds of small bugs bouncing off of our bare faces, chests and legs. Sure that they were nothing more than harmless but obnoxious gnats, we simultaneously hit the bottom of the hill and the entrance into our campground. We walked our bicycles into the grassy camping sites.

"What the..."

SLAP. SLAP, SLAP, SLAP..."MOSQUITOES!"

They were indeed mosquitoes, thousands and thousands of now swarming mosquitoes. I thought that I had grown up in the mosquito capital of the world, but I had never been attacked by so many and bitten so ferociously. It was a losing war.

I quickly set up my tent, my fortress, my safe haven. Steve was a blur of motion as he too sought refuge from our relentless swarm of attackers. Once inside and zipped shut as darkness fell, I exhaled my first sigh of relief. I scratched itchy spots all over my body. Hunger pains then hit hard. I grabbed some bread from my bike bag and then found a 39-cent can of chicken spread. Using a flashlight and a can opener, I dug into the can. It looked like dog food. Famished and cautiously hopeful, I spread it on the slice of wheat bread and took my first bite.

It tasted like dog food. I scratched more bites on my back.

"I can't eat this garbage!" I was discouraged and suddenly really sad and frustrated.

Steve was finally lying in his own tent munching on some raisin bread.

"You? Can't eat something? Mr. Garbage Disposal?"

"I never throw food out but this is disgusting! I should have known that 39 cents was too cheap for a can of chicken. Yuck!"

I slipped the open can and three-quarters of my sandwich out of my tent. I hurriedly zipped the tent door shut in an effort to keep what little blood I still had left in my body. I was a prisoner. Starving, exhausted and bored to tears, I had no choices. I drifted off to sleep as a chorus of crickets lulled my senses to black.

THE ICE CREAM BAR SOOTHED AND COOLED MY OVERHEATED body. It must have been close to 90 degrees on a sunny, dusty afternoon, our 50th afternoon of the trip. The quaint little general store seemed to sprout out of nowhere, but Steve and I were awfully glad that it had.

"How's your water holding up?" Sometimes we were low and other times our water was simply too hot to quench a parched throat.

"I need some cold stuff." Steve looked tired. His colitis was getting worse and taking a lot out of him. I was whipped as we continued to bicycle 10 – 12 hours a day in desolate country on 90-plus-degree days. I couldn't even imagine how Steve must be feeling.

I glanced towards the storekeeper. He was a kindly old gentleman who seemed happy to share his air-conditioned store with his only two customers.

"Sir, where could I refill our water bottles with some fresh water?"

"Outside around to the left. There's a faucet and a hose on the side of the building. You can't miss it."

"Thanks."

I grabbed the water bottles off my bicycle and then Steve's and headed for the side of the building. As I turned the corner I saw that I had to wait. Two guys were filling up a gallon jug of water. Eight feet away stood their beat up old Chevy, hood up and a trickle of steam rising from its overheated radiator. They filled up their jug and shut off the faucet.

I quietly walked to the hose, turned it on and started to fill my bottles.

"You in a f****ing hurry or what?" Startled by the loud question and the ugly language, I looked up. There stood one of the men who had been filling his jug for the Chevy. He was about 6 feet tall, 240 pounds, fat, bearded, dirty and very ornery.

"What do you mean?"

"I mean what in the hell is your problem? We were using this hose, meathead!"

I could now smell the beer on his breath.

"I know you were. I waited until you were done and now I'm filling my water bottle. I'll be just a minute."

"You know somethin'?" He was snarling. "I oughta beat your f****ing head in!"

I now sensed real danger. This was quickly and unexpectedly becoming ugly. I finished my two bottles and then reached for Steve's. I looked towards the car. Three more men were waiting impatiently. Steve wasn't in sight. It was four against one. I hadn't done anything wrong. I held my ground.

"Hey man, life's too short. I just need a little more water for our bicycles and we'll be on our way."

I must have said the wrong thing. He squared his shoulders and clenched both of his fists. He took three more steps towards me, close enough to connect with a punch.

"You do not want to f*** with me!!"

He kept using the "F" word and always said it loudly and in a very menacing way. His eyes were glazed. He was drunk. His buddies stayed by the car waiting for somebody to make the first move. I was now in too deep to back down. I stared him right in the eyes. I thought that I could kick his butt, however I didn't know for sure. I sized up the situation. Again, it was four on one. Possible weapons, alcohol for sure and maybe drugs. I finished filling Steve's water bottles and handed him the hose. He wouldn't take it. He looked over his shoulder back at the Chevy.

"Hey Bobby, I think I'm going to have to kick this guy's head in!"

I had to think fast.

"Hey guys, I don't want any trouble. I thought that you were done with the water. You turned the hose off. I've been bicycling for 3,000 miles and I'm hot and tired. Just take the hose and let's forget it."

I made a point not to apologize. But I was appealing for logic and a little help. My hope was that I made some sense to "Bobby" and friends and that they would take their Cro-Magnon gorilla friend and stuff him back into the car.

"Ah, let's get the water and get the hell out of here. We got a party to get to, Marty."

I could now see that these guys weren't up for a fight. They all seemed to be drinking and up for partying. Only this big ape still three feet from my face seemed sour.

"Naw, I want to kick his head in." He was sounding boorishly stuck like a broken record.

"Have a good life." I smiled and walked away. I didn't feel good about turning my back on him but I determined that it was the only way to get out of this now senseless situation. He was still blurting threats when I heard his buddies try to pour him back in the car.

"What was *that* all about?" Steve had come out of the store and had been watching the end of my confrontation from a distance. I handed him his filled water bottles. I was furious!

"Stupid jerk." I told Steve the whole story. As I finished up, the old beat up Chevy spit gravel and dust and roared away. Gorilla man flipped me off from the back seat and threw an empty beer can out of the window.

I stared at the dust gently falling back to the ground onto the road.

"Man, I would love to have a brown belt in karate so I could know for sure that I could have beaten him to a pulp."

"You would have, Ken. You would have today. He was a fat, stupid slob. But, you did the smart thing in walking away."

"Damn it!" My face was burning red and I still felt a very rare emotion for me: rage. I hated him for being such a jerk. I hated that I walked away from him. And I hated the fact that I wasn't sure if I could have handled him or not. I was not a fighter but I really wanted to know in my heart that I could have handled myself today. Steve listened quietly and let me blow off steam. I didn't normally have such a hot temper but this was eating me up.

I felt so sorry for Ken right then. He could have beaten that guy senseless if he had wanted, but he did the smart thing. He told me later that although he wanted to strangle the guy, all he could picture was them catching up to us a few miles down the road and either running us over or shooting us.

I finally told Ken, "I wish you would have at least pulled the guys shorts up over his head, tied his socks together, shaved his head and finished him off by throwing him back into his car through the wing window. Now let's go get some miles!"

I slowly smiled back and then laughed. It was a great word picture! Steve had said all the right things. My mood was shifting. I wasn't going to waste any more anger. We had 36 states to get for our promised pledges to the eventual kids of Make-A-Wish.

That should keep us busy and challenged for a few months.

CHAPTER 17
SAVAGE AND BRUTAL COLITIS CONTINUES ITS TOLL ON US

"Courage does not always roar. Sometimes, it is the quiet voice at the end of the day saying, I will try again tomorrow." ~ **Anonymous**

SEPTEMBER 8. DAY #51. STEVE'S BICYCLE SUDDENLY JERKED TO a stop. From 50 yards behind him, I slowed to a stop to keep our distance. I knew exactly what was happening. It was becoming a routine sight, gut wrenching, but common. Steve's head was bowed down. He was frozen, standing and straddling his bicycle. Ten seconds passed. Suddenly Steve lifted his left leg over and off. His beautiful machine collapsed to the pavement. He then ripped off his bicycling gloves and threw them towards the middle of the highway. Turning to his right, he marched to find a little scarce privacy and cover in the desert. My gut and heart hurt as I watched the scene before me unfold once again.

I eased back on my seat and slowly bicycled by without a word or a glance in his direction.

THIS MORNING WAS ALREADY TURNING INTO A BRUTAL DAY. The sun was searing our blackened skin at only 11 AM. But the intense summer heat was not my concern. Steve was getting sicker and sicker by the hour. I couldn't even spell "colitis" four weeks ago. Now I saw it firsthand tortuously destroying my friend. I felt so helpless. I could not really do anything for Steve except to be patient, but it was becoming a terrible and complicated drain on me too. I even felt guilty because I was so physically healthy.

Steve was deteriorating before my very eyes. Something had to be done.

"Well?"

Steve looked as if his worst fears had been realized.

"What did he say?"

Steve had called his doctor back in Minneapolis and explained what had been happening the past two weeks.

"Well, he wants us to check into a hospital in Reno. He actually scared me. He said that I could be becoming dangerously anemic."

He stared intently at a hole in the dusty pavement.

"He said that I could collapse out in the desert and be in big trouble."

Damn. This was even more serious than either one of us was imagining. Plus the fact that Reno, Nevada was still a long, grueling 60 miles away.

"Well, let's drag our butts to Reno and figure this mess out. You up to puttin' on some more miles?"

Steve looked up at me. Listless and dazed, he nodded his head.

Two long, quiet but uneventful hours later I bicycled into Doyle, California. Reno was still another 40 miles or so southeast of this little town. I was parched. My drinking water was bath-water-warm again and I needed something ice cold to keep my legs churning. I found a small hotel and grocery store and parked my bike where Steve could see it. He was behind me, but not far as I had been afraid to lose sight of him for too long today.

I chugged 12 ounces of Diet 7-UP in about eight seconds flat. The cold carbonation stung my throat but it felt unbelievably refreshing. It "hurt so good" all the way down! Grabbing a cold quart of orange juice, I thanked the owner and headed for the cool shade of a tree.

Three minutes passed. Finally Steve pulled in and glided to a stop next to the hotel. He trudged into the store without saying a word and grabbed a Coke and joined me in the shade.

"How ya holding up, buddy?" I asked. He looked miserable. Beaten.

"I'm just sorry, Ken."

"Sorry for what?"

"Sorry that you have to ride with a 'sickie'." Tears started to well up in his eyes.

"It's not fair that you have to put up with me and all this. I mean I'm going slower every day..." His head dropped into his hands. He was devastated. His pride and dignity, once so strong and determined, were broken.

I started to cry too. My heart ached for him.

Ken listened intently as I poured out my bottled-up fears.

"This colitis has got me whipped. It has gotten to the point where I'm miserable from the time I wake up to the time I go to sleep. Besides wondering what's going on inside of my body when I see all of that blood come out, I'm so sick of being afraid of being farther than 20 feet from a bathroom. Maybe I should catch a plane as soon as we get to Reno. It just kills me to think that I wouldn't be able to finish this trip but I am really sick. Again I'm just sorry about all of this."

"Hey buddy, I love you! We're in this thing together. Your colitis could just as easily have been my bad knee. You've been an animal to have gotten this far. We'll work this all out. Just don't ever feel bad for my sake. You're the one going through hell."

Steve looked up and stared at my face.

"You're going through the same hell. No less and no more than mine. I'm no hero to have gotten this far. Not any more than you."

I closed my eyes and let his words slowly sink in. In some respect he was right. This had been a miserable month for both of us, physically draining and fearful for Steve and emotionally draining and fearful for me. I gave him a teary bear hug.

We spent the night six feet away at the Doyle Hotel. We both lavished in our first showers in six days, a new trip record.

Before hitting the pillows, we quietly discussed all the options we thought we had in front of us. I suggested that Steve fly home from Reno. I'd bike south to Las Vegas and wait for him before I left the state. That way we would not miss bicycling into a new state without each other. Steve could get better and I could keep the trip moving. It sounded like a good game plan for both of us. The idea of bicycling alone for a few days was very appealing after all of the stress of the past few weeks. Steve said it all sounded okay. Bottom line I told Steve that we were going to finish this trip together, no matter how long it took us.

We turned out the lights in our little room. Thirty minutes passed with no snoring sounds like usual after a hard day battling the elements.

"You sleeping?"

"Obviously not, Steve."

"I've been thinking."

"Proud of you buddy."

"Thanks. Flying home. It's sounding worse and worse. I'd feel like I was running home. You know, couldn't cut it, ran home to make it better, leaving you behind…"

He paused. I reflected on Steve's words in the blackness. I put myself in his shoes.

"I see your point. I guess…I guess I'd feel the same way. I remember how I felt hitching those miles in Oregon. Ah…bottom line, I want you better. And bottom, bottom line, I'll support whatever decision you make. Let's just weigh everything when we get to Reno tomorrow. You call it and we'll live with it."

"Sounds fair."

"Good night buddy."

"Good night buddy. I am really glad to end this one."

CHAPTER 18
THE 1st WISH IN MAKE-A-WISH MN HISTORY IS ANNOUNCED!

"You have not lived a perfect day, unless you've done something for someone who will never be able to repay you," ~ **Ruth Smeltzer**

"LORI, I NEED YOU TO CALL DR. PIZINGER AND CANCEL MY appointment for Friday. Ken and I are going to bicycle to Las Vegas and take it easy getting there, stopping in motels for one solid week."

A major decision was made. Steve was in the best spirits I'd seen him in several weeks. It was a beautiful day and only 46.5 miles long as Reno was our only destination. We had state #13 under our belts and we were "home" before lunch!

"How'd she take the news?"

"Not too well. I'm sure that she was psyched to see me plus she thinks that I'm crazy not to be in a hospital. But I know that I am the best judge. And I don't honestly believe it myself, but I do feel better today!"

"Well, the *team* will roll down the road then!"

I felt wonderful too. It was fun being with Steve again. He was child-like in his joy for the day. We prayed that he would stay better and finally clear himself up.

"Truisms" that I have noticed in my life:

- It always seems that when I go to the dentist because of a sore tooth, it doesn't hurt when I am in his office.

- When I go to the barber because I can't stand the way my hair looks anymore, it looks great to me right before he starts clipping.

- When I bring my car into the shop because it's making a weird noise, it will never make that particular noise while I am there.

- And whenever I plan to fly home from Reno, Nevada in the midst of a 48-state bike trip because of a severe case of chronic ulcerative colitis, my colitis won't bother me at all that day!

From the moment that I woke up that morning, I felt healthy for a change. A normal day in the last few weeks meant at least ten bowel movements, or more accurately blood movements before noon. Today I did not have to go once. I knew that this remission of my affliction was very temporary, but it was all the excuse that I needed to postpone flying home. Ken seemed real upbeat today too. I am sure that was because I was in a much better mood.

STEVE AND I LOOKED INCREDIBLY OUT OF PLACE FROM THE moment that we rolled into "America's Biggest Little City," full of beautiful people in their Mercedes and Cadillacs and dressed to the max heading in and out of luxurious casinos. But we didn't care as people stared at our loaded-down bicycles and us in our tennis shoes, shorts and dirty t-shirts.

I put another nickel in the slot machine. I had fed all of 65 cents into the one-arm-bandit, who was living up to its name. The hotel lobby of the Plantation Casino was an explosion of action and colorful people. I was really excited this morning.

I eagerly grabbed the lobby phone and placed our weekly Friday call back to Minnesota.

"Kenneth?"

"Hey Dick, good morning!"

"Good morning. Where are you?"

"Well, last week we called you from a gas station in Oregon surrounded by trees. This morning we're calling from Reno, Nevada surrounded by slot machines in a casino."

Dick roared his famous high-pitched, infectious laugh. I loved it when I could do that to him.

"Did you pull up on your bikes?"

"We pulled up on our bicycles."

"Did they look at you like you were a little odd?"

"Well this is an odd city, Dick. I think you can get away with anything in this town."

Dick roared again. He must have been in a really good mood because I knew my last comment wasn't that funny.

"Kenny, I'm going to put you on hold. I need to take a quick break and when we come back I'm going to put you on hold with someone else and you will hear his story in a minute and I think you two will be incredibly gratified.

"Okay."

I heard Dick doing a quick weather report and then brief his listening audience as to what was about to happen. I was getting curious as to what he was up to, but all I could really do was listen to the phone.

"We are going back to Reno, Nevada to Ken Rogers and Steve Anderson who are bicycling around the United States on behalf of Make-A-Wish of Minnesota and at the same time we are going to a school in the Twin Cities and I'll be talking to 13-year-old Jamie Keller and Mary Lou Keller, Jamie's mother."

"Ken, you there?"

"I'm still here, Dick."

"Mrs. Keller, are you there?"

"Yes, I am."

"Jamie, are you there?"

"Yeah."

"Good. Jamie, tell everybody, because nobody knows why Jamie Keller is on this particular program and I'm talking to you and you're talking to Ken and Steve right now. What's happened to you the past couple of days?"

"Well, some people asked me if I wanted to be in Make-A-Wish and ah…that's a thing where…you can…"

He sounded young, nervous and searching for the right words. I was hanging on each and every one that he found.

"…I can't think of anything to say. I'm trying as best I can."

"I know you are." Dick's reassuring voice intervened.

"Why don't you tell the public a little bit more about Jamie Keller. You're 13 years old. Right?"

"Yeah, I'm 13 years old and I got MD."

Boom. He spit out the fact he had muscular dystrophy like it was his shoe size.

"And at one point, am I wrong or right, you used to be the poster child?"

"Yeah, I used to be."

"Where did you want to go, Jamie?"

"California."

"Where in California?"

"Disneyland."

"Mrs. Keller? Has this been a dream come true?"

"We're so high up in the clouds and I don't think we'll ever come down. It has been a dream come true, one of the most wonderful things that has ever happened in our whole lives."

There was a long pause. Mrs. Keller continued. "You've got me crying now."

My eyes were watering too.

"Last night they called Jamie on the phone and after he hung up I said, 'Jamie, what do you think?' And he said, 'I wanted to say more, mom, but I knew I would cry so I couldn't.'" Mrs. Keller started to cry again.

Dick interjected. "Jamie, don't be shy about crying because I think all of us will be crying with you when you go out there to Disneyland. I'm going to put everyone back on hold…"

It was really happening. A wish was about to be granted. My body tingled.

"Ken?"

"Yeah, Dick, I'm here. My body is one big goose bump. We all knew that it was going to happen sometime but there he is! He is going!"

I was now lost in my thoughts as we wrapped up the call. I was feeling a humble pride to be a part of what was all happening back in Minnesota. I knew a lot of people in Make-A-Wish, Chairman John Rubel, board members Kermath and Mary Beth Ward, Joe Coppersmith, Tom Reid, Karla Blomberg…they were behind the scenes thanklessly and selflessly making great headway in building this all-volunteer organization from the ground up. And Dick Pomerantz had started the entire thing moving with his impromptu and heartfelt call to arms on the air all those many months ago.

What an incredible moment in time!

CHAPTER 19
NEVADA DESERT, WILD DOGS, A BROTHEL & TARANTULAS!

"My most beautiful moments are not of scenery, but of serenity."
-Steve Anderson somewhere in Nevada on Day #43

WE HAD OPTED TO TAKE U.S. HIGHWAY 95 ABOUT 50 MILES out of Reno, through Fallon, Hawthorne and Tonopah into Las Vegas. We knew that this route wouldn't be much more than open desert, snakes, spiders, atomic testing sites and desolation. However, it seemed better than the only other alternative. If we headed to Las Vegas by going through California we would be encountering the Sierra Nevada Mountains and Death Valley, one of the hottest places on earth with common air temperatures in September over 120 degrees!

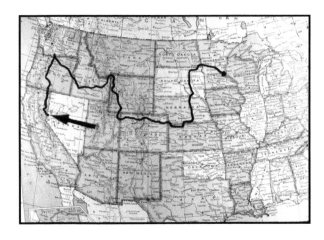

We covered the 450 miles to Las Vegas in five days. My colitis, as I knew it would, came back, but not with the severity it was in Oregon and California. I decided to postpone my plane ride home until it really started bothering me again.

"GRRRAHRERRR!"

The hair on my neck shot out. The sounds were savage, unearthly, menacing and close. I turned to look in back of my bicycle. There, two wild black labs were literally foaming at the mouth and bearing down on me.

Where in the world? We were in the middle of the Nevada desert for crying out loud! Where had they come from? I was shook up and hammered down on my pedals. Thankfully the grade of the road was gently sloping downhill. Fear of my own mangled death propelled my legs furiously. Adrenaline was pumping throughout my body. Foaming at the mouth cannot be good. Ever so gradually I outdistanced both of them. I still had absolutely no idea where they could have possibly come from. There were no towns, no woods, nothing but barren desert and occasional cactuses.

I was done with any daydreaming and focused on intently watching the road.

"THE MOTELS ARE FULL?" WE WERE 71 MILES DOWN THE ROAD and looking to shut down early. This town in the middle of nowhere was perfect. I asked Steve again.

"You mean to tell me that there is absolutely no vacancies in this town?"

"Yup. She said that there was a Harley Davidson convention in town. They do it every year and book everything in town and nearby to the max."

"I don't believe it! We come to town in the middle of nowhere on Saturday, September 11 for probably the only time in our entire lives and the Hells Angels are here for a once-a-year meeting. I mean there must be ten motels in this little town!"

I was beyond frustrated. What were the odds?

"Let's look at our map again. What's our best bet?"

"Y'all looking for a place to spend the night?"

I glanced up and saw a woman in her late 40's strolling our way. She was blonde, classy, shapely and dressed to the nines. Her suggestive eyes quickly roamed my entire body. Uh, oh, I thought.

"Maybe I can help?"

I felt like a country bumpkin on his first trip to the big city. What in the heck was going to happen next?

"I own the Mustang Ranch, but that's quite a ways for you boys and your bicycles. Your best bet is in Mina, about 35 miles south of here. You won't find much open until you get there."

"Well, thank you. We appreciate your help."

"No problem, honey. And if you're ever back my way at the Mustang, you be real sure to look me up." She beamed, batted her eyelashes and sort of "slunk" away. It was classic. I smiled and looked back at *my* world, my buddy Steve.

"Can you believe that?" I asked Steve incredulously.

"What was that all about?"

"Don't you know what the Mustang Ranch is? She was the owner of one of the most, if not *the* most famous brothel in America!"

I was by no means a brothel expert, having never been even near one, but you had to have been under a rock for most of your life to not have ever heard of the infamous Mustang Ranch. It gave us yet another taste of this unique part of the country. We were so many miles from home and familiar surroundings. Out here with the barren brown desert country, cactuses, legal gambling casinos, legal prostitution and brothels, real cowboys and...HOLY COW! I slowed my bike and stared in amazement.

There on the pavement slowly crossing the highway was a hairy, huge tarantula!

I looked for Vincent Price to come out from behind a cactus. I eased my bike closer. There was no traffic and so I could gaze in awe. It was without a doubt the largest, hairiest spider that I had ever seen in person. It felt like I was in a real horror movie. Dang it! Steve had the only camera and he was long gone ahead of me digging for a town with a place to stay. I watched the tarantula make it to the other side of the highway and slowly walk into the desert sand, seemingly unconcerned that I was staring at his every move.

Minnesota mosquitoes were indeed many, many miles away.

"I WISH THAT I WAS BACK IN MINNESOTA MAKING NEW account calls!" Now I knew that Steve was really angry. He **hated** making new account calls in a suit and a tie. But the wind was savagely in our face making for a miserable day of riding. A mind-numbing and endless brown desert, searing heat again and Mother Nature were all doing their best to keep us from getting our final 66 miles to Las Vegas.

The bright blue tow truck passed us on our left and gave us several feet of room. We really appreciated it when drivers tearing down the road at 70 to 80 miles an hour in a ton of steel moved over to give our vulnerable little bodies a chance to bicycle undisturbed. Suddenly the truck jerked to the shoulder and stopped. We eased up to the driver's window.

"You guys look like you're crawling in the wind! Are you heading towards Las Vegas?" She was a big woman with an even bigger smile. We nodded.

"Well, how about throwing those bikes in the back and I'll drive you both into town. You got a ways to go yet and it's only going to get hotter."

Steve and I looked at each other. Steve's colitis was really beating us both down. Who would ever know that we spent a few miles in a truck? It was a very tempting offer. But we also knew our answer without exchanging a word. Cheating was not an option. We had gone through too much hell already pedaling our bicycle rubber over 3,500 miles of America. We explained our mission to our road friend.

"Okay, no problem. Good luck guys."

We watched our could-have-been-painless-ride roar away. The tow truck's engine sounded like a fighter jet as we continued to limp south. Almost out of view, the truck pulled to the shoulder again. We slowly rolled alongside.

"Hey guys, my name's Joni. Here's my address and phone number. My husband Bill and I would love to have you spend the night and enjoy supper with us."

Now that was an offer that we could use! She roared away once again. We resumed pedaling into our punishing wind.

The miles hurt a little less knowing that today they led somewhere friendly.

CHAPTER 20
THE MOST PUNISHING DAY OF THE ENTIRE TRIP

" My strength lies solely in my tenacity." ~ **Louis Pasteur**

THEY SAY THAT YOU CAN TELL A LOT ABOUT A MAN BY WHAT pleasures in life make him happy. Mine are simple. A huge bowl of hot-buttered popcorn or watching my Minnesota Vikings football team was near the very top of my list. Tonight I would have one, if not both. I'm sure that I woke up with a smile already on my face.

The day started with our nemesis, "Mr. Wind," blowing in our faces from the south once again. But we were only mildly irritated today. We already had a 7:30 AM start and had only 76 miles to Kingman, Arizona where we planned to rent a motel room for the nationally televised Vikings vs. the Bears. Monday Night football at 6 PM on the west coast seemed weird vs. 8 PM in the Midwest, but that still was 10 ½ hours away, half hour lunch stop, so…if we averaged a mere 7.6 miles an hour we would be eating popcorn and sipping on a cold beverage by kickoff. No problem. We were pumped. Steve and I were both overly-zealous Vikings fans and we really missed the weekly Viking football games back home. We were lucky to get scores out here much less see any football game.

This would be a very special treat. We charged south on highway 93.

The early morning hours went quickly as we bicycled next to the famous Hoover Dam and into state #14, Arizona. Highway 93 then pointed directly southeast and directly into the teeth of a howling wind. The road seemed to deteriorate as we bicycled our first slow miles of Arizona.

10:30 AM, 16.7 miles. No shoulders and lots of traffic. 11:45 AM, 22.6 miles. We were behind schedule and losing ground. I pushed harder, angrily on my pedals. The wind kept swirling around my ears. Precious minutes kept ticking away. The miles were not. I had not seen too much of Steve, as he was behind and out of sight most of the morning. The "Big C", as we now called his colitis condition, must have been hitting him hard today.

We pulled into the roadside convenience store and out of the wind. Steve looked awful.

"You look awful!" These first words out of Steve's mouth were directed *at me!*

"How you doing?" I asked Steve with great concern as I had hardly seen him today.

"Between the 'Big C,' the wind in my face, the most belligerent and obnoxious drivers I've seen so far and a road so full of potholes I'm amazed that my wheels are still sort of round, I'm great! Are we anywhere near on track?"

We were increasingly aware of kickoff time and the many miles to go.

"We're near, but we are not going to make it at this rate. Let's just keep at it."

The pickup roared by at 70 MPH and gave me all of two feet of room to bicycle. I screamed a rare obscenity.

3:06 PM. Only 49 miles. Simple math and our progress told me that we were not going to make it. I felt the first quarter of football slipping away. I lowered my head and painfully pushed my pedals toward the deteriorating asphalt. I was frustrated. I was bitter.

The first drops of rain were now falling on my head.

"I DO NOT BELIEVE THIS!" I screamed at the top of my lungs! I yelled at drivers, at my odometer for not moving and at God. We had worked so hard to make good time yesterday so that today would be easy. We could not catch a break. I continued to pedal as fast as I could, propelled by rage. Rain continued to batter my head, now in drenching sheets.

6 PM. Kickoff time. My legs ached, but kept pumping. We still had eight miles to go. The sun had set and darkness was settling all around us. Steve and I were about 300 yards apart. Six miles to go. We were now soaked, cold and starving. Five miles to Kingman. I looked up.

I could not believe my eyes.

There, straight ahead, was a small...mountain! I swear the road went straight up! I started to laugh and cry for the first time in my entire life. I had nothing left inside of me. I had given my guts to this incredibly wrenching stretch of road.

"He's to the 30, to the 20, 10, TOUCHDOWN VIKINGS!"

I inhaled another handful of Fritos. I was too tired to get excited. But I sure was happy and secure to be tucked in our little motel room with our color TV set. Steve and I were quietly sharing our thoughts and private misery of the past 76 miles.

"I've been going through a lot of hell with my colitis this past month, and it's been a real lonely hell. Today we both went through hell together."

Steve and I warmly shook hands. We had indeed bonded our friendship to a deeper depth today. We had gone through, collectively, the most maddening and frustrating day we had ever experienced together. But we had done it.

The bad guys scored. Our Vikings were now down by six. We booed along with 50,000 Viking fans at the Metrodome. They eventually lost the game.

For tonight, one night, Steve and I were both in the same place, back at home in Minnesota.

CHAPTER 21
A NEW PLAN AND KEN FIXES A FLAT TIRE FOR <u>THE 1ST TIME!</u>

"It's hard to beat a person who never gives up." ~ **Babe Ruth**

"HEY, CAN WE GET SOME SHOTS OF YOU GUYS ON YOUR bicycles?"

I looked at my half-eaten hamburger and then at Steve. Our café lunch in air-conditioned comfort was being interrupted and I was not in the mood for it. I looked up at the two men in their 30s or 40s with cameras the size of cannons. I started to think of a way to politely explain to them the immense joy of eating food and sipping on a cold diet coke after 40 miles of Arizona desert bicycling.

"We're from *Life Magazine* and we're doing an article on the history of Route 66."

I stopped chewing my burger.

"If you guys are up for it, we'd like to get some shots of you on your loaded bicycles actually on Route 66."

National exposure. Wow. We could make some time. My adrenaline was flowing. I left my burger at the table.

SUNDAY, SEPTEMBER 19. THIS WAS A DAY OF REST FOR MANY. It was seventy-nine miles so far for us and the end of two months on the road with 4,036 miles of bicycle riding between us.

We were incredibly tired.

In two months we had never had a whole day off for fun. But over the past few days Steve and I had put together a game plan. We would bicycle to Independence, Missouri where my sister Mary and her husband Mark would pick us up in a truck. Steve would fly home to Minneapolis and see a doctor in the hospital. I would stay with my family until Steve felt better and was road ready again. The thought of family, rest, Lori and a doctor for Steve and home cooking kept us bicycling East in the stifling heat.

The 10,000-mile-challenge that we had undertaken in July seemed so incredibly overwhelming at times. The tedium was relentless. The trick to keeping us sane was to break it down in achievable chunks. Missouri was an achievable chunk to shoot for.

I could smell my sister Mary's baked chicken as I saw a shooting star rocket across the desert night sky.

"STAY OFF THE INTERSTATE AND ON THE SHOULDER!"

Deep in thought, I was startled by an unfamiliar voice issuing a stern command. Where did the voice sounding like an intercom…?

"Thank you."

I looked up to see a highway patrol car speed away. Steve moved back away from the white line. Since leaving Kingman, Arizona, Steve and I had no choice but to pursue the lives of outlaws. It was expressly illegal to ride a non-motorized vehicle on the interstate system throughout the United States. But Interstate 40 was just about the only east/west road to take through Arizona and New Mexico. One look at a highway map told us that options were few to none traveling in this direction. There were mountains to our north and desert to our south and so we proceeded to break the law day in and day out until we would finally get to Texas and off of the interstate.

The road was long, straight, boring and life threatening..

"Albuquerque 325 miles." "Albuquerque 307 miles." "Albuquerque 286 miles."

I hated seeing all of those distance signs. They made us so distance conscious and aware of the snails' pace crawl of bicycling 70 miles in a ten-hour day. It was not our idea of enjoyable bicycling. Semis and general traffic roared by at 60 plus miles per hour every second for days. Eighty percent of the shoulder width had some sort of engraved ridge one inch deep and two inches wide, that gave us all of about nine inches between the end of the ridged concrete and the white line of the highway. Bottom line is that we had exactly nine inches of width to travel on for hundreds of miles, with one to two tons of traffic flying past us twelve inches away! It was noisy, dangerous and incredibly tense for the entire day pedaling. Steve and I were not talking to each other. I spent my many hours dreaming of being home in Minnesota in an effort to survive the day.

We were really getting sick of this whole damn thing.

NOTE TO SELF. TODAY WAS SEPTEMBER 22. DAY #65 AND month number three on the road.

At exactly mile 4,155 I repaired a flat tire for the first time on my own!

I had woken up from a relatively good night's sleep and after packing up my tent, I saw seven burs sticking out of my back tire and noticed that it was flat. The front tire had one bur in it and as I pulled it out, I heard the ugly sound of a loud hiss. Great. We bicycled 65.3 miles yesterday on a sweltering summer day straining to watch out for and successfully avoiding broken glass on the road and shoulder for almost nine hours. I then end up getting two flat tires simply walking my bicycle to a grassy spot at the end of the day to camp and sleep for the night! That was pretty dumb.

I borrowed Steve's tire patch kit and I finally fixed my first flat tires of the entire trip. I knew what to do and starting off the day at our campsite versus on the road really helped me on my first tire repair.

If I ever made it back to Minneapolis, I would be able to tell people that anybody can get around this country if this inexperienced big palooka could do it!

CHAPTER 22
ALBUQUERQUE OASIS AND CLEARING THE AIR

"Being convinced one knows the whole story is the surest way to fail."
~ **Philip Crosby**

THIS WAS SUPPOSED TO BE AN OASIS IN THE DESERT. A WELL-deserved treat. Answered prayer.

It was not happening.

"What did he say?"

Steve had just hung up the phone in a pay phone booth in downtown Albuquerque, New Mexico.

"He didn't know who in the heck I even was!"

"Dang it!"

It was now rush hour. We had bicycled right into the middle of a city of 240,000, all of them driving their cars tonight, or so it seemed. After two months of bicycling the back roads and rural communities of America where 10,000 citizens were too many to us, the quarter of a million people living in Albuquerque was staggering!

"What do you mean he didn't know who you were? You talked to him this morning. The idiot gave you directions on which exit to take!"

I was exasperated, exhausted and baked by the New Mexico sun. Steve and I had been instructed by the station manager of KSTP radio back in St. Paul, Minnesota to call the station manager of KOB in Albuquerque, Bob Stanfield, as soon as we were close to town. They were sister stations, owned by the huge Hubbard Broadcasting and together they were going to put us up in a local hotel for the night. Our $10 a day budget had not allowed us many comforts besides hearty breakfasts the past two months, so a promise of indoor accommodations paid by somebody else for the very first time was an incredibly uplifting and tantalizing thought. It was like a peek down the stairs at the unopened gifts around the evergreen tree Christmas morning, many, many years ago. We had been psyched for a week.

Steve looked washed out and dazed.

"No one knows where the guy is that I talked to this morning. They don't know about any hotel."

"The guy is the damn station manager! What do you mean they don't know where he is, for crying out loud?"

This was maddening. We were five miles away from the radio station in rush hour traffic and we felt like Rod Serling was just around the corner smoking a cigarette and telling the camera,

"Consider if you will, the plight of two young bicyclists, tired, sweaty and hungry, promised a hotel room by a man who does not exist. Like a mirage of water to a parched desert traveler, these two men have found a town not listed on any map. As they will soon discover, Ken Rogers and Steve Anderson have bicycled into…The Twilight Zone."

As car after car blew by, armed with directions to the radio station, we headed into the sun for a five-mile ride that would hopefully end with a promise of comfortable beds, TV and much needed rest.

"Bob Stanfield was fired about an hour ago. He is no longer in the building and I am unaware of any hotel or motel room for you guys." Steve and I stood in the lobby stunned and without a clue as to what to do next.

This was beyond anything that Rod Serling could have even imagined. This was actually happening!

My head swirled in what was a bizarre situation, somebody finally allowed me to call the station manager, Bob Oakes, back at KSTP in St. Paul in an effort to untangle this mess. After almost two hours of chaos, waiting and slowly evolving answers and apologies, we discovered that indeed the head honcho down here had been fired and escorted out of the building within an hour or so of talking to us earlier in the day! We were finally told that we would be put up at a luxury 15-story hotel only a mile away. We also walked out of the building with two sets of exceptional rain gear donated and mailed to us here at the radio station by a local Minnesota company, Burger Brothers *and* a goose down sleeping bag donated to me by an anonymous KSTP listener back home who had heard on the air by me that I had been freezing! We hit the sunlight and pedaled our one-mile ride to our oasis, spirits soaring for the first time in a long, long while.

I thought to myself, "What's wrong with this picture?" as I watched Ken with a two-month growth of beard push Acabar into the Regent Hotel of Albuquerque, while a doorman held the door open for him. I hadn't seen myself in a mirror for well over a week, but I figured I probably looked just as ragged as Ken and just as much out of place walking into this luxury hotel.

We wheeled Betty and Acabar into the giant lobby, rested them against the pillar and walked over to the desk to check in. As we approached the girl behind the desk, she seemed to be looking over our shoulders for the security guard that would help her eject these two bums.

"May I help you?" she asked warily.

"Yes, my name is Steve Anderson and this is Ken Rogers. Radio station KOB has made a reservation for us to stay a couple of nights."

Her face then lit up like a Christmas tree.

"Oh, you're the bikers!"

"That's us. Our bikes are parked right over there." I pointed a few yards away as she now saw them for the first time.

"Holy cow! How far have you come?"

"Oh, about 4,200 miles so far. We started in St. Paul, Minnesota."

I proceeded to tell her our objective as I had so many times on this trip.

"Well you guys sure deserve a good rest. I've been told that KOB will be paying for your lodging, meals and anything else you want. They've just asked that you try not to order the most expensive champagne or have milk-fed veal flown in from Argentina. Other than that, relax and have a great time!"

Our suite was huge, with double beds, a huge bathroom and plenty of room to park Betty and Acabar without tripping over them. To my horror, there was also a full-length mirror in the bathroom. This was the first time in 66 days that I had seen a full-length view of myself. When I left St. Paul I weighed 166 pounds. Now I looked like I weighed less than 90 pounds! I hit their scale in the bathroom and found out that I was actually about 143 pounds, but on a thin frame like mine, 23 pounds is a lot of weight. I had not had a haircut for over two months and the bushiness of it exaggerated my sunken body even more. My shoulders looked so narrow and bony. I had no chest and my dark brown, whiskered, weather beaten face made me look years older than I was.

For the first time I saw how devastating my colitis had been to me.

"My God, look at me! I look like I just came from a concentration camp and you look like you just came back from a health resort. We've both lost a lot of weight but you look great and I look dead!"

Ken laughed and then shared his own observation.

"It's been real hard not telling you for the last 2,000 miles that you've looked like a hairy beach ball on top of a broom handle. Let's go down to the bar and get you fattened up on those free chicken wings!"

We headed to the little bar/grill off of the main lobby. I was euphoric. After many nights painfully drifting off to sleep in humid, 80 degree temps, grimy, sweaty, eating a supper of raisin bread and water, scratching mosquito bites from head to toe on the rock-hard ground trying unsuccessfully to find a comfortable position…and days of freezing our butts off in the mountains still soaked from an all day rain, no comforts and nothing to look forward to but getting up and bicycling all day all over again…to now staring at two nights in a luxurious all-expenses-paid hotel was overloading all of our senses.

Steve and I were beyond giddy.

We pounded down the chicken wings, vegetables and cooled off with some tasty cold beverages, including something our beautiful waitress Toni called, "The Toni Tantalizer." Our hunger and thirst satiated in air conditioned comfort and an open-ended expense account at our fingertips, we were more relaxed and content than we had been in a very long time. It was impossible not to reminisce and share some significant thoughts and feelings that had been left unsaid over the past few brutal weeks.

"Doesn't it feel unreal to be here in Albuquerque – just another place to flop for the night? It's like this is our new life now, almost like a job. We get up early every day but instead of working for money we're working for miles. Of all the jobs that I've had in my life I have never wanted to achieve goals, our daily miles for example, like I have on this trip. I tell you, Ken, I've never felt more alive in my life, even though I look dead!"

"No kidding, buddy. When we get home and get back to work we'll have to remember what we have been applying on this trip; getting a crystal-clear vision of the goals we want to achieve and then attacking them relentlessly one day at a time. That 'one-mile-at-a-time' thing is exactly how we are going to get home."

"It's kind of hard to think of getting back to a normal life again. About the only thing I miss back home is Lori."

Ken seemed genuinely surprised by my statement.

"I've had the feeling for the past month that you would rather be home than be with me."

"Of course not! Why do you say that? We've covered this before."

"Oh, I don't know. It just doesn't seem like we have much fun anymore and you seem mad at me a lot. Sometimes...I...uh...feel like I forced you into this and I almost regret that I just didn't go by myself."

That really hurt. I was a little mad and really shocked but I could also understand what and why he was saying this.

"I'm really sorry that you feel that way, Ken. The only excuse I have for the way I've been acting is 'The Big C.' I'm miserable most of the time. I'm still scared to be more than 20 feet from a toilet. The whole time that we were riding through the desert, all I was looking at were possible places to go to the bathroom in case I felt an attack coming on. Any time we stop in a town, we always have to go to a place that we know also has a toilet. It's an awful way to live, Ken, and it's made me very ornery. Think back to the good time we were having before my colitis came. We had a great time, didn't we?"

"We sure did." I was glad that he replied instantly.

"Believe me, Ken, you're my brother, you're my best friend in the world and you always will be. I'm sorry I've been such a creep, but I promise that it's nothing personal."

Ken breathed a very apparent sigh of relief. "Wow, that's a mouthful. I feel 100% better now that we cleared the air. I just thought that you were really angry with me."

"No way. Even if I have to finish this trip with my intestines hanging out of me like a tail, we're doing it together. There is absolutely no one else in the world that I could do this trip with or would want to."

Ken reached out his hand,

"Friends to the end?"

"You got it buddy." We warmly shook hands.

We eventually covered many, many topics that night as the air was finally completely cleared between us. We were so relaxed and secure with our plush suite on the eighth floor. I enjoyed the best night of sleep since I had left home.

I COLLECTED MY THOUGHTS AND HIT THE RECORD BUTTON again. "Our ride into Albuquerque yesterday covered 72.2 miles..." As of three days ago, thanks to a small recorder that my mom and dad had sent me, I stopped keeping a hand-written journal of our trip and started to create an audio journal. This was so much easier after an exhausting day of bicycling. Steve and I had both kept journals since the day we bicycled out of town. I was sitting comfortably in an overstuffed chair in the deserted lobby of the Regency Hotel and tried to capture the last two days on tape. Tomorrow the doorman at the Regency would once again classically hold the door open for our bikes, only this time we would be heading back to sweating and avoiding semis on another 175 mile stretch of Interstate 40. We would also be back to warm water bottles, peanut butter sandwiches and sleeping on the desert ground. Yikes. This luxury living thing had been just what the doctor literally ordered.

"Steve was told by the station manager at KOB radio to take the Rio Grand exit."

"Sir?'

I turned off my recorder. A gruff sounding and burly looking police officer or security guard interrupted my train of thought.

"Are you a registered guest of the hotel?"

"Yes I am."

"Can I please ask to see your key?"

"Sure."

I nervously fumbled for my room key, unaware of why I was feeling uncomfortable. He glared at me still searching my pockets and then backed off his stern demeanor as I finally produced a big brass key to my room.

"Sorry for the inconvenience, but since we are in the downtown area we have a lot of street people. I have to check people out on occasion and..."

"That's okay. No problem."

As he slowly left my vicinity, I realized how much my outward appearance had changed over the last few months compared to my clean-shaven, three-piece-suit days as a salesman. As I sat there comfortably in my bib overalls, t-shirt and full beard, it also hit me full force that although I was still the same on the inside in terms of my honesty, integrity and trustworthiness, apparently I was initially judged by my changed appearance on the outside. I was giving my body, heart and soul to raise thousands of dollars for terminally-ill children, but that man thought that I was a major problem, a "street person," a "vagrant."

Now I better understood how good people down on their luck might feel when stared at by people who don't know the person on the inside or how they got into the situation.

I went back to recording into my new audio journal. I was sadly aware that I had lost my vitality in retelling the events of the past 48 hours.

CHAPTER 23
KANSAS CITY, KANSAS CITY HERE WE COME

"I have always been delighted at the prospect of a new day, a fresh try, one more start, with perhaps a bit of magic waiting somewhere behind the morning." ~ J.B. Priestly

WE WERE NOT ONLY MOVING AGAIN, WE WERE FLYING. Putting together a string of three record-setting days was awesome bicycling. Near the end of our first day out of Albuquerque, we climbed a fairly long hill about 40 miles west of Santa Rosa, New Mexico. As far as we could see ahead of us, and to the north and to the south…it was FLAT! For the first time in 50 days of bicycle riding we couldn't see a mountain anywhere. Steve and I knew that we would miss the mountains, but this was a huge turning point and a relief. We kicked cow pies out of our way in order to pitch our tents on a flat surface, a far cry from our soft double beds in an air-conditioned suite we had awakened to earlier in the day.

The second day we smashed our existing mileage record for a single day and kicked out 146.5 miles! The next day the wind was still at our backs but it was even stronger. We rode 136 miles in a mere six hours! The wind was howling out of the southwest and our road angled northeast. Perfect. That morning we had started in Nara Vista, New Mexico, then cut across the chimney in Texas and actually ended our day in Hooker, Oklahoma, grabbing states #16 and #17.

I had never experienced a tailwind like this in my life. Ken had stopped to fix a flat tire. Before he was done I told him that I was going to see how far up the road the wind would push me. I had gone three miles without pedaling even once. The wind was so strong that it was actually pushing me up small hills! I think I could have gone for 20 miles without pushing on my pedals, but it was so exhilarating to be effortlessly pedaling in high gear at better than 30 MPH.

We very seldom ever rode side by side together. We would each ride at our own pace. Because of my diminished strength, I was always picking up the rear. Sometimes I would actually be miles behind Ken. When I would finally catch up with Ken he would usually be laying along the road with his head resting on one of his panniers, sleeping, writing a letter or talking into his tape recorder.

One late September day in Oklahoma, as usual I was riding way behind. We were traveling on US Highway 64 on a fairly rolling section of road. I was up at the crest of a hill and I could see Ken up the road, just a couple of hills away. From where I was, I could see his bike Acabar lying on one side of the road and he was on the other side, directing traffic around something IN the road. It looked like trouble, definitely out of the ordinary. I picked up the pace to see what the problem was.

When I got close I could see that what Ken was directing traffic around was his sweatshirt. As I pulled up to a stop, he said with a big smile,

"I've got a little surprise for you buddy."

At that precise moment a large tractor-trailer rig approached in the other lane and when it roared by it blew Ken's sweatshirt aside to reveal my "little surprise"...

...AN EIGHT-INCH-LONG HUGE, HAIRY TARANTULA!

I have a real phobia with spiders; even small ones and Ken knew this. He got a real kick out of seeing every hair on my body stand on end as I watched this big, hairy spider slowly cross the road heading for the desert, lifting and placing each leg very carefully as it went.

"You missed the last one in Nevada, so I wanted you to see this little guy. I kept trying to stall him with my bike tires but he kept running around me and so I whipped out my sweatshirt to stop him so you could share this moment with me."

What a great buddy I had. I only wished that I could have returned his "thoughtful gesture" and pulled a bull snake out of my bags and thrown it at his feet.

We camped that night in Buffalo, Oklahoma, only nine miles from the spider crossing. I slept on a picnic table with my tent zipped up around me.

THE OFFICIAL DEFINITION OF WHAT STATES CONSTITUTE THE "Midwest" only includes those as far south as Kansas and Missouri. However, as Steve and I bicycled through Oklahoma, a mere 20 miles south of Kansas, we *knew* that we were back home and that we were indeed back in the Midwest. We were again experiencing small towns, closer together, green grass, trees, mailboxes at the end of driveways and most importantly, very friendly people. Now when drivers honked at us it was to say "Hello" and "Good luck" instead of "Get the hell out of my way!" People were constantly waving as we approached mile 4,800 and always curious about our adventure and our mission.

The gusty winds crossed our paths once again instead of being at our backs, Steve's colitis had resumed in full force and we were battling hard for every mile. However, we knew that we had a break planned in Kansas City and we were psyched for our goal, now only two days away.

The press was also picking up. The more miles we achieved, the bigger the story was becoming. By the time Steve and I bicycled into Arkansas City, Kansas on October 1, the press had already been notified that we were heading their way and they had a photographer and a reporter meet us at the city limits. It was also Steve's turn to make our weekly call to KSTP back in Minnesota and so our morning was full beyond the usual meals and miles.

Stressed by time constraints, we finished our newspaper interview at their office so that Steve could use their telephone to make our phone call. In a unique circumstance for us, we were able to flip on a speakerphone so that we all could get in on Steve's conversation with KSTP's host Dick Pomerantz.

"Here's Dick Pomerantz."

"Thank you, John. 11:10, 53 degrees. I have Mr. and Mrs. Keller and Jamie Keller, they are going off to Disneyland, they are in the studio and I have Steve Anderson. Mr. Anderson along with Ken Rogers, they are not a song-writing duo, they are traveling around America, by bicycle for Make-A-Wish. For those who do not know what Make-A-Wish is, Make-A-Wish of Minnesota is a foundation which has been established to provide wishes to come true. We now go to wherever Steve is."

"Stephen?"

"Yes."

"You doing okay? We are now on the radio."

"Yes, I'm fine, thank you."

"First of all, where are you?"

"We're in the land of Dorothy and Toto in Kansas. It's called Arkansas City, Kansas. Actually Kansas was our fourth state but we were in Oklahoma yesterday and the wind was so bad that we decided to head northeast and go with the wind for a while so we went up into Kansas. It's just nice to be back in the Midwest again."

"Now as far as I know you have not been primed for this particular interview, have you?"

"I have not been...what?"

"Primed. This hasn't been rehearsed, has it?"

"No."

"Okay, well you may not be aware of it but I've got the Keller family, who are going off to Disneyland, and they are in the studio."

"Oh, great!"

"So, I have Mr. and Mrs. Keller and I have Jamie, Jamie's on my left, Mr. and Mrs. are across from me and you're somewhere in…wherever you are…"

"Kansas."

"Kansas, right. Well that's your problem, not mine, Stephen. Jamie, these two fellas are bicycling around America on behalf of Make-A-Wish. Do you want to talk to them at all?"

"Uh, okay."

"Go ahead, you can talk to Steve. He can hear you."

"I want to thank you for what you're doing."

"My pleasure Jamie, my pleasure. When are you going to be leaving? Is it October 11?"

"Yeah."

"Wow. I hope you have a great time."

"Thank you."

Dick directed the next question.

"Jamie, have you ever thought about, I'm serious about this, if somebody said to you that it could be done, would you want to wheel yourself all over America? (Jamie was wheelchair-bound). I mean if it physically could be done, we put like an umbrella on top of your head or whatever and there was a truck following you providing food, did you ever think about that? Did you ever think about just getting on the road and getting out there?"

"No, but it sounds like it would be fun."

"Do you think it would be fun?"

"Oh, yeah!"

"Steve, is it fun bicycling?" Dick asked over the airways. Even I was curious as to how Steve was going to answer this question for the listening audience.

"Well, let me tell you Jamie, I wish that sometimes you and I could trade places. It is fun. I tell you, I've had this dream for many years and when you dream you only think of the good things. And there's a lot of miserable times but overall, I would say that it's a lot of fun and I feel very fortunate to be able to do it."

"Anderson, there's a difference between the kind of dreams that you and Rogers have versus the kind of dream that Jamie has. He's not stupid. He's the kind of individual who says, 'I know what I want to do with my wish; I want to go to Disneyland. There ain't no problems there, it's got good weather, there's palm trees, he's going to have a lot of fun. You guys take the hard way. You guys decide you want to try another different kind of dream or a wish so you decide to bicycle."

"Right."

"Says something about where you're coming from, right?"

"Right."

Dick let out his trademark hysterical, high-pitched laugh. It was contagious and then Steve started to laugh heartily too.

"I don't know if I'll ever have a dream like this again, either!"

Dick laughed again and almost drowned out Steve's next words.

"It's more like a nightmare!"

I started to laugh so hard in that newspaper office that I could hardly breathe! Finally the truth was on the table. We had kept Steve's colitis from every radio interview and newspaper article that we had ever done. Even though today Steve's "nightmare" line was still in code and not truly understood by the majority of Dick's audience, I got it and loved his candor. It was a classic moment and a great emotional release.

"Let me give you an idea as to what their itinerary looks like. On Monday, October 11 they're flying via Northwest Airlines to LA, they have the evening off, then Tuesday they'll be at the hotel, they then go to Disneyland when the park opens, they will spend the day at Disneyland and then they go back to the hotel. On Wednesday they will be driving off to Universal Studios for a tour, they will spend the morning at Universal, have lunch at their own leisure, they will then report to NBC Studios for a tour, they will have dinner there and then go back for the evening to the hotel. On Thursday it's totally open for Jamie to spend a complete day at Disneyland and then they will fly back on Friday."

"Oh, that sounds great, Jamie."

Steve and Jamie and Dick continued on for several more minutes. It was fun to listen in on the happy banter between the three of them and to again better realize that our bicycling for Make-A-Wish was no longer a vague hope for a dream for an eventual child. Jamie and his family were real and within ten days they would actually be getting on a jet and flying to Disneyland.

I intuitively knew deep down that the image of them in California would really sustain us on the bad days that certainly lay ahead of us on the remaining 5,000-miles-plus and 31 states through the winter months.

I started listening in to Dick and Steve again as my instincts picked up that they were making fun of me on the air as Steve retold the story of me capturing the tarantula in my sweatshirt two days ago.

"What does a tarantula look like?"

"Well, I'm sure you've seen pictures of them and they look exactly like their picture. They're really big and they have hairy legs and just the way they crawl across the road kind of gives you shivers up your spine."

"Did Kenny then put the sweatshirt back on his body?"

"Hard to believe, yes he did."

"That is hard to believe."

"I told him, 'Hey, that thing might have laid eggs in there,' but he didn't seem to care."

Dick and Steve roared. I had to admit it was funny.

"Give our regards to Ken."

"I will do that. We'll see you, and we'll see you, Jamie."

"Yeah, goodbye."

Steve and I sort of piddled away the next few hours, grabbing endless snacks, purchasing a bicycle air pump to replace the one I had lost and because the time was now so close, waiting for the paper to come out. I finally grabbed six copies of the afternoon edition. I was happily surprised to see that we were on the front page with our story and our photo. Even though Arkansas, Kansas was only a town of 14,000 people, hitting the front page with our adventure was a great ego boost.

Our goal was now to bicycle 32 miles to the next town of Cedar Vale, Kansas before nightfall. I started out ahead of Steve and bicycled at a comfortable pace. Over the months we had both discovered that there is a natural pace, flow or speed to any day and in any condition. It is a rhythm that is natural for that stretch of road and to go faster or even slower saps your energy. Although it was hard to do, I tried to bike a little slower as to not get too far ahead of Steve, but I still had not seen him for about an hour. There were no shoulders on this stretch of road and so it was tough to pull over and wait for him.

Getting more and more concerned, I finally stopped about halfway to Cedar Vale and lay down next to my bike in a driveway to wait. Several minutes passed in the tranquility and I started to ever so slowly doze off.

SCREECH!

A dark blue late-model sedan pulled over in front of me on the shoulder and the driver leaped out of the car.

"Are you alright son?"

As I worked through my fog, I quickly realized what was happening and I was immediately embarrassed.

"I'm fine, sir. Sorry for the concern. I'm just waiting for my buddy."

He smiled and walked back to his car. I again realized why I loved this part of the country. People cared. I had forgotten how much and how easily.

Another ten minutes passed before Steve slowly bicycled to a stop next to me on the driveway. The look in his eyes told me the whole story.

He not only looked terrible, he looked bitter.

It had been a draining 16-mile stretch of road for him and he just vented. He was so sick of using his energy and thoughts to plot for bathroom stops in case he cramped again. He was frustrated and angry. He told me how much better this trip could have been to this point if he wasn't battling this colitis. There wasn't much that I could say but I was glad to let him blow off steam. With each passing day I better understood what a pure, tough and lonely hell this was for him. He needed to get home and to get medical attention in the hopes that the second half of our trip would be not just tolerable for him but the exhilarating adventure we had planned together.

Bicycling more closely to each other, we managed the final 16 miles into town and got a motel for our final night on Part 1 of the trip. The next day we would be bicycling into our planned safety net of family and a plane ride home for Steve to see a doctor.

Relaxed and secure in our little refuge of a room, we split a six-pack of Coors. Steve then surprisingly and refreshingly shared with me all of the things that he *loved* about this trip and what we would miss when we got back home after bicycling all 48 states.

"Ken, do you realize that when we finish this thing we are going to go through serious 'outdoors' withdrawal? Can you even imagine working inside again or being cooped up in an office?"

"Are you kidding? The lights in this room already hurt my spirit. Fluorescent bulbs actually strain my eyes now and carpet fibers give me a headache!"

Steve took another sip and munched on some Fritos.

"I'll be honest; I love being noticed for doing something that I am really proud of. This trip does my soul good. Plus I am really enjoying the fact that we have absolutely no idea in the world what each day will bring."

"Kind of a feeling of really being 'alive' isn't it?"

"Exactly! 'Alive.' That really is it. Man, I am excited about the second half of this trip."

"Well after today and even the past month and a half, that's great to hear coming out of your mouth. Let's get you to a doctor and get back on track."

CHAPTER 24
HALFTIME AND CANCER FEARS

"Rest when you're weary. Refresh and renew yourself, your body, your mind, your spirit. Then get back to work." ~ **Ralph Marston**

WE WOKE UP EXCITED. THIS WAS A BIG DAY. AFTER BICYCLING 18 miles in the crisp, cool early morning fall sunshine, Steve and I hit our 5,000th mile. By our closest estimation, this was the midway point in our adventure. As we bicycled east of that mile marker, I felt a distinct sense of courage and confidence.

Something inside of me changed again. Lingering doubts were gone. Bicycling over that first mountain had produced the same confidence.

We had prearranged to meet my sister Mary and her husband Mark somewhere around Independence, Kansas. They were going to pick us up in their green pickup truck and drive us to Kansas City, Missouri where they lived, about 150 miles away.

As we got closer to Independence, every hill that we crested, we searched for a green Ford 150 long-bed, step-side pickup. We had already spotted two green pick up trucks, but they did not turn out to be them. My heart continued to be filled with breathless anticipation. Finally, seven miles southwest of Independence, Kansas, we spotted them as they spotted us.

Half time had finally arrived.

I hugged my precious sister Mary with gusto! Tears trickled down our cheeks. This was an unbelievable moment. I gave my brother-in-law Mark a bear hug and then made introductions. No one in my family had previously met Steve. Before we hit our 48th state, they would all meet him as they were spread out from Vermont to Florida. Mark and I jumped into the cab of the truck and Steve and Mary jumped into the truck bed. To my amazement and joy, next to me on the seat was a huge bowl of hot-buttered popcorn! This was my favorite food group in the world and there it was!

This break was going to be lifesaving for both of us.

On the following morning I caught a Minneapolis-bound airplane. It was finally time to get my colitis taken care of. It was so bad that I wondered what could be done besides surgical removal of the inflamed portion of my large intestine to make it better. I tried not to think about it as I soared north.

I looked out my window to see all of the ground below me. It finally struck me as to how much ground Ken and I had covered in the last 75 days. To travel all those miles on a scrawny little bicycle seemed almost unbelievable. I felt so proud of what we were doing, knowing that very few people would ever give up perfectly good jobs to attempt something of this magnitude.

I wondered how long it would be until I saw Ken again. I knew that he would wait for me in Kansas City for as long as it took for me to get better.

It was wonderful to see Lori again, but I had this very uncomfortable feeling that I shouldn't be in Minneapolis yet. When I left town back in July, I hadn't planned to see Minneapolis for a year and I sure didn't plan to make my return by plane.

On October 5, I went into St. Joseph's Hospital in St. Paul early in the morning. I was scared. God knows I needed help. I was down to 142 pounds and nothing but skin and bones. I lost lots of blood every day and had become anemic. My colitis was so bad I thought that the only way to get rid of it was major surgery. I was all too familiar with what the procedure is when you have an advanced case of chronic ulcerative colitis. They would remove the inflamed part of the colon and reroute it to a colostomy bag that is worn on the outside of your body. This is a real traumatic event to go through, from what I had read, and I knew that it would be no easier on me.

But what really scared me most was the chance of them finding cancer.

Anyone with a history of colitis is a much greater cancer risk. I also knew that during the examination Dr. Pizinger would be taking biopsies, specifically looking for any change in the tissue of my colon showing the first signs of cancer.

I was given an anesthetic that would help me make it through the very uncomfortable colonoscopy exam. It didn't put me out but it made me very relaxed. During the examination Dr. Pizinger showed a real interest in our trip and our main purpose in doing it, Make-A-Wish of Minnesota.

The examination showed that the last 12 inches of my colon was severely inflamed but the rest seemed okay. I would find out the results of the biopsies in two days.

Before I left the hospital that day, Dr. Pizinger asked if I had any health insurance. Before I left town last July I made sure that I was covered. About two months into the trip I learned that my insurance company had rejected me because of my past history of colitis. I was obviously a poor risk as far as they were concerned. My answer to Dr. Pizinger was, "No."

He patted me on the shoulder and said,

"That's okay, kid. I'm not going to be sending you a bill. I just want you to lie flat on your back for a couple of weeks. I'm going to write you a prescription for prednisone. I'll give you directions on how much to take each day. Call me in two days for the results of your biopsies. We'll get you back on your bike in no time."

I left the hospital feeling pretty good. It sounded like I would definitely be continuing the trip before too long. I also left astounded and very appreciative of Dr. Pizinger's generosity.

For two days I did nothing but lie down, drink fluids, take my medicine and wonder what the results of my biopsies would be.

On October 7th I called Dr. Pizinger. I am sure that he knew I was anxious in hearing the results and so he wasted no time in telling me the check for cancer was negative. I'm not sure if I yelled into the phone but I know my insides were screaming, "YAHOO!"

For two weeks all I did was work at getting better. That consisted of no physical activity and massive doses of prednisone. Five days after my exam at the hospital I started noticing the first signs of improvement. I had put on a couple of pounds even though I wasn't eating much and there was a marked reduction of blood in my bowel movements. I think what helped me to get better so fast wasn't just the prednisone. It was my change of attitude.

For the first time in about two months I knew that I was going to be okay.

I also got to spend a lot of time with Lori. She was very proud of our efforts so far and was very helpful in helping to cure this bout of colitis. She was anxious for me to rejoin Ken in Kansas City, thinking that the sooner I got back there, the sooner the trip would be over.

I tried to keep my return a secret from KSTP because I thought that maybe our fundraising efforts for Make-A-Wish would lose some impetus if the public found out that I was back.

They found out soon enough. Dick called to see how I was. He was very concerned. He was also a lot of help because someone close to him had occasional flare ups of the same condition that I had.

He felt differently than I did about the public knowing I was back. He believed it was a good idea to go on his show and explain why I was back. He thought that if anything, it would encourage his audience to donate more for Make-A-Wish.

"Ken Rogers and Steve Anderson have been bicycling around America touching all 48 states, the continental United States, on behalf of Make-A-Wish of Minnesota. If you have been reading about Make-A-Wish recently in the newspapers, it began, 'knock, knock' touch wood, on this program. It is an organization set out to provide wishes to come true for young people who have been diagnosed as having a serious illness of a life threatening nature. Now, as to how many young people have already had their wish come true, at least one, Jamie Keller, is presently in Disneyland. He returns today, he went on Monday and you may have seen it reported on a number of television stations and in newspapers here. I do want to publicly acknowledge and thank those publications and those media broadcast outlets for being so kind to be nonpartisan in that endeavor to give exposure to an organization which truly deserves it, which is Make-A-Wish. We're now going to go to Kansas City, Missouri, I believe, to Ken Rogers."

"Kenny?'

"Good morning, Dick."

"Are you in Kansas City?"

"You bet I am."

"Okay. You explain to the public, and you know that Steve is across from me, and so I'm going to be brief with you if it's all right, and then Steve's going to talk a little bit about himself so that people can understand why Steve Anderson is here and you are there and why for at least a week or so your rather grand odyssey had to be put on hold. Why are you in Kansas City?"

"Well, Dick this is something that we had originally planned about a month ago anyway, was just to take a break. The last time I think I talked to you in Albuquerque, New Mexico we were running really ragged. It had been a really relentless trip and it was time for us to take a break. But it goes a little deeper than that in that Steve had contracted an intestinal inflammation of some kind about three states into the trip. The trip itself was full of enough adversity for two healthy bicyclists, and Steve was just not doing that well. So we made a decision that when we got to Kansas, which is in our estimation, halfway through the trip mileage-wise, or about 5,000 miles of our estimated 10,000 miles, that we would take a break here. Steve would get some medical attention and I would pretty much take some R&R and do some regrouping financially. I've been painting a house for the past two weeks and I've got another job tomorrow. So it was just a break for both of us to do what needed to be done, get some home cooking and kind of relax before we tackled what will prove to be probably a tougher part of the trip as the weather gets colder."

"It was one of the best-kept secrets. In fact most of the people you and I are familiar with didn't know about it. Not only the audience but even people we know at the station and the like. It was something that we had to keep under wraps because you guys wanted it, uh, you didn't want any sympathy. Correct?"

"Well, that's correct. It's not a big ego, pride, hero thing or anything like that. It's just something we felt we could keep dealing with and we did.

We didn't want to alarm anyone. We wanted to keep people excited about what was going on and it didn't seem to be the time and the place to let people know. Like I said, it was our own little personal battle and we just fought through it and took care of it the best that we could while we could."

"Well Kenny, since Steve is sitting across from me and unbeknownst to probably most everybody, he and I and my wife and Lori, his girlfriend have had a long talk, if it's okay with you I'm going to put you back on hold and I know that Steve is going to be rejoining you and I'll ask him to continue the story that we've just begun, okay?"

"Okay."

"Are you doing okay by the way?"

"I'm doing great. I'm sitting here kind of getting used to home cooking again and fattening up. I lost about 20 pounds and I've gained about 8 back in the past two weeks. I've been taken care of by my sister and her husband. It's been wonderful."

"Ken, thank you. Don't hang up."

"Right across from me is a guy who, and I'm not just saying this because he and I both know what the fear was...you were frightened weren't you?"

"I sure was."

"Why were you frightened? You were bicycling around America. What happened?"

"Well, what happened was about 1500 miles into the trip I contracted ulcerative colitis. I've had trouble with it the last eight years but I was just hoping that I wouldn't have a flare up on this trip and sure enough, I did. But I didn't realize just how severe it was until I got back."

"Explain how ulcerative colitis manifests itself? I know that this is going to get a little embarrassing but let's be open about it."

"Okay, well, whenever you go the bathroom there's blood. It starts out with just a little and as it gets worse, it gets to be more and more blood."

"The harder the trip, the worse it gets?"

"Ah, yes I guess so. It seemed to come and go. For example I was going to come back when we hit Reno, Nevada."

"You were scared?"

"Yes, I was. I didn't want to take a chance with my health. As important as this trip is to me, I didn't want to risk doing anything to my health. So, I was going to come back in Reno and something happened; it just seemed to clear up for a couple of days. I decided that I should be able to ride, and I estimated that the next biggest town if it comes up again is Phoenix, Arizona or something. Well, we decided to take the northern route of Arizona so we weren't going by Phoenix and it got worse again. Then we decided that we were going to take a break halfway through and I would fly home no matter what."

"I want to say to the audience, and I am not into drama, both my wife and I had to yell at you on the phone last Friday when we talked because, without getting into personal stuff about my family, we kept saying the most important thing you have to do is take care of yourself, and you kept saying, 'I'm really committed to do the trip, not only for myself but for Make-A-Wish.' And we kept saying, in language which I will now sanitize for radio, blankity-blank Make-A-Wish, your health is more important, and you kept saying I'm committed to Make-A-Wish, I've got to go back. And we said at least see what the doctor says. You saw the doctor on Monday, right?"

"Right."

"What did the doctor say?"

"The doctor just, well what really scared me was, and I never thought of this before, but what they were checking for was the possibility of cancer."

"You had a colonoscopy right?"

"Right. He took five biopsies and on Tuesday the slides were developed and the diagnosis was chronic ulcerative colitis. He said, 'No cancer.' So I asked him, 'Does that mean that I am going to get better?' And he said, 'Yes, it does.' My doctor has been great through this whole thing and he really wants me to go back on the trip. I like to thank him personally on the air, Dr. Pizinger, as he's not charging me anything for the services he's done and he's seen me about four times, saving me a lot of money."

"And you're going back?"

"I am definitely going back Wednesday."

"This coming Wednesday?"

"Right."

"With doctor's permission?"

"Right."

"You feel good about it?"

"Oh, I sure do! I'm just so anxious to get back there. I'll be wearing long underwear and mittens for the next half of the trip but I'm really excited to get back and I know Ken is too."

"When will you leave Kansas City?"

"I think we will leave either Wednesday or Thursday. I'm going to fly back to Kansas City to where Ken's staying and then his sister or brother-in-law are going to run us down to where they picked us up at and then we're going to just continue the trip from there from where we ended it."

"As if it never stopped."

"That's right. And I just wanted to tell Ken not to put too much weight on because he's had some trouble breaking spokes and we don't want that to happen again."

I was laughing on the other phone line although no one could hear me. If he's making good-natured fun of me over the airways I knew that he was really back. Steve sounded so pumped, relieved and giddy that I was already chomping at the bit to see him and to get rolling again.

"Ladies and gentlemen, that is the kind of devotion and dedication to Make-A-Wish these men have. Here you have both Ken Rogers and Steve Anderson who are bicycling around America and you've just heard Steve's personal story. He's going back to continue it because so many of you have committed yourself to a pledge of "x" amount of dollars for every state the two gentlemen touch with their bikes during the next eight, or ten or twelve months. We need you, Make-A-Wish needs you and this is a personal thing to Stephen, because I probably won't see him before he leaves, do my wife Bobbi and me a favor, just stay healthy."

"Okay, I will."

"Good luck and we will be talking every Friday."

"Okay. Thanks Dick."

"We'll be back."

On Wednesday, October 20 the time had come to rejoin Ken. It seemed like a miracle that in just 17 days I was back to normal again. I had put on 11 pounds in that time and my bleeding had completely stopped. Obviously two weeks off my bike accompanied by large doses of prednisone was just what the doctor ordered.

Saying goodbye to Lori was much easier this time for both of us than it was in July. We knew that if Ken and I kept up the pace we were riding it would only be about four months before we would be together again.

As our 737 landed in Kansas City right on schedule, I exited the plane and thanked the flight attendant for a comfortable flight. Looking around for Ken or someone in his family, something hit me. I never realized it before, but when I pictured Ken in my mind, I always got an image of him before the trip. I remember of course that he had a beard now, which had been growing for three months. When I finally saw him off in the distance for the first time in almost three weeks, I was amazed at how long his beard was and for the first time I realized how much he had trimmed down.

He looked incredibly healthy.

I reached out to shake his hand and Ken just pushed it aside and gave me a big, ol' bear hug.

"How ya doing little buddy? You're looking great. Looks like you might be back up to 120 pounds again!"

"Oh yeah, ya big goon? You look like Grizzly Adams times two!"

We were both grinning from ear to ear.

"Let's say we do a little bike riding?"

"Sounds good. Where to?"

"Oh, how about all of the United States east of the Mississippi?"

"Let's do it!"

Then Ken yelled, "Heeee, Haaaa!" and we instantly had everyone in the airport staring at us. Needless to say, we were a little excited to see each other.

Since we had left St. Paul over 90 days ago, I had grown a beard and cut it off three different times. Ken hadn't shaved once. In the three weeks that I was gone it seemed to have grown another three inches. During the summer, Ken's traditional garb, whether he's riding a bike or not, consisted of shorts, socks and tennis shoes and no shirt. When the weather is cool, you will always see Ken in his faded Oshkosh bib overalls and a flannel shirt.

He really did look like Grizzly Adams.

CHAPTER 25
ON THE ROAD WITH A HEALTHY STEVE FOR PART II

"On the road again, going places that I've never been, seeing things that I may never see again." ~ **Willie Nelson**

After a final comfortable night's sleep in a bed, Steve and I and my sister jumped in the pickup truck Thursday morning with all of our gear and headed south. Mary had taken a day off from work to drive us back to "our spot."

It had been a wonderfully warm and renewing few weeks with my family. Mary and Mark had their first baby, Gabriel Peter six months ago, and for the past several days I had a chance to cuddle and play with the little guy for the first time and to hang out with my family. I had also painted the wood trim on the exterior of their brick house, which helped rebuild my finances for the second half of the trip.

Making money again really felt great.

I had left Minnesota back in July debt-free and with my total life savings in travelers checks totaling $500. Although I knew that wouldn't get me through 48 states, even at our allocated budget of $10 a day, our original plan was to stop for the winter and work in Florida until the snow melted up north so that we could bicycle again. With our new plan to finish the trip without stopping, I was in a financial crunch. The most imperative thing that happened over our break was that Steve got physically healthy. But it sure helped that I was able to get fiscally healthy too, adding another $230 to my stash. Both of us got a good shot in the arm of self-esteem. Steve and I had also been loved and cared for by our friends and family in very practical ways.

I had also bought my own tire pump and tire repair kit while in Kansas City. That purchase would make us both more independent of each other and less stressed by each other's temporary absence on the road. I was going to surprise Steve with my new "survival kit" tonight wherever we ended up.

The scariest part of my time In Kansas City was getting my initial updates from Steve. I finally got ahold of him four or five days into our "break" and he shared some pretty unsettling news. His colon was severely inflamed well past his historical first six inches and his doctor was now concerned about cancer. *Cancer.* That was an ominous word that Steve had never used with me and I had never considered. For the first time ever I was not only concerned about the possibility of Steve's health preventing him from finishing the trip, which would have devastated him, but now I was worried about my buddy's life!

Steve told me that Dick and his wife Bobbi had advised him not to continue the trip.

Make-A-Wish was also considering telling him that he could not continue but Steve just knew deep down in his heart of hearts that he would rejoin me. Thankfully his updates got better and better, even making a sparkling presentation to the entire Board of Make-A-Wish and the trip was back on!

It was great to see Steve again. He looked and acted like the Steve that I had come to know and love over the past many months. He seemed genuinely healthy. We had both forgotten what that was like. I was excited again.

I believed that we were ready for the open road and 5,000 more miles.

As ready as we were and as healthy as we felt, the cab of that truck heading southwest was also filled with a vague nervous tension. When we left back in July we had absolutely no clue as to what lay ahead or what living on the road for months was like. I had no understanding of how my body would react to bicycling for 12 hours and then trying to get comfortable, much less sleep on a rock-hard surface. Now we knew. We both had very vivid and recent memories of pain and extreme discomfort. We were incredibly apprehensive.

The trip went too quickly, as Steve and I enjoyed our final moments of my sister's warm cab, 6- mile-per-hour speed and total protection from the elements. Mary was obviously sad. She knew that not only was I leaving her and her family, but we were also about to reenter a world of risk, danger and the unknown.

As our truck ride was about to end right around 3 PM, we experienced a neat little "miracle" that made all of us laugh. We slowed the truck down to get close to where we thought we had been picked up, when we spotted the exact truck tire tracks that Mary and Mark left on the soft shoulder of the road weeks ago! Now we were assured that we would not miss even one foot of this trip.

As all of our belongings were slowly dumped on the road, I realized that Steve and I were literally being thrust back into our adventure and all of the elements. Mary and Mark's Ford 150 pick-up, our security blanket, was about to drive north without us.

It was very unsettling.

I kissed Mary goodbye. I then watched as Ken hugged and kissed his only sister goodbye. When Mary started crying I got a little choked up myself. Ken had always described Mary as a genuine sweetheart, and now after meeting her, I totally agreed.

As I watched her drive north, I already missed her. Quietly packing our bikes, Ken finally said,

"What do you say we fake the rest of this trip?"

"What do you mean?" I asked with sincere curiosity.

"Well, we'll take a bus back to Minneapolis, get an apartment for a few months and then call Dick every Friday making believe that we are still pedaling!"

"Wow! That could be more interesting than riding another 5,000 miles. We would have to find some way of making a long distance hookup through whatever state we're supposed to be in when we call KSTP."

Ken was now putting the front wheel back on Acabar.

"We'd also have to put on disguises whenever we went out for groceries."

When we were done packing our bikes, we pointed them towards Maine and I took some photos.

Ken finally summed up our new "plan."

"The more I think about it, we're both too dumb and too honest to pull it off anyway. Let's ride!"

"Hi Ho Betty, Hi Ho Acabar, Awaaay!"

We put our feet in our pedal stirrups and pumped our trusty steeds eastward for the start of the second half of our big adventure!

We only bicycled 17 miles on our first day back. We had a very late start but I don't know if that made much of a difference or not. Ken and I were back to being IN PAIN!

My right knee started feeling the same pain that my left knee had felt at the start of the first half.

Once again it was obvious that Ken and I were not professional bike riders. We were just a couple of ordinary salesmen out for a little adventure and bicycles were our form of transportation.

I guess that Ken and I were proud of this all along.

We believed that those bicyclists who wore skin-tight Gortex riding pants, brightly-colored, tight-fitting bikers shirts, biking shoes and painters caps with the bill flipped up, while riding their skinny, lightweight bikes every spare moment, could have physically done this trip very easily and in a lot less time.

We had absolutely nothing against these guys, but we didn't want to be identified as one of them. We were adventurers. Our riding gear consisted of gym shorts, sweat pants, baggy windbreakers and tattered tennis shoes. When it got cold Ken wore bib overalls and flannel shirts and I wore mismatched sweats, long underwear and galoshes.

If we were away from our bikes, no one would ever know that we were bicyclists.

That first night back we camped on an old abandoned farm, right next to a decrepit barn that was mostly caved in. It was a very typical Midwestern setting with splashes of fall colors all around us.

Once again we unpacked our bikes and set up our tents by flashlight. We then sat up for about an hour underneath the stars and got caught up on everything that had happened while we were separated. We were both missing our families. I was also missing Lori and some incredible homemade meals, as I sat there alone in my tent eating my supper consisting of a Snickers candy bar and water.

It was also hard to believe how much colder it had gotten in just two weeks.

"Ken, did you get a chance to hear any forecasts for the area?"

"Unfortunately I did. They were talking 35 degrees in the area tonight."

"35 degrees?"

"Yup. Buddy, I think that's going to be about the new normal until it starts to really get cold. I don't know if you've looked at a map for awhile but the state of Maine is north of here and it will be November in about a week!"

We finally crawled into our cozy sleeping bags and signed off with our traditional banter adding a couple of variations, spoken only after a rare easy day or a relaxed, upbeat evening.

"Good night, Steve."

"Goodnight, Ken."

"Good night, John Boy."

"Good night, Mary Ellen."

"Goodnight, Grandpa Boy."

"Goodnight, Grandma Boy."

"Glad you're back, little buddy. Sleep well."

"Glad *you're* back, big buddy. Thanks for waiting for me."

"There's no way that I could do it without you anyway."

THERE WAS FROST ON THE GROUND AND 28 DEGREES IN THE air. It was cold! We did not want to get out of our warm, cozy sleeping bags.

"Ken, you awake?"

"No!"

"Ken, it's time to rise and shine."

"Go away, Steve!"

I persisted. "This is your mother. It's time to go to school!"

"Leave me alone, MOM!"

"Ken, get up or I'll set your tent on fire!" I yelled.

Ken was laughing somewhere in his tent.

"Remember last night when I said that I was glad you were back?"

"Yes."

"I lied!"

We packed up quickly and sang a silly song we called, "Jack Frost roasting on an open fire, chestnuts nipping at your nose..."

MY KNEES HURT. MY BACK HURT. THE KINKS OF BEING LAID off of our biking "jobs" the past couple of weeks were readily and painfully apparent. Ever since high school football so many years ago, I have been saddened and amazed by how hard and long it takes to get into shape and yet how easily and quickly it takes to get out of shape. It's not fair but that's how it works.

The entire bicycling motion of pedaling seemed weird. It was as if I was on somebody else's bicycle. The early morning temps were also a new discomfort. My feet, dressed in white socks and cheap tennis shoes were freezing. What a difference a mere couple of weeks made! We would have to make some sort of wardrobe adjustment to keep our feet warm in the morning. Steve at least had on winter galoshes and long underwear. I had chopper mittens and we both had stocking caps. It was unnerving as we realized that it would only get colder as we bicycled north. Once we made our decision several weeks ago to bicycle this new nonstop, figure eight route heading to the northeast in November, we were going to have to experience much colder weather.

We were not sure if anyone had *ever* bicycled cross-country in the snow.

As the morning wore on, however, and our muscles slowly loosened up, the ensuing hours and then the next few days proceeded wonderfully. Temperatures rose with the sun, fall colors were peaking and the autumn smells and sounds were everywhere. I loved the fall, and experiencing this season on a bicycle with the new confidence that Steve and I both had knowing that half of the trip was already behind us, was awesome. I often thought while bicycling that if I could figure out how to somehow package up and sell the "smells" of fall, that I could easily make a million dollars.

The biggest highlight of all was Steve. He was back. The exuberance and camaraderie that we experienced those first few weeks leaving Minnesota were a part of our lives again. There was also a very noticeable lack of tension. Even though we both understood that the colitis wasn't anybody's fault and the stress between us wasn't personal, at a minimum there was a constant edge. That was completely gone.

We were having fun again.

Steve was also now engaged to Lori. I believed that because his relationship and health were now secure, he was genuinely more relaxed, confident and in less of a hurry to get back home. We had both pushed and pushed hard to get to the halfway point in the trip. That was now behind us. I could not have been happier for Steve, Lori or me.

For the first time in the trip we **both** now had watches, flashlights, tire repair kits and refurbished spirits. There was no more, "What do you think we should do now? How much daylight do you think we have left?" Ending our day was a simpler decision. We watched and then marked when the sun dropped. As of yesterday, the sun set at 6:35 PM, it got dark at 6:45 PM and by 7:00 PM we needed to be "home."

Our first full day bicycling again got us 68.9 miles down the road. During our initial break of the day, we stopped at a little general store and warmed our hands by a pot-bellied stove. We then proceeded to experience two new "firsts" on the trip.

First #1; at lunch in a little café, the waitress asked us if she could put some more ice in our water. We promptly and adamantly replied, "No!"

First #2; as we bicycled leisurely through the beautiful fall scenery of Kansas, we noticed for the first time ever, smoke coming from several chimneys. Summer had indeed slipped away and Fall had taken over.

We ended our day in Pittsburg, Kansas, and together decided that we did not want to be cold at night again. We learned some new indoor strategies and attempted to stay overnight at a college Newman Center, a police station, Salvation Army and a YMCA. In a rare scenario, two places actually ended up wanting us and we decided to accept an invitation to stay at a college student's house where a party was in progress. Steve and I were the celebrities of the evening.

It was now quickly becoming apparent, that after 5,000 miles of bicycling for Make-A-Wish and heading north in late Fall, people were really starting to take more notice of us and remarking that what we were doing was pretty unique.

Steve and I found ourselves still answering a lot of fun and unusually sharp questions at 3 AM, about five hours past our bedtime even for a Friday night, and so we said our goodnights. We were heading for our sleeping bags on the floor in the living room when the young man, Ken, who was our host, said,

"Either sleep in our beds or sleep in the street." It was typical 'guys talk' and we immediately got the message of hospitality. He pointed to a nearby bedroom.

I gave a goodnight hug to a man named Mike whom we had both been talking to for awhile. He had confided to us that he had been struggling with his faith. Mike told us more than once "you guys are my heroes!" He even gave us a five-dollar-bill for food down the road, a significant sacrifice on a college student's budget. As we said goodnight and goodbye, he made a point to tell us that he was now at peace with his faith issues, inspired by our mission and thankful for our encouragement.

Drifting off to sleep moments later in my comfy bed and warm room, I tried to think of how we had helped this man. I could not think of any one thing that we had told him that would have given him "peace" or even "encouragement." I just knew that somehow, someway, faced tonight with multiple options as to where we could have spent the night, we were exactly where we were supposed to be.

CHAPTER 26
ALL-GIRL COLLEGE LEADS US TO AN INCREDIBLE OVERNIGHT

"Life is all about timing…the unavailable becomes available, the unattainable, attainable. Have the patience, wait it out. It's all about timing."
~ **Stacey Charter**

IT WAS ANOTHER BEAUTIFUL DAY AS WE BIKED OUT OF Pittsburg, Kansas, warming to a comfortable 65 degrees in the sunshine with a gentle crosswind. It was hilly and we worked for our miles but it was a doable stretch of road after enduring the often-tortuous terrain out west. The leaves were again exploding in all of their resplendent orange, red and yellow colors and the smells were invigorating by themselves. It was also comforting having these little towns closer together in the rural Midwest.

It was a pure delight to be bicycling with Steve again. Apparently, Dr. Pizinger's care, massive amounts of prednisone and a couple of weeks on his back had done wonders. I had felt guilty in the several weeks before our Kansas City break that I always, and I mean always bicycled ahead of Steve. In the early days of our trip, Steve and I discovered that there was a natural ebb and flow of strength and speed. We developed a pattern of each taking turns handling the lead throughout any given day. People I am sure assumed that two buddies traveling the country must be bicycling side by side for the better part of a day. That rarely happened. We were too busy concentrating on traffic, obstacles like broken glass on the shoulder or road and involved in our own thoughts. Our bicycling had a nice rhythm to it. We were both very competitive as athletes but since our bicycling was not a race like the Tour de France, our egos were in check and we just simply "bicycled." If a reporter would have ever asked me back then who led for more of any given day, I am sure I did not know. It was probably 50/50. There was even an adventurous and dangerous feel of the road when you led and a comfortable and relaxing feel when you followed. It was refreshing and routine busting to do both.

But now I could not keep up with Steve to save my soul! He was rarely in sight. Yes, he knew that I now could change a flat tire on my own and I am sure that helped. But I also knew that he was strong and healthy again and in all probability, sick and tired of looking at my rear end. He was flying!

Although we had a lazy, late start, we worked our way through the hilly terrain bicycling to Missouri, and eventually 50 miles to a quaint little college town of 9,000 people, Nevada. Right on Main Street, Steve spotted three young women heading into a dorm. Steve laid down his bike and raced to catch up with them.

Several minutes later, he walked out of the building and back to his bike and me.

"Haven't seen you move that quickly in months," I chided him. "What did you find out?"

"No luck here, of course. It's called Cottey College and all of the dorms are female only. The girls I ran down made some phone calls for possible places to stay, but they couldn't get ahold of anybody. They suggested the police station down the block."

We were really hooked on the idea of sleeping indoors in the colder weather. I was convinced that we still were not "road ready" and tough like we were the months before we stopped and got soft from the comforts of a home again.

"Good afternoon, Sergeant. My name is Ken Rogers and this is Steve Anderson. We are bicycling all 48 states in an effort to raise money for children with life-threatening illnesses. A couple of young women at Cottey Colley suggested that you might know of somewhere where we could stay for the evening. We're financing this trip ourselves and so we are on a limited budget and staying away from motels."

She was a heavyset, sharp-looking woman who looked like someone who would get my immediate respect and attention if she pulled me over for any reason. She smiled, closed her eyes for a few seconds and then finally told us about a campground two miles outside of town. You could tell by her smile that she thought she had given us a great answer on the spot. We, however, were disappointed that it was an outdoors thing. She would never know that we were discouraged with her answer.

As we headed back to our bikes unsure of our next move, a police officer was closing his door to his squad car and heading for the building. Our paths crossed and he asked us if we had been helped. We said we had.

As he reached for the handle on the glass door heading inside with his back now to me, I thought to myself, "Turn around and take one more shot by asking him a simple question." I don't know why I didn't just let him walk through that door. I spun around.

"Excuse me sir, but do you know where two guys could stay for the night?" I had to shout, as the door was about to shut with him inside.

"Not really. But, let me think. You know, there are some fairgrounds north of town with some shelters. Why don't you come in and I'll draw you a map?"

As we followed him back inside, I was now really mad at myself. He was a very helpful and well-intentioned man, but we still didn't want to stay in a primitive wooden shelter. We should have been out checking churches and other options but now we were committed to wasting more time and at least getting his map.

We followed him to his office, past a quizzical-looking sergeant who thought she had already hooked us up. We sat in his office feeling stupid. The officer painstakingly drew us a detailed map as to how to get to the fairgrounds from the police station.

Off in the distance, the phone rang. I easily heard one side of a conversation.

"Yes, they are here. Uh, huh. Nope. I think they are planning to stay at a campground. Sure. Okay, go ahead. Uh, huh...got it. I'll let them know. Thanks for calling."

"You guys got a sec?"

We found out that the girls at the college had called and had found a little family that wanted to put us up for the night! Hooray! What an unbelievable turn of events. We really wanted to stay inside and with people tonight, maybe because it was still the weekend on a Saturday night. Whatever was going on inside of us, we both felt it and we were incredibly happy that we had followed the police officer back inside the building and gotten the unexpected news. There was absolutely no other way for anybody to have located us.

Steve and I bicycled the short distance to meet Grace, the mom, her adult son Jim, her daughter-in-law, Jaqualene and her little three-month-old baby, Kelly. It was an unusual situation. Out of the blocks, they were all Mormon, a new situation for us. Secondly, Grace's daughter-in-law, Jaqualene was living there because her husband, Grace's other son, was awaiting his trial for second-degree murder. What a loaded situation for innocent little Steve and Ken!

But they were wonderful to us and fed us a spectacular meal, allowed us to bathe, openly shared their faith and were incredibly hospitable. As we relaxed on the couch after supper, the doorbell rang and in walked eight young women from the college that Steve had originally met and who had put this little overnight together for us. It was great to see them and to be able to thank them for connecting us with this little family. But, there was another reason for their visit.

"We have a surprise for you!" a beautiful young brunette named Julie beamed.

We were just so happy that they had set us up that we had no need for any sort of gift. But they each handed Steve and me an apple and a Snickers bar for our trip. Eight apples and eight of my favorite candy bars! We were touched!

"That's not the surprise."

We now were sincerely puzzled and totally unaware of what might happen next.

"After Steve told us about your mission and then left us today, we were so moved that once we found you again, we took up a collection in the dorm. We collected $50 for you so that you can afford some places to stay down the road and some hot food."

She then handed us an envelope with a ten-dollar bill, a five-dollar bill and thirty-five one-dollar bills. We were overwhelmed.

Steve finally broke the emotional moment with an, "Ahhh..."

We then started at each end of the line of young women standing side by side for this presentation and gave each and every one of them a heartfelt hug. No group had *ever* extended this kind of generosity towards us and what we were trying to do. Yes, we had met some incredible people on the road who had helped us in very tangible ways. But this, the time and effort to take up a cash collection from an entire dorm of struggling college kids blew us away.

They eventually left and after more conversations on the couch, Steve and I finally retired to our bedroom. I went to bed again thankful that I had inexplicably asked that police officer if he knew of a place to stay.

We came within seconds of missing this entire evening. Thank you God.

CHAPTER 27
RELAXED FALL PEDALING IN GALOSHES

"Nothing compares to the simple pleasure of a bike ride." ~ **John F. Kennedy**

"THANKS, MOM. THE BISQUITS AND EGGS WERE AWESOME AND we will devour the four sandwiches later today."

It was another golden day and Steve and I were more than ready to ride. Grace, after only 15 hours together or so, already called "mom" by both of us, was hugging us as we prepared to take on this Sunday. We had said no to church this morning. The sky was so beautiful and the wind calm that the road was calling us to ride ASAP. It had been a positively delightful several hours together. We both kissed little baby Kelly goodbye and told them that we would pray for a good outcome on the upcoming trial of her son and Jaqualene's husband.

We flew down the road.

For the second day in a row, I could not catch Steve. He was not only fast, he was in an exceptionally playful mood. He was ahead of me and out of sight as I looked to my left at an intriguing-looking abandoned farmhouse near the road. Deep in thought on this tranquil and serene stretch of highway, I heard ape-like screeching and then felt two bananas bounce off of my back. I was momentarily confused with the disruption of my view of the farmhouse because of feeling things bouncing off of my body.

It was Steve hidden behind a little hill on the right, his bicycle completely camouflaged from view. As I stopped my bike he started giggling. Thirty-years-old and he's getting a kick out of hiding and throwing bananas at me while doing his best impression of an ape.

I laughed so hard so many times throughout the day that I momentarily forgot that this bicycling for ten hours in a row thing was grueling.

When we stopped around noon to eat our sandwiches from Grace, we were in for another unexpected surprise. Between the cheese and bologna she had slipped a ten-dollar bill into each of our sandwiches! Ken and I actually unsuspectingly bit into the currency! It didn't taste good but the bills were still in one piece when we backed our teeth off. She also wrote a little note to us saying that she wished that she could have done more for us.

This was just one more act of human kindness bestowed upon us, convincing us once again that this country is as great as it is because of its people. We both finished our sandwiches agreeing that Grace had indeed done enough. This family had surely been a very real Jesus to us.

Our day wound down 70 miles later in a town of 154 people called Preston, Missouri. A town of this small size presented a new challenge for staying indoors. We got to town, found a phone book, focused on the only two churches in town and placed a phone call.

Our first call was to the local Baptist church, Olive Point Baptist Church. A young youth pastor answered, heard our story and then offered us a trailer out in back of his church to stay, along with an invitation to attend their evening service, which was just about to start.

We happily accepted both offers.

Steve and I had recently talked about trying to get to church on Sundays. That was how we both had been raised but lots of Sundays had slipped away since going to church with our families years ago. Here in Preston going to church simply felt like the right and reassuring thing to do. Considering the dangers we potentially faced week in and week out, with traffic alone, we were pretty darn thankful to make it to the next Sunday.

Steve and I parked our bikes in the lobby and inauspiciously slipped into the back pew of the service. The pastor looked up from his reading and gave us a warm smile.

"Slipping" unnoticed into the back pew didn't last three minutes.

"We are privileged this evening to have two guests from out of town in our midst. They have quite a story to tell. Ken and Steve, would you stand up, introduce yourselves and explain why you are traveling the country on bicycles?"

We humbly stood up and briefly told our story. You could see by the smiles and sparkling eyes that people were really excited with our mission and how far we had already traveled.

Unlike the first 5,000 miles that we shared with a lot of bored desert lizards, it was already becoming obvious that the next 5,000 miles were going to bring about a much different reaction from real live people.

As the congregation filed out several minutes later, each and every one of them warmly shook our hands and wished us well. We had also upgraded from an unlighted, abandoned, uncarpeted trailer in back of the church, to the lighted, carpeted and *heated* church itself. The youth pastor also would be picking us up at 7 AM to take us to the home of a little old lady, a church member, who loved to cook a big, scrumptious breakfast. It had been a very good day.

"IS IT ME OR IS IT JUST A TOUGH ONE? IT EVEN FEELS LIKE A Monday," I gasped, huffing and puffing.

Steve had been patiently waiting for me at the top of another steep hill.

"No, it's been tough. The wind isn't our friend today, the hills don't seem to be letting up and I honestly think wearing all of these extra clothes isn't helping us either."

"Do you think it's finally time to buy some of that skintight Gortex gear so that we are more aerodynamic and…"

I started giggling as I stared at Steve in his unzipped 1950-style winter galoshes, bright yellow sweatpants and three-layered t-shirt, hooded sweatshirt and grey coat. It was too stupid to even attempt to make a joke about being more aerodynamic. We looked more like poster children for a Good Will drive.

Thank God we weren't racing anybody.

"Well at least it is a beautiful day, we've stopped trying to break mileage records and nobody is waiting for us down the road. Let's keep getting some miles."

It was true. Steve and I were no longer in *any* kind of hurry. We used to always be trying to bicycle more than yesterday, last week, last month and shorten the time between each 1,000 miles. Now we were playing more, taking it all in and shooting many more photos. We also loved finding places to stay inside without cheating and getting a motel. This way we were meeting with many more people and enjoying the journey significantly more.

We rolled into Brazito, Missouri early evening with 74.6 tough miles under our belts. This was our best mileage since we restarted the trip. Without a word, Steve headed for the Laundromat and I hit a nearby pay phone and phone book. We were getting this down to a system.

After a wrong number and two no answers, I saw Steve saunter out of the Laundromat with a smile and a thumbs up. He had secured a one-room carpeted shed right out in back of the Laundromat. I laughed as it hit me! Since we had restarted the trip, Thursday we had camped in the middle of nowhere, Friday we had stayed in an off campus party house with six college kids, Saturday with a Mormon family, Sunday in a Baptist church and tonight, Monday, in a carpeted shed behind a Laundromat. What a run we had going. I wondered if Tuesday night had any shot of keeping up this string of diverse and unusual inside overnight accommodations.

CHAPTER 28
OUR NIGHT IN THE HAUNTED HOUSE

*"Many of the most successful men I have known have never grown up.
They have retained bubbling over boyishness. They have relished wit
and indulged in humor. Youthfulness of spirit is the twin brother of
of optimism...Resist growing up."* ~ B.C. Forbes

KEN GOT TO HIDE FIRST, SO I SAT THERE NEXT TO THE casket, plugged my ears with my fingers so I couldn't hear where Ken was hiding and counted to 100.

"Here I come ready or not!"

From not too far away Ken yelled back, "I'm not ready!"

I just broke out laughing. There was an abundance of places to hide in this huge house with no electricity in the blackness at 10:05 PM and he *still* needed more time.

"I'll give you another 25!"

I put my fingers back in my ears and counted to 25, all the time laughing at how immature we were and loving every minute of it.

"22, 23, 24...25. Here I come, ready or not!"

This time there was silence. Ken must have found his hiding spot. I flicked on my little flashlight. Now I could see the casket I was sitting next to and all of the cobwebs in the corners. Through a doorway to my left I could see the dummy filled with hay with a bloody stump where his head should be.

My plan was to systematically look through every room and behind every door in the house until I found Ken. I figured that I would start with the room that I was in, even though I knew that he wouldn't be here.

There was a closet door right behind the casket and so I opened it and shined my flashlight in. Just around the corner were the legs of the OSH-KOSH bib overalls that I had grown so accustomed to seeing every day. I roared with laughter.

"You're not too good at this game are you?"

Ken was laughing so hard he had tears running down his cheeks. He finally was able to talk and said in mock anger,

"Anderson, you dummy. You weren't supposed to look here first! Did you really plug your ears?"

"Of course I did. I just figured that you would be too scared to hide upstairs so this seemed like the most likely place to start looking."

We laughed and we laughed and we laughed.

What was so funny to me was the whole situation. Two "mature" adults playing hide and go seek and one of the mature adults was no better at the game than my little sister was when I used to play with her when she was about five-years-old. I remembered going to my parents' house every couple of weeks and my little sister Kim, always wanted to play hide and seek and always wanted to be the one to hide. When I would look for her she stood out like a sore thumb, her legs hanging out in full view, or her arm, or the top of her head. Then I would act as if I didn't see her and walk right by her. If I went too far by her she would always say in a loud whisper, "Steve, I'm over here!" We played until we exhausted about every possible hiding spot in the house. Childhood memories were adding to my fun tonight.

Ken and I continued to play hide and seek in the dark for almost three hours in this very spooky old mansion.

We hit Montgomery, Missouri at 72.6 miles. It was a relatively uneventful day. But once in town, we wanted to continue our string of staying indoors and out of motels. It was quickly growing into a fun little challenge. We had developed the strategy of asking the question something like, "Do you know where two guys could flop for the night indoors?" We then smiled and kept quiet until they spoke first. It was effective about 80% of the time, even though some people fumbled for words or eventually asked to hear more about what we were doing.

As we hit town today, we started our quest by checking in and asking a gas station owner, a police station sergeant and a Catholic Church rectory where the priest was not due back until tomorrow. We were striking out but at least we were striking out quickly. We finally sauntered into a little neighborhood tavern that advertised exceptional sandwiches and asked the female bartender if she knew of a place where two guys could flop for the night. She slowly and thoughtfully said no, but then opened it up to everyone else in the bar. A lot of people seemed to hem and haw as they checked out our grungy appearance after 99 days on the road. Finally two guys to my immediate left sipping on bottled beers started asking us a couple of questions.

"What's up with you guys anyway? Where you from and why do you need a place for the night?"

He asked somewhat warily, as if he could help us out if he decided to, but for now he needed more information. We knew at this point that we were in. Experience had consistently taught us that if they were interested enough to ask questions, our story always softened their hearts and ultimately clinched a home for the night.

Steve humbly shared with the two men what we were doing and why.

"I think that we can help you out."

The other young man chimed in, "As long as you guys aren't scared to spend the night in a haunted house!"

Now everybody within earshot was laughing. Steve and I were confused and unable to decipher what in the heck was really going on. It was an awkward moment. We were not sure who was serious about what and how we should react.

"My name is Richard and I am the President of the Montgomery Area Jaycees. What our chapter treasurer, Gary, is referring to is that we are putting the final touches on a haunted house project that opens tomorrow to raise money for the area. There really is no heat or electric but it's yours for the night if you would choose to spend the night with us. With what you guys are doing for kids, we would be honored if you would spend the night at our house."

In my past I had been a Jaycee, a great organization, and Richard and Gary shared our bond of helping other people in need. We were on the same page.

We gladly accepted their offer, and as we patiently waited for Richard to draw us a map to our destination, about half the bar patrons offered to buy us a beer. We politely refused most of them, but took them up on one cold beer each. We still had a few miles to bicycle before our day ended at our "haunted house."

Steve and I enjoyed an incredibly fun evening, playing hide and seek among the "ghouls" for just over three hours.

CHAPTER 29
TABLES ARE TURNED AS KEN FINALLY GETS SICK

"Health is not valued till sickness comes." ~ Thomas Fuller

ONE OF THE SPOOKS IN THE HAUNTED HOUSE MUST HAVE given Ken the flu bug. For the next two days he was sick. We should have quit riding but Ken wanted to keep moving. In those two days we put on 130 miles, but very, very slowly. We would ride for three or four miles or so and then my buddy would feel a wave of nausea coming over him. He would immediately get off of his bike and lay down on the nearest grassy shoulder. Since I had nothing else to do, I would document the fact that he could get sick too by taking pictures of him lying there. Back on the first half of the trip when I was plagued with colitis, I envied Ken's health many times. I remember telling him once,

"I'll bet that you could eat rotten, uncooked pork sprinkled with asbestos, on moldy bread and wash it down with a jug of nuclear waste without getting sick."

He seemed so invincible then that I almost got angry. But now, I felt bad for him because he really was sick, and yet I also couldn't believe how wonderful and different it was to have the roles reversed.

I recalled the times that Ken would ask me, "How's my bloody buddy doing?" or "How are the entrails hanging today?" as I snapped pictures from many angles of my sick, pale friend laying along the road outside of Ashley, Missouri.

"Have you ever seen lutefisk, Ken?"

Lying flat on his back with his eyes closed, he answered,

"Yes, Steve. Where is this going?" He knew me too well.

"That's what you look like right now. The color is about the same and to tell you the truth, you smell like it too." I clicked two more photos.

Ken smiled weakly, "Steve did anyone ever tell you that you have a lousy bedside manner?"

"Oh, I'm sorry buddy. I guess that I'm just a little excited that you are sick and I am not!"

"Well, I'm happy for you, Steve. If I had enough strength, I'd throw you out on the road in front of the next 18-wheeler that came by."

For those two days it was really nice to take care of Ken for a change, since he had done it for me so many times during my sickness. I would take care of finding a place to stay for the night and would go out and buy whatever food Ken thought that he could keep down.

I felt weak, feverish and achy, had a sour stomach, headache and alternately wanted to either throw up or poop. The smell of any food nauseated me. It had been literally years since I had felt this physically crummy. I drank fruit juice, took aspirin and downed Maalox the entire day. Nothing helped to get me beyond three or four miles down the road before I had to get off of my bike and lay down on the ground.

I now better understood Steve. Getting sick on the road, in a word, "sucked." You are weak, miserable, the miles go by excruciatingly slowly and you are *always* behind. I quickly realized that the "always behind" thing is psychologically devastating.

You are also in no mood to contend with the weather, the wind, stray dogs trying to run you down, broken glass and all of the typical daily nuisances.

I gutted out 49.1 miles. I honestly don't believe that I could have bicycled 50 miles no matter what I was promised once I got there. We ended our week in the little town of Louisiana, Missouri, a town of about 4,000 people right on the border of Missouri and Illinois.

Steve asked at the first gas station if the owner knew of anywhere where we might be able to spend the night.

"There's a Catholic Church two blocks up and the priest lives right next door."

The priest answered the door on the first ring of the doorbell. We told our story. As he briefly hesitated, I asked him,

"Is this something that you usually do?" I don't know where that question came from.

"No, I actually don't but I will tonight. Let me get the keys to the church. You guys can sleep in the basement. It's carpeted, has lights and even has a bathroom."

We kept our record string of indoor accommodations at six and counting.

Steve and I chatted in the dark before I drifted off to sleep first, processing the trip for a few minutes. Steve had checked his log a few minutes earlier and discovered that it had been exactly 100 days since we left home back in July. We both agreed that the past seven days of bicycling since our break was remarkably the best week of the trip so far. We realized that at some point in the first half of the trip neither one of us was really sure what was wrong and why the trip had increasingly become so stressful and uncomfortable. Was it the colitis, was it Lori, was it the grueling months of being on the road or was it possibly me?

We both understood to our core that now that Steve was healthy he was enjoying the trip and so was I. The bicycling was still hard and days long but we were having a gas and were certainly more confident than at any other point in the trip. With 5,400 miles behind us, spending the nights inside and often with people, all combined for an awesome and renewing week.

I felt a great sense of optimism, despite the taste of Maalox backing up into my mouth from my rumbling stomach.

While Ken was sleeping, I turned the lights back on and wrote letters. Then I shaved off my moustache for the first time in nine years. Ken was shocked when he saw me the next morning and immediately started making fun of me. He told me that I looked just like Beaver Cleaver. I hoped that he was wrong.

CHAPTER 30
BICYCLING DIVERSIONS, PRANKS & A THREE-LEGGED DOG

"I thought of that while riding my bike."
~ Albert Einstein, on the Theory of Relativity

TRAFFIC WAS CLEAR. I REACHED OVER FOR STEVE AS HIS outstretched hand clutched mine and we bicycled past the Illinois border sign.

It was state #19.

"YAHOOO!!"

Although every state line that we crossed was monumental to us, this one seemed particularly sweet and well deserved. It was a psychological milestone after the weeks of stop-and-go in Kansas and Missouri. Bicycling into Illinois was a good, clean break from all of that confusion and meant we were charging east. More importantly we had pedaled one more state closer to Maine.

Steve raced back to the border sign for our traditional two celebratory symbols. First and foremost, Steve quickly took out his world atlas and opened to the two page-sized map of the contiguous United States. He then took out a black marker and put about seven lines diagonally across the entire state of Illinois. It was an enormously liberating exercise after bicycling for days and often days at painstakingly slow speeds to get through another state in our country. It was uplifting for me just watching him draw the lines!

Then we once again took our border shot of one of us holding up "Number 19" on poster board that we carried with us next to the "State of Illinois Welcomes You" sign. As I climbed back on my bike, I thanked God for my much-improved health this morning that I had taken for granted these past months on the road.

It was a relatively routine day of bicycling through the countryside of Illinois.

Later in the day, however, my neck hairs literally stood on end. I heard the unmistakable sound of a dog ferociously chasing me. This one caught me off guard as most of them do anyway when I am deep in thought. Although he was not barking I could tell by the increasing volume of his panting that he was getting closer. I turned to check out who my opponent was on this particularly peaceful and cloudy fall afternoon. I had to look twice.

The mutt that was bearing down on me and closing the gap only had *three* legs!

How was he moving the three that he had so quickly? His "handicap" was not slowing him down in the least. That scared me all the more. My adrenaline shot to a new level and I smoked down the highway until I could no longer see him. Once he was out of sight I still kept bicycling in my fastest gear! What an inspirational adversary. There was a lesson here somewhere about overcoming limitations or something but I was too spooked for too long to put it all in perspective. I turned around to check the road again and again.

The rain started to trickle down on my head. The skies were looking like they were about to really open up and so I pulled over to the side of the road and reached for my new rain gear. Until Burger Brothers from Minneapolis gifted Steve and me with two sets of complete rain gear back in Albuquerque, I had only had a $7.99 windbreaker to protect me from the elements. As I slipped on my rain pants and hooded rain top, I started singing in the rain, as predicted by the smell in the air and color in the sky. It was now pouring. Thank you Burger Brothers! I eased back onto my bike and securely headed east.

"Beardstown, Illinois, B-E-A-R-D-S-T-O-W-N, I-L-L-I-N-O-I-S," my fingers would type out on my imaginary typewriter. Every sign that I would see would send my mind breaking every word down into letters and instantly computing how many letters in that word. Then my fingers would start typing it out.

It seemed that since the weather had turned cold and I had started wearing my stocking cap, I started to play this particular mind game. The cap shut out most of the noises from the world around me and left me with the sound of my own breathing.

I trudged along, one stroke at a time, occasionally changing gears, and listening to the hollow sound of my breathing. I marveled at how easily Betty and I meshed together as one, as though I had ridden her all of my life. At the beginning of the trip I would always look down for the shift lever and then back to see what gear I had shifted into. I would occasionally screw up when shifting into my largest front sprocket and the chain would then become derailed.

With 5,400 miles and 101 days of riding behind me I could shift without looking and know just from the tension on the pedals what gear I was in. I could also tell from the cushiness of the ride if my tire pressure was less than 100 pounds. Yes, Betty was indeed a good old girl. I took good care of her, cleaning her up every couple of days and she rewarded me by never breaking down.

Acabar and Ken had become close too, but she had a few problems now and then. We both had our share of flat tires, but I had not had even one other problem. Acabar, on the other hand, had popped seven spokes, lost her rear wheel bearings and had broken her seat, forcing Ken to ride lopsided until he got it replaced. You really couldn't blame Acabar. She was a top-of-the-line TREK bicycle and Ken's hulking 215-pound frame was proving to be a little much for her to handle.

I used to feel the same way about poor Hoss Cartwright's horse from the classic TV show, Bonanza.

I passed through Meredosia. "MEREDOSIA 17 MILES." Lunchtime "S-E-V-E-N-T-E-E-N"...oh no! Now I was starting to type out numbers alphabetically! "Stop it, Steve! Just stop this." I had to start thinking some productive thoughts. I rolled up my stocking cap so that my ears were exposed. Immediately the sounds of the outside world roared into my ears. I knew that my ears would get cold but I didn't care. I rolled along past corn field after corn field and the only sounds I heard were rustling cornstalks, an occasional car or truck and birds chirping loudly as they gathered together for their flight south.

I was in heaven.

I started singing, "Oh beautiful for spacious skies, for amber waves of..."

SPLASH!!

From out of nowhere I was by a large stream of water! I looked around and then...up. In a tree right next to the road, halfway up in its branches was a big, hairy vulture, Ken, with his half empty water bottle in his hand. He was giggling.

"You better plan on staying in sales, Steve. You'll never make it as a singer!"

Since the start of the second half, this had been an almost daily occurrence. Each of us would ride as far ahead of the other as we could, just so that we could jump out of nowhere and scare the rear rider as he came by. Ken had totally taken me by surprise with the water-bottle-in-the-tree-sneak-attack, but in recent days whenever he would get ahead of me and out of sight, I would spend most of my time looking for him around every corner.

Riding by a bridge abutment one day, I was sure that he was further up the road when an arm reached out toward my bike from underneath the guard rail; Ken doing his troll impersonation. Another time I waited in a cornfield for about 15 minutes waiting for Ken to come by so I could do my best impression of an angry, snarling dog. I could tell by the way his bike swerved that I was convincing as a wild dog!

This second half found Ken and me in a totally different frame of mind. Life was so enjoyable. A big factor of course was my return to good health. But the biggest fact in our renewed spirit was that we no longer even considered that we wouldn't accomplish our goal of bicycling all 48 states. We had already overcome what once seemed like insurmountable odds to get this far. We had made it through mountains, torrential rain, blistering deserts, debilitating sickness, bike trouble and homesickness. We knew that we would make it now. It was just a matter of taking it one bicycle stroke at a time, one mile at a time, and one day at a time and eventually we would make it back to Minnesota.

"WELL *THERE* YOU ARE, STEVE! I WAS STARTING TO GET A little worried about you. Did you get lost, little buddy?"

"You dog! How long have you been here?" Steve was smiling. As competitive as we both were, his smile was a bit anguished. I decided that I wasn't going to push his buttons tonight.

"The truth? A little fib would be a lot more fun to tell you. I've been here about 20 minutes."

"Oh, good." He looked relieved.

"That was refreshing, scary, exhilarating and a little unsettling. Made me better understand how thankful that I am not alone out here. Let me get you our waiter."

Our long, first day in Illinois was ending in the small, folksy town of Chandlerville, exactly 80 miles from where we awoke in our little church basement this morning.

Steve and I finished the day experimenting in a way that we had never done before. With roughly 20 or so miles before we got to Chandlerville, our decided destination for the day, we literally came to a fork in the road. Together we decided to each take a road and see who could get there the fastest and easiest. Since we now both had bicycle repair kits and I could change a flat tire by myself, we could be independent of each other for a couple of hours.

My route ended up faster and longer. Steve's was slower and his pavement full of more holes we discovered as we shared notes. It was a fun diversion and adrenaline rush.

We soon found out that our waiter, Chad, was a junior in high school and a stringer for the local paper. With a young ear and eye for news, and living in a town of about 2,000 people as well as noticing our loaded down bikes, he kept asking us questions. He was a polite and personable young man, and as our meal progressed, he retrieved his camera and notebook and interviewed us and asked if he could take some photos.

Eventually people in the small café started to take notice of us. A man in the next booth asked us if we had a place to stay for the night. My, oh my, how we loved that particular question! When we said that we did not, he had an idea.

"I bet that the mayor can help you two fellows out."

"And how and where do we find him at this time of night?" Steve politely asked.

"Hey mayor, you got a minute?"

Dining two booths down from us was the mayor and his wife. I *loved* small towns.

After photos with the mayor and then with our bikes all loaded down with gear, we happily took the key that the mayor gave us to the local community center and bicycled "home" for the evening.

As I hit my pillow on a table in the center, I again was amazed at just how exhilarating and even eventful our lives were on "uneventful" days on the road.

CHAPTER 31
A LESSON LEARNED IN NORMAL & HOME WITH KEN'S FOLKS

"Happiness is having a large, loving, caring, close-knit family in another city."
~ **George Burns**

OUR WAITRESS PUT TWO FULL ORDERS OF BISCUITS AND GRAVY in front of Steve and me. It already seemed like a mistake to have allowed her to talk us into this meal. I loved starting my day with my omelets and hash browns and stacks of pancakes at a delicious greasy spoon diner. But our vivacious waitress this morning in Chandlerville told us that we had to try the legendary and delicious biscuits and gravy "breakfast of champions" to anyone in the south. Although central Illinois didn't seem that "southern" to us, we were up for some indigenous culture and a gamble.

We lost.

"Never again, buddy!" I moaned to Steve. "My Lord in heaven these things are filling and already just laying there in my stomach. I'll be lucky to give you 20 miles today! You see that gentleman over there? Now he just got an order of like half of this and then got some scrambled eggs. Maybe that's the ticket."

We labored down the road never feeling so full in our lives. Thankfully the day was gorgeous with blue skies, high 60s and a good wind at our backs all day long pushing our ever-so-slowly digesting biscuits and gravy closer to Maine.

We hit a bike shop in Normal, Illinois at mile 90.3, where Steve needed to buy a new tire. He went inside to make his purchase and a small crowd of people started to form around my bike. The questions and curiosity around us was mounting by the day. Two young guys suggested a campground just outside of town for an overnight possibility.

"Where do you guys usually stay?" The question came from a good-looking, mid-30s young man who seemed very down-to-earth and genuinely interested in our story. Steve walked out of the bike shop with his tire as I was giving my answer.

"Well, for the last week or so with the cooler weather, Steve and I have been trying to find places to spend the night indoors."

"You can stay with me and my family if you want."

His response was warm and not overbearing. Steve and I hadn't given much thought to tonight, Friday, nor had we had the chance to talk about it. I looked at Steve's face looking for some help. The young man continued.

"My name is Phil Kearney, this is my son and supper is at 6:30 PM. My wife Kathy and I live about three miles from here. It's up to you guys. No pressure."

Steve smiled at me. That's all I needed. We knew the subtle code of agreement.

Phil later told us that as he drove home after Steve and I had accepted his invitation, he had told his son, "You know, we are going to get a lot more out of this tonight than they are."

A spectacular home-cooked meal, hot showers, an opportunity to wash clothes, spend time with a family including children and pets, great conversations and a warm bed, and yet he told his son that they would get more out of our time there then we would.

These were the kinds of people that continued to serendipitously bless our lives.

We sipped hot chocolate after a great meal and all of us enjoying each other's company. Phil gratefully explained to us that we were living a life with our adventure unlike anybody he and his wife had ever known, worked with or known socially. He intuitively knew that by taking a risk and inviting us over and engaging Steve and me to share our stories and experiences, that his family's thoughts and hearts would be expanded, enriched and possibly even inspired.

His point was significant and explained why he felt so fortunate and blessed to have us in his home. So often in life we only hang out with people like us. That happens in part because we socialize with people from work or with family or with those who share our interests, theology, hobbies, politics, etc. It was refreshing and invigorating for all of us to be together that evening. He reached out to us at the bicycle shop, trusted us and then made the evening happen.

Steve and I were very humbled by Phil's thinking and trust. This was a lesson I hoped that I would keep close to me long after I got back from this trip.

WE BIKED 86.5 MILES TO KANKAKEE, ILLINOIS WHERE KEN'S dad had prearranged to pick us up. He met us with bear hugs, three chocolate éclairs for Ken and me (Ken's favorite desert in the world as I later found out) and then drove us to their home in Arlington Heights, Illinois. We were going to take a quick "refueling" stop of a couple of days with his mom and dad and 17-year-old brother Stan Jr.

They treated me like one of the family and I really did feel like part of it. However, what I really enjoyed was watching Ken, his mom Dorothy and his dad Stan enjoy each other's company. There was lots of love in this family and they were never timid about expressing it.

It was really fun sitting back quietly as they shared stories and memories. I could see where a lot of "Ken" came from.

"Dad, remember when you helped Tom and me build one of my first model ships, that big aircraft carrier and then we put it in a big tub of water in the backyard, you poured gasoline on it and then set it on fire? That baby sank faster than the Titanic!"

We were all roaring with laughter and the image in my mind of a dad helping his two sons sink a model ship with fire was fantastic. In fact, I could really relate, as my dad seemed a lot like Stan. Both born in the late 1920s I could see where Ken and I got our sense of play and childlike spirits.

"Thank God your mom wasn't home," his dad laughed. "I think she would have been mad even before I poured the gas on it. That wasn't too smart on my part. Forget you heard that story, Stan Jr."

The next couple of days were full of great food, conversations, deep sleep, bike cleanup and gaming with Ken's extended family.

"SORRY KEN. I DON'T HAVE A SINGLE POINT."

Uncle Bob roared with laughter.

"Steve! Blanked out again? How can you *do* that?

The four of us were laughing often and loudly. It was a Sunday afternoon cribbage game on Halloween, played on a card table in our game room. My Uncle Bob, my dad's only brother and his wife Kay were down for the day to meet Steve and to spend some time with us and mom's precious older sister, Marian, who was also in for a few days. Steve, mom, Marian and I had started our day with a great Mass at St. James Catholic Church. Now only hours later on a day full of thunder, lightning and pouring rain, we were playing cards and sipping on a few cold beverages.

"It's bad when you have to do it without a partner, Ken," dad laughed.

"That is tough hey, that is tough," Uncle Bob chimed in. "Doesn't this guy know that he's paying us cash after a loss?"

I could not stop giggling at the humorous abuse we were taking. Steve and I were very competitive card players. But over the years when playing four-handed cribbage against my dad and his younger brother Bob, as much as I always wanted to beat them, there was nothing more fun than losing to these guys. They were like a well-rehearsed vaudeville act. Stan and Bob effortlessly played off of each other as if they had practiced their lines for weeks on end.

"Fifteen-two, fifteen-four and a run of three for seven. I got half of them!" Dad exclaimed to his brother.

"That a baby!" Bob shot back with glee.

It was my turn to count.

"Well, I don't have a whole lot. Fifteen-two-four-six and a pair is eight."

"Not too bad for a beginner." Dad was playfully digging at me, his oldest son who had been playing cribbage ever since he taught me about 20 years ago.

"I'm sorry Ken." Steve was laughing but you could tell he felt bad. This game had come down to the wire and he had absolutely no points to count when we needed them the most. Steve was an exceptional card player. No points meant he was dealt zero and didn't get a needed cut.

Now it was time for Uncle Bob to count to see whether they had won the game or not. It did not look good.

"Well, all I know is that I have six here. But I haven't counted the crib."

They needed a mere two points to end this disaster. He peeled his crib over one at a time. The first two cards he rolled over were a pair of fours for the win.

Dad started counting how much we had lost by and consequently how much we owed them. The stakes were big at a quarter a game and a penny a hole.

"Twenty-five, thirty, thirty-four cents this time."

"Hey you guys are building! You're getting better!" Uncle Bob was on a roll.

Steve and I were laughing so hard that tears were rolling down our cheeks.

"That's 78 cents total guys for the two games you've lost."

"Well, why don't you guys discuss it a little and we'll try this again. Let's see, how about trying a few moments of meditation?"

"We didn't seem to scare them even a little in either game, Steve," I said.

"I think we've got to talk a little strategy here, Stan. They got a little too close to us last time. What we're going to have to do is to get off to a little faster start."

The good-natured repartee continued. It was great to be home with family, safe, secure, loved and silly on a rainy, memorable Halloween afternoon off of our bicycles.

CHAPTER 32
TWO OVERNIGHT CHOICES - NUDIST CAMP OR PASTOR JOHN?

"I was just thinking, if it is really religion with these nudist colonies,
they sure must turn atheists in the winter time." ~ **Will Rogers**

"YOU WERE RIGHT. YOU HAVE A BROKEN AXLE AND SOME crushed bearings. It could have been a lot worse down the road, messed up your wheel hub and gummed everything up. It will cost you about $14 and 30 minutes to get you back pedaling again."

Great. Dad had just dropped us off back in Kankakee at a bike shop and hugged us goodbye. It was already a miserable day in the pouring rain and I had a major bike challenge and we had not bicycled a single mile yet.

This was really depressing.

Saying goodbye to family and hugs was never fun and leaving the comfort of warm food, housing, beds, running water, toilets and hot showers never easy. Our first "transition" day back on our bikes after a break of any duration was unsettling. The word "vulnerable" fit our moods well.

Thankfully I had discovered that there was too much give in my axle last night while I was cleaning my bike at mom and dad's in the comfort of a warm house. I had a problem that was beyond my ability to fix.

"Thanks. Let's get it done."

We had a late start, miserably wet weather and our 20th state border under our belt as we eventually bicycled 33 tedious miles to the town of Roselawn, Indiana.

We warmed up in a little tavern, sipping on our hot chocolate and finally asking the bartender if he knew of a place that we might be able to stay for the night.

He responded with the most intriguing option of the trip so far.

"Well, I got a buddy, John, who's a minister in town, great family, or if he's not home or not up for putting you guys up I got another buddy who runs a nudist camp. This is their slow season and I know that he would have some room."

Now I had to admit I had never heard all of **those** words in a single sentence! The bartender noticed our eyes bugging out at this strange combination of overnight possibilities.

"No, no, I know what you guys are thinking!" He was laughing now. "This nudist campground is totally on the up and up. They're good people. But let me call John first and see what he's got going on."

A nudist campground. That sure would be an intriguing addition to our string of indoor accommodations if they had a pavilion or indoor shelter.

"John's good with this, I think. He's on his way over to talk to you guys."

Within minutes, Pastor John settled in next to us and introduced himself. Then he started asking us questions. In the past, people and potential overnight hosts asked us about our adventure, our experiences on the road and our mission. John wanted to know if Steve and I were Christians, were we saved, how did we know that we were saved and more about our beliefs and our theology.

I was really put off with this "interrogation."

Although I believed that Steve and I were giving him all of the "right" answers, and I knew that we were both Christians, I became increasingly defensive. Why did he need to know this? Was he going to base his decision on whether or not he would put us up for the night by the answers to his questions? Would he treat us differently depending on how we each responded? And finally, what if he liked Steve's answers but did not like mine? We were sort of a package deal these days!

He eventually must have liked what he was hearing and he slowly relaxed. Once John felt at ease with us, we started to feel at ease with him and Steve and I finally and without reservation accepted his invitation to spend the night at his home with his family.

"JESUS LOVES ME THIS I KNOW, 'CUZ THE BIBLE TELLS ME SO. Yes Jesus loves me; yes Jesus loves me..." Precious little 7-year-old Johna and 5-year-old Jennifer sang into my little tape recorder. Johna was Pastor John's little girl and Jennifer was their even younger foster child. They were both cute, dressed in matching pink pajamas and pretty shy until they caught me catching up on my day's events on my little audio log. I invited them to talk into it and they spontaneously broke out in the famous children's Christian song. What else did I expect from preacher's kids!

Steve really had a soft spot for Jennifer. When we found out that she was a foster child in part because she had been abused and abandoned by her real parents, Steve surprisingly mentioned to me that if he was home, in a stable situation and the opportunity presented itself, he would love to adopt a little girl like her. That was a side of Steve that I had never seen before. I also knew that if Steve said it, he meant it. He was so good with kids of all ages I don't know why I was even surprised. It was a fun revelation for me.

John's wife, Willie, then found me and we chatted for about an hour and a half. John was gone for the evening with church business. As we shared life stories and values with each other, I slowly realized how stupid I was for questioning John's motives in his perceived relentless questioning back at the tavern. My gosh, he was gone for the evening and yet he invited two bearded 30-year-old men on bicycles to spend the evening with his wife and two little girls! How many men in America would do that with people that they had known for about 20 minutes!

It made me realize that in spite of the evil in the world, I believed even more firmly now in a life philosophy of trust. It is far easier and more beneficial to believe in people and live by the golden rule than it is to be cynical and afraid. The people of America were certainly showing Steve and me that they can and do live this way by how we had been treated again and again.

As Willie and I wound up our conversation for the night, she reminded me that we had an "obligation" to write a book someday about our exploits on the road. She had seen my little tape recorder and heard of some of our stories.

"It sounds as if you have inspired a few people already on this trip. But if you write a book about what happened out here and even one person reads your story and decides to pursue their dreams, or take their own adventure-for-a-cause or even seeks the Lord because they were inspired by your exploits, they could change the world. Always remember that you now have an obligation. And also know that I want to read it when it comes out."

She smiled and hugged me goodnight.

A day that started with a sad goodbye, a broken axle and a miserable pouring rainfall, ended on an incredibly different note; actually an entirely different song!

CHAPTER 33
IF YOU CAN <u>PROVE</u> YOU ARE A BELIEVER YOU CAN SLEEP HERE

"The greatest proof of Christianity for others is not how far a man can logistically analyze his reasons for believing, but how far in practice he will stake his life on his belief." ~ T.S. Elliot

"MORE BAD NEWS, BUDDY. NO ONE'S ANSWERING AT THE United Methodist Church either. That's a 'No' from the police, the Boy Scouts, the Mennonite Church and now a 'no answer.' We still have the First Baptist Church to try and the Church of the Brethren, whatever that is, is still busy. Man, this isn't easy tonight! I do not want to pull out my tent and stop this indoor string."

We were vegging out at another little pub in North Liberty, Indiana. It had been a weather-beating 73-mile-day and we were pooped. At the end of our day we were now looking for a friendly-looking café or tavern to try to get a good sandwich, a cold beverage and a local phonebook or a friendly face. When we'd arrive in a strange town on a bicycle, exhausted and looking for help, we were discovering that our options were limited. Our first stop tonight had been the local police station. They were not helpful at all and so then we bicycled to this little pub. The few patrons who asked about us seemed disinterested in our story. So far this had been a very rare unfriendly town.

Tonight was my turn to find us a spot and Steve looked so tired and relaxed that I'm not sure if he would have been much help anyway.

I took two more bites of my cheeseburger.

"It's getting dark and so I'll go and give this one more shot. Keep your eyes open for a friendly smile from anyone. I can't get rid of the chills and the tent thing does not sound good. I'm getting spoiled and I don't care."

Reluctantly I headed back to the phone booth. I hated it when I felt like I was begging or groveling but I was determined tonight to find us something warm.

"Bingo!"

Steve's mood immediately picked up as he saw me spring back into the bench.

"You found us a home?" His grin was expectant and hopeful.

"I think so. I finally got through to the Baptist preacher and he wants to meet us first. Unless you are really motivated, I think that I can make this happen faster by myself. Besides, it looks like you and that bench are melting into one! His church is close so hang in here and I'll be back with a warm home for us."

Steve smiled weakly as I finished off my burger.

"I will be your hero tonight, you weather-beaten noodle. See you in about a half hour."

MY FIRST IMPRESSION WAS THAT HE LOOKED LIKE JIMMY Swaggert on TV. He ushered out the last person from his small, cramped and messy office.

"Come on in, young man."

He sternly introduced himself, asked me to sit down and then said that he wanted to know a little bit more about me. He started by asking me what Steve and I were doing and why. I told him our entire story, as I had done countless times before. As he listened, it was strange to me that he never registered so much as a smile nor did I get a sense that he appreciated anything that I was saying. When I finished my short explanation, he stared at me and then asked,

"Ken, if you died tonight, do you know where you would go?"

I disappointedly thought to myself here we go again. I have to sell myself and my faith like a beggar to simply get inside any place warm.

"Yes, I would go to heaven."

"How do you know?"

"Because I have accepted Jesus Christ as my Lord and Savior."

"Are there words that say that in the Bible?"

I was beginning to seethe but I also knew all of the answers that he was looking for. Seriously considering walking right out of his office, I thought of pathetically tired and hopeful Steve sitting back at the pub and then of both of us setting up tents and shivering all night in the cold.

"I can't quote bible verses or even tell you whether it's in Matthew, Mark, Luke or John but it goes something like, "I am the Way, the Truth and the Light and no one comes to my Father except through Me."

He said nothing and stared at me still not smiling.

I finally irritatingly said, "Why, is there more than that? What's the deal?"

"No, no, that's right, you're right. I just wanted to check out and find out if you knew. Now, is your friend saved? If he died tonight would he go to heaven?"

"Does it make a difference?" I was now flat out angry and finally he could tell. I not only had to defend my faith I had to defend Steve's faith? I wondered what he would have said if I told him that Steve was back in a bar.

"No, not really. If you weren't saved, I would want to talk to you and witness to you and save you now. If you are saved, it makes me feel a little bit better about me trusting you guys. You know, you really can't trust anybody these days, you know what I mean?"

"I know what you mean. I just don't feel that way."

I did not like this guy.

"Well, maybe you're right. Hebrews chapter 13 verse 2 states, *"Don't forget to show hospitality to strangers, for some who have done this have entertained angels without realizing it."* Maybe you guys are angels for all I know!

He laughed. I smiled weakly. It's a good thing that we were not angels. If it had been any kind of a test from above, he was flunking badly.

After some more grilling, he finally seemed to accept that either I was an angel or at least an okay person.

"Well, I can't give you the keys to the church since I don't know you *that* well, but...'Honey'?"

His wife was just outside the office at a small desk. I thought that she was his assistant but apparently she was his other half. The office door had been opened this entire time and she must have heard our "chat."

"Do you think the boys can stay at our house tonight on the floor?"

"On the floor," I thought. This guy is giving anything to do with God a bad name.

"They'll be gone first thing in the morning."

She nodded an indifferent yes.

He then started to give me verbal directions to his house, not bothering to write anything down.

"You head three miles south of town; we're out in the country..."

"South? We need to head north in the morning." I was still pulling for the church floor that was about 100 feet away.

"Well, that's where we live. What's three miles out of your way, anyway, after all the miles that you two have put on?"

What a presumptive jerk. I finally left after writing his directions down. It was now totally dark, he lived south of town in the country, no lights or streetlights to guide us, a "floor" awaiting us and maybe even more questions about our characters or about our knowledge of Paul's letters to the Corinthians.

We never attempted to bicycle back to his house.

I went back to Steve and shared my story. We then called the two remaining churches with no luck, Steve personally tried the police station again with no better fortune and then we bicycled about a mile north of town to a Church of Christ, no lights in the church, nobody answering doors, no lights at the parsonage and no good moods in either one of us.

"The way I see it, Ken, I'm willing to go one of two ways unless you can come up with more options. Let's either camp right out here on the church lot or let's bicycle 13 miles north to South Bend and find a motel."

I thought right then and there that we were not going to get a motel out of desperation. When we got a motel it was going to be because we were psyched up and that's what we really want to do. We also promised each other awhile back to talk each other out of bicycling in the dark.

"Let's check this out together one more time." I finally said.

We again knocked on the church door, rang the parsonage doorbell and tried any and all doors. No luck. I finally spotted a little building of some kind on the other side of the parking lot. As we got closer it appeared to be a one-room schoolhouse. I tried the door. It opened. I looked at Steve.

We laughed, hooped and hollered and hugged and gave each other high fives. What a celebration for a carpeted floor! We had hung in there, not given up and we were now home and *inside*.

We loaded our bikes into the room, kept the lights off and Steve wrote and left a nice note on the outside of the door. Since we had never gotten permission, we did not want to alarm anybody. We settled quietly into our sleeping bags.

I made a commitment to myself right then and there on that floor in my bag: My door to my home will be open to anyone at anytime, period. Whether it was a bicyclist, or a friend of mine who had kids coming home from college that need a room, whatever…done deal. I decided in the dark that I would always have an open door to anyone in need.

It had been so phenomenal this entire trip when people trusted us and let us in into their homes. Maybe someday those people will get burned and maybe someday I would too. I hoped not. But, I hoped that if I did, that I would turn around and live life exactly the same way as I did before I was hurt. But this not trusting people and making it such an issue to share a garage or tonight even a church floor, when there are folks like Pete Matthews back in Nebraska and Phil Kearney in Illinois and many other assorted people across the country who had taken us in based on a five-minute conversation, was misguided and wrong.

I would continue to trust people. I was going to give them the benefit of the doubt until they proved me wrong. I refused to live any differently. Hopefully the good Lord would give Steve and me people in our lives that wouldn't harm us. It really meant a lot when people took us in. It meant a whole lot. It was no fun begging. That's basically what we had to do; we had to sell ourselves and beg every night for a place to stay.

Just as I started to drift off, I remembered that the Baptist preacher might still be waiting for us at his home. Although it was a farfetched idea, I hoped that he now believed that we really had been angels from above. I wanted to beleive that he was finally ashamed as to how inhospitable and suspicious he was and that he knew deep down that we finally had found a warm home with a more deserving host.

In a shack, by ourselves, we had indeed.

CHAPTER 34
PEDALING KNUTE'S CAMPUS AS TEMPS & FIRST SNOW DROP

"Let's win one for the Gipper." ~Knute Rockne

EVERYBODY IS LOOKING AT US. DON'T WE LOOK LIKE students?"

"Yeah right, Ken. They probably think we're big eaters and the 50 pounds of baggage we're each carrying is just our lunch."

Once again, we did not fit into our surroundings as we biked through the grounds of Notre Dame Campus in South Bend. The fall leaves were in full fiery display, accentuating the beautiful old buildings of this grand old legendary school. For all I knew Knute Rockne himself walked on this campus road, or George Gipp (or was that Ronald Reagan?) and countless other athletes, coaches and students over the past century.

It seemed like the beautiful fall colors were lasting extra long this year. Ken and I believed that autumn was moving east across the country and we were almost magically matching its pace.

Our ride through campus brought back warm memories of my failed college career. I thought I was going to do so well after I breezed through high school with no major effort, but unfortunately in college I discovered girls and parties. My adventure in the hallowed halls of higher education only lasted a year.

I was a natural in math so I figured that a week of skipping Algebra 101 wouldn't hurt me one bit. When I came back to class, the professor may have just as well been speaking Hebrew. I failed.

History should have been a snap. No calculations, no logic, just memorization. However, every class I caught myself watching the antics of the professor, who was obviously intoxicated, instead of listening to his words. At the start of every class he would take a cigarette out of his pocket, put it in one hand and have a lighter in his other. He would then put the cigarette to his mouth, bring his lighter up to light it, when a flash of insight about Ulysses S. Grant or something else would pop into his mind. He would bring the lighter down having never flicked it, take the cigarette out of his mouth and start talking. He did this time after time after time, driving me nuts. I was often close to standing up and yelling, "WOULD YOU PLEASE LIGHT YOUR CIGARETTE BEFORE I GO CRAZY!" I realized that I wasn't the only one who felt this way when one day he finally lit up and everyone in the room stood up and clapped. I failed this class too.

With no teachers around checking for hall passes and no parents around telling me that I had to go to school, I was a total failure in every subject that I took except for Physical Education and English.

In my first semester of English, our assignment was to choose any subject we wanted and write an essay. I scoured through several Readers Digests and decided on writing about heart transplants. I titled it, "A New Heart-A Breath of Ecstasy." You could call it blatant plagiarism. I just took out the big words figuring that my professor would think something was up, seeing those words coming from the hand of a nineteen-year-old. I aced the class.

Physical Education classes were my only legitimate successes. I got A's in skiing, basketball and volleyball. Unfortunately, I was light years away from being good enough to make money at it.

The University of Minnesota did us both a favor and told me I couldn't come back unless I took night courses for a year and maintained no lower than a 2.5 GPA. I decided to get into sales.

I looked around at all of the young men and women walking between classes and wondered if any of them were going through right now what I had gone through eleven years ago.

As a frigid wind picked up from the west, we bicycled north from South Bend and headed towards Michigan.

I COULD FEEL ICE FORMING IN MY BEARD. MY WATER BOTTLES were freezing up and my bicycle tire skidded ever so slightly for the first time in my entire life. Then it happened.

Snow dropped from the sky.

The inevitable was finally happening on November 4th with 28 state borders to yet bicycle through. Could we really bicycle through snow on these skinny high-pressure tires? We were going to find out.

For the 21st time on this trip, I grabbed for Steve's hand as we bicycled through the Michigan border sign. I was freezing. I took off my fall jacket and grabbed my goose down parka, packed in my panniers, for the very first time. Steve looked at me disheartened. We jumped back on our bikes.

When we reached Michigan Ken broke out his goose down jacket. Unfortunately, I hadn't thought ahead. Mine was still back in Minnesota.

We were now consistently hitting days like today when it didn't reach 40 degrees. I was forced to wear a couple of sweaters, a windbreaker and my rain jacket. Tomorrow after talking to Dick on our weekly phone call, I would ask John Rubel, the chairman of Make-A-Wish, to call Lori and have her mail my goose down jacket, my ski mask and my deerskin woodchopper mittens to some town up the road.

This had been an unexpected problem almost the entire trip. We obviously could not carry all of our changes of clothing with us, and so we would call home and have them sent to a predetermined town. It was difficult most of the time to choose a town we would be going through and when we would be there. We never really knew what our exact route would be because we would usually determine our routes based on what the people in that area would tell us. Countless times they really helped us out. They would steer us around mountain passes that outsiders like us would not know were closed because of snow or even too steep for our faithful 18-speed bikes. They advised us to avoid certain roads because they were so heavily traveled and had no shoulder. They also told us to avoid some high-crime areas in certain cities that we rode through.

The first mail drop that we missed was in Jackson Hole, Wyoming. Because of an almost dizzy-like run of changes due to several factors including my colitis, that mail followed us all around the country until we got to Kansas City.

Tonight Ken and I would figure out where we might be in about a week and then cross our fingers. Normally we would pick a town a good two weeks up the road, allowing time for possible post office error, challenging weather and hills affecting our forecast and any other hazards and variables two lowly bike riders might encounter. But it was cold and I hated wearing my rain jacket. It was rubber-coated and didn't breathe at all. I kept soaking in my own sweat and freezing. I wanted my real winter clothes NOW!

"SMELT BASKET FOR YOU AND A BOWL OF CHILI FOR YOU. Enjoy guys."

As my toes warmed up under the table and I took in the aroma of my fish and homemade French fries with the skins still on, I knew I had made the right choice. So many times on this trip when Steve and I ordered two different entrees on the unfamiliar menus in unfamiliar towns, we had a winner and a loser. This afternoon in our small little café in the middle of rural Michigan, Steve and I were both winners and happy with our food choices.

My toes were still numb as Steve glanced out the window at our bicycles, purposely in full view of our booth. The snow continued to accumulate on our bike seats and saddlebags.

"I'm getting that sick feeling again. Makes me nervous," Steve grumbled.

"What's that? Nervous?"

"Well, maybe not exactly nervous, but unsettling, I guess. Do you realize how many more times you and I have to get back on those bike seats and keep pedaling? Not just today, obviously, but tomorrow, next week, next month and the month after that?"

As my body continued to enjoy the warmth of the café, the smells of the food and the taste of another deep fat fried scrumptious smelt before sipping on some hot apple cider, I slowly, reluctantly and agonizingly realized what Steve was saying.

"Yikes. Now that you put it that way, this feels like Aberdeen, South Dakota Part II! I was pretty happy about 20 seconds ago but now…"

"I'm sorry. It's not that bad. I'm having a blast now that I'm healthy and our nights indoors are great. It's just that as I'm warming my body up and looking outside I think, man, we still have about 5,000 more miles of this and it's getting colder and snowier and the wind's starting to have an almost fierce bite to it."

Steve stopped venting and gobbled up another spoonful of hot chili.

"No, you're right, buddy. In some ways this isn't going to get any easier. It's going to continue to take immense motivation, almost daily, to get back on that bicycle seat, especially after we've warmed up. But on a positive side, I think that everything that we are doing is shaping us somehow. And getting back on those dang bike seats and heading back into the wind and snow has to be making us tougher emotionally and mentally. This will pay some dividends when we get back home. That or it will kill us."

"Actually," I continued smiling, "it will probably kill you first. You don't have enough meat on your bones. Then, in the middle of a blizzard in say, Iowa, stuck in a snowdrift, no food, I'll start a little fire, roll your dead, stiff, frozen body over…'Timothy, Timothy, where on earth did you go?'"

We were both giggling as I sang the stupid lyrics from an old song we both remembered from the 70s.

"Seriously, Steve, you and I already know the drill. One day at a time. How's your chili?"

"Awesome. It was the perfect food on a day like today to thaw and satisfy."

We headed to the register. The new owner of this place, It's the Pitts, in Union City whom we had chatted with earlier and briefly told our story after he noticed our bikes, waved off our attempts to pull money out of our pockets.

"It's on me today, guys. Take care of yourselves."

We headed back to the cold and I thought of the unfriendly townspeople of North Liberty, Indiana who would not help us out last night. The police station, multiple churches, indifferent bar patrons and finally the Baptist preacher had saddened and disappointed us. Yet in one casual, "It's on me today, guys," our faith was restored and our hearts lifted.

The thought of a brand-new and probably struggling business owner spotting us a free warm meal and words of encouragement would keep me warm and optimistic on our blustery path today until we found a home tonight.

I brushed the snow off of my bicycle seat.

CHAPTER 35
HOW OUR "CHURCH STRATEGY" LED TO BEAUTIFUL NUNS

"Friends are angels sent down to earth to make good days and help us find our way." ~ Unknown

KEN AND I SPENT THE NIGHT IN THE BASEMENT OF A FIRST Congregational Church in the little town of Orland, Indiana. Churches were quickly becoming our mainstay for indoor lodging.

Ken and I both realized the value of a first impression. These past several nights when we would knock on a minister or priest's door we had nothing to sell but ourselves. We realized that with beards, Ken in his Oshkosh bib overalls and me in my sweat pants and hooded sweatshirt, our physical appearance did nothing to enhance someone's trust or receptivity to us. As in sales or dating, nobody likes rejection and so Ken and I took turns with our nightly "sales presentations."

It was pretty standard fare, something like, "Hello, my name is Steve Anderson and this is my partner Ken Rogers. We're about 6,000 miles through a bicycle trip covering all 48 states while raising money. This town is as far as we could make it today. We were wondering if you knew of a place where a couple of tired bicyclists could sleep for the night?" Then we smiled and waited without saying another word. We never wanted to put them on the spot by asking if we could stay with them or at their church.

Ken and I were convinced that it was not our presentation and it certainly wasn't our appearance that got us a place to stay so often. It was our smiles, our pleasant, polite manners and our ability to not put them on the spot.

We loved churches. We certainly felt safe, but another huge benefit is that they almost always had full kitchens. When we left Kansas City we left our little cook stove and eating utensils behind. We needed to make room in our limited baggage compartments for extra clothes to keep us warm in the fall and winter months. We ate so many meals in restaurants now that when we had a chance to make a homemade meal, we always took full advantage of it.

We had only pedaled 48 miles, as we battled a headwind most of the day. We rolled by a big Catholic church in Custar, Ohio and noticed the sign in front said, "SATURDAY NIGHT SERVICE 7 PM." It was now about 5:30 PM and Ken said, "Why don't we get a bite to eat at a pub or café and then go to the service?"

"Well, I don't think that there's anything good on the tube tonight and besides, I don't have a TV. Sounds like a plan to me."

We sat near the front. This was our fourth weekend in a row that we had gone to church. We had not been that consistent for years back home! There were families scattered here and there. Most of the congregation was probably home watching television or out socializing. The few of us that were there sang some rousing hymns. I was surprised with the volume that we could muster. I noticed shortly into the service how comfortable I felt in this house of God. Calm engulfed my body and I felt so much at peace. I noticed that I wasn't just saying and praying. I was actually paying attention to every word and they touched me deeply.

Father's homily continued. "Whatever you do to the least of my brethren, that you do unto Me." Ken leaned over and whispered.

"I hope that the few people here are taking his message to heart. I'm happy to be 'the least of my brethren' for tonight. We could get a warm bed and someone here could be getting closer to Jesus in the process!" He started to laugh. I wanted to but I didn't want to get a case of the giggles in church.

Since I have been old enough to remember things, I've always gone to church. Every Sunday morning my family would be at the Fredenberg Chapel, which was just a mile from my parent's farm. I learned all of the books of the Bible, heard all of the classic Bible stories and memorized many Bible verses every summer in order to get a free ride to church camp. I hardly missed a Sunday until after I graduated from high school and moved to Minneapolis. Of all those church services I could only remember a few that touched my heart.

In the eyes of my church, I was saved. I was a born again Christian. It happened at summer camp when I was thirteen-years-old. It was a feeling of comfort to know that no matter what happened from then on, I was going to heaven. All I had to do was to believe that Jesus Christ died on the cross to save me (and anyone else who wanted to believe this) from going to Hell. I believed that he was the Son of God and I believed that he died on the cross because of His teaching.

On that sunny day at summer camp I felt strangely at peace and I quietly said to God, "Take me, I'm yours. I'll try to be a good servant," and I cried tears of happiness.

As the years passed I always tried to live by the golden rule and the Ten Commandments. I did a pretty good job at obeying most of the commandments but I really butchered some others. Whenever I messed up I always tried to remember to say a small prayer like, "I'm sorry God. I'm trying to be like your Son but he's a tough act to follow. I'll sure try to be better though. Thanks for listening."

Where I was having trouble with Christianity was the fact that all I had to do to gain passage into heaven was to believe that Jesus died on the cross for me. This alone seemed too easy a task to get such a great reward.

I also had a hard time believing that people of other faiths could not make it to heaven because of their beliefs. I found it very hard to believe that a great man of peace like Mahatma Gandhi who did so much with his life would not make it to heaven. I had a hard time believing that some of the Mormon people we had met like Grace back in Illinois were not going to heaven because they studied and practiced the writings of Joseph Smith. They were some of the most loving and caring people I had ever met in my life. They were sincerely seeking the truth and that is what they discovered and believed. I couldn't help but think that God was looking down at these people and saying, "You are living your life exactly as my Son suggested you should almost 2000 years ago. I am pleased." All I knew for sure is that God was a big God and I knew that He would sort it all out.

I sat through the Catholic service in Custar, Ohio feeling closer to God than I had in years. Despite all of my doubts, I knew somehow that if I died this very instant, I would go to heaven. Not because I was as good a person as Gandhi or some of the Mormons and ministers that we had met on this trip, but I was at least trying to be the best person that I could be.

The priest had gone to the back of the church at the end of the service to shake the hands of everyone that showed up. When my turn came I was going to thank him for a wonderful service and then ask him if he knew of a place where a couple of cold and lonely bikers could stay for the night.

Before we reached the back of the church, a very pleasant looking woman wearing a huge grin approached us.

"Do you guys belong to those bikes out there?"

"Yes we do," I replied. "How did you guess?"

"Oh, just a wild guess," she laughed heartily.

"I'm Sister Di. I'm glad that you made it to our service."

"So are we," Ken said. "My name is Ken Rogers and this is my friend Steve Anderson."

We chatted a while longer with Sister Di and she brought up the subject before we had the chance.

"Where are you guys planning to stay tonight?"

"I'm not sure," I said. "We really don't like to travel when it's dark, so I guess we'll be looking for a place in town somewhere."

"Well, why don't you two meet me over at my place across the street in about a half hour. I'll talk to Father Jim and see if you can stay in the rectory with him for the night. I know that he's got plenty of room. In fact, Father Jim?"

We had been talking and slowly drifting to the back of the church as we followed those in front of us out. Now, Father Jim was right in front of us. We all shook hands as Sister Di introduced us.

"This is Ken Rogers and Steve Anderson. I think they deserve some kind of award for traveling the farthest to get to Mass tonight. They have bicycled from Minnesota!"

Ken and I took over and explained our situation and finally I asked if he knew of where we could stay for the night.

"There's really not that much in town. But I've got room over at the rectory. After preaching about loving your neighbor tonight I better not turn you guys away! There's room at the Inn. I've actually got a wedding to perform out of town and so my rectory is yours to come and go as you please. I would be proud to have you under my shingle."

"That sound's great! Thank you, Father." That was easy.

Sister Di then turned towards us and asked us a new question.

"Now, have you guys eaten yet? How about dinner? I can't promise you anything fancy but it will be good!"

I looked at Ken. I was personally elated and relaxed by the thought that we had a place to stay for the night. Sister Di had been exceptionally friendly and helpful. But now, it was Saturday night and a little relaxing in town sounded like the best idea. We had already munched some hors d'oeuvres before Mass and I for one, wasn't that hungry. Ken smiled and gave me a look that I recognized immediately.

It was called RULE OF THE ROAD #3 or something close to that. "Never say NO to any reasonable offer."

"Thank you very much, Sister" we almost said in unison. That's very thoughtful of you. That same half hour we talked about before?"

"Perfect. We will see you then."

Steve and I meandered over to Sister Di's house at the planned time. There we immediately met Linda, a neat young woman who was studying to be a nun too. I had grown up with 12 years of Catholic school and I never remembered nuns or sisters looking like these two. They were attractive, casually dressed and immediately engaging and personable. You would never point and think, "NUN" if they walked down any street in America.

We had delicious broiled hamburgers and veggies for supper. Dessert was vanilla ice cream topped with some green Crème de Mint Liquor. I chided them both for being nuns pouring liquor on all of our innocent bowls of ice cream. They laughed unabashedly. It tasted great.

For the next three hours we chatted in their living room over hot chocolates. It was one of the most mesmerizing and exhilarating conversations that I could ever remember having. They both asked us incisive, thoughtful questions about our times on the road, our faith, our mental toughness needed to bicycle thousands of miles. They were then great listeners. It was refreshing for me to hear Steve's answers and perspective to many of these questions. It hit me that Steve and I had spent literally hundreds of hours in thought over the months on the road and significantly fewer hours actually talking to each other. I learned a lot about Steve and his thinking these past months thanks to Sisters Di and Linda's insightful questions.

Finally, as Steve and I were preparing to leave with a promise to meet them for a home-cooked breakfast before we hit the road Sunday morning, Sister Dianne, her full first name we discovered, made a final point as we were hugging our goodbyes for the night.

"You both are being impacted by this trip in ways that you simply cannot know until you finish this thing and have the perspective of being off of your bikes for awhile. Believe me when I say that you are changing and growing and only later will you understand what that all means. What I know tonight is that Linda and I were blessed to have you with us and we will see you two adventurers in the morning at 8 AM! Goodnight!"

They were wise beyond their years. Their encouragement and affirming words would never leave us. And to think that once again we had almost missed this entire evening with them.

Our rules of the road had saved us again in spite of our desires and ourselves.

I STARED AT MY PLATE OF EGGS, BACON, BISCUITS, ORANGE juice and hot cocoa. I caught myself starting to drool. Sister Di said a short prayer before we ate the breakfast that she and Sister Linda had prepared for us. Just like last night, I caught myself hearing and listening to what was being said and I realized I still felt that same peace as if I were a little closer to God.

Half done with my cocoa, I was taking a sip when I noticed the head of a frog in the bottom of my cup. With a shock, I jerked my cup away, almost spilling all over myself.

Sister Di and Linda roared with laughter.

"I thought that you would never drink your cocoa. We've been waiting for you to see our little friend in your cup."

It was a little ceramic frog cemented to the bottom of the cup. Now knowing Sister Di and her sense of humor, I am sure that I was not her first victim.

As had happened so many times on this trip, the time had come to say goodbye to some people that, in a very short period of time, we had become very attached to. Sister Di and Linda gave us each a candy bar, a package of M&M's and a little homemade gift to be opened when we hit Mile #6000, which we anticipated would happen later today. "I will be in a group praying for you guys every day at 9 AM," Sister Di cheerfully exclaimed with her hug.

We mounted our trusty steeds, turned back one last time to wave goodbye and then rode off into the sunrise.

THE DRIVER MUST HAVE BEEN DRUNK. APPARENTLY SHE HAD taken a right out of McDonald's and then missed the actual road and ran up a huge rock in her small car. Only two wheels were even touching the ground. She was wedged and could not move her car. She was also drop-dead-gorgeous, about 22-years-old, stunning face, long, thick blonde hair and a beautiful shape. Steve and I leaned our bicycles against a building and joined two other men as her gallant rescuers. We slowly got her car down off the rock as the police arrived on the scene.

Since she appeared to have some 'splainin' to do with the police, we thought to quickly ask the officer if he knew of anyplace we could stay for the night. We had just finished bicycling our 68th mile of the day and exactly our 6,000th mile of the trip as we hit the city limits of Willard, Ohio, population 5,800.

"Well, you guys can go down to the police station, we'll give you a Salvation Army slip and you guys can stay at the YMCA tonight."

Wow! This was great and a first. We bicycled through town to the police station and walked in to the reception desk. As we started to explain our story, the sergeant told us that the police officer from the McDonald's scene had already called it in. We were given two passes to the YMCA, told where to store our bicycles at the station's garage and then directed to the YMCA a block away.

"You're all squared away guys. Enjoy a good night."

This was magical after the many evenings of working the phones, the bar and café crowd, knocking on doors, begging, explaining, reciting Bible verses. This had all effortlessly fallen in our laps.

We walked into the YMCA, handed the person at the desk our slips and he handed us *two* room keys.

I excitedly put my key in the lock, turned the key and opened the door.

There was my own single bed, clean sheets, soap, towels, washcloths, a chair with a reading light and a cozy atmosphere. There was a bathroom with showers and stalls down the hall and TV rooms and pool and ping-pong games downstairs. The cost was ZERO.

Steve and I had a quick supper across the street, played eight games of pool, watched a little TV and then retired to our respective rooms to read, write, and for me, tape these words into my little audio log. It was so very relaxing. As much as I enjoyed nights like last night with soulful and stimulating conversation, I also needed nights like this where I didn't have to be present to anybody and I could just relax. Last night! I reached for my saddlebag that I had carried from my bike with my personal things for the night. I pulled out a homemade card from Sister Di and Sister-in-training Linda that we were supposed to read at mile 6,000. We had forgotten to pull it out in the confusion of hitting that exact mile as we hit the city limits and witnessed an accident before the police were even at the scene.

Realizing that we were at mile 6,002 at the most, I climbed into bed, turned on my little reading light and opened the card.

"CONGRATULATIONS! YOU MADE THE 6,000^TH MILE!

I couldn't believe it. It was a 10-page homemade card, full of humor, inspiration, notes from Diane, Linda and Father Jim and over 20 cut out images from magazines that were glued in and which told a story. They must have been up half the night creating this wonderful little masterpiece! The card ended with three personal notes that read in part:

"Dear Ken and Steve,

I always find it interesting when people come into my life, stay awhile and then move on. I always seem to grow and change because of those encounters. I must say that is true of you two. First of all, we shared Eucharist together. What better place to get to know someone than in the Lord. He is the one who calls us to be brothers & sisters in Him. Then Linda and I were able to share our humble food and our warm home with you. I was so happy to see you so relaxed and at home in our home. You shared a profound part of yourselves with us. Thanks. Just remember, as you move on, you've left a little bit of yourself here, but you've also taken a little bit of us with you. We are all richer because you risked asking for a place to stay.

...Peace my friends, Diane"

"Dear Steve and Ken,

You two truly have been a gift to me. May God continue to gift both of you with safe travels, warm hearts and friendly faces. I know that you will reach your goal and that all will go well. Cherish the good things in your hearts and 'shake the sand' of the lesser experiences 'from your feet.'

...St. Francis had a special greeting that he used and encouraged others to say. It's a simple phrase, but please hear it from my <u>heart</u>: Peace and all good to you!

Love, Linda"

"Hi guys...Sorry I didn't get a chance to share with you, but I'm glad to be able to share my house. Best of luck in your travels. Remember us as we will remember you, especially in prayer. May the Peace of Christ go with you...Father Jim"

I turned off my light and slept blissfully until morning.

CHAPTER 36
MEDIA COVERAGE GROWS PEDALING THROUGH MILE 6,200

"I always turn to the sports section first. The sports section records people's accomplishments; the front page nothing but man's failures." ~ **Earl Warren**

THE NEXT FEW DAYS WERE A MIX OF MEDIA INTERVIEWS, dreary bicycling and finally passing vehicles on the road: Amish horse and buggy carriages.

As the miles kept mounting and we continued bicycling north in November, the press came after us more and more. One day alone we did three separate interviews with photos. With shorter days and hillier terrain in western Ohio and heading towards even hillier West Virginia and Pennsylvania, the press was actually starting to slow us down. We always tried to be cordial and patient and we were committed to generating good publicity for Make-A-Wish, but bicycling even 60 miles a day was getting tougher and tougher without answering questions and posing for pictures.

Further complicating our bicycling was the fact that Steve's other knee was starting to bother him. One day he flat out asked me, "Do you realize how many total days of this trip I have been 100% healthy?"

He was still in pretty good spirits but I again appreciated how much more he was enduring physically than I was over the past 6,200 miles. It was rough enough out here without one's body holding you back.

The Amish people, rustic farms and horse-drawn buggies were breathtaking sights for several days. We learned from some of the families that we spent our evenings with that the Amish were a strict Christian community, very family-oriented and basically good people. They also tried to separate themselves from the world, believing for example, that modern electricity was the devil's work.

One afternoon Steve and I found an empty buggy near the road and stopped to take a photo. A newly-married Amish couple came out of their farmhouse and actually allowed us to sit in the buggy while they took a picture of us. They would not, however, allow us to take a picture of them. They told us that if we did we would be stealing their souls. I have since learned that for many of them to "take a graven image" of them while they pose for the camera is simply against what they believe. They are often okay if it is a candid shot.

We bicycled into a little town of Zelienople, Pennsylvania just as the sun was setting. We had only gutted out 55.8 miles but we were pooped. We pulled up to a Catholic Church and rectory situated right next door. It was Steve's turn.

"We were wondering if you knew of a place where we could stay for the night," I asked the man with the collar.

"Thirty miles south in Pittsburgh!" he said and slammed the door in my face.

I could see where the expression, "He was in an ugly mood," came from. I think that most people actually look ugly when they are in a bad mood and this priest must have had one bad, horrific day.

I decided to blame the priest's rejection of me on Ken.

"Hey buddy? Maybe from now on when I'm trying to find a place for us to stay, you should just stay back in the shadows somewhere. You're starting to look like Charles Manson!"

Ken broke out in one of his huge laughs and before he could catch his breath I persisted.

"I'm sure that poor priest is in there right now calling the police, telling them that there was a really nice young man at his door but directly behind him was this big huge goon with beady red eyes and hair all over his face trying to get in. Because of you, we are going to find a place to stay indoors alright, IN JAIL!"

We both laughed and climbed back on our bikes.

A little further down the road we found another church with all the lights on. Obviously, there was something going on in there. We went inside and informed someone whom we were and what we were doing. There were several women in the front of the church practicing Christmas songs with bells. The man that we were talking to interrupted the beautiful music and relayed our story to the women.

Marietta Reeb was gracious enough to offer her house to us. We ended up spending the night with her and her husband Wayne and their three children, Rob, Heather and Melanie in their huge house. One of the few church services I remembered growing up was the pastor's message about the gifts that each of us possesses and how we should share them with others.

Some of us are blessed with the wonderful gift of being able to create music. Some of us are blessed with the ability to be a good public speaker. Some of us are blessed with the skills to make a lot of money. And thank God, some are blessed with the gift of hospitality. Wayne and Marietta had that gift in abundance.

Although Steve and I had met some unbelievably friendly and remarkable people, Marietta and Wayne had a unique gift. We never engaged in a lot of conversation in our short time with them; however I have never in my life been made to feel so comfortable physically, emotionally and mentally. We discovered that besides their own three beautiful and well-mannered children, they had hosted several foster children over the years. Nothing could have made more sense to me.

They fed us, washed our clothes, made us popcorn, allowed us to take showers, watch television, gave us both our own rooms and in general, in a way that I simply cannot accurately describe, were as down-to-earth and relaxing to be with as anyone I had known. They actually gave us the gift of NOT asking us a lot of questions. We never felt for even a second that we had to do anything that we did not want to do. This was exactly what we needed to renew ourselves.

We awoke Thursday morning to a hot breakfast waiting for us on the table. Steve and I were refreshed and ready to tackle the day. We all hugged goodbye soon afterwards and received kisses from Marietta and her two young daughters.

We got directions to our first stop of the day, the local town post office. Steve was anxiously awaiting his winter clothing. This is the town we had targeted a week ago. I had my fingers crossed as Steve stepped up to the service counter.

"I'm sorry sir, there's no package here under the name of Steve Anderson."

I cringed, as I knew how brutal those words were to Steve's heart. He looked like he wanted to burst with some sort of emotion, but there was no one to blame but ourselves. Apparently once again we had miscalculated and bicycled a little too quickly.

I looked into Steve's forlorn face. Now we needed to decide on another town.

"Sorry buddy. I know that news sucked. My only thought is that they forward your package to Tom and Deb's place in Vermont. We will stop in there for a day at least. I'm thinking we should be there in eight to ten days. If that's too long, let's look at a map and you make the call."

Tom was my brother and Deb his wife. I knew that Steve was beyond discouraged, not to mention cold, especially as he thought about at least another week until he got his good chopper mittens and goose down jacket.

"Let's go with your brother's place. I'm sick of the guessing game."

I CRESTED ANOTHER HILL AND LOOKED AT THE SKY. THE RAIN was not going to stop. It had been raining relentlessly all day and there was no relief in sight. Steep hill after steep hill and soaking wet in my drenched clothes made for a grueling day with miles ever so slowly rolling over on my odometer. Steve and I exchanged the lead several times, grimacing as we took the lead or trying to generate a weak smile to each other as a pick-me-up for the other guy. This was without a doubt the toughest day of bicycling since the day we pushed over 90 miles in the desert with no services and crossed from Utah into Wyoming.

It was brutal bicycling.

The day was made worse by the fact that we were on a narrow, two-lane road with no shoulders and in non-stop traffic. One of our fears of the northeast part of the country was the lack of quiet, relatively untraveled roads that we had so often found out West and in the Midwest. It was the beginning of a threatening and unsettling era.

Our goal for the day was the town of Clarion, 61 miles away. At the 30-mile marker, Steve and I were convinced that we would never make it. At about mile 42 we believed that we would and finally, thanks to both of us working hard and not giving up, we rolled into Clarion in the dark.

Our legs were incredibly tired and sore but our spirits were high with the welcoming sight of city lights. Today was the kind of bicycling that inspired clichés like, "This separated the men from the boys."

Our normal first stop in town was a police station, church rectory, tavern or a café. This night it was a Laundromat. We used their small bathroom to literally peel off our drenched clothing and change into semi-dry clothes from what didn't get soaked in our saddlebags. Steve was better than I with packing all of his clothes into plastic bags *before* putting them in his saddlebags. I paid the price for that omission, as virtually everything that I owned was soaked.

We changed dollars into dimes and then headed to their huge, tumbling dryers.

As our clothes dried, and it was time to figure out a home for the night, I remembered seeing a sign for Clarion University. I made a few phone calls that eventually led me to dorm directors. Within 20 minutes I found a young man in charge that was originally from Minnesota. After hearing our story we immediately had complimentary college dorm rooms for the night. Dry, warm and exhausted, we both slept like rocks.

MY FRONT TIRE EXPLODED. UNLIKE A TYPICAL PUNCTURED inner tube, I knew that as soon as I hit the sharp rock imbedded in the shoulder tar and heard the loud pop that this was different. I quickly braked in the pouring rain.

"What's up?" Steve coasted to a stop alongside of me.

"I think I have more than a flat tire. I heard a good, hard pop when I hit something stuck in the tar back there."

As I examined my front tire closely, I discovered that I was on the money. My rubber tire had a shredded hole that was not repairable. I checked out my odometer and then flashed Steve a big smile.

"Well, I just broke a record, for us anyways. That is exactly 6,242 miles on one TREK tire! Can you believe that! I should do a commercial for these guys."

As weird as it sounded, I loved that tire. You get attached to strange things when you bicycle over 6,000 miles. I was a little sad. This was also my first flat tire of any kind since leaving Kansas City. At least it was a good one. I pulled out my repair kit to fix my inner tube and pulled out a fresh tire that I had backing me up. As uncomfortable as I was doing bike repairs in the pouring rain, the second day in a row of this drenching weather, I remembered what a young man had told me at breakfast earlier back at the college cafeteria.

"They are expecting 6"- 12" of *snow* north of Pittsburgh tonight!"

Steve and I were already north of Pittsburgh. As we headed north and east to Maine, bicycling through lots of snow was probably inevitable. Changing tires in the freezing white slop didn't sound like much fun.

Seventeen miles later my back tire blew a flat. "When it rains, it pours," was at the moment a figurative and literal expression.

At 12:10 PM, now Eastern Standard Time, Steve slid into a phone booth and checked in with Minnesota.

"...It must be about 47 degrees today, Dick, but right now we are outrunning a snowstorm."

"How many miles did you guys do this week?"

"Oh, we probably biked only about 350. We've been into a lot of hills and a lot of rain."

"You're in Marionville, Pennsylvania. Where do you go from there?"

"We're going to head northeast towards New York. We should hit that probably Sunday. Then we will go all the way across New York to Vermont, New Hampshire, then Maine and then back down the east coast."

"Now you better explain to the public when you get to New York why two guys, in the middle of a possible snowstorm are bicycling, because New Yorkers have a strange makeup."

"We've had to do a lot of explaining already!" Steve was laughing on the air.

"Have you really?"

"Oh, yes! People just can't believe it. We get the same story from people. They always say, 'You're going the wrong direction. You're going the wrong direction!'"

"And when you say, 'Make-A-Wish', what do they say?"

"Well, they still think we're a little nuts for doing this."

"You are!"

"Yeah, I think we are! Now tonight they are predicting about six inches of snow, too."

"Seriously, how will you bicycle in six inches of snow?"

"We won't. We will have to wait until the roads are plowed."

"Do you know where you will be staying overnight?"

"Yeah, I think we will be staying in Kane. It's about 30 miles north of here. We're only going to do about 60 miles today."

"Because of the hills or the weather or what?"

"Because of the weather *and* the hills. Pennsylvania is a really hilly state. They say if you would flatten out Pennsylvania it would cover half of the United States. This is the hilliest country that we have been in so far."

"Well as usual, as I say on the behalf of Make-A-Wish and the public and for what the two of you are doing for Make-A-Wish in bicycling, in touching all of the continental 48 states, all we can say is God Bless and I look forward to speaking to you next Friday."

"Okay, Dick."

"Take care and give my regards to Kenny."

"I will do that."

Steve stayed on the line to talk to our good buddy, John Rubel, who always updated us on many levels. I sat under a tree as patiently as I could, waiting for Steve to finish up with John. Part of the reason we seemed to make such poor mileage on Fridays was because of these phone calls and then the extra time that we spent with Make-A-Wish after we talked to Dick.

I was getting more and more anxious and wet under the tree waiting for Steve to finish. Steve finally stepped out of his dry phone booth.

"That took forever. You didn't seem like you were in too much of a hurry in that covered phone booth as the rain kept pouring into my undies!"

Steve laughed hard. He knew I was giving him grief but I could also tell he was really happy. Our Friday calls always picked us up, especially for the guy on the call. But I thought I detected a little extra lift from Steve this afternoon.

"Sorry for taking so much time. But considering the fact that you and I contemplated last night not even talking to John today because it slows us down so, it was a great call. Give me five minutes and then let's keep riding so that we can get warm and dry in about 30 miles."

Steve quickly told me that John had told him about three media exposure possibilities. A major columnist for the Minneapolis Star and Tribune, Jim Klobuchar, wanted to do a telephone interview with us next week for the paper, a brand new network TV show called *Fantasy*, a national magazine show wanted us to call Amy somebody next week and finally *Good Morning America* was interested in our story if we got to New York City.

It was all very exciting news and a great lift in a pouring rain. We were soaked and shivering but still thankful that it was in the 40s and not snowing yet. The snow thing was growing into a huge mystery, a "monkey on our back" that we were growing restless thinking about and wondering if we could bicycle in. But today, we just had to turn our pedals until we moved 30 miles down the road in the rain on a Friday afternoon to Kane, Pennsylvania.

I WAS SITTING IN THE ONLY DRY THING THAT I OWNED AT the moment, the bottom half of my rain gear. I was writing a long-overdue letter to Lori while my clothes and Ken's were tumbling around in the dryer, when Ken came charging in wearing his dripping rain gear and soggy stocking cap.

"I scored! I got us a hotel room, and it's free!"

We had ridden about 50 miles in a cold, soaking rain all day and so by the time that we reached a small Pennsylvania city of about 4,800 people called Kane, we were thoroughly whipped and our spirits were dampened, along with all of our belongings.

But the words "hotel" and "free" immediately cheered me up.

"Way to go buddy! How did you do it?"

"I just walked into this little hotel a few blocks away and started talking to this bartender. His name was Darrel, and it turns out that he owns the place. I told him our story, and he basically said that he would take care of us and that we could stay upstairs above the tavern. It's sort of a bar, restaurant, hotel combo."

"Great job, buddy! I was not up for looking for a place tonight. I was seriously prepared to fall asleep right here on this table until someone kicked me out."

Our Friday night was the totally opposite of our day. We had fun.

By the time that we got our fluffy, warm clothes out of the dryer and reached the Arlington Hotel, our host Darrel Goodman had told all of the patrons in his tavern about our adventure. Most of our Friday nights were pretty uneventful. In fact, we really didn't look forward to them because we knew that our friends back home were celebrating the end of another week of work. We sensed that tonight might be our turn.

Darrel gave us the key to our room and told us to come down after we got settled in and he would have his cook make us supper. Our first order of business was to take a nice, hot shower and finally steam out the chill that our day in the rain had driven right to our bones.

We came downstairs like a couple of clean, warm, happy "noodles." We both could have crashed on our beds and fallen asleep instantly, but we did not want to miss out on what sounded like a great meal.

Darrel's cook whipped us up a couple of giant broiled steaks with mashed potatoes, coleslaw, green beans, warm bread and all served with a couple of beers. It was awesome! Had someone brought out another steak for each of us, I am sure that they would have been eaten.

As we ate, the waitress kept bringing over beers, pointing out the different people that were buying them for us. By the time that we finished our last delicious bites of steak, there were more beers on our table than we possibly could or would want to drink.

We went around thanking the people. They graciously told us that it was their pleasure and thought that what we were doing was really something.

Darrel was some kind of host and was obviously a very gifted man in many ways. It was also apparent that he was a very compassionate person. He was not all that impressed that we pedaled over 6,000 miles to get to his little establishment. He was, however, very impressed that we were riding for the kids of Make-A-Wish of Minnesota. Our cause seemed to touch him deeply.

Then, at about 8 PM, we found out how talented Darrel really was.

He sat Ken and me down at a table in front of the stage in the back of the tavern. What had earlier been the dining room was cleared out and turned into a dance floor. Darrel stepped out of his role as a bartender and into his role as a musician. He strapped on his accordion and was backed up by an older gentleman on rhythm guitar, a kid in his late teens on bass guitar and another young man on drums.

They started wailing on those instruments and played a lot of 50s and 60s music. Darrel would be singing, playing his accordion with one hand and playing a keyboard with another. They were unbelievably good as everybody in the room was either dancing or tapping their feet!

It was a rare and wonderful Friday evening for us, but exhausted from an incredibly challenging day in the rain and hills, Ken and I left the bar early and headed to our beds for a hopeful good night's sleep.

CHAPTER 37
BICYCLING THROUGH OUR FIRST SNOWSTORM!

"No one would ever have crossed the ocean if he could have gotten off the ship in a storm." ~ **Charles F. Kettering**

I RAN AND PEERED OUT THE WINDOW. MY WORST FEARS WERE realized. The temperature had dropped during the night and the pouring rain was transformed to at least four inches of snow lying on the ground and in the road. I was as apprehensive as I was the day that Steve and I woke up at the foot of the Rocky Mountains, unsure of how we would be able to pedal 10,288 feet up and over a mountain for the first time.

This was just as frightening. We had absolutely no idea if we could do it.

What we knew for sure was that today, Saturday, November 13th was going to be our first attempt to bicycle in and through snow.

Unsettled, nervous and candidly a little fearful once again, we both headed across the street from our hotel to a little café for some breakfast before we attempted to bicycle. Darrel walked over to the same café minutes after we arrived and topped off his generosity by buying our breakfast and sitting down with us. Almost everybody who walked into the café stopped by our table and said hello to him, obviously one of the most popular people in town.

We reluctantly hopped on our bikes at just after 9 AM. The snow was still coming down in big, wet flakes. We were not sure if it would even be possible to ride in these conditions.

We headed east on State Highway 66 on our way out of the Allegheny National Forest. It took only a couple of blocks of pedaling for us to realize that we could actually ride in this slop. Then, without even trying, Ken gave me my first good laugh of the day. A car that had just passed by me plowed through a big pile of slush in the middle of the road between the two lanes just as it was passing Ken. He was splashed with this dirty snow from head to toe. It slid off of his legs, which were covered with the bottom half of his rain gear, but it stuck right to his goose down parka, his stocking cap and half of his beard-covered face.

I didn't even get a chance to thoroughly enjoy the soaking of my biking buddy, when...WHOPPP...another car came by and caught me off guard. I'm sure it must have looked like an instant replay of Ken's soaking.

I immediately realized that it wasn't that funny. It was humiliating.

I caught up to Ken who had already stopped to brush the slop off his face and clothes. He looked at me full of wet snow and spoke first.

"Fun, huh?" We both started laughing looking at each other, so fresh, warm and dry only minutes ago and now wearing cold, icy buckets of slush.

"Yeah, it's going to be a great day," I said. "I think this is going to be one of those days again that we'll have to dedicate to the kids."

This was the first time in 116 days of riding that I realized that we made the right decision in opting to buy low-rider front racks. They helped us carry our gear closer to the road, giving us a much more stable ride. The weight that we carried really helped our bikes plow through the snow and the icy ruts the cars left behind. We could not ride very close behind each other either. Neither of us had fenders on our bikes so we kicked out a pretty good rooster tail.

The ice built up in our sprockets and any attempt to change gears would have derailed the chain. We had to get off of our bikes every few miles and chip the ice out of our gears, chains and derailleur with a screwdriver.

It was a whole new experience bicycling in the snowy unplowed roads and shoulders. I bicycled extremely tentative initially, not sure if my skinny high-pressure touring tires would have any traction or if my bike would slip out from underneath me. Steve and I had *never* fallen off of our bicycles on this trip for any reason. I wanted to keep that streak going today. When I went to shift gears as I normally did several times in any given hour, I found out almost immediately that I only had two gears available out of my normal eighteen. There was so much ice clogging up my back six sprockets, that I could not move them. I had two sprockets of the three on the front wheel working and so I only had two gears for the day. Although I missed being able to use my other 16 gears, as long as I was moving forward and down the road I was happy.

I heard the unmistakable sound of an 18-wheeler approaching me from behind. Pedaling on our still narrow and curvy two-lane road, I got completely off of the highway, onto the shoulder and braked to a complete stop until he passed.

There was no room for error today.

Visibility was poor because of the snow pelting down on us, piling a good fresh inch on the roads. We wore sunglasses to keep the snow out of our eyes so that we could keep a close eye on the very dangerous traffic.

As the day wore on the snow slowed down, and with each mile we bicycled, our confidence picked up. With that confidence came a feeling of immense satisfaction and joy as we charged forward through the elements. We finally stopped about four miles from the New York State border at a small gas station.

The sky was clearing and the sun was trying to shine.

"Hey man, I think we're through it for the day! That was actually sort of fun!" I was grinning at Steve and he was smiling right back.

"Easier than I thought it would be that's for sure. Betty and Acabar were really impressive today."

Steve and I certainly knew that colder and snowier days lay ahead of us, but at that moment, we felt strong, confident and secure knowing that we had once again successfully tackled a part of the trip that we were not sure we could do. It was a major, major accomplishment.

"Excuse me guys, but what in the heck are you up to?"

The older man had walked over from gassing up his car and looked incredulously at our loaded bikes. We were used to this attention but you could quickly tell by his intuitive questions that he must have been a bicyclist, adventurer or both.

"I own the bicycle shop in town."

"Hey, then you are the perfect guy to ask." I had a question that had been nagging me for almost a week.

"When are we going to hit the mountains in New York or better yet, where and when will we start to run into them?"

"Son, you are *in* the mountains!"

"Huh?"

"Look out there. Those are mountains!"

All he was pointing to were the same size hills we had been climbing in Ohio, Pennsylvania and now soon-to-be New York.

"You have got to be kidding me! That's just a hill!" I told him.

"No sir. Those are mountains. That's as bad as it will ever be."

Steve and I looked at each other with a tremendous sense of relief. This was unbelievably good news. We had been psyching ourselves up for "mountains" and "mountain passes" that we would again climb to the heavens like the Rockies out West with elevation signs of thousands of feet. We even envisioned getting stuck in snow-covered passes, but these were only big hills!

Ken said in his wild and crazy Steve Martin impression, "Wow, this is gonna be a piece of cake! I could climb that with two flat tires and both feet tied behind my back."

After successfully negotiating the snow and slush, and learning that very same day that the mountains people had warned us about were only big molehills that barely caused us to sweat, we were euphoric!

We ended our day a monumental 40 treacherous miles down the road in the town of Portville, New York, our 25th state. That was a significant border for us to celebrate as it officially put us over the halfway mark in our quest for 48 borders.

I started looking for a home at the first gas station. I heard about a young Catholic priest from someone and scribbled down the address when another young woman suggested her Methodist minister, Dr. Doug Wilson.

"He's a great guy and he's a marathoner."

Steve and I looked at each other and knew immediately where we were heading.

After Dr. Doug answered his door and heard our story, we happily discovered that our instincts were correct. He offered us his church and then bought us supper at a pizza and sub place across the street. He also invited us to his 11 AM service the next day. Although a service that late in the morning was a long shot for us, as we needed to be moving down the road by then, he told us that he would split half the collection basket with us to send to the children of Make-A-Wish back in Minnesota whether we attended the service or not.

This was a first. We were blown away by his generosity and his thoughtfulness.

Later that night, settling comfortably into my sleeping bag, I felt a tremendous sense of peace. More than well-earned exhaustion, we had experienced a day of achievement and overcoming the fear of the unknown once again. I wished that more people in their lives would risk and do whatever it was that they were afraid of and find out like we did that it wasn't that tough after all. Asking for a date, a job promotion, running a 5K or whatever it was that someone might be unsure of doing, we were finding out again and again that as Ralph Waldo Emerson said, "Do the thing and you will have the power."

We really enjoyed our day in the snow and the people staring at us throughout the day as if we were nuts. That was setting us apart from everybody else and we were taking great pride in that fact.

A day that started out focusing on the kids of Make-A-Wish in order to calm our fears and deflect our struggle, was now ending peacefully with a sense of pure sweet satisfaction. I had never known this calm.

CHAPTER 38
VERMONT W/FAMILY & A SLICE OF LIFE IN NEW HAMPSHIRE

"There is no other love like the love for a brother. There is no other love like the love from a brother." ~ **Astrid Alauda**

"WOULD YOU BE EMBARRASSED OR BOTHERED IF I SOMEDAY wrote a book about our adventure out here and talked about your battle with colitis?"

Steve and I were sipping on a couple of cold ones after another long day on the road. We had already secured a church for the night and it was great to be warm, relaxed and full of a great supper. My question to Steve caught him off guard. I said nothing as he slowly gathered his thoughts.

"No, I guess not. To be honest I was sad the other night when I overheard you making a tape for your friends back in Minnesota and you mentioned that my colitis took some fun out of the trip. So, as I think it through, I'm not embarrassed or ashamed that people know about it, I'm just embarrassed that it happened and that it detracted from our trip in any way."

I knew that it was still a tough subject so I dropped it quickly. Steve however once again repeated his assertion that we had gone through it together and he would not ever accept my belief that he had it tougher than I did. I let it go as our waitress checked back in with us.

"Yes, we'll take two more."

"Can you believe this, 90 cents for a round of two beers? I'm getting change back from a dollar bill! Even though our total budget is ten bucks a day we could get in trouble and have way too much fun here!"

I laughed at the thought. At this time of the day after battling the wind, the cold and 70 miles or so of bicycling, you could normally just pour Steve and me into a chair or bed without any food or drink. It was great to just relax and share our thoughts after bicycling for hours lost in our own private thoughts. It was a time of very special camaraderie.

"You know this is in our blood."

"What do you mean?" I asked Steve.

"Everything about the road; the recognition, the cause, the feeling of achievement, the physical challenge, the 'alive' feeling that we've talked about, the incredible people, the whole lifestyle of this thing. I thought that by being out here I would get it out of my system but now my desire is actually getting bigger and hungrier. I already know that there's going to have to be adventures for both of us down the line. I'm even starting to worry about the withdrawals when we get back!"

"Well, this is sure fun hearing from you. You're right, though. It may not necessarily be with each other, although it would be fun to pull off something with you of a smaller nature down the line, but you and Lori, or me and my buddy Foge in Alaska; it's exciting to think about."

"Let's toast to our adventuresome spirit. May it never diminish and only grow stronger!"

WE KEPT ANGLING TOWARDS BENNINGTON, VERMONT. THERE, my brother Tom was planning on picking us up to bring Steve and me to his home in Burlington, a city roughly 125 miles further north. The weather and traffic varied wildly with sleet, rain, snow, and sunshine in mild temperatures with congested traffic as we negotiated around larger cities like Binghamton and Schenectady in New York. We slept in our record-setting 24th indoor accommodations in a row last night and today my bicycle pedal ripped off my bike and onto the road for excitement.

One evening I called Amy Carr, the producer of the brand-new ABC show called, *Fantasy*. Their very first show aired in September, after we were on the road, on their tagline was "The show where dreams come true." It seemed like a good fit for us, and the people behind the scenes at Make-A-Wish in Minnesota were trying to make an appearance on their show a "reality."

Amy was delightful, vivacious on the phone and very excited about our trip and our travel plans. She wanted to find an NBC affiliate out east to film us on our route and then the plan was to fly Steve and me to California for the on air segment with co-hosts Peter Marshall and Leslie Uggams.

"I suppose that you and Steve wouldn't necessarily want to come out here and leave your bicycles behind on the road but could we work something out with you guys?"

A national network executive was asking *us* for permission, aware of the inconvenience of their request and acting as if it would be a favor for Steve and me to fly to Burbank, California all-expenses paid to get some national exposure! It was a humbling experience that really wasn't sinking in.

Amy concluded the call with a great sense of optimism that we could pull this together and a promise that we would all keep in touch. I excitedly told Steve,

"We may get to that infamous California coast yet! Let me tell you a story."

"HEY TOMMY! MAN IS IT GREAT TO SEE YOU!

My brother Tom had suggested that we all meet at a particular monument just outside of Bennington, Vermont. I remembered the challenge of trying to hook up and spot each other on the road with my sister Mary and her husband Mark in Kansas and with my dad in Illinois. There was a reason why we always thought that Tom was the smartest one in the family. The Bennington Battle Monument, at slightly over 306 feet tall, was the highest structure in the entire state of Vermont! There is no way that any of us could have missed each other nor have been confused as to exactly where to meet.

"My gosh! You have everybody with you!"

"Deb's doing her thing, her craft show today. I just came from the baby sitter's."

As Steve and Tom formally introduced themselves, I was busy opening car doors and kissing my six-year-old Godchild Jaime, two-year-old Sarah and little one-year-old Becky. What a fun reunion for me.

"I hope that you have room for us and our gear."

"I have a roof top rack for your bikes. I've never used it before so we'll see what happens."

Tom peered curiously at our bikes, then our equipment and finally took in our bicycling "attire."

"Sooo, this is the professional equipment and look of long distance touring bicyclists?"

"Whadda you mean?" Steve asked, as he and Tom were now laughing heartily and already playing off each other.

"Tom, we don't like the biking look, okay? We actually *fight* the biking look."

"Well, Steve, you certainly have fought it well!"

The next couple of days were a great break from bicycling. Once again, Steve was easily and effortlessly embraced as one of the family. We enjoyed more chocolate éclairs, a phenomenal early Turkey dinner, long winding conversations and the rich and warm opportunity to live in a "home" with a loving mom, dad and three precious little girls. We also squeezed in a church service, proudly saw Deb marketing her beautiful homemade Christmas dough ornaments at a craft show and both Steve and I efficiently handled several media situations.

The Burlington Free Press came out to Tom and Deb's house and did a nice newspaper article on us and shot some photos. Steve called Amy Carr with the show *Fantasy* and discovered things were not as optimistic as they were only a few days ago. Steve also talked to Robin, the executive producer of *Good Morning America* and that live interview option near New York City looked more promising than before. Steve and I hoped that the national media possibilities, constantly in flux, were not simply feeding our egos. We decided that if they happened, great. If not, that was okay too. We were focused on KSTP and Minnesota media as all the money for wishes was going directly to Minnesota children. National exposure was a secondary priority that brought positive attention to the need and hopefully inspired other chapters to be created. Bottom line, national media exposure results were all out of our hands.

Finally, I got a nice relaxed chance to talk to Dick Pomerantz back in Minnesota. Not having to race for a phone after bicycling for hours and fighting the clock, I made a conscious effort to slow my words down on the air and really reflect on my answers to his questions.

"Kenny?"

"Hey, Dick. Good morning."

"Where are you?"

"State #26. Last night we rolled into Bennington, Vermont."

"That's beautiful countryside."

"It truly is! I mean this is supposedly the time of year where it's not the prettiest because there's no leaves left on the trees and the snow's not in yet but it is so gorgeous; the rolling hills, temperature was in the 50s today, it's just a beautiful, beautiful part of the country. You are correct."

"There was a rather lengthy article about you and Steve last night."

"We just found out about that, the Jim Klobuchar thing in the paper."

"The implication of the article was, from a positive point of view, that the two of you are sort of enjoying America. I am wondering whether that was the columnist sort of reading into it, because he put a lot of his own self into it, or is that what's happening? Are you kind of enjoying it?"

"Dick, I guess maybe that doesn't come out often enough because we've been convinced since the first week out on this trip that if this is the way things truly are and if this is the way people are, there's so much hope for this world. It seemingly is a fact that the press publicizes a lot of the bad things that go on in this world but Steve and I continually, I don't care what part of the country or what state we are in, meet just wonderful, wonderful people. Obviously people are receptive to the cause, but even before they know who we are and what we're doing, they're curious, helpful, loving and kind. It's been a really 'up' trip in that respect."

"Are you getting any more feedback about Make-A-Wish? Are people still asking you why two weirdoes are bicycling north?"

"Yeah, it happens more and more. In earlier states people waved at us and gave us the thumbs up. This past week in New York people seemed to just stare at us. In fact, the day after Steve talked to you last week we did hit about four inches of wet snow the next morning, and so we continue to look a little more nuts out there to begin with in our galoshes and tracking through the snow. But the publicity and the reporters are increasing more and more as we continue to head north and add more miles. We are now at mile #6,670 and the Make-A-Wish thing keeps coming up. So we are telling the story more often now. It's heart rending for us to be able to talk about it. People are more interested all of the time. I don't know if necessarily people are going so far as starting their own chapters yet in their parts of the country but we are leaving newspaper articles in a lot of the towns and states we're going through so hopefully some positive things are happening in parts outside of Minneapolis."

"When you say that reporters keep asking the two of you, how do they hear about you?"

"When we first started on this trip we literally went and called on reporters ourselves. Now an assortment of things happen. Over the past months, for example, we would have a lunch at a café, then the owner or waitress hears our story and then has called the town up ahead without our knowledge after we leave the restaurant, and then when we would hit the town, there's a reporter. Or people just see us on our bicycles or see us in town walking two loaded bikes and they introduce themselves as reporters and ask for a story and some pictures. So I guess it's because, again we are hitting towns anywhere between 200 and 10,000 populations and people are seeing us and telling someone else down the line and we are being met literally on the road these days."

"Hmmm. Tell me the map for the next week and where you think you'll end up."

The interview was always winding down with this type of question, a question that I was always ill-prepared to answer. Steve and I lived day-to-day, and to project a destination seven days away, especially as we approached the east coast with all of our variables increasing even more with travel routes, weather and shorter days, was an exercise in futility. I usually made something up. Today I got caught.

"Rhode Island?"

Dick knew this part of this country better than I did. His response surprised me in a funny way.

"Rhode Island?"

I immediately changed my answer. Unfortunately I had the same level of confidence.

"Connecticut?"

"Connecticut."

At least it wasn't a question. We had a few laughs together as he realized that it was now a complete guessing game and we soon wrapped up the call.

MONDAY MORNING AND ANOTHER GOODBYE CAME ALL TOO soon. We left in the dark, as Tom had to drive six hours roundtrip to return us to our bicycle tracks and needed to be on time for a critical IBM meeting back in Burlington.

I kissed my precious little Godchild Jaime goodbye. Although she was only half awake, it was as usual tough for both of us to say goodbye. Jaime was the first grandchild, my second Godchild and for me, still single at almost 30, as close as I could feel to having my own little girl. We shared a very special bond.

As we drove back to Bennington, Steve drifted to sleep and Tom and I got some rare one on one brother time. It was a priceless three-hour car ride.

"YOU ARE THE BEST FIRST-TIME CONTRA DANCER THAT I HAVE ever met in my life!" I glowed, thanks to her comment. As I twirled my pretty 26-year-old brunette dance partner around on the sanded wooden floor of Keene, New Hampshire's 1786 Town Hall, I was mesmerized and transported back in time to another era.

What a difference once again, a single day makes.

Having slept a mere 3½ hours after late night conversations with my brother Tom and our early morning start, it had been an especially tough day climbing hills in the cold. Steve and I had decided to stop at the little town of Spofford, New Hampshire, but it was so little that Steve, in the lead at the time, missed it completely. We were at mile 58, dark starting to surround us, when a car pulled over to the side of the road ahead of us and a young man jumped out.

"Hey guys, I'm a bicyclist but I didn't know that people still bicycle this time of year! What in the heck are you guys up to?"

After hearing our story and realizing that we had no home yet, he introduced himself as Norm and offered to take us to his place in the country. We knew that he was a good guy as he had a double bicycle rack on top of his car! Norm was house sitting for a millionaire couple who had a huge cabin in the woods including horses, a stable and was surrounded by 200 acres that they owned.

The huge, rustic cabin was stunning.

Norm invited a buddy, Ben, over and we ate chips and burritos by the old potbelly wood stove, drank a little home-made wine and heard stories about this evening's "contra dancing" event at the old town hall. Live music, lots of active, friendly folks who loved to dance and we were invited. Steve declined and stayed behind to wash dishes, write letters and to work out. I was exhausted and going on no sleep for almost two days. But this sounded like something a tourist could never find on his own without being connected. Always up for new experiences and adventure, off I rode into the night with Ben and Norm.

The fiddler, the flutist, piano player and the rest of the six-piece-band played away as the caller kept barking out the dance instructions.

"Swing your partner round and round. Star left and let her go!"

I had never met so many friendly, outgoing, active and helpful people in one place in my life! I was having a riot. Unlike square dancing, which I knew just a little about because my mom and dad were participants, this contra dancing was simpler, didn't require a partner and I got to dance with every woman in the room! They were all very encouraging to a newbie like me. It was a family atmosphere with youngsters dancing, no booze and no sexual overtones. Everybody was there because they loved to dance, loved the music and loved people and life. I had a complete blast.

Norm and I said good night around the little wood stove after our late night snack of homemade pumpkin pie and discussions about making maple syrup. As my head finally hit the pillow, I knew that my first day ever in New Hampshire had given me a true and honest flavor for this incredibly beautiful state.

CHAPTER 39
THE THIRD CORNER OF THE COUNTRY & FINALLY THE OCEAN

"A smooth sea never made a skilled mariner." ~ **English proverb**

"I'LL HAVE THE $4.95 CATCH-OF-THE-DAY-SPECIAL WITH A BIG bowl of clam chowder."

The waitress turned to me and asked what I wanted. Nothing on the menu sounded better than what Ken ordered and besides, since we were in Maine, it would have been a crime to ask for anything but fresh seafood.

"I'll have the same."

The catch of the day was "scrod." It sure tasted better than it sounded. The clam chowder was the best that I had ever had. After I finished every single bite, I said to Ken, "That's the best piece of fish I have ever eaten and certainly the best lunch I can remember having since we left."

Ken was in one of his feisty moods where he purposely takes great joy in playfully disagreeing with me.

"Oh, I don't know about that. I can still remember the peanut butter sandwiches and warm water that we had for lunch back in South Dakota. And then there was that cold can of SpaghettiOs with the squished brown bananas; my mouth is watering just remembering that delicacy, back in the Kansas heat and..."

"Ken, did I ever tell you that you give new meaning to the phrase 'incredibly obnoxious?'"

He laughed loudly and then asked in his feigned innocent voice, "What do you mean buddy?"

"You know what I mean. Now, promise me that you won't talk to me again until we get back to Minnesota!"

Our good-natured mood was typical of our entire day. Our 28th state, Maine, had been a major goal and our focus ever since we headed east from California months ago. We had been anxious and excited to reach Maine because we knew that this was our third corner of the United States and as far northeast as we would have to ride. We would now be heading due south to Florida, our final corner of the country.

With the change of direction we would soon be running away from the snow instead of towards it. We would hopefully stop hearing the everyday berating cry of "You guys are heading the wrong way!" that we had been hearing for over a month. Looking at a map we observed that we would tally up another ten states by the time we reached Florida. Checking the north/south mileage of states like Rhode Island, Connecticut, Delaware and Massachusetts we also determined that we could probably pass through states in a single day, compared to a week or more out west in the larger more desolate states. That would be a great psychological boost and would allow us to feel like we were making great progress while "charging" south at ten miles per hour.

We celebrated our achievement and new direction with our unbelievably delicious fresh seafood lunch.

We only bicycled into Maine as far as the first highly-recommended seafood restaurant that we could find. We left Warren's Lobster House not filled but happily satisfied. These days it took an incredible amount of food to fill us up. The constant cold weather added to the physical exertion of bicycling all day and ripped calories from our bodies. We ate as much and as often as we were able and could never get enough. I even had food stashed in all the pockets of my jacket.

We still drank lots of water. The possibility of becoming dehydrated was actually greater in the cold weather because although we didn't get as thirsty, our bodies were still losing water. We would try to consciously be aware of this fact and take in water whether we felt thirsty or not. We also had to carry water on the inside of our clothes or the water turned into a solid chunk of ice. This was quite a switch from the days back in Kansas when our water got too hot to drink!

We bicycled back into Portsmouth, New Hampshire and then east and southward towards the ocean on Highway 1A. I could feel those old familiar stirrings of excitement, as we got closer. The wet, salty smell became a little stronger and as we approached Odiorne Point I could hear the surf pounding on the rocks.

I dropped Betty, probably a little harder than I should have, and ran over the rocks toward the water. Looking out over the vastness of the Atlantic Ocean, I kept repeating the word "awesome" over and over in my head. Ken picked up Acabar and carried her over the rocks and headed for the water. He wanted a picture of him sitting on his bike in the water, proving that we had bicycled as far east as we could possible go. The waves lapped at his feet, occasionally going over the tops of his boots and then splashing up on his panniers, I'm sure soaking most of what was inside. I had to laugh at him as I took the pictures. My big buddy really was a crazy man, but I wouldn't want him to be any other way.

We sat on a rock overlooking the ocean, trying to decide what was more beautiful, the ocean, the Rocky Mountains or a good-looking woman. The good-looking woman won, hands down. The ocean was a distant second followed closely by the Rockies.

The waves relentlessly bashed against the rocks. Every so often an extra large wave would crash and the rocks would pulverize it into a fine spray that hit me softly in the face. I thought of a fellow Minnesota adventurer named Gerry Spiess. In June of 1979 he set out alone across this same North Atlantic Ocean in a ten-foot sailboat named, Yankee Girl. Despite many harrowing experiences he reached England 54 days and nearly 3,800 miles later. I admitted to myself that it took a certain amount of courage to do what Ken and I were doing, but I could never imagine myself brave enough to venture out alone in such a small boat across this huge, treacherous body of water.

Once again I was feeling guilty about depriving us of the chance to bike all the way to the Pacific Ocean. I was just hoping that Ken wasn't thinking about it right now.

We could have sat there a good while longer but there was only a little more than two hours of daylight left and we had to start looking for a place to stay tonight.

We headed south towards Hampton Beach. Along the way we saw some guys who were crazier than we were. We were dressed to the max with our goose down jackets, boots, hats and mittens and they were out in that frigid water surfing.

New Hampshire has only 18 total miles of coastline, but the whole stretch of Highway 1A where the state meets the ocean was a ghost town. Virtually every house was boarded up. From the size of some of the houses and mansions that we saw, this had to be one expensive piece of real estate and an even more fun place to be in the summer. One of the most unbelievable sights that we saw on this stretch of road was a McDonald,s that was closed. A big sign in front said "See You Next Summer." That was a first. Somebody that day told us that this particular franchise did more business during the three months of summer than in any other McDonald's in the world!

As so often happened to us on this trip, we slid down the coast and we got caught riding well past sundown. We stopped for a rest in the resort town of Hampton Beach. Sitting next to our bikes we contemplated camping on the beach and hung out for several minutes.

"What a day! I'll tell you one thing. As much as I love Minnesota, this may be the most beautiful state I've ever seen. Reminds me of northern Minnesota with all of the pine trees, curvy roads, old farms, lakes *and* they have mountains, sort of, and the dang ocean! What a great package." I never thought that I would say those words out loud or even to myself. Steve nodded his head in agreement with me.

"It's got a lot of things going for it, that's for sure. It's sort of like Oregon with the mountains, high desert, the ocean and whatever else. Boy that seems like a long time ago!"

"I think it was!"

"Did I tell you that I found out as we left Warren's back in Maine that a 'scrod' is not really a fish at all?"

"No you didn't. It sure tasted better than something called a 'scrod'. What in the heck is it?" Steve asked me.

"Well, according to a guy that I chatted with in the parking lot, a scrod is simply a small white fish or haddock fewer than three pounds. I didn't have an encyclopedia on my bike to check his answer out, but makes more sense than going out 'scrod fishing.'"

"Well, aren't you quickly becoming a New Englander! Anything else 'Mr. East Coast Rogers' would like to share and enlighten me?"

I laughed. I think I was more tired than Steve was funny but it had been a wonderful day so far and we were both in great moods.

"As a matter of fact, I thought the proverbial 'New Englander' was supposed to be grumpy or at least indifferent. So far, everybody's been great to us. Once again we are smashing the stereotypes. More people ought to get on bikes and pedal 7,000 miles and figure this stuff out for themselves."

I laughed at my own little joke as a policeman in a squad car slowly drove by for the third time since we had sat down. He threw a light on us. Thinking we were vagrants, he started asking us some terse questions. We answered them and told him our story. He finally suggested a motel a couple of blocks away with very reasonable off-season rates and then graciously offered to drive us five miles from that motel to "the best seafood place in the state!"

My eyes lit up.

We heeded his suggestion and splurged on a room with our own money for the first time since we had left Kansas City. We had no money for a nice meal but Ken shared a big surprise with me. He had been saving for weeks to buy us a lobster dinner. I was really psyched with this unexpected gift. We then cleaned up, took police officer Russ up on his offer and called "our cabbie" to drive us to the restaurant. I don't know if he could have gotten in trouble for driving us to a restaurant and back while on duty, but he sure was a friendly and hospitable man that we greatly appreciated.

"I'm sorry sir, but we don't have any lobster today. We only had three yesterday and none came in today."

Ken was devastated with the news!

I told him that I was not disappointed. It was just nice of him to buy me a dinner and I appreciated it a lot. He still protested.

"Yeah, but it makes me mad! I've been planning on buying you a lobster dinner when we got to the Atlantic practically since we left California. I slowly stuffed $40 away just for this shot tonight. You'd think a seafood restaurant practically on the ocean would have lobsters coming out their ears."

I laughed because his voice was getting louder with every word.

"Yeah," I said, "You would think that there would be lobsters crawling all over the floors and walls!"

Ken started to loosen up and almost smiled.

"You're right. You would think that even the waitresses would be lobsters!"

"It's like Mr. Steak not having steaks!"

"It's like Taco Bell not having tacos!"

We were laughing pretty well playing off our goofy analogies.

"It's like Burger King not having burgers!"

We didn't stop till Ken finally said,

"It's like Domino's Pizza not having dominos!"

Despite the lack of lobster, we each had mixed seafood platters of crab, shrimp and fresh fish, a couple of Heinekens, a plate of hors d'oeuvres and a dessert.

As Officer Russ chauffeured us back to our motel, I thought about what a fitting end it was to a phenomenal day.

CHAPTER 40
THANKSGIVING RAGU, BEANS AND A CRACKED BIKE FRAME

"Good people will be remembered as a blessing." ~ **Proverbs 10:7**

I REMEMBERED AN OLD 1960S BLACK AND WHITE SCIENCE fiction movie starring Vincent Price titled, **The Last Man on Earth.** Because of some catastrophic event, he was the only human being left on the face of the planet. It felt eerily the very same to both Steve and to me.

I had thought that the day before, the deserted ghost towns of the off-season New Hampshire coastal community were strangely ominous and mysterious. This morning, with almost nothing open including service stations, restaurants and grocery stores on the quiet roads that we needed to travel, we were even more alone and depressed.

It was Thanksgiving Day.

We bicycled south during the early afternoon hours, noticing that what few service businesses had been opened were now shutting down. Even accessing drinking water was becoming a concern. I grew sadder as the day wore on. I knew that everyone was heading home to be with family, to enjoy the feast that accompanied this traditional day and to watch the Dallas Cowboys beat up on the lowly Detroit Lions. Memories of past Turkey Day celebrations flooded my mind: remembering my brother Tom and me challenging dad and Uncle Bob in cribbage, the football games, the scrumptious food that my mom prepared over the years, Auntie Kay's famous banana cream pies, the hugs, family and kids everywhere, the catching up with relatives…a sharp piece of glistening glass on the shoulder brought me back to my harsh reality. I swerved sharply back into the road to avoid a blowout. Thankfully, there was almost no traffic to worry about.

The best thing that had happened is that we grabbed our 30th state. In fact, the motel we stayed in the night before was exactly 2.2 miles from the border of Massachusetts and so we were within three miles of crossing three state borders in one day; Maine, New Hampshire and now Massachusetts. That certainly would have been a new record.

The day provided us with a little sunshine, which certainly felt good, but it was also very hilly. We grew weary over the miles because there was nothing open to stop and get food or to sit down and get a sandwich. We finally spotted a small grocery store that advertised it was open until 3 PM. As Steve and I bought some bread and sandwich meat, I struck up a conversation with a young man exiting the store and admiring our bikes.

"That's quite a story. Hey, not to throw a kink in your travel plans but if you guys want to come over to our house and have Thanksgiving with us, we're just around the corner. My son is in California so we have room. Don't have much and it's not too fancy but we would be more than happy to share what we have."

Steve and I beamed. His generous offer made our day. He had known us for a full ten minutes and he was prepared to share whatever he had with both of us. We graciously turned him down as we felt compelled today to move on and experience this special day in a very unique way, but he sure warmed our hearts and uplifted our spirits.

We kept working the hills. We periodically stopped to make a cold sandwich and eat next to our bikes. It wasn't the same experience that we had become accustomed to, warming up with a cup of hot chocolate and a warm meal in a little café or service station. We realized for the very first time how our little 30-minute breaks inside the past several weeks, renewed us mentally and physically for getting back on our bikes and tackling the weather and more miles.

It continued to be a day that we simply had to gut out.

We bicycled exactly 50 miles to the little town of Bedford, Massachusetts by nightfall and Steve, thankfully, just flat out took charge.

Ken and I were both drained and pretty darn tired when we rolled into the little town of Bedford. Within minutes of entering the city, we saw a church with someone closing a door to a small house right next door. I quickly approached her, found out that she was indeed the minister and I ended up doing a very, very rare "hard sell" on Pastor Jamie. I felt so vulnerable on Thanksgiving Day and I did not want to work the town for a place to stay. Although this was something she obviously was not used to doing, she gave us permission to stay in her church basement. I was elated.

We thought that not only would we not have turkey dinner tonight, we eventually believed that we would not have anything to eat tonight! We could not find even one store that was open in town.

Pastor Jamie really brightened our dismal day when she stopped by the church basement with some freshly baked bread that was still steaming. The aroma filled the room! She also brought us some Ragu spaghetti sauce and some dry noodles, a can of tomato soup and a can of baked beans.

"In case you guys can't find anything tonight, at least you have this. Just keep the place locked up. I have a dinner engagement and I just want you to know that I am really sorry that I can't make you guys some supper or at least offer you some meat on Thanksgiving for your spaghetti sauce!"

We assured her that just trusting us enough to let us stay here and bringing over the food that she did was more than we expected and we really meant it!

We then spent a quiet night eating our Thanksgiving meal consisting of spaghetti and bread, cleaning our very dirty bikes and writing letters.

It was a very different Thanksgiving. It was good for both of us to be away from family and friends, be a little lonely around the edges and experience a unique kind of holiday. Life on the road had been teaching us to be more empathetic and compassionate to so many different needs, causes and situations in life. Hopefully we would both be even more sensitive to people who were homeless and tired and lonely, needing whatever it is that they need. The Lord says, "Whatever you do to the least of my brethren, that you do unto Me." We thankfully had been helped many times throughout this trip. On this particular Thanksgiving Day, more than ever I knew that I had so much to be thankful for.

Before I fell asleep I thanked God for my wonderful family, a safe day of biking, a warm place to sleep, my spaghetti dinner and warm bread, for Jamie trusting us and for my very special friend sleeping in the next room.

"THERE'S A SCHWINN DEALER. LET'S STOP IN SO THAT I CAN find out why my dang axle is bent again."

This was beginning to get really old. Last night while cleaning my bike in the church basement, I noticed that my axle was bent, again. I was really ticked off and it made absolutely no sense to me why this was continuing to happen.

"Yeah, she's bent all right. You said that you've had problems with this before so I checked a little further and the problem is that your bicycle frame is bent. See this right here? That's why you're continuing to have problems."

I was relieved but confused. Then I heard words that shocked me.

"No, wait just a minute. My God! *Your whole damn frame is cracked!* Look at this at this little dropout. She's cracked right through! I can't believe that you haven't lost the back half of your bicycle on the road somewhere! Let me call TREK. This should never happen and I'm guessing that this frame has a lifetime guarantee."

I was stunned. Initially I felt blessed that any bicycle shop would even be open on the day after Thanksgiving to help me straighten out my axle. Now I was imagining my bike breaking apart going down some steep hill in the middle of nowhere! I knew that a lot of people were praying for Steve and me around the country and those prayers were obviously working.

"Yep, TREK said that's their problem and this never should have happened even if you weighed 300 pounds. They can ship you a new frame free of charge but they need to know where. It will take about a week."

This was one hell of a way to start a day. My emotions were all over the board. Steve and I had planned to stop in Gainesville, Florida where my last family member, my brother Paul lived, for a Christmas break. That was a long way away, and after all of our missed mail stops, made the most sense. The bigger challenge was how would I bicycle one more mile?

Ninety minutes later I left the bicycle shop with a straightened-out axle and a welded brass overlay on my frame to temporarily insure, sort of, that I could keep going. TREK was shipping my new bicycle frame free of charge to my brother's house in Florida. How many bicycle shops in the world have the capacity to torch and weld a piece of metal onto a bicycle frame? Total cost to me for our little unscheduled stop? Fifteen bucks.

As we bicycled south, I remained confused by a lot of complex emotions, but predominately I was incredibly grateful by our good fortune.

Thanksgiving Day had been extended one more day.

CHAPTER 41
HITTING "THE WALL" AT MILE 7,000

"The next mile is the only one that a person really has to make."
~Danish proverb

HAD I BEEN BACK HOME IN MINNESOTA, I NEVER WOULD HAVE left the house. I was tired, grumpy, weary, sick of bicycling, unsocial, homesick, sad and missing security and the people I loved. I was even uncharacteristically short with the press. I wasn't in the mood for much of anything. I kept thinking that if I was at home I could crawl back under the covers of my bed, take the phone off the hook, turn on the TV or read a book and simply tune the world out for a day and recharge my batteries. On the road, I had only one choice. I had to bicycle through it. This was not the only day that I felt this way lately. Thankfully Steve and I were experiencing the same phenomenon at the same time and it only served to bond us even more.

We had now been on the road for over four months and 7,000 miles.

I'd never been a marathon runner and I never planned to be one. However while bicycling down the East Coast, I finally shared something in common with them. As a marathon runner hits the "wall" at about 20 miles, we hit our wall at 7,000 miles.

I'm not sure how hard that 20-mile wall is to run or break through, but our 7,000-mile-wall was incredibly tough. Our wall was more of a state of mind than it was physical exhaustion; in fact we were in such

great condition, I'm sure that we could have ridden 24 hours a day if we had lights and a good reason to do it. Despite the mission behind our riding, we were having a terrible time finding the motivation to do just that. Our depressed state of mind was brought on by several factors. The weather was near the top of my list. We were getting rained on almost every day. Our daily regimen was to eat breakfast, ride, get wet, find a Laundromat, dry out, ride, get wet and so on and so on. We were also experiencing a new surge of unexplained flat tires. When we first started getting flats out west, thorns almost always caused them. Now up to 25 flats and counting, we had no idea what was causing them. Finally, our dark mood was being caused by relentless, unavoidable and God-awful heavy traffic.

We were skirting all of the major metropolitan areas of the east coast. We had ridden by and around Boston, Providence and Hartford. Dead ahead were New York City and Newark and then Philadelphia and Washington, D.C. We were giving all of these major cities a wide berth but not wide enough to avoid all of the commuter traffic.

I thought to myself, "If there's a chance of getting killed on this trip, it will probably happen out here." I was growing very anxious and irritated. I even admitted to Ken that I had discovered that I could be a nervous person in this traffic. I could feel my gut tighten.

It seemed like all the roads had narrow shoulders and were in terrible condition. We were riding on roads that anyone living out here would never dream of riding on. I also knew that the people driving the cars and trucks would not be expecting to see bicycles on these roads, especially at this time of the year.

Bicycling out East I was painfully reminded that there are people in this country who do not like sharing their highways with bicyclists. I now personally know some of these people. We thankfully encountered relatively very few of them. Ken and I called them "highway hogs," and although we ran into more than our share out East, the majority of people who passed us in cars were extremely respectful to us. Some of them were so respectful in fact that they would blow their horns as they passed, warning us that they were there. Little did they know that more times than not, this sudden and unexpected blast would make my heart jump to my ears, my stomach jump to where my heart had been and I would very nearly go careening off of the road.

I constantly wore a pair of sunglasses with an attached rearview mirror. It looked goofy sticking out from my head like a little antennae but it was an accessory that I could not do without. Whenever I saw a car coming toward me in the other lane, I would look in my rearview mirror. Inevitably a car would be coming up from behind me and would meet right alongside where I was riding and squeeze me off the road.

The scariest monsters of the road, as they had been since mile one, were the big tractor-trailer rigs, the eighteen-wheelers. I didn't even need my rearview mirror for these big trucks. I could hear the roar of their huge diesel engines above the steady din of the Chevrolets, Fords, Volkswagens and other cars. When I could feel the ground shaking I knew that it was time to bail out and get over, shoulder or not. When they passed, the first wall of air they were shoving ahead of them would momentarily make my bike lurch forward. When the wall of air passed, I would be caught in their draft and be pulled toward the truck. Finally, as the truck zoomed by, its back wake of air blew Betty and me every which way but loose.

The worst truck was the cab-over, the flat-nosed kind. The worst time to meet this breed was when you had a tail wind and they were coming at you in the other lane bucking a head wind. I found that the best thing to do was to put your head down on the handlebars and cut through that blast of air like a swimmer diving through a big wave. The only conditions that seemed to render these big brutes harmless was when I was riding with the wind and they were passing me going in the same direction.

The Peterbilt-style trucks, the kind with the long hood on them must have been more aerodynamic. They could be bad too, given the right conditions. But they were never as bad as the cab-over trucks.

The truly harmless giants of the road were the Greyhound and Travelways buses. They could pass within inches of us and they never seemed to make us sway a bit. They looked as flat-faced as the cab-over trucks did, but all of their rounded corners on the front and the rear must really have let them slip through the air.

As proof of these buses' gentle nature toward bicyclists, they always left us with the same sweet smell. It was obviously diesel exhaust, but it always smelled like a sweet perfume.

The damp weather, unexplained flat tires and the horrific traffic were the bricks and mortar that made up "the wall" that Ken and I were trying to break through.

We were just so incredibly tired of bicycling.

The 3,000 miles we knew that we had left may just as well have been 30,000 miles. Either number seemed unattainable. We were both also becoming very unsociable. We got along just fine with each other; in fact, sharing the same feelings caused by "the wall" even drew us closer. We just didn't feel much like talking to strangers.

We knew all along that the best way to break through this wall was to not think about how far we had to go, but rather to think about how far we had come. For the time being we had to abandon our goal of Minnesota and just take it one state at a time.

As we knew that it would, we gradually started to beat our way through this mental wall and we ever so slowly began enjoying ourselves again and became normal, fun-loving, sociable human beings.

"I'M EXHAUSTED AND SICK OF WALKING THESE STREETS.
I don't care who or what is in there. That's our pub."

Steve and I had bicycled 60 miles to Peekskill, New York and had already secured our first overnight in a Salvation Army. We were tired and thirsty. Both of us were on the lookout for a friendly, cozy pub to have a couple of brews before retiring for the night.

"The Tiki Bar. There are BUD signs in the windows and it doesn't look lit up on the inside like a pizza joint. I'm heading in. I'll see you inside."

As I opened the door, I quickly observed that the bartender was black and that the ten bar patrons were also all black. I was the only white person in the entire bar. All eyes turned my way. The bar became silent, just like in the movies. As a city boy from Minneapolis, I suddenly felt uncomfortable. I was in the solid racial minority for the first time in my entire life. I believed that I did not have a prejudiced bone in my body, but I also knew that I was very ill at ease. Steve soon joined me. I took a deep breath and reminded myself that I had firmly stated before I opened the door to the bar that this was our place.

I noticed that everybody was drinking bottles of Budweiser beer.

"We'll have two bottles of Bud."

As we headed to a nearby booth without a word, I continued to feel eyes piercing my back.

"For once on this trip I wish that our bikes were not locked up and secure somewhere else. At least with our bikes we look like we're from somewhere else and not just stupid or looking for a fight."

I started to relax and reminded myself that there was absolutely nothing to worry about. Suddenly two young men stood up from the bar and briskly walked directly towards our booth. I braced myself. I had no idea as to what was about to happen.

"My name's Will, my friends call me "Kid Flippo" and this is Ronny. You guys up for taking us on in bowling on this machine right next to you?"

Thus began over two hours of fun and camaraderie at the Tiki Bar. "Kid Flippo" was a wonderfully charismatic and hysterical 30-year-old man from New York City, married with six kids. Ronny was his 40-year-old buddy; Howard was the bartender; Shorty, Jasmine and other colorful characters filled this little pub. Everybody tried to buy a round of beer for us. Every single person there also wanted to know our story and eventually wished us well. Ronny and Will wrote down their addresses and asked us to drop them a line after we returned safely back home.

We headed back to the Salvation Army. Then it hit me. By the end of the night Steve and I had still been the only white people in that bar. However, we were the only ones who saw color. Nobody else cared.

We were all just folks relaxing after a long hard day, sharing stories, laughs and encouragement.

"The Wall" was slowly crumbling down, in more ways than one.

BY LATE MORNING WE HAD GRABBED OUR 32ND BORDER, NEW Jersey. We were charging south to Florida. Traffic was very congested as we bicycled south on Route 202 into Wayne, population about 50,000 people. My odometer read exactly 46 miles. I slowed to a stop at a light and waited for Steve to catch up to me. There were several construction guys working on the very road on which we were pedaling. The popularly asked questions started one after the other.

"Hey, where are you going? What for? You started...*where*?"

Steve finally saddled up next to me and these guys, friendly in their demeanor, continued to pepper both of us with questions.

One question came from what looked like the stereotypical construction worker – over six feet tall, healthy-looking, around 40-years-old, graying hair, checkered flannel shirt and a slightly-portly physique which suggested that he occasionally celebrated Miller Time. He introduced himself as Freddy Balbo.

The light kept changing from red to green back to red as we continued to patiently answer their questions. They could not believe how far we had traveled and were blown away by our cause.

Freddy and his crew were in the process of resurfacing the road and we were now slowing their progress down for the day. They were certainly slowing us down, too.

"Hey, I have an idea! Let me and the boys buy you a beer at The Penguins Restaurant. It's only a couple of blocks away. That's the least we can do for you two."

Ken and I protested and protested. It seemed like forever since we had put on even 70 miles in one day and we were on a good roll today. It was still warm and sunny and we wanted to put on miles and get this traffic and urban congestion behind us.

"Come on. You guys can watch the New Jersey guys drink and we'll buy you a pop or Perrier water. You two need a break. We'll tie up the bikes and have you back on your way in a few minutes."

He wore us down. It was 3:45 PM. We left The Penguins Restaurant seven hours later.

Once inside the restaurant, Freddy introduced us to his good buddy Walter Oset. Between the two of these characters we had a lot of laughs and a clear understanding within minutes that our productive day of bicycling was down the tubes.

This crew must have been working on this job for quite some time. Freddy and Walter knew every waitress, bartender and customer that walked into the place.

In the course of many conversations, we learned that we would probably never bicycle out of traffic in this state, since New Jersey was the most densely-populated state in the country at almost 1,000 people per square mile. All night long Freddy and Walter told us fascinating stories about New Jersey, the culture and many preconceived ideas we had about people "out East."

"You're wrong, Ken, about people not being friendly or helping each other out here," Freddy blathered. "Now in New York City itself, that's another story. If a guy dies right next to you, you shove him out of the way to get at what you're doing! But not in Jersey!"

I had to agree that people in New Jersey, of all places, were some of the downright friendliest people we had met on the trip. Ken and I were both impressed.

Finally at about 9 PM Freddy and Walter prepared to leave, but not before introducing us to The Penguins' owners, George and Nick. Great guys as well, they told us that we would now be their guests for the specialty of the house. Freddy and his crew headed for the door after giving us hugs, addresses and having us sign their placemats. What a memorable bunch of guys. Ken and I then feasted on our huge plates of lobster, shrimp, stuffed crabmeat, filet of sole and huge buttery baked potatoes. It was an incredibly delicious meal and generous offer of hospitality.

An unknown dishwasher speaking in broken English and thick Italian dialect shook our hands and told us to "take care of ourselves" as we walked out the door. We smiled and waved.

Steve and I hit the night air at close to 10 PM and were jolted back to reality.

We were still only 46 miles down the road, it was dark, we had no place to stay and it was too late to knock on minister's doors. However, with a moonlit night, a light breeze at our back and very little traffic, we decided to tentatively bicycle down the highway.

Thirteen miles later, we biked into the little town of Morris Plains. We quickly found a little church and pulled out our sleeping bags. Laying down our tents like a blanket over the wet grass, we crept into our bags and slept under the stars for the first time since the first night we left Mary and Mark back in Kansas last October.

I was confident we wouldn't get rained on as I drifted to sleep under the stars.

"YOU LOOK LIKE HELL." STEVE LOOKED UP FROM HIS BOWL OF oatmeal and smiled at my remark.

"Well you smell like chicken urine so I'd keep your thoughts about my appearance to yourself."

Ouch. That hurt. After months of bicycling through farmland, Steve and I were both in 100% agreement that chickens and their waste products were hands down the worst odor of the entire trip.

"We made a great choice last night. We darn near disrespected our rules of the road and turned down Freddy's offer for one beer, pop or water. We ended up having a blast."

"Wholeheartedly agree." Steve was now into a plate of scrambled eggs.
"But, as I sit here in the same clothes that I have worn for the past three days, *three days,* same black and white Minneapolis T-shirt, same overalls, same sweatpants over my overalls, same socks, same underwear, same…"

"Ken, I'm trying to keep my food down."

"Sorry buddy. Seriously, I don't know when the last time was that I washed clothes or had any water rinse over my body. I cannot ever remember feeling this grungy. Can we agree that we will get a motel room tonight, regroup and get back on track?"

Steve kept taking in deep breaths in an attempt to smell me and then started giggling. I did not even want to hear what was about to come out of his mouth. I was only happy because I already knew that he agreed with me and that our day would end with hot, soapy water.

"I agree."

I waited for his punch line. It never came. It would have been too easy.

The day was full of rain and some dangerous patches of fog, but Steve and I were in great spirits. I coasted to a stop at a traffic light in the town of Flemington, NJ, right behind a big garbage truck. The man standing on the back with a Jersey accent shouted at us.

"Hey! Where you guys going?"

We told him.

"Cross country? Geez! My kid brother biked the length of the state of Jersey and thought that he was hot stuff. Wait 'till he hears this! Good luck fellas!"

We waved, smiled and yelled, "Thanks!" As I pushed hard to get my bike moving forward after a dead stop, I thought again about the challenge Steve and I were going to have when we got back home, adjusting to not being treated like royalty and heroes wherever we went. The past month of accumulating miles and our Make-A-Wish cause had brought us a lot of positive attention. With today being the first day of December, I knew that the newsworthiness of our adventure was only going to grow.

CHAPTER 42
HORRIFIC TRAFFIC, GRAVEYARDS & FOUL BICYCLISTS

*"When the morning's freshness has been replaced by the weariness of midday
and the leg muscles give under the strain, and the climb seems endless, and
suddenly nothing will go quite as you wish – it is then that you
must not hesitate."* ~ Dag Hammarskjold

WE LITERALLY FEARED FOR OUR LIVES. BICYCLING ON HWY 202 back into Pennsylvania, the traffic was so congested and horrendous that Steve and I were punchy. There were hundreds of exits, on ramps, off ramps, four lanes of traffic and shoulders in such terrible shape that we were afraid that riding on them would literally rip up our tires. To top it off traffic was really, really scary. The entire afternoon was so horrific that for the first time on this trip, we both imagined that we could easily get injured or worse on that stretch of road.

Finally, we were able to get off highway 202 near West Chester, Pennsylvania and regain some sense of relative security.

My knuckles were white, arms numb and head pounding from the stress.

The next two days we bicycled through the rolling hills of Pennsylvania on our way to our focused goal of the Virginia border. We still had Delaware and Maryland in our sites, but Virginia represented the northeast and all of its major cities and congestion firmly in Steve's rearview mirror.

"ARE YOU AFRAID OF GHOSTS, BUDDY? SERIOUSLY, IF THIS graveyard is too spooky or weird we can check out somewhere else nearby." I was serious.

Steve slowly surveyed the assorted tombstones and then gave me his honest opinion.

"I'm good if you're good. It will be one more intriguing overnight option to add to our growing list. Just don't tell me any scary stories or put your sleeping bag right on the gravesite. I read once where that's either disrespectful or it summons them out of the grave to violently harm whomever is on the plot. I forgot which one it is but either one is ominous and the harm or maim thing could really slow up our bicycling."

It was a warm, balmy night in Madonna, Maryland. At least the name of the town made us feel safe and unthreatened.

Actually, our entire day had been miraculously safe and unthreatening. Having battled ferocious traffic and terrible shoulders in the rain for days, we crossed into Maryland and were overjoyed to once again experience lazy back roads, gentle rolling hills, the sunshine of a gorgeous day and only sparse traffic. It set a laid back tone for the day. It had been a good long while since Steve and I had enjoyed a day of bicycling.

We bicycled 55 miles to Madonna, crossing the Susquehanna River, climbing possibly the single steepest hill of the trip that had us huffing and puffing as we *walked* our bikes to the crest and excitedly took a photograph at border #34.

We rolled into Madonna at dusk; a town with no population listed on the sign and immediately spotted a very small country church. Right next to the church were a patch of trees and the little graveyard.

"Then this is home."

We rested our bikes against the church wall, pulled out fixings to make sandwiches and sat down, immensely satisfied. For fun we played some trivia games. At one point as we started to yawn and wind down our day, Steve correctly figured out 45 of our state capitals. I was impressed. Then it was time for me to figure out where to sleep without disturbing the dead.

I laid out my tent for a blanket and then rolled out my sleeping bag on top of my tent. I checked to see exactly where I was. I finally determined that I was between two rows of headstones and not on any actual graves. I crawled into my bag, honestly feeling a little apprehensive. Thankfully I was able to fall asleep to the sound of crickets in the distance and not to the sounds of a hooting owl or a howling coyote.

In fact any noise other than crickets and Steve's breathing would have been very unsettling.

IT WAS A DAY OF RELENTLESS, INTENSE BICYCLING. SUN, HILLS and a wind in our face, Steve and I were razor focused for a 70 mile charge to the Virginia border. As the day wore on, we were both starving and stripped of needed carbohydrates to fuel our quest. We were easily burning up 6,000 calories a day. The back roads we traveled simply had no services and no supplies. Finally, as the sun was setting and our daylight quickly leaving us, we saw the Point of Rocks Bridge over the Potomac River descending into the state of Virginia.

"Isn't that a beautiful sight? We are at 74.2 miles and there's a tiny grocery store right over there. Perfect!"

We were tired but pumped. I'm not sure what was better, the sight of the bridge or the thought of some bread. We bought two submarine sandwiches, chips and pop. Then checking the sky, we sadly realized that the sun was completely down and our border crossing would have to wait until first thing in the morning. We sought out a nearby church to camp or to get inside for the night.

"Pastor will be back in about an hour." We were at the church but nobody available could make a decision for us. I was troubled and a little frustrated.

"Are you up for taking on this bridge right now and waking up tomorrow in Virginia?"

I looked intensely at Steve for his response. I knew that what I was proposing was legitimately dangerous. I had set a personal goal to be in Virginia tonight and my spirit and body were both willing. However, it was now nighttime. If Steve hesitated in any way I was not going to push him.

He didn't have to say a word. I saw the answer in his eyes.

There was no moon or stars out and the two-lane Point of Rocks Bridge had truck traffic in both lanes. This was not only the latest border crossing we had ever attempted; it was undoubtedly the scariest bridge conditions that we had ever undertaken. My adrenaline was pumping wildly in the darkness.

Steve flew right by the huge four foot by six foot, "Welcome to Virginia" sign. He never saw it. The only reason I did was because a truck passed by me illuminating the words with his headlights.

Once we got to the other side and could move a little to the right and relax, Steve and I held hands as was our border crossing tradition and whooped it up. There was a little more energy and volume in our voices than usual.

Five miles later, tents erected in the backyard of a little church adjacent to another graveyard, we heard the drops of rainfall, in the state of Virginia.

This was a 79-mile-effort for the books.

THE NEXT TWO DAYS WE POUNDED OUT 176 MILES. WE WOULD get on our bicycles as early as 5:45 AM and just pedal. I couldn't believe how tranquil our lives were again after the congestion and stress of the northeast. Steve and I loved the people that we had met this past month, but the bicycling part of it was brutal. We constantly had to pull out and check our maps, figure out how to get around the next metropolitan area, reconnect every two miles or so in order not to lose each other and be aware at all times of traffic and road conditions. Now we just got on our bicycles and biked for hours over rural back roads without strategizing or thinking too hard.

Steve and I were not in the best of moods nor were we particularly enjoying the beauty of Virginia or the experience of bicycling. We were shooting for a prearranged and needed Christmas break in Gainesville, Florida and we were very cognizant of our miles and how many days until December 24th. One night we bicycled a solid 40 minutes in complete darkness in an attempt to bicycle 100 miles in a single day, something we had not been able to do in these shorter days for months.

We missed our goal but we biked an incredible 94 miles. If we enjoyed anything during this stretch it was the achievement of putting on miles and creating a solid day of getting closer to another border.

6:30 AM. I WAS STILL SO TIRED THAT I COULDN'T OPEN MY eyes. Then a foul odor filled my nostrils. My dear Lord in heaven, it was me! I sat there in my tent unable to get up. I was freezing, ornery, hadn't slept well and I stunk. I had planned to wake Steve but he was already up and waiting for me. Now I was mad at him and presuming he was mad at me for having to wait. Why didn't he simply wake me up? I tried to sit up. I didn't even want to be awake. This was already not a good morning.

I was mad at the world.

It had now been five days since I had been in a shower. The last two nights we'd spent in tents. Yesterday I broke a spoke, determined that my bicycle axle was bent again and fixed a flat tire. As I sat there, unable to clear my head from a fog, Steve left and told me that we'd connect at the next town for breakfast. My hair matted to my head, I crawled out of my tent. It was more than just me that smelled. Life stunk. The very last thing in the world that I wanted to do was to get on my bicycle and pedal 70 or 80 miles down the road.

This was my life.

Steve and I met for breakfast and we both perked up a little bit. Nobody was mad at anybody but we were in sour and unsocial moods. My eyes were still like slits and not opening up without focused effort. For the rest of the day, Steve and I put the blinders on and ground out the miles. We rarely saw each other.

Eighty-two miles later, thanks to a kind police officer in Blackstone, Virginia, we stayed inside a minister's home focused on outreach in the community, with some great young people and enjoyed an Advent service and Christmas songs.

We took hot showers and slept in warm, comfy beds. It made all the difference.

CHAPTER 43
BEHIND BARS IN NORTH CAROLINA

"It is definitely no fun when that iron door clangs shut on you." ~ Barney Fife

I TALKED INTO MY LITTLE TAPE RECORDER LOGGING THE DAY'S events.

"Day #142, Wednesday December 8th, 82 miles, Enfield, North Carolina, State #36. We are now at 7,500 miles or 75% done with this trip, we are inside at the Enfield Inn and it's not costing us anything but…"

"WE ARE BEHIND BARS!"

"That's right, we are in jail! It finally caught up to us. Fast living, rolling down the road, the 'big house', up the river"…I broke out laughing.

Steve and I really were behind bars, and it all started with an innocent conversation at supper tonight.

We were eating a southern supper of biscuits and gravy in a tiny little café. I thought it was pretty good but Ken vowed once again that it was the last time biscuits and gravy would ever pass his lips.

There was a policeman sitting a couple of tables away. We hadn't found a place to stay for the night and so after I finished eating I walked up to the officer and gave him our standard speech explaining who we were, where we had come from, where we were going, why we were doing it and finally, "Do you know of a place where we could stay for the night?"

As the days went by and the miles piled up, our little speech gained impact.

"You mean y'all rode bicycles, the pedal kind, from Minnesota to here?" the big police officer asked.

Not sure if he realized that we got here via Oregon, California, Kansas, Maine and all of the states in between, I said, "That's right. We bicycled over 7,500 miles so far."

Everybody had their own way of expressing how impossible that fact seemed to them and this officer was no different.

"Man, I think that I would die if I rode a bike across the street!"

Our conversation seemed to gain the attention of everybody in the small café. Before we knew it, we were fielding questions from everybody there.

"When did you leave Minnesota?"

"How much weight you two carrying?"

"Either one of you married?"

"You guys brothers?"

"You ever hit any snow?"

"Where y'all stay at night?"

Bingo. That was our opening and I knew that we would have a place to sleep indoors for the night. I directed my answer to the policeman.

"Wherever we can find it."

Once again I asked him, "Do you know of a place like a church, YMCA or a Salvation Army where we could stay tonight?"

He mulled it over for a minute and finally suggested, "Well, there's always the Enfield Inn!"

Several people in the café started laughing and so we figured that this Inn must be some awful, seedy motel of some sort.

"What's wrong with the Enfield Inn?" I asked.

"It's the jail. But if there's an empty cell, you fellas are welcome to stay there for the night. At least it's indoors, dry and you'll have a bed to sleep on. You sure as hell will be safe, too!"

There were more snickers. He didn't have to sell us on the idea. It sounded fun and different and something we could write home about.

CLANG!

The sound of cold, hard iron rang out as our "innkeeper" locked us into our cell for the night. I knew that we were only in for the night but the sound of that heavy metal door slamming shut was still ominous.

"I'm going to have to lock you in for the night. There's nothing to worry about. It's regulations."

He explained that it was their policy to lock us up for our own safety. If a real criminal got loose, they couldn't get to us and do us any harm. This sounded like a great idea to us as long as they remembered to let us out in the morning.

We then passed our camera to the police officer through the bars. We put on our best "jail bird" faces and the officer took our picture.

When he left us for the night, the jailhouse humor started up.

"What you in for, pal?" I asked Ken.

"First-degree murder. I killed some punk."

"Why?"

"Because he talked to me!" Ken replied in the lowest, meanest voice he could muster.

"What are you in for, punk?"

Feigning my newfound inability to talk, I mouthed a few words.

"Hey! You talk to me when I talk to you!"

I did my best Barney Fife-trying-to-be-a-tough-guy impression. I hitched up my pants, cleared my throat, stuck out my chest and said in a low, shaky voice,

"I'm in for treason, robbery, assault with a deadly weapon, forgery, kidnapping, jay walking, kicking a dog and killing a guy just because he was big and had a beard!"

We could no longer stay in character. We laughed at our own pathetic silliness. We then settled into some serious letter writing before they turned the lights out at 10 PM.

There was a time in my life several months ago that I considered luxury accommodations for a night away from home to be a Radisson, Ramada Inn or Embassy Suites. Life on the road had dramatically changed all of that. The only two factors that constituted luxury living for us now was a roof over our head and a bed to sleep on.

Tonight, locked behind bars on our two-inch-thick mattresses, we slept like rocks.

Chapter 44
AWAY IN A MANGER, NO CRIB FOR A BED

"I think we may safely trust a good deal more than we do."
~ Henry David Thoreau

THE NEXT SIX DAYS WE BIKED 442 MILES AND DID IT WITH relative ease. We took the path of least resistance; the pine tree-filled flatlands between the mountains and the ocean that ran the entire way from North Carolina through Georgia. Almost all of those 442 miles was spent on US HWY 301. In this stretch we had passed through 51 towns that at one time had been prosperous. As happens so many times and in so many places in this country, progress changed that for many of these towns. Progress here was the advent of Interstate 95. This new major freeway saved drivers a lot of time but it also destroyed the economy of many of these communities. Gas stations, motels, restaurants and many other retail businesses that drivers had to pass by if they wanted to go from North Carolina to Georgia were completely bypassed by I-95.

HWY 301 was for us, however, one great stretch of road to bicycle! It often had double lanes and always had beautiful shoulders to ride on. Traffic was minimal and I assumed that was because everybody was on the Interstate.

The weather had finally started to cooperate with us too. We bicycled through rain in North Carolina but the balmy temperatures made it much more bearable. The rest of the time it was calm, warm and sunny. It was the first time since Kansas that we were able to ride shirtless for part of the day.

I COULD NOT BELIEVE MY EYES. AS I SLOWED DOWN TO CHECK as to why Steve had biked to a complete stop, I followed his eyes staring down at his tire.

"You have a flat tire. I do not believe it."

To the casual observer, my words made no sense at all. What they would not have understood was the fact that Steve had not had a flat tire in over 3,000 miles! 3,000 MILES! My tires were getting flats left and right in the northeast and Steve had not had a flat or a blowout of any kind since before he flew home to get his colitis checked on back in Kansas. This was truly a remarkable feat.

"What did you hit?"

"I don't even know. I didn't see any glass."

"So help me God, I was starting to honestly believe that you would never have another flat tire. It was like I was in the dugout in the eighth inning of a game and you were pitching a no hitter. I was afraid to bring up the subject in case I jinxed you! I wasn't going to say anything until we were back in Minnesota. I'm almost relieved!"

Steve laughed as he stripped off his spare inner tube and put a new one on his back tire. It was getting late and he would actually repair the hole in his inner tube some evening when we had some time.

We bicycled into Ludowici, Georgia with just about 80 miles under our belts. Although we both felt strong, the sun was setting and we had set our sites on the city of Jesup, exactly 11 more miles down the road. We needed to hustle.

Steve spotted a convenience store and we quickly refilled our water bottles, bought a loaf of bread and a package of ham and packed them into our saddlebags. We bicycled south to get our last ten miles.

"Steve! Hold up!"

Steve looked at me as I stopped alongside of him, now straddling his bike. He spoke first.

"Are you thinking what I'm thinking?"

"Probably. Every car I've seen the past three minutes already has their headlights on. There is absolutely nothing between here and Jesup."

Steve smiled broadly.

"I saw a café about a mile back advertising a cheeseburger basket special of some kind."

Now I was smiling. Life on the road could be as uncomplicated as possible when you and your traveling buddy routinely thought as one mind and heart.

As we chomped on our cheeseburgers and glanced at the darkness out the café window, the only restaurant in town, we were even more relaxed.

"Excuse me, officer. Do you have a minute?"

Steve took the lead, gave the police officer sitting at the next table our background story and then asked the critical question about possible overnight accommodations.

A smiling Officer "Elliott" excused himself to make some phone calls on our behalf and said that he would be right back.

"Well, I might have something for you guys. Did some checking around with some friends and a couple of churches and had trouble getting anybody to pick up the phone. I thought that our police station was a possibility, but my sergeant told me that if we book you in and don't charge you with anything, we're 100% liable for anything that happens to you. You get up to go to the bathroom in the middle of the night and trip and split your head open, we don't have any good answers for your folks when they find out that you were in our jail but never committed a crime, we're in big trouble. The good news is that if you guys can handle about 40 degrees or so tonight, I have a safe place to at least throw down your sleeping bags."

Officer Elliot had put forth some serious effort and so we were game for whatever option he was about to present.

"We have an old railroad platform about a mile from here. Years ago they put offices in the railway station and it's now actually our city hall. The platform though is safe and all lit up for Christmas with a life-size nativity scene. You should be comfortable enough and nobody will bother you."

That sounded unique and fun. Steve and I heartily agreed and thanked him for his effort and his time.

"You know, I've spent the past eight years as a private investigator and now a police officer. There are a lot of rough people out there and I had to learn how to sort out the sincere people from the insincere people pretty damn quickly. I knew right out of the blocks that you guys were okay."

The fact that he trusted us and did it quickly was one of the best compliments that he could have given to us.

"Well, you should have seen us about six months ago!" I said. "We were clean-shaven and dressed daily in three-piece suits. Now look at us!"

We all laughed.

"You've heard it before, I know, but you truly can't judge a book by its cover." He then reached into his wallet and pulled out his drivers' license and showed it to both of us.

"No way!" Police Officer Elliott had hair down to his shoulders with a beard that was as long as Moses.

"Yup. That's me and not that many years ago. I could write a whole book about my days as a private investigator."

With that, he put his license back and reached for something else. I was sure it was going to be a business card to be able to contact him after we got home."

"Here's ten bucks, guys. Grab a meal down the road on me. I love what you are doing and I will keep you in my prayers."

He then gave us directions to the train platform and warmly shook our hands goodbye.

Wow. As I climbed on my bike I was almost speechless.

I thought about how as a young boy in grade school we read the legendary, "See Dick and Jane" reading primers. I still vividly remembered the old depiction of a policeman in his blue uniform and his blue hat. "The policeman is our friend." I believed that to my core. He was there to protect and serve me in every sense of the word. Then as I hit my teenage years and then started to drive, the "policeman" turned into the "cop." His sole purpose now was to try to catch me messing up, speeding, missing curfew. He was someone out to cause me pain. That image stayed with me all of these years.

However, as Steve and I traveled the country, each and every single police officer we met was kind to us, respectful and exceptionally helpful. We were bearded and often filthy but we always received the benefit of the doubt and ultimately, like tonight, a lot of needed help.

The beautiful sight of the lit-up train platform startled me out of my thoughts. We pulled our bikes up onto the station. Sure enough, there was the nativity scene with life-sized cut-out figures of the three wise men, Mary, Joseph and a real crib with hay and a baby doll replicating Jesus.

Steve and I were overwhelmed. Because of all the lights, I wasn't sure how well we would sleep but we felt incredibly safe, secure, and in a strange way, reverent in our surroundings.

We took photos, made a tape recording singing Christmas carols for Steve's family and eventually laid our sleeping bags in the manger next to the baby Jesus and slowly drifted to sleep.

We got very little sleep that night. Besides all the lights around us, there must have been 20 trains that roared by within 20 feet of us during the night. Freight trains were carrying cars full of lumber, Amtrak passenger trains carrying cars full of people...all of them blasting their train horns to alert car drivers stopped at nearby railroad crossing signs.

They mercilessly shook Ken and me out of any possible deep sleep.

In addition to the unbelievable noise of 80 MPH trains roaring past us, sleeping next to Mary, Joseph and the baby Jesus in the manger was one of our most unique campsites and overnight experiences ever.

CHAPTER 45
MY GOD, HE'S TRYING TO KILL ME WITH HIS CAR!

"Man could escape danger only by renouncing adventure, by abandoning that which has given to the human condition its unique character and genius among the rest of living things. ~ **Rene Dubois**

MY MIND WAS EMPTY. I COULD NOT CONJURE UP EVEN ONE single thought. I had never been so mentally drained in my life. Although earlier we had bicycled into our 39th state, Florida and our Christmas break was quickly approaching in Gainesville, my mind was clean. It was exhausting and impossible to put into words. Five months and 8,270 miles of bicycling alone with my thoughts had drained my head down to zero. It was the strangest kind of tired that I had ever experienced in my life. There was nothing to ponder or think about. I was mentally stuck. We had hit "the wall" several hundred miles earlier and eventually snapped out of it, but this was different.

I was now on a deserted stretch of highway 121 bicycling south in Florida. Steve was up ahead and out of sight. I slowly looked up to see a dark sedan traveling northbound ease into the southbound lane to pass a car.

In a horrific split second, my internal radar went off telling me that something was deadly wrong. The dark sedan was not parallel in the southbound lane as it should have been. My brain screamed. There was no car for the sedan to pass!

He was angling for my bicycle! He appeared to be trying to kill me!

Had he already hit Steve up ahead? What do I do? The distance between us was closing terrifyingly quickly. I headed for the ditch, preparing to get off my bike and race to protect myself behind a tree.

I ran out of time.

He roared by me, coming within a mere few feet of my bicycle and me. As I stared at him through the driver's window, I saw that he was wearing sunglasses concealing any intent in his eyes. I then observed a slight smirk.

I waved at him wildly, spewing forth frightened, angry and I am sure unholy words. In retrospect that was a dumb move. I was still on a deserted road with no Steve in sight. He could have turned around and attempted to run me down again and again.

Slowly bicycling south, still shaking from my first near miss of this entire adventure, I was deeply convinced that the dark sedan's actions were not accidental.

His motives were malicious. My mind was again engaged. Welcome to Florida.

CHAPTER 46
CHRISTMAS BREAK IN FLORIDA

"The only blind person at Christmas time is he who has not Christmas in his heart." ~ Helen Keller

A MINUTE AFTER WE PASSED THE GAINESVILLE, FLORIDA population sign someone behind us beeped his horn. It was my brother Paul! Christmas vacation had officially arrived with his bear hug. Steve and I were exhausted on all levels and more than ready for a short break. "How you doing bro! You're looking like I used to look in sales! What in the heck happened to you? Shirt and tie, the whole nine yards and me on the other hand?"

"You got the grizzly look, Ken!"

Paul looked great. It was funny though that the last time I had seen him was when he was at college; longhaired and dressed in casual clothes. Today he was a young, dynamic salesman for a local radio station. I had never seen his hair this short and overall so clean-cut and corporate-looking. Steve and I now had the grungy, hairy, college look.

"Steve, this is my brother Paul. Paul, Steve. That's the last of my family, buddy. You have now met each and every one of them. I wish that I could say that I saved the best for last but...."

We all laughed. It wasn't that funny of a line but we were excited for a break.

I had heard a lot about Paul from Ken and it was great to finally meet him. Ken once referred to Paul as a "media child." It was a fitting label apparently because he used to watch television a lot when he was a kid. He not only memorized all of the commercials, TV shows and movies that he saw, he also imitated many actors right down to the subtlest mannerisms. When he was in college, Paul saw his favorite movie, Caddy Shack, about twenty times. I had only met him for about ten minutes and Ken baited him to do imitations of Bill Murray and Rodney Dangerfield repeating their exact scripts from the movie, leaving me in stitches and gasping for air!

Paul sold commercial time for a local radio station. He would occasionally do his own spots for the station, speaking as one of the

many characters that he imitated. His Clint Eastwood and Howard Cosell impressions were so dead-on that he blew me away.

No one seemed more custom-fitted for their job than Paul Rogers.

For the next couple of days we did a lot of sunbathing. Our only job for a week or so was to match the color of our bodies to the dark brown color of our faces.

One day while we were lying there on our lawn chairs, the mailman walked up to Paul's door and left a large package. As I suspected, the package was for me. It was my goose down jacket! It was 39 days and four snowstorms late but I was still thrilled to finally get it. Ken laughed when he saw me return to my lawn chair wearing only my shorts and my big, fluffy, blue goose-down jacket.

"The top half of your body looks like the incredible hulk and the bottom half looks like a skinny chicken. Maybe you should get yourself some goose-down pants so that you look like a normal person."

Normally I would have retaliated with an insult of my own but I couldn't think of anything. Without saying a word, I laid back down in my lawn chair, still wearing my jacket, reached over and cranked up the volume on the radio, completely drowning out his voice.

"Hey guys! Good news, I think."

Paul had just gotten home from work and joined us on his sun-drenched patio.

"Steve, that's quite a unique tan you're working on there, hey. It looks like kind of an Oreo thing; dark legs, white middle and dark face."

Steve did look silly.

"So as I was starting to say, I've got you both booked on our new talk show, *To the Point*, tomorrow night. If you guys want to do it, I need to know by tonight. We had a guest cancel and they were pumped when I told them about you. It runs for 90 minutes with callers able to phone in with questions. It's brand-new for us and so I don't know how many people would actually call in but our host is a riot. It would be relaxed and fun for you, that I can promise."

It sounded good to Ken and me. We couldn't work on our tans at night anyway.

"THEY LOOK LIKE MOUNTAIN MEN, STEVE ANDERSON AND Kenny Rogers, and of course, he does not sing. I am sure that he gets that wherever he goes. These two guys have gone 8,300 miles and not in an automobile but on bicycles. What a feat it is that you're not dead yet. I don't know if y'all been in Gainesville long enough but I think the motorists here aim for the people on bikes. These guys have wheeled into town for a very good cause. It's called Make-A-Wish of Minnesota. It is a program that grants wishes to children with terminal illnesses. You talk about injustice; I think that's injustice, children dying of diseases that overtake them. These two guys are raising money and getting suntans and avoiding the hazards of the road. And they're going to join us in a few minutes and tell us about their adventures. We'll be back in a minute."

Steve and I joined our host Laura for the segment, put on our headsets and positioned our microphones. The atmosphere in the studio was very relaxed. The last time that Steve and I had nervously sat in a studio together was six months and 8,300 miles ago. This was going to be fun. We could immediately feel the difference.

"Like I mentioned before we broke, we have two hairy guys here in the studio with us. You *look* like you've been on the road! We've got Steve Anderson and Kenny Rogers, who doesn't sing. He's not *the* Kenny Rogers but he is the brother of the famous salesman, Paul Rogers. These two guys have been on the road for how long?"

"About five months." I loved those tough questions out of the blocks.

"Let me find out a little bit about what you're doing for these people. Make-A-Wish of Minnesota is the name of the program and it grants, last wishes?"

I quickly corrected her.

"We never say, 'last' wishes and we never use the word 'terminal.'"

"Of which I've done both."

"Well the reason being is that with children anything can still happen. We use the term 'serious and life threatening' diseases. So, any child that has been diagnosed with something like cancer or leukemia, very, very, serious diseases…"

"I already see where that is a more hopeful scenario." Laura interrupted.

"…and they are being referred to us and nobody wants to refer a 'terminally-ill' child."

"So you guys are biking around the country to raise money for wishes for these children. What kind of wishes are they? Do you know? Off the air you said that four have been granted so far. What kind of stuff?"

"First off, the ages of the kids have been anywhere between four and seventeen. They can't be adults so we go with the legal term of under eighteen. The most popular wish always has been Disneyland or Disneyworld. But we had one little guy, Dustin, for instance, who wanted to meet Barry Manilow backstage.

"Really, why?"

Laura and Steve were both laughing pretty hard. It felt a little mean but not being a Barry Manilow fan either, it was funny.

"So he was able to do that?"

"Barry's people were very, very nice. I'm not particularly fond of Barry Manilow's music but I now think he is one heck of a good guy to do what he did."

"So that was an easy wish. He was in town and the boy wanted to see him and afterward he went backstage and met him and Barry was really great with him."

It was an hour or so that literally flew by. We took some excellent calls from listeners, even one where we were forced to explain our training regimen in preparation for the trip. The answer was still zero going in, but we shared that revelation with confidence from our 39th state as opposed to hiding that fact at the start in Minnesota.

"You're heading back to Minnesota. It's snowing there according to our meteorologist. Are you going to ride through the snow?"

"We have no choice because that's home and that's where we have to end up."

"What's the weather been like on this trip?"

"All in all, it's been glorious."

"Steve, how many days have we been rained on while we were bicycling?"

"That was one of my next questions."

"Sixteen."

Laura laughed at his quick and firm response.

"I forgot that this is the statistician. Is it true or did you guess?"

Steve was laughing.

"No, it's true."

"He really knows this stuff!" Laura exclaimed.

I backed up Steve's credibility. "No, he's not making these things up. We used to have a stat on how many squished bunnies we saw on the road. How big has that grown to, Steve?"

"That's up to 1,218,112. It's really fun trying to see the different little contortions their little bodies are in; two legs out of their ear..."

Laura couldn't breathe she was laughing so hard. I chimed in. "We try to figure out what that animal used to be."

Laura composed herself. "It is apparent that these long days in the sun have totally fried your sensibilities here if you could find any sort of humor in squished bunnies! Why bunnies?"

"I don't know. Bunnies must be dumb. I really don't know. Steve?"

"They are really dumb. I guess they just can't judge the speed of cars at night. They get confused when they see headlights or something."

Steve and I shared more "biker anecdotes" as our host affectionately called them and we slowly wound down our segment. It had been a buoyant, hopefully inspiring and for the first time often-irreverent and humorous interview. Although Laura had set the tone for tonight, being relaxed, confident and closing in on our last leg of the trip had a whole different feel to it. It was a good one.

We spent a solid week or so off of our bicycles and enjoyed a very wonderful and renewing Christmas. Friends, family members and even people we had met the previous five months wrote letters and notes to us while we were at Paul's, greatly renewing our spirits for a final push north.

UNFORTUNATELY IT WAS OUR LAST DAY OF RELAXATION, IF you could call it that. It was comparable to the feeling I used to get on Sunday afternoons when I knew that I'd be in school the following morning or any jobs I ever had too.

The next day would be the start of our final stretch. We had 1,700 miles and nine states to go. Most of those miles would be ridden in extremely cold weather.

I cleaned up Betty about as thoroughly as I had all trip long and outfitted her with some new rubber. I was also tempted to replace the chain and a few of her rear gears. The chain was really stretched out. Normally you should replace a bike chain every 3,000 miles. I had passed that mark 5,300 miles ago. The middle three gears in my rear gear cluster had lost their sharp edges and were pretty much rounded off. I had a feeling that before I reached Minnesota my stretched chain would start losing its grip on those rounded gears and start slipping over the top of them.

The smart thing to do would be to replace them, but I wanted to remain consistent with the way that I did most everything on this trip. I wanted to see if I could make the whole trip with all of Betty's original equipment. She had been a truly amazing bike up to this point. She had not broken one single spoke yet. I had not even had to true the wheels once. The only problems of any kind that I had were flat tires.

Ken spent his day about the same way as me. He would be starting the last leg of the trip with half of a new bicycle. As TREK had promised, they had a brand-new frame waiting for him when we first got to Gainesville.

CHAPTER 47
THE $20,000 RANSOM IDEA & OUR CAUSE BECOMES PERSONAL

"When you are sorrowful look again in your heart, and you shall see that in truth you are weeping for that which has been your delight." ~ Kahil Gilbran

"FOLLOW ME. I KNOW A SHORTCUT OUT OF TOWN!"

I shouted over my shoulder as we pedaled out of Gainesville. Ken followed me as I zigzagged my way down alleys, through parking lots and finally through the doors of a Winn Dixie Supermarket. The doors opened automatically as my tire hit the black mat in front of it. Ken kept following me as we rolled through the store attracting the attention of many curious shoppers, then did a quick 180-degree turn back out the exit doors.

Ken, who had played it straight up to now finally laughingly said, "Hey buddy, if we keep taking your shortcuts we won't make it home until next July!"

Our first day back on the road got progressively worse at a very rapid rate. The morning sunshine and blue skies gave way to gray skies and rain clouds before we had even left the city limits. We proceeded to head northwest on US Highway 441.

An uneventful but tough day back on our bikes got us 62 miles closer to Minnesota and ended in Mayo, Florida. I told Ken that I was a wimp today.

We were both indeed soft again. We looked for a motel out of the rain and off of the hard ground.

With the only two motels in town completely full, we ended up accepting the hospitality of a family of four that Ken had met and offered us their office cubicle in a service station that they owned. This was a new accommodation for us. No TV, music or entertainment of any kind but it was warm, dry and the price was right considering our dwindling funds.

One aspect of this trip that was always hard for me to deal with was the lack of things to do at night. Back in my normal life my evenings were never long enough. In the summer I was on two softball teams, in the fall I was on a football team and in the winter my evenings were especially full with hockey and racquetball. On the nights that I wasn't playing one of these sports, I was out visiting a friend or a friend was visiting me.

Life on the road was completely different. There were no friends to visit and no sports to play. At night the only things that we could do were to write letters, read or do our pushups and sit-ups. In our gas station we didn't feel like doing any of those and so we talked.

It was amazing to me that Ken and I never ran out of things to talk about. We were together more than most married couples but we never ran out of things to say. Tonight we got on the subject of Make-A-Wish of Minnesota. From the beginning, this was of course one of our main topics of conversation.

Having never participated in a fundraising venture like this before, we had no idea how much money we would be able to raise. On July 1st when we first announced on KSTP radio what we would be doing, we had gained about $4,000 in pledges in 45 minutes. That was an incredible achievement at the time! Every Friday since then when we would call into the station, the head of Make-A-Wish John Rubel would talk to us off the air and keep us apprised of what was happening with the fundraising. As of about a week ago, there was approximately $10,000 in pledges on our behalf for the children of Make-A-Wish of Minnesota.

As we sat there amongst the fan belts, oil filters and vending machines inside this gas station, we were questioning why we had raised only $10,000 in six months since we had raised $4,000 in our first 45 minutes on the air?

Since the inception of Make-A-Wish of Minnesota, they had relied heavily on KSTP as their primary media source for promoting them. It seemed to Ken and me that all the other radio and television stations in the Twin Cities had adopted a hands-off policy regarding Make-A-Wish, almost as if they considered them the property of KSTP. We knew that they were not anybody's property but it sure seemed like most of the other media had deliberately avoided our story since we left town over five months ago.

On the day that we left, there was a press release inviting all of the radio, TV and print media to see us off. The only press that was there was the Minneapolis Star and Tribune, KSTP-AM talk radio and KSTP television. At the time, Ken and I didn't care. We were half in a daze anyway. I know that there were people in the Make-A-Wish organization who were disappointed with the poor media turnout.

As far as we could tell, KSTP was doing a tremendous job for Make-A-Wish, promoting all of their fundraising events and doing many public service announcements for them. The only problem with being almost solely connected with KSTP talk radio was that they were only reaching a small percentage of the Minneapolis and St. Paul's vast radio audience. Many, many people listened to the large assortment of available music stations. In fact, I think that most of the people in the Twin Cities area had never heard of KSTP talk radio. I had been one of them. Before Ken told me about Make-A-Wish on the Dick Pomerantz Show on KSTP, I had never tuned to their call letters at AM 1500.

As time passed and miles mounted, Ken and I started taking this lack of pledges personally. We had no idea if $10,000 in pledges was low, high or about right for the time that we had spent on the road. However, deep down somewhere in our souls we were beginning to have this nagging and disheartening feeling that the pledges on our behalf were way below what they should be.

When people would find out about our trip, their initial reaction almost always was, "What a wonderful thing you are doing for those kids!" I would always feel guilty when people responded this way. I felt like a hypocrite. I knew that in my heart, I would have taken this trip with or without Make-A-Wish. Ken was the one who convinced me that since we would be embarking on such a massive undertaking, we should at least be doing it for a good cause.

I would think of all of those kids with the life-threatening illnesses and for the parents who had to watch the child that they loved so very much suffer and struggle with their diseases. The parents couldn't feel their child's physical pain, but I could not imagine their emotional pain being any less.

I would feel compassion for these kids and their parents, but I always believed that my compassion wasn't as gut level as it should be. I think that my problem was that it was too horrible for me to even comprehend a child with a life-threatening illness and the excruciating pain the parents felt.

That all changed for me about a week ago on a call with John Rubel.

John told me that Make-A-Wish had been in contact with some good friends of mine, Craig and Nancy Campbell. They were going to be granting a special wish to their little girl, Katie, who was suffering from a brain tumor.

In the blink of an eye, my compassion reached "gut-level."

I first met Craig and Nancy about ten years earlier. We had a mutual friend who had a cabin on beautiful Lake Sylvia just west of Annandale, Minnesota. They had met each other at St. Cloud State University, and at the time that I met them, they were still unmarried. If there were ever an All-American-looking couple, they were it. Craig and Nancy would show all of us their athletic ability at the cabin by performing some great stunts on water skis.

It was obvious to everybody they were made for each other and they would some day get married, be successful and raise a family as good looking as they were.

As the years passed, their life went about as everyone had expected. At times it seemed that Craig wasn't that satisfied with his job and a couple of times he had to be brought to the hospital for stitches when he got a little nuts on water skis, but otherwise it seemed like their life was pretty darn good.

Then Katie got sick.

I had only met Katie a couple of times and their son Christopher once. I remember Katie as being a little miniature replica of her mom. It was difficult to swallow, talk or even think about when John told me about Katie's condition. My mind drifted back to those fun-filled, sun-drenched days on Lake Sylvia when life seemed so promising for all of us. But the unimaginable was happening to the Campbell family and it made me sick at the thought of how unfair life could be.

As Ken and I sat in that gas station and tried to figure out how we could raise more money, I finally said jokingly, "Let's just tell Dick on Friday that we are not coming back until we've raised $20,000 in pledges."

Ken's eyes got big and he sat up straight as a board.

"That's it!"

"What's it?"

"We just don't come back until we've raised $20,000! I love it! We'll ransom ourselves! Every Friday that we are on the radio, we will tell our listeners that we will not be back until we get more donations. From what Dick and John have been telling us these past months, we've got lots of faithful listeners and continue to get more every week. They'll be behind us all the way. I can see it now. If we get to Hudson, Wisconsin and we haven't raised $20,000, maybe even $25,000 yet, we'll camp there in the snow right on the banks of the St. Croix River and won't cross into Minnesota until we do. You can't tell me that won't generate some donations if people know that we're sitting in Wisconsin freezing our butts off. And just think of all the national publicity that would be generated for Make-A-Wish!"

Ken was really excited and his little speech got me excited. This sounded like it would work. I really couldn't see us spending the rest of the winter camped on the banks of the St. Croix River because our fellow Minnesotans wouldn't contribute to Make-A-Wish.

We got ourselves so fired up that we decided to call John Rubel right then and there on the gas station office phone and bounce this new strategy off of him.

We reached John at home. He was a little surprised to hear from us on any day other than Friday. We told John about our idea. John was extremely devoted to Make-A-Wish and would always be receptive to any idea that could generate more donations for the kids. He heard us out, but his response wasn't quite what we had expected.

"That sounds real good but what would happen if we couldn't raise $20,000?"

"We just won't come back until we do," Ken answered.

There was a moment of silence on the other end of the phone and John finally said, "We've got a Board meeting next Wednesday night. Why don't you hold off saying anything on the radio until I talk with all of the Board members?"

Ken agreed but he was obviously disappointed when he got off the phone. John did not seem to share our enthusiasm. Ken, being the eternal idealist said, "We won't say anything this Friday, but no matter what the Board says, they can't make us come back sooner if we don't want to!"

I, being the eternal pragmatist, thought that if John was a little shaky on this idea, that it must not be a good one, but I did not share this with Ken.

It was great to be sitting on the floor of our carpeted cubicle in a gas station, of all places, as Steve and I shared concerns and brainstormed about how we could generate more funds to grant wishes for the kids. It had been a tough day bicycling again as we battled the mental part of pedaling all day long. The thrill of bicycling was gone, despite the weeklong break off our bikes. But tonight our minds and hearts were really engaged as we struggled with doubts about our fundraising efforts and then got excited brainstorming ideas on how to change that.

It had started in my brother Paul's kitchen the week before, when I first brought up my frustration about our lack of increasing pledges. It seemed as if we had been stuck at around $9,000 - $10,000 in pledges for easily three months. I caught Steve off guard with my thinking, but he readily agreed with me. It was as if we were bicycling to honor the initial burst of pledges, but that we were no longer growing the pledge base. Make-A-Wish of Minnesota was expanding and growing back home and we knew that they were branching out doing multiple fund-raising events. We agreed that this was not about our egos. We simply believed that we might be being overlooked and underused. Part of the reason could have been that we were only on the radar screen for about ten minutes a week with our Friday phone call. Another reason might have been that it was tough to keep people motivated and reaching into their wallets for over half a year! But now, with only weeks to go and a physically challenging push through winter and the Midwest to get home, this was the perfect time to give this our attention.

Our minds also desperately needed to engage and be creative and this focus was ideal.

Out of nowhere, Steve laughed and announced his "hostage" strategy. I loved it! It was the perfect idea and a hugely mobilizing force for all of us with 1,650 miles to go! My adrenaline was pumping immediately.

Steve got more and more excited the more I talked about all of the positives, ranging from pledges to national publicity. He birthed the idea and then I was sprinting with it. It reminded me of his very first brilliant idea of bicycling all 48 states. I then took the same approach that I did with him back on a fall evening over a year ago.

"Let's shake on it, buddy!"

"Now wait a minute. It sounds good but I'm not shaking until I think about this a little more. What if we can't do it?"

"Out of the blocks, Steve, I don't want you to shake unless and until you are ready. This is not about pressuring you. I just believe that when you set a goal for yourself, you tend to realize it and make it happen."

I tried to calm down but I remained excited. We each only had one beer apiece to last for the entire night, and so I knew that my excitement was being induced by nothing more than a phenomenally great idea by Steve.

Several minutes later, Steve turned to me, extended his arm and proclaimed,

"Alright! We are in for $20,000 or we will sit in Wisconsin!"

We shook hands and whooped and whooped. Then ideas started to almost gush from inside of both of us.

"On this Friday's phone call to Dick, let's first thank everybody for their support up to this point and for this past year. Then, I think it's my turn this week, I will announce that the following Friday we will BOTH be on the call for the first time ever, to make a special announcement."

This was getting good. We knew we were on to something big.

Then we started to brainstorm what we could add to the mix of fundraising possibilities outside of KSTP.

"We could get a team of Make-A-Wish volunteers, our friends, family, new volunteers that could do door-to-door solicitations."

"That's good Steve. Even better yet or in addition to, our friends could bring brochures and pledge sheets to their workplace. At a minimum Lori or my dad or John could create a brochure and we could get them mailed to our closest friends and they could start displaying them at their companies."

"Perfect. You and I could even create the verbiage and mail it to Lori for example. How about local churches? We could at least have folks drop them off with a pastor or minister and leave it up to them. My gosh, we got an entire congregation out East to split a collection basket with

Make-A-Wish and the money didn't even help out kids in their own state!"

This was great. On and on we went, writing it all down. When we couldn't contain our enthusiasm any longer, we decided to call John Rubel on the spot and share our plan.

"Well, what do you think, John? Are we on to something or what? In fact, what do you think about a $25,000 goal?"

"No, no, don't do that. Stick with the $20,000 goal. Well, before I tell you exactly how I feel about this, you're not going to believe this but your brother called me today!"

"My brother? Which one and why?"

"Your brother Tom. He was in Minneapolis on a job interview. He called me up from a pay phone in a hotel and asked if there was anything that he could do to help. He said that he had talked to you recently and you had mentioned being frustrated about the lack of pledges to this point."

"Wow! That's Tom. He has always been one to speak whatever is on his mind. Yeah, we chatted briefly earlier this week. What else did he say and what in the heck did you tell him?"

"I told him that we had raised about $10,000 solely on both you and Steve's efforts and that we were really pleased and that you had been a tremendous kickoff to our nonprofit organization."

John started to laugh.

"Yes, John?"

"Well then he told me that although he didn't want to be argumentative..."

"Uh, oh, here it comes!"

"He told me that we have two guys that quit good, full-time jobs to do this, that you and Steve will be about $6,000 total out-of-pocket expenses by the time you finish this thing and that we've only raised about 50% more than your expenses so far and we're *satisfied?*"

I started laughing at my brother's machismo. God, I loved him for it.

"Finally he said that you and Steve could have kept your jobs and donated part of your salaries and we would all be further ahead by now!"

I couldn't believe it. I was so proud of Tom. Sadly, though, he was right.

"I told your brother let's then come up with a better 'count down' strategy. I agreed with him. And so I've been thinking about you guys today."

This was weird. My brother Tom, who lives in Vermont, was in Minneapolis today on a job interview, he calls John Rubel, John starts thinking about how he can better use us on the road down the stretch, Steve and I are sitting on the floor of a gas station somewhere in Florida brainstorming ideas, and we are on the telephone talking about it.

"So, Ken I have to go. But as to you and Steve and your 'ransom' idea, let me run it by the Board this week before you go announcing anything on the air with Dick. I will keep you posted on what comes out of my phone calls."

"That's okay. But for now, what do *you* think about it?"

'Honestly, I'm not sure. But we'll talk later this week. Stay excited and I promise you that we will come up with something. Nobody has forgotten about you guys."

We hung up and I conveyed everything with Steve. I was very disappointed. As much as I was glad that John was giving additional fundraising some effort and thinking, I expected him to see the big picture and the incredible publicity potential of Steve and me in Wisconsin, as the pledges exploded with tons of fresh media exposure.

It was hard getting to sleep. I was disappointed but determined. At least Steve and I were in this together.

CHAPTER 48
NEW YEAR'S EVE DEBACLE

"Be at war with your vices, at peace with your neighbors, and let every New Year find you a better man. " ~ Benjamin Franklin

IT WAS NEW YEAR'S EVE. MOST FOLKS WERE LOOKING forward to partying tonight. Steve and I were looking forward to our Friday call. Dick was on vacation but I went ahead with our scripted plan with the substitute host, Dave Hellerman.

As the call was winding down, I made our move.

"I'd like to say thanks to everyone this past year that has been supporting us and helping us. I realize that this is the last day of the year and we have really appreciated the funds, the support and the prayers that have been given to us by all of the listeners and the people supporting us behind Make-A-Wish, KSTP and the listening audience."

"In fact this past week or so while we were taking our break, some of your listeners sent us thank you cards and letters encouraging us. It has meant an awful lot to both Steve and me. It's many times very lonely out here and it feels good knowing that besides the pledges, which are going to be increasing in importance to us as we count down the way home, we are very, very thankful to the people who are pulling for us and those who have written."

"Well we're all thankful to you for going out there and doing this. Despite the fact that you are getting your bodies in great shape, and we're envious of that, I'm not sure that most of us would like to be out pedaling through 48 states because that's a lot of work! Well good luck on the last leg here and I will be mentioning the phone number for those of you who would like to pledge based on the remaining states as soon as we end our call here."

"And David I would like to just say one more thing."

"Yeah, go ahead."

"Next week, Steve Anderson and I are going to be calling in jointly with a special announcement. So, I would like all of those who are listening now, or if anyone knows of someone who normally listens to the show or has been following this Make-A-Wish Bike-A-Thon, if they would tune in next week for our announcement that Steve and I will be saying over the air for the first time."

"Thank you very much. Pedal carefully and have a great New Year's Eve!"

"Happy New Year to everyone!"

Our plan was set in motion. I was now going to get patched in to John Rubel, as was customary after our live on-air call. We were anxious for the reaction from the Board members on our new strategy.

"Hey John!"

"Great call, Ken."

"Thanks. Well?"

"Well what?"

"Don't mess with me! What was the reaction from the Board?"

My excited anticipation ended abruptly. I could not believe my ears. John proceeded to tell me that some of the Board members figured that we would still be in Wisconsin in late summer. Others did not know what to think about our ransom idea. Still others were concerned about our safety in the cold weather if the pledges did not come through. I was dismayed and angry.

"John, believe in us!" I pleaded. "Assign a committee person to head this up! I'll get back to you on Wednesday. Get us the exact pledge totals to date and let's together figure this out and what we can do. I'll talk to you next week."

Steve had heard my every word and could surmise the other half of the conversation. I was bumming but Steve was flat out shocked by the Board's reaction. He was the first to speak.

"Never in a million years did I figure this. I was sure that Make-A-Wish would get excited by our plan, that John would get pumped, call an emergency board meeting, brainstorm ideas like we did and figure out how to generate another $10,000 in pledges."

After a delicious but sullen breakfast, we bicycled side by side for a short while.

Steve sadly told me again about his unexpected disappointment. He was so sure about the board's reaction, but now that it wasn't apparently generating any enthusiasm back home, he started talking about backing off of our pledge to not come back unless we hit $20,000.

I was dumbfounded.

"How can you back off? This was your idea! *And we shook hands on it!* I will do this by myself if I have to. I won't come home to Minnesota."

I felt alone and bicycled up ahead for a while. I cooled down within only a few miles and rejoined Steve at his pace. He immediately apologized and I quickly added my own apology for being so brash with my comments.

Steve later reminded me that we had been playing off of each other for the entire trip. He was the pragmatic realist and I was the idealistic dreamer or something. Steve figures it all out and then sets a goal and I set a goal and then figure it all out. Maybe that's a major reason why we got along so easily. We did approach things differently and I knew that our styles complimented each other very, very well.

We relaxed and agreed that it wasn't worth getting angry over. We had both been getting miffed at each other on this one but then we very quickly realized that if we were not on the same page, then who in the heck else was there? We were all we had out here! We usually thought like one person so on this idea we decided to shake it off for now.

We let it go for today.

We celebrated a "wild" New Year's Eve with Steve's first pizza of the entire trip! That's pretty much a colitis no-no, but with him feeling so healthy and counting down the days, we splurged with a motel room, two pizzas and a couple of brews. I called my best buds Brad and Kari back in Minnesota at midnight to carry on our New Years Eve tradition of ten years, and then went to bed.

The most incredible year of my life was officially over.

THE DEBATE ON OUR $20,000 RANSOM WAS A TIE; A DEAD HEAT. I wanted to do it. Steve did not want to do it. My bottom line was that all I needed was for both of us to be in this together. Steve's bottom line was that he needed both of us in this together *and* he needed to know that Make-A-Wish was behind us. Steve wanted us to cover our butts and was concerned about us being able to afford a stand in Wisconsin living, working or whatever if an additional $10,000 could not be raised. I believed that telling people on next week's call that we would not come home showed them our commitment, resolve, created a huge human interest story for the nation and had more impact possibilities. I enjoyed burning the bridges behind me and Steve needed a Plan B.

Steve and I continued to feed our faces at this unbelievable all-you-could-eat seafood buffet for only $4.95 each and firmly discussed our positions for an hour and a half. It was not a heated argument but it was apparent that we both felt very strongly. One of our rules of the road that satisfied us about 99.8% of the time was that we would listen to each other and "sell" our respective viewpoint or need or desire for that particular situation. Whoever did the better job of selling the other one acquiesced. It almost always worked. Not this time.

Steve and I finally agreed on the obvious; we simply approached life differently. I summed up my position as we prepared to find a home for the night.

"This is a stalemate. Let's consider this. We both want a minimum of $20,000 in the wish fund before we put Betty and Acabar into storage this winter. Let's together do whatever we can on KSTP and with every other option that we've already discussed that generates the awareness and enthusiasm to hit our goal. If we can agree on that, then I promise to let go of *your* unbelievably phenomenal idea of a $20,000 ransom!"

We were both laughing as I got my final dig in. It was, after all, his dang idea that I was defending and trying to make happen against his will!

"Perfect. I can do that. You okay with this?" Steve asked earnestly.

"Yup. Promise. Let's find a place to lay down a sleeping bag for the night."

It had been another cold rainy day in the panhandle of Florida and we were initially up for a motel. As we exited our little restaurant, we noticed that the sun was setting because the clouds were opening up.

It was a stunningly gorgeous evening. We headed for the beaches of the Gulf.

At 43.8 miles we rested our bicycles near the sand. Another .2 miles and we would have hit our third consecutive day of exactly 44.0 miles. That was a mileage coincidence and oddity. As we walked towards the water, Steve let out an almost delirious whoop and holler. He had once lived in the panhandle of Florida and he traveled back here years ago with his brother. This very beach was a part of his old stomping grounds and background for some poignant memories. He had an affinity for this area and loved the ocean and the gulf.

For the next two hours, Steve and I soaked up the sunset and the lapping "ocean" on the rocks, a mere 50 yards away. We talked about our dreams for the future and our mistakes of the past. There was no hotel in the world that we would rather have stayed in. Finally, we rolled out our sleeping bags in the sand and slept under the stars of Florida.

CHAPTER 49
OUR FINAL PUSH NORTH & GOODBYE TO WARM TEMPS

"Never go on trips with anyone you do not love." ~ **Ernest Hemmingway**

"I'VE MADE MY PEACE. YOUR TURN TO SAY GOODBYE AND then we go," I said to Steve. We had bicycled to the little town of Navarre, Florida, where we were saying goodbye to the Gulf of Mexico. It was literally a sacred experience. It certainly was bitter/sweet. We were also officially turning our bicycles north for the final push home.

I had gotten there first. It was already a spectacularly beautiful morning, highlighted by a rare appearance by the sun that was warming the day by 9 AM. I walked to the ocean's edge and took a few pictures. After Steve and I met up back on the road, I followed Steve down for a final look, smell and experience. We did not say a single word to each other. As we slowly walked back to our bikes, Steve finally spoke.

"Are you ready to bust up the middle of this unbelievable country of ours, explode through snow and ice and grab nine more borders for the kids?"

All I could do was smile my approval and point my bike north with the morning sun over my right shoulder for the first time in months.

I WAS STANDING BY MY BICYCLE OUTSIDE OF A GAS STATION and convenience store in Allentown, Florida, munching on a candy bar. A farmer in his mid 60s pulled up in his old blue Ford pickup. I could tell the minute he came to a stop that our loaded bikes had caught his attention.

"Where y'all headed on them bikes?" he asked

"Minnesota."

"Why?"

His very simple but straightforward question made me laugh. I was used to questions like, "Wow! You mean that you're gonna ride that bike all that way?" or "Are you two nuts?"

But this farmer in the crusty bib overalls and camouflaged hunter's cap had reduced all the possible questions we were used to into a single word, "Why?"

My explanation as to why we were doing this left him shaking his head. I wasn't sure if he was impressed or if he thought we were unbelievably stupid.

"Where do y'all sleep at night?"

Oh how I continued to love openings like this. It was like having a potential office supplies customer asking me, "What do I have to do to establish an open account with you?"

"Basically anywhere we can find a roof over our heads," I answered.

"Do you know of any place nearby where we could stay for the night?"

"My name's Earl. I've got a farm about ten miles up the road. You guys are welcome to stay in my barn."

We had stayed in a few barns on this trip, so I had a picture in my mind of spreading my sleeping bag out and over a soft bed of hay again and getting a rare good night's sleep.

"That sounds perfect!"

He gave us directions on how to get to his farm. Fortunately it was on the exact same route we were planning to travel anyway. We quickly grabbed some supper, a typical convenience store meal for our night in the barn. Ken bought a can of beans, a bag of Fritos, a quart of orange juice and a little pecan pie. I bought a can of sardines, a bag of Doritos and one beer. This may not have sounded very exciting back home to us, but after a long day of bicycling these really were two delicious meals!

Earl met us in front of his house and told us to be sure to come and ask him if we needed anything. It was a big red barn, basically no different than most of the barns I had seen over the past 8,400 miles except for one thing. It only had two bales of hay. I felt like going back to his house and taking him up on his offer and asking him for more hay.

My vision of having a warm, cozy barn with lots of soft hay had burst. The barn had a dirt floor, a few scattered farm implements, an old pick-up topper set up on blocks and those two lonely bales of hay. If we had broken the bales apart and spread the straw out it would have made plenty of bedding for the both of us. We were pretty sure that our host would not like us to spread his straw all over the floor. He had been kind enough to offer this shelter to us and since we thought it would be rude to ask him for anything else, we made an executive decision. We flipped a coin to see which one of us would get to sleep on the hay bales. The loser would have to sleep on the dirt floor.

I won. Or so I thought.

The hay bales set end to end were just barely wide enough for my body to fit on and just short enough for my head to hang over one end and my feet to hang over the other end. My victory was not as sweet as

I thought it would be.

I couldn't help but laugh as I watched Ken spread his tent out on the dirt and lay his sleeping bag on top of that. When he was finally settled in for the night I snickered gleefully, "Goodnight Pigpen."

"Anderson, I may wake up covered in dirt tomorrow, but at least I don't have to sleep shaped like a twisted pretzel."

It was 6:30 PM.

Neither one of us slept very well that night as I was tormented by dreams that felt too real and Ken was hacking and coughing with a bad cold. I did, however, get to enjoy Ken spending a half an hour beating the dirt off of his tent the next morning.

CHAPTER 50
THE PREMONITION WARNING STEVE'S LIFE WAS IN DANGER

"You do not know what will happen tomorrow." ~ James 4:14

"YAHOO! THIS ONE WAS A LONG TIME IN COMING, BUDDY!
Hey let's have some fun with this border shot."

It seemed as if we had been in Florida for a month and stuck on state #39. Our Christmas break had added to that feeling of not making any progress. I slept horribly last night, but today was easy on the system as it was sunny, gorgeous and we had finally broken through heading north to border #40. It was really an exhilarating moment.

"Man, it is fun bicycling again today." Steve looked really happy.

"I can't go as far as 'fun' but it is a great day." I started laughing out loud.

"You up for an even more creative border shot than usual?"

It was Steve's turn for the pose and so obviously I was the camera guy. He looked a little concerned regarding my laughing, knowing that it was his body that would be involved when I used the word "creative."

"Ah, it's not like I don't trust you after hanging out with you for 40 states but what in the heck are you thinking of doing?"

The idea hit me hard and funny. It was only a question of whether we could physically pull it off. I knew that Steve was game. He always was up for anything that would make someone laugh today or tomorrow. It was a quality that all of Steve's friends had always loved about him and one that got him in trouble occasionally when he would push the envelope to get the laugh. This one would be fun and not dangerous.

"Perfect!" I yelled through the viewfinder.

"Now, 'Smile!'" He was laughing at my ridiculous request in his particular posing position.

As he climbed down from the border sign, we were both laughing hard at our own joke.

"I am already thinking about how I will set this up when I do a slide show. This will be a riot!"

Bicycling our first miles in Alabama, an uneasy feeling swept over me. I vividly remembered that I was given a specific warning about potential danger in this state.

Our first night in Gainesville, we went to Paul's office Christmas party. Late that evening we were sitting at a piano bar listening to the piano player as he took requests from everyone around him. I was seated next to his wife who struck up a conversation with me. She had found out from someone there that I was one of "the bike riders" and seemed very interested in what we were doing and why. During the course of our conversation she said, "You should avoid going through Alabama."

I explained to her that if my sixth grade geography teacher had been correct, Alabama was one of the 48 continental states and we had to bicycle through it to achieve our goal.

"You are going to have trouble in Alabama," she repeated again.

I was stunned to hear her say this so emphatically and so I asked her why she thought this was so. Her explanation was,

"You have this aura around you that doesn't seem right for you. I feel very strongly that trouble lies ahead for you in Alabama."

"Do you mean bicycle troubles or people troubles?"

"I mean that your life could be in danger."

I did not stick around long enough to get the details. As far as I was concerned, our conversation had dropped way below what I considered inspiring and encouraging. I wished her a "Merry Christmas" and excused myself.

I never believed what this woman had told me, but as we crossed the border I could see and hear her as vividly and ominously as the moment she said it.

"I MEAN THAT YOUR LIFE COULD BE IN DANGER."

I laughed nervously recalling the moment and then I forgot about it.

Later that night, after bicycling a strong 72 miles to Gosport, Alabama, we camped under a stand of pines next to a little grocery store. I then told Ken for the first time about the woman's premonition. Lying in our own tents talking back and forth in the darkness, it came out like one of those campfire ghost stories.

"That aura that she saw must have simply been the fumes rising off your body from rarely bathing anymore." Ken did not seem to be taking my story too seriously. I was sort of glad of that.

However, as the night wore on he admitted that when I first told him about it in the darkness, the hairs on the back of his neck stood on end.

I was getting tired. I heard Ken taping into his tape recorder about the day's events. He was up to suppertime, sharing the specifics of his meal.

"It was another great supper. I had my second can of beans in two nights, some peanuts, cheese and a V8. Steve, I don't even remember now, I think he had a fruit cocktail, some chips and..."

I thought I'd help him out. "Some dirt!" I could hear him laughing.

"...and some dirt. He's down to 87 pounds now. Even cars passing him blow him into the ditch. I'm getting worried about him."

I laughed listening to Ken ramble on and on. As my lids grew heavy, I hoped that I would at least dream about steaks and lobster.

That sure would beat a dream about fruit cocktail in a can and chips.

STEVE PULLED OUT OUR MAP OF THE UNITED STATES AND pointed to our route as three college students huddled around Steve in awe. I snapped a photo.

Today we decided that during these final days bicycling north, we needed to shoot a lot more photos of the little things that we did every day and had only been captured in our mind. Steve showing our map to intrigued local folks had transpired scores of times. Finally, I took a picture of it as it happened.

"Thanks guys. We really appreciate it."

"Well that looked great in the viewfinder Steve. Let's stay aware. Eighteen-wheelers, dogs, you and I eating out of a can, filling water bottles--all the things that we always do and see that will help tell this story. You know the more I think about it, there are hundreds of moments we've missed. I see them in my mind but I bet we would be shocked with how few photographs we've actually taken."

It was another gorgeous day. With our good morning start and the light breeze, we were hoping for a break in the hills and a shot at 70 miles or so to get us to Mississippi by nightfall. It was amazing to me how almost the moment we left Florida, we were back in new terrain with hills every few miles. The Florida panhandle had been easy to take as far as pedaling. I swear that there were days that I was in only in one or two gears from morning to night. Alabama had us back to working again and using most of the 18 gears on our bikes.

Steve was ahead of me today and moving pretty well. He told me last night about this psychic lady in Gainesville predicting some major issues for him in this state. It was a pretty creepy story in that this woman, nutty or not, totally believed what she told Steve. I had also been told at some point in the trip to be wary of rednecks in Alabama, especially because of our appearance and bicycles. All I knew from experience was that every single person that we had met one-on-one while in Alabama was about as kind and friendly to us as anyone could be.

cannot understand why anybody is satisfied with only raising about $6,000 more dollars the last five months that we've been pedaling."

I was incredibly disappointed. I was angry and did not know where to focus my anger. Make-A-Wish was growing back home. That was great. They were doing more and more fundraisers with incredible income possibilities. Local TV, radio and sports personalities were now getting involved. Super. This was never about Steve and me. But bottom line, we were 8,700 miles into a bicycle trip that had ripped the guts out of us and we felt underused and nearly forgotten this past month. We were about to fiercely battle what could be the toughest part of the trip, and nobody could get excited about the opportunity sitting right in front of them--Steve and I generating at least another $10,000 bicycling through the bitterness of winter.

We had slowly become the spokespeople for other Make-A-Wish fundraisers back home, plugging other events on our weekly calls. During this final, once-in-a-lifetime stretch drive in January, we thought that their strategy with us at least, was misguided.

"Finally I asked John for Dick's home telephone number. I really trust his perspective and I want to hear from his mouth what in the heck is going on and what his opinion is on all of this. If he really thinks that this is a bad idea, I want to know why. And if it is, then what in his opinion *is* the best way to take advantage of these final states? Remember I told all of his listeners last Friday that you and I would be doing the call together tomorrow and making a special announcement. At this moment I don't have a clue what we would even say!"

Silence consumed us both for well over a minute as I calmed down and all of this new information slowly sunk in.

"Ken?"

"Yeah?"

"This might sound like a long shot, but hear me out. What if we go on the air and ask for $20,000 or we stay in Wisconsin, but we get to the border and the best Make-A-Wish can generate is $16,432 for example. Instead of getting screwed in the snow of Wisconsin, how about you and I taking on the $20,000 Challenge personally and figure out a way that we can raise the rest when we get back? We can call on churches or businesses in Minnesota and do free slide shows or whatever we need to do to get it done."

It took me awhile to really listen to what Steve was saying. I slowly realized that I loved his idea. Bottom line, Make-A-Wish did not seem to share our enthusiasm. I chose to believe that they were simply concerned for our safety in case our pledge goal fell short. Nor was it the responsibility of our friends to make up the difference, or to go out and try to raise the funds in their respective circles of influence. This was not their deal. This was not their dream. It was ours and nobody else's.

"Let's think on this. I'll call Dick tonight and we'll get a plan together by tomorrow's phone call. As my buddy Pack Palmer always tells me, 'Never make a decision until you have to.' I think that's a Patton, Eisenhower or a Margaret Thatcher quote."

"Margaret Thatcher?"

"Oh yeah. She's known for saying lots of neat stuff. Now let's ride while we have sunlight. We need about 70 miles or we'll be sleeping in a dirt field again."

We eventually gutted out a hard day and bicycled 73 miles into Waynesboro, Mississippi. In looking at the map first thing in the morning we realized that there were no other towns within 15 to 20 miles of Waynesboro in any direction and so it was imperative that we got there before the sun went down or else we had nothing. It was a tough day but we happily made it before nightfall.

I asked the first police officer that we saw for any overnight ideas.

"Well actually boys, the churches in town pool part of their money together and put it into a fund for transients and give it to our department to distribute when and how we see fit. I can put you up in a motel for the night. How's that sound?"

I looked at Steve. As usual, I knew exactly what he was thinking. I put our thoughts into words and immediately told the policeman, "We appreciate the offer. But we're not transients or bums. We have the money for a motel but we're on the last leg of bicycling the entire country for sick kids and we are trying to stretch out our remaining dollars. All we need is a dry floor somewhere. Can you think of anywhere else we could try?"

"Honestly, no. But I'll say it again another way. We have the funds for a motel and to be honest, I'd be proud to handle that for you."

That did it. It had been a long day and we had held our ground and our pride. We checked with each other again and finally told him that we greatly appreciated his offer.

As Steve took a hot shower, I put in a call to Dick. No answer. After repeated attempts, I drifted off to sleep with the resolve to catch him in the morning and to figure this out one way or the other before we went on the air.

This money-raising thing was now more challenging than any amount of biking.

"DICK, WHAT'S THE DEAL ON ALL OF THIS? MY HEAD HURTS trying to figure out what the heck is going on back there."

It was Friday morning, January 7th, exactly 9 AM. I had hoped to catch Dick in his office before he went on the air and definitely before we called in for our "special announcement" in a mere two hours.

"Kenny, do me a favor. Call me back at 10 AM at the number I'm about to give you. It's in my office. I will be able to talk much more candidly at that time."

"I'll do it. I'm ready for the number."

I slid back to our table where Steve and I were wrapping up breakfast.

"I need to call him in an hour. Exactly how far is the next town?"

"Twenty-four miles."

"That makes it easy. Even if you sucked down that bowl of oatmeal in the next three seconds we would never cover 24 miles in one hour. When we're done here let's go meet the mayor."

We leisurely finished our breakfast and then meandered the eight blocks over to City Hall to meet the mayor of Waynesboro as we had promised our officer friend of the day before. After hearing our story last night he was excited that we meet with officials from this town of about 5,000 people.

The mayor wasn't in but several council members warmly greeted us, peppered us with questions and then introduced us to a reporter from the local paper. Keeping a close eye on the clock, I finally excused myself to call Dick at 10 AM and let Steve finish the interview. It was incredibly comfortable and efficient to be so leveraged with Steve. Today he could have just as easily been the one to have a heart-to-heart phone call with Dick and I could have been just as articulate and engaging with the interviewer. We rarely thought about how interchangeable our roles had become on this trip.

10:01 AM. I placed my phone call to Dick's office using my calling card. The line was busy. I dialed all the numbers four more times and got the same busy signal.

10:04 AM. The line was still busy. I started to panic. I imagined Dick leaving his on-air show at the top of the hour newsbreak to take my call *that I requested* back in his office down the hall. Dick would be pressed for time and the dang line...wait a minute. The busy signal was too fast. I thought that maybe it was my card, or busy circuits on this number or something.

"May I use your phone and dial long distance direct? I have someone waiting for my call and for some reason I am not ringing through. I can leave you money for the charges."

They assured me that it was not a problem.

10:07 AM. I dialed direct and it was still busy. I was beyond stressed.

I ran directly across the street and used the pay phone in the public library. The line was still producing a fast-ringing "beep, beep" tone. By the time I ran back to City Hall I knew that any possibility of talking to Dick before our big "announcement call" at 11 AM was gone. Somebody in the mayor's office made some phone calls and finally told us that sometime between 9 AM and 10 AM a construction worker had accidentally severed the long distance cable on a telephone pole. There was no long distance access for a radius of at least 24 miles from town, indefinitely!

Then it hit me. We not only could not call Dick for his advice and perspective on how to proceed on today's call, we couldn't even make today's call! Heck, we couldn't even phone anybody to alert them that we could not make the call! Someone in the office generously offered to drive us to the next town down the road and back so that we could at least make our scheduled weekly call. We graciously declined. Too much time had elapsed and we had no pre-call plan.

Steve finished his interview with the reporter and then sat down next to me on a chair in the lobby. We both took a collective deep breath.

"This just isn't happening today, is it?"

"Can you believe how excited we were in that gas station that night and today long distance phone lines are severed and we cannot even make the phone call to the radio? We haven't completely missed a phone call since we started this thing in July of last year! This is bizarre. If we were looking for a sign from God, I think he's hitting us over the head with a sledgehammer."

As we said our goodbyes to the very friendly and helpful folks at Waynesboro City Hall, one young man warmly shook Steve's hand and said, "Man, I sure wish you guys were sticking around for lunch because I'd like to buy anyone who has bicycled 8,000 miles a meal."

He then slipped Steve a ten-dollar bill and told him to grab lunch down the road on him.

His kind gesture lifted our hearts as our weary bodies climbed back onto our bikes and headed out of town. It was a very long day of bicycling after digging so hard yesterday to get our second 70-plus-mile day in a row. We were beat out and still tired in our muscles from climbing yesterday's hills, rarely stopping for breaks in an effort to get to a town for the night. We gutted out another tough 63 miles through our blues and got to our goal of Taylorsville, Mississippi.

It was 5 PM on a Friday night. It would be dark in about 45 minutes and Steve and I were up for something. A friendly-looking "big ol' boy" in bib overalls walked out of the gas station. I was more up for something to do on a Friday night than a place to stay.

"Excuse me sir, do you know where a couple of tired guys could get a cold beer and a good burger?"

"Nowheres around here. For starters, this is a dry county. You can't buy a beer or even more importantly, even have a beer on you! There's a $110 fine for one beer or $660 for a six pack!" He was laughing. I wasn't.

"No sir, we don't even have a movie theatre."

Great. Friday night on the road. Six months of rural weekends was getting old. I really longed for the cities. I was starving for the people, the energy and the options. I started to psychologically prepare myself for a can of cold beans and sleeping in my tent by 8 PM. I was really disheartened.

It was back to the basics.

"Well, then do you know where a couple of guys could safely pitch a tent for the night?"

"You can pitch it at my house. I'm about a mile from here on six acres. You guys are more than welcome. The name's Carl. I own this gas station."

We shook his outstretched hand and introduced ourselves. Steve quietly took me aside and told me that he could not imagine bicycling one more foot, much less another mile. We were floundering.

"I feel exactly the same way, buddy. I'm going to give Dick a quick call at home while we figure this out. There's a pay phone right over there."

I left Steve with Carl and walked across the street. I reached Dick and he called me back on his nickel. Initially I apologized for any concerns and confusion we caused by missing my promised call to him in his office and then our scheduled on air interview. He certainly understood as I explained the unavoidable severed lines.

"I wasn't too concerned. My first thought was that Steve was battling another colitis attack and you guys couldn't make it to a phone. He *is* okay isn't he?"

"Steve's fine."

"You sure?"

"Yes, Dick, I promise. We're done holding back the truth out here, especially with you. He's physically great."

We then chatted for well over an hour. To say that it was an eye-opening conversation would be the understatement of the year.

I sadly discovered that there were a lot of conflicts behind the scenes including power struggles and differing agendas between the management at KSTP and Make-A-Wish. A non-profit volunteer's mission and a radio station's ratings did not always mix well, despite everybody's good intentions.

"I believe that you guys should have raised over $50,000 by now. If this had been done differently and if we had used even one single hour a week on my show to implore my listeners to continue to pledge, who knows where we would be today. In fact, one week I spontaneously asked Steve to focus on a plea for pledges instead of our normal human-interest travel focus, and after that particular show the phones rang off the hook. We generated a fresh $1,500 in new pledges within an hour and I got in trouble! I was told that the spontaneous plea for pledges resulted in understaffed phones and several other problems."

"At the end of the day, I hope that you and Steve don't feel bad about this thing. The people who *do* know that you are out there admire you, care about you, are pulling for you and are pledging their money. The sad thing is just that there are so many people out there who don't know who you are and would feel positive and encouraged and inspired and would be pledging money if they did know that you were out there!"

By the time that I had hung up, my head was spinning. Our conversation certainly explained a lot of things that had been bothering us. The other bottom line was that I realized that Dick was indeed in our corner. He even told me that our ransom idea *was* a great idea. He thought that it had the needed dramatic "flair," as he called it, to generate both money and publicity. The problem with it was that the needed support to make it happen sadly wasn't there to back it up at this particular time.

I had a lot to tell Steve. But for now it was first things first. He and Carl were still talking when I got back to the gas station.

"Sorry guys. I had no idea that I would be gone that long. Just a second, Carl."

I walked Steve a few feet away.

"What are you thinking? Do you want to take Carl up on his offer?"

"Honestly, I'm not up for it. One mile sounds like ten right now."

Carl must have suspected what we were discussing. He shouted over to us.

"If you guys still want to do this tenting thing, I can throw your bikes in the back of my pickup and drive y'all over to my place."

Steve gave me a weak smile.

"Man, I think that we have to do this now. You okay with this?"

"Yeah, I'm good. I was always alright with Carl; it was the bicycling."

We drove to his house and he showed us his backyard. The three of us chatted in the dark, getting to better know each other and creating some time for Carl to better trust us.

"Hey, come on inside for a little bit. Let's all grab a cold beer."

So much for a minimum $330 fine.

The three of us sat in Carl's kitchen for a couple of hours learning about the ways of the Deep South and of this wonderful man, his lifestyle and his world. Carl was a welder, a gas station owner, a patriot and a true "southerner" in a very wonderful way.

344

Steve made a quick call from the kitchen to John Rubel back home to explain why we had missed today's scheduled call to KSTP. He was greatly relieved to hear Steve's voice as he had been really, really upset and concerned about us today.

"Dick told me today in the studio that even he was worried. "I actually called the Mississippi State Police and had them keep an eye out for you today and make sure that you were all right."

The people of Mississippi had hands down been the friendliest people statewide that we had met since we left Minnesota. Everybody, black and white, smiled at us, honked at us, waved, asked us questions and overall was welcoming and engaging. We were truly being served up some wonderful southern hospitality.

It was somehow liberating and restoring at that very moment to be sitting in the middle of Carl's kitchen sipping on a cold "illegal" beer with our new friend from Taylorsville, Mississippi.

When it was finally time to say goodnight, Carl brought us back outside. However, instead of directing us to a flat area in order to pitch our tents, he pointed at a beautiful camper trailer and said, "She's yours for the night. See y'all in the morning."

CHAPTER 52
ALONE IN A NAUSEATING SPIDER-INFESTED DUNGEON

*"Along came a spider, who sat down beside her
and frightened Miss Muffet away."* ~ **Anonymous**

"IT SURE IS A BEAUTIFUL DAY! BUT WE BOTH KNOW THAT
before it's over it is going to turn into pure and living hell!"

We were a mere 400 yards out of Taylorsville, heading west Saturday
morning after a great night's sleep. The sun was rising and it was indeed
a glorious morning. However Steve's sentiment shared with me only
seconds earlier both made me laugh and made me sad. It was true.

There was no longer any joy in bicycling.

We thought that we would regain some giddiness and enjoyment after
our Gainesville Christmas break but it was simply not happening.
Bicycling was now a chore, mentally draining and old stuff. We just
ground out the miles during the days and looked forward to our
evenings off of the bikes.

Within the hour clouds started to periodically cover the sun, cooling
down what little heat we had. Then the first drops of drizzle started.
Twenty minutes later, we were bicycling in the pouring rain. I hated it
when Steve's thoughts turned into literal predictions that were so
immediate, harsh and uncomfortably accurate.

Later that afternoon, we sat under a beat-up awning at a gas station,
quietly listening as the raindrops pelted the metal over our heads.
Sipping on two pints of orange juice, I finally broke the silence to share
something with Steve that had been building in me all morning long.

"When I first bicycled west out of Minneapolis last July, I was
apprehensive to say the least. I was full of a lot of fear, not sure if I was
physically capable of doing this, afraid of the unknown, insecure about a
lot of stuff. My biggest fear, as you know, was whether or not I could
survive 24 hours, seven days a week for a full year living side-by-side
with you."

Steve smiled.

"Today, the exact same thing is hitting me. Only this time my fear or concern is about going home. I'm good at what I do and this trip now is where I get my sense of worth and purpose. I'm all about getting the next mile, the next state line and the next dollar for the kids. As for you and me, there is no tension, despite constantly living in tight quarters and literally being forced to make hundreds, *hundreds* of decisions together. We even know when and how to back off and get out of each other's way and *not* say things. In a month or so, you're going to go head in one direction and I'm going to head off into another. I am brutally tired of bicycling and so excited about getting home, but I'm telling you, even today in this cold slop, I'm starting to understand what a damn challenge it is going to be when we get home!"

I was getting really chilly as I was soaking wet. The pinging sound of the rain on the awning picked up the pace.

"We sure do know how to do this thing," Steve replied. "I am really, really excited about being with Lori and I too am sick of the bicycling all day. Plus the snow and bitter cold is still in front of us. But as we've talked before, I will miss this. I also know that there are too many things back home that will keep us connected. Do you know what you're doing for money when you get back?"

"This will sound a little strange, but I don't. I am so focused on raising as much money as we can and seeing that Minnesota border sign that I don't know. Probably won't be a job that keeps me inside, that's for sure. You?"

"The only thing that pops into my mind these days is to get after putting a slide show together and maybe being self-employed and telling our story. I'm figuring it will all work itself out." Steve's answer was reassuring.

We were getting downright cold in the damp, chilly afternoon and we needed to bike some body heat back into our bodies. We reluctantly and slowly got back on our bicycles and headed northwest.

WE GUTTED OUT 72 MILES AND TWO MORE STATE BORDERS; Louisiana #42 and Arkansas #43. It was an ornery, nasty day that included fog, a spirit-breaking wind out of the north and in our face, and a black, savage, relentless dog that chased me for miles through puddles and over hills. After I finally outdistanced him, a semi-truck blasted his horn and then never moved over even a foot as he roared by me at 70 mph. What a jerk! I swear that I would have thrown punches at him if he had pulled over after I shook my fists at him. People were not being friendly and Steve and I agreed it was a rotten day. I was proud of both of us for persevering through 70-plus miles. However, as we pulled into Eudora, Arkansas for the night, it was about to get even worse for me.

The police in the town of Eudora were kind enough to let us stay in their jail. The officer in charge had warned us, "It's not much but you're sure welcome to stay."

That was the understatement of the year. The lock-up area resembled a dungeon. Right next to the lone jail cell that was offered to us was an old kerosene furnace, blasting out way too much heat for this small area. The jail cell itself was approximately 8' x 10' and really filthy. There was a pungent stench of urine that was almost overwhelming. I had reservations about staying here but I was reluctant to tell the officer, "Thanks, but no thanks." I didn't want him to think that I was ungrateful for the free lodging. I lost all concern for the policeman's feelings when I looked up at the ceiling. In one corner was a huge mass of spider webs.

For a person like me with a real phobia towards spiders, this was a nightmare. That large tangle of webs must have taken years and several generations of spiders to make. For the brief moment that I was able to look at it, I saw a couple of large spiders.

"Sorry Ken, but I can't stay here tonight."

"It's pretty bad, isn't it?"

"Bad? Vincent Price would never be able to think up something this awful!"

With his true adventurer's spirit, Ken stated, "Well, I'm going to stay. At least it will be something to tell my grandkids about some day."

"If my grandkids are anything like me, they wouldn't want to hear about this place anyway. I'm going. I'll call you in the morning to find out where we should meet."

I ended up in a small motel just outside of town. The first thing that I did when I walked into my room was to check out the ceilings. They were free and clear of all crawly things.

The room only cost $17 but I would have paid anything. I took a long, hot shower, then flicked on the TV and crawled into bed and then felt really guilty about my friend being in that horrible jail cell while I luxuriated in all of this bug-free cleanliness. I phoned the jail and asked for Ken.

"What are you doing, buddy?"

"Killing spiders. Where did you end up tonight?"

"In a nice clean motel room just outside of town with a great hot shower, two double beds and it's already paid for. You wanna stay over at my place tonight?"

He paused a few seconds before answering me.

"Boy does that ever sound tempting, but I better not. I just got done taping into my journal about how brave I was for staying here tonight while you ran out of here crying like a baby because of a couple of little spiders."

"Oh yeah Mr. Macho? Maybe tomorrow night you can journal about the 50 or so spider bites that you got while you were sleeping and about the spider family that made a new nest in your hair. Now take a few deep breaths of that stench and try to get some sleep."

I laughed after I hung up. Ken was where he truly wanted to be but I still felt a little sad for him.

The next morning at 7 AM Ken met me at my room looking haggard and immediately took a hot shower and burned all of his clothes. Well, he took the shower anyway and I wished that he had burned his clothes. After getting all cleaned up and looking around my sanitized and comfortable room, he smiled and said, "You sure made the right call last night!"

The warm sun hit my face. I really did feel like a free man. I had survived my night in jail. I had been colder, dirtier, less comfortable and in more pain on some nights since last July, but I had never been in a worse place. The smell of urine had kept me up half the night and I had seen several cockroaches scurrying about in the darkness. My jail cell was sleazy, filthy, nauseating and degrading. In the morning I learned that even the police did not keep prisoners in that cell overnight! It was merely a detaining area for temporary transfers. It was horrible. By the time I finished showering at Steve's motel, I was convinced that several layers of stench and grime had washed down the drain. My overnight stint satisfying the journalist in me was thankfully over. I had made it.

CHAPTER 53
WASHATERIA, DORM ROOM, FIRE STATION & LOCKED UP!

"The World is a book, and those who do not travel read only a page."
~ Saint Augustine

After breakfast Steve and I flew down the road. The wind was at our backs! We were averaging about 16 MPH and even with a late start we had 46 miles on by noon. The speed and easy riding in high gears lifted our spirits immeasurably. It was a wonderful stretch of bicycling, a morning sprint that allowed us to focus on the joy of speed, the beauty of the scenery and the smells of the country. Momentarily gone were our concerns about raising money or our desires to be home. Even partial days of a good gust of wind at our backs could be counted on two hands over the past half-year. We were flying and deservedly lost in the all too rare experience.

Late morning we crossed the Mississippi River and back into the state of Mississippi as we angled towards Tennessee. We had bicycled about ten yards past the welcome sign when a young black man on the side of the road yelled,

"How y'all doing? Good morning!"

This was uncanny. Steve and I had shared with each other on more than one occasion how we believed that the state of Mississippi had been without any doubt the friendliest people that we had met bicycling the past 9,000 miles or so. Once again, less than one minute back in her friendly borders, we were being warmly greeted. We smiled and waved back to him.

At exactly 12 noon, I experienced my first flat tire in quite a while. It eventually proved to be an omen that our day of enjoyable bicycle riding was now over.

The wind shifted and started blowing from the northwest. Miles 46 to 70 peeled off excruciatingly slowly. We were back to the pace we were used to. Our goal was the only decent-sized town on the map, the city of Drew, at mile marker 81. The last 11 miles of the day, the brisk wind now directly blowing in our faces, were as brutal as any we had experienced in over a month.

Thanks to the friendly hospitality of Captain Malone of the Drew Mississippi Police Department, Steve and I again spent the night locked up. Only this time, thankfully, it was not in a spider-infested jail cell. We were safely locked up in our first "Washateria." With a black and white TV and only one station, we wrote letters home, sad that for the first night in a very long time, all of our clothes were already clean as we slept on the floor of our own little Laundromat.

"STEVE, CAN WE PLEASE CALL IN SICK TODAY?"

"There's no one to call and no place to call in to."

"But I don't want to go to work this morning."

"Sorry, buddy. We got to get up."

It was 7 AM. As I lay there in my underwear, curled up in my sleeping bag on the Laundromat floor, I could not imagine a worse plan for my day than to get on my bicycle seat and pedal anywhere. Then I heard the key lock turn. We quickly realized that staying in our sleeping bags for even a minute longer was not an option. We were now wide awake and scrambling for a plan.

A black lady with a ring of keys was slowly entering the building. She must have been the owner or the manager and we were still in our underwear with nowhere to hide. I hoped that she had at least been tipped that we were sleeping inside with permission from the police. As soon as her back was turned, we hopped safely into our pants. If we weren't so nervous about getting caught with "our pants down" it would have been pretty funny.

We shopped at a nearby convenience store for our breakfast. Still groggy and aware that the checkout girl was watching me unable to make up my mind as to what I was going to purchase, I blurted out what I thought was an innocent observation.

"Sorry that I'm taking so long, but I'm not from around here."

Her big brown eyes rolled to the heavens as she mockingly exclaimed with a smile, "*that's* kind of obvious."

Then it hit me. Her comment had nothing to do with my inability to decide what to eat from an unfamiliar set of food selections. Steve and I sounded funny to her! To these wonderful drawling southerners with their unique twangs, we sounded like we were from a distant land. I had to laugh as this was the first time that it had dawned on me that we were actually the ones with the accents.

We headed north into a good wind for the first 35 miles. Steve called it another "Gut-out-shut-up" day. It was a perfect description as we put our heads down, focused and pedaled. Eighty miles later we rolled into the college town of Oxford, Mississippi.

Steve tried to catch the attention of some college students to inquire about overnight possibilities. Resting near my bike, I had a funny thought. We had gotten a late start, had three food stops, fought a headwind for over three hours, endured the coldest day in weeks and had to shut down at 5 PM because of darkness. Yet we still had a solid 80 miles to show for our efforts. What in the heck were we doing those first months when the sun set around 9:30 PM? We should have easily bicycled over 100 miles each and every day! We must have taken a lot of breaks. I smiled as again I realized how far we had come and how much stronger we were physically, mentally and emotionally.

Steve finally rejoined me.

"I met a jogger named Crystal. She's a sophomore, from Nebraska, a nursing student and loved what we were doing."

"Did you get her shoe size and a rundown as to what she had for lunch?"

"Stuff it, wise guy! She directed me to the men's dorms. They're close."

As we headed to the front desk to inquire about the possibility of staying for the night, the young man already knew who we were, what we were doing and told us that a reporter was on the way to interview us. He also finally told us we had a free room to stay for the night. We had been on the campus of the University of Mississippi for less than 30 minutes and the word that we were on campus had spread like a grassfire.

Tomorrow we would be finally bicycling out of the "Magnolia State." Her southern hospitality and gracious people would be greatly missed.

IN FOUR CONSECUTIVE NIGHTS WE STAYED IN A COLLEGE dormitory, a washateria, a fire station and another jail cell. Our night at the fire station in Bolivar, Tennessee was a fun one, as I held center stage in the firehouse answering scores of questions from the 25 or so volunteer firefighters around me. But this morning in Trenton, Tennessee we had our first real taste of what it would be like to be a prisoner without freedom locked away in a cell. Last night the police department of Trenton, population 4,000, allowed us to stay in our nicest jail cell so far of the trip. As usual they locked us in for our own protection. It was "lights out" at 8 PM.

Ken and I slept well. However, the night crew eventually went home while we were sleeping and forgot to tell the morning crew that we were not locked up because of any crime!

Our cell was about ten feet down a hallway away from a door that the officers used to go from the office to the parking lot. We were tucked far enough out of the way so that they could not really see us. We tried to get the attention of every single officer that walked into or out of the doorway. Our voices got louder and louder with every passing officer until one officer finally glanced our way and noticed our bikes inside the cell. He yelled to the desk officer, "Hey, who are the guys with the bikes?"

"Oh, that's right. They're just staying overnight. Let them out when they want to go."

"We wanna go!" Ken and I yelled in unison.

The officer came over with his keys.

"Sorry boys. I thought that you were in for something until I noticed your bicycles. As far as I know, we've never had a criminal locked up with his bike before!"

CHAPTER 54
OUR FINAL ON AIR KSTP FUNDRAISING PLEA FOR $20,000

*"With these changes in latitudes, changes in attitudes,
nothing remains quite the same..."* ~ Jimmy Buffet

THE TIME TO SEIZE THE MOMENT WAS TEN MINUTES AWAY. WE biked up to the two phone booths that were within a half block of each other. Steve and I had discovered them almost an hour ago in preparation for what we hoped would be our historic call together to KSTP. We each called in on our own phone lines and got set up with Dick's producer, Deb.

"Ken and Steve, as you well know, are the two bicyclists who are bicycling around America on behalf of Make-A-Wish of Minnesota…and so without further ado, we go to Steve Anderson and Ken Rogers, and for the first time we have them together; the odd couple. Gentlemen?

The call started like many of our previous exchanges with bantering back and forth, anecdotal stories about our string of strange overnight accommodations, weather conditions and travel paths, all fun and games. I was getting anxious and concerned about running out of time. Up to this point it had been Steve answering all of Dick's questions. Steve finally took some control.

"I'd like to explain to the audience too, that the reason that we did not call last week was that a construction worker cut through the long distance telephone line in the small town in Mississippi that we were in at the time. There were no lines out of town and the next town was about 35 miles away. That's why we were not on last week."

"Just a couple more quick questions. How many miles have you done since day one?"

"Since day one, we are up to 9,330 miles. We believe that we have just under 900 miles to go."

"The 9,000 odd miles have been over how many days?"

"That's been about 180 days. We left on July 20th and so on January 20th it will be exactly six months. We will be arriving home about the first Saturday in February."

"Do you know how cold it's going to be the first Saturday in February and between now and then?"

"Yeah, it will be real cold. We're not looking forward to that at all!"

Dick finally, *finally* threw out the line that we had talked about and planned together.

"Gentlemen, I am going to ask both of you to be the salespeople here and I will give out the appropriate phone number. I'd like to raise some more money for Make-A-Wish on your behalf. So why don't you, and we'll begin with Ken, ah Kenny, by the time you finish it will have been 48 states. Now there have been a fair number of people who have made pledges for the 48 states, you've got four left, you can talk about the 44 that you've already covered and the four more to go...you take it anyway that you want to take it. I will give out the phone number."

"OK Dick, thanks. I guess bottom line, during the course of the trip Steve and I worked out what we felt would be a successful pledge goal for our efforts. And that goal was and still is $20,000. The fact is that current pledges to date total just about $10,000. We're very thankful for everyone who has pledged those dollars because those have enabled us to get the organization started with the first couple of wishes but as Steve said, we've been on the road for a half a year, we're counting it down with less than three weeks to go and I guess what we're asking from everyone is this: If you've not pledged, but are hearing our voices and you've heard about the cause, I would ask anyone today to consider pledging. It's a tremendous cause; otherwise Steve and I would not have committed ourselves to a half a year on a bicycle seat. I hope and pray that people understand that every penny of these dollars does not go to Steve, does not go to me, does not go to any of the tremendous people back in Minneapolis and St. Paul who are making the behind the scenes things happen for these wishes to come true, but every penny goes towards granting a wish for a child in the state of Minnesota to come true. It's tax deductible. I guess I don't know what else I can say but that if everyone would just pledge either an amount for the states that we have crossed or about to cross, or pledge a flat dollar rate. Even a couple of dollars helps. If everyone pitches in, if everyone tells people about us being out here that don't listen to Dick's show, tell a friend and just gather around during these final weeks of an adventure for all of us, we can make even more wishes come true."

"Okay, Steve, your confrere talks a lot and he makes a good point. What else would you like to add?"

"Well, Ken pretty much said it all. I guess I never realized what a need there was back there in Minnesota but unfortunately there are more kids who are bedridden or confined to wheel chairs or hooked to life-sustaining machines than there are dollars to grant them special wishes. I never realized it myself before but there is a tremendous need there. If people could just see how happy the wishes make these kids and their families. Anybody who knows these kids wouldn't have any problem pledging some amount."

"Gentlemen, Let me take it over from there. For Steve Anderson and Ken Rogers, they are asking for your help on behalf of Make-A-Wish. We need your money. There's no other way. We can't not make the wishes come true, there are no special deals; nobody makes any money on it and if the kids are going to have their wishes come true then we need your help. Let me give all of you a phone number. Just think it through. You've heard the two gentlemen. They've made an incredible commitment; six months on their bikes, not because they're sane individuals but because they're nice people. There are people here to take your pledges. We have three weeks left, unless these guys get caught up in snowstorms. You can pledge by the state. By the time they finish they will have gone to 48 states. They are in 44 right now, 9,000 miles. By the time they finish, it's like halfway around the world. Go to your conscience. Think of your own children."

"Ken and Steve, I'm going to say goodbye but I'm going to keep you on the phone. Don't hang up. I'm going to keep you on here. I have two other individuals who are here as a surprise and they have a special announcement.

"Gentlemen, something is happening a week from tonight. What is it?"

…900 miles south of the KSTP studios in St. Paul, I was on the line in a Tennessee phone booth suddenly dejected. The wind was out of my sails. I could not believe my ears. I was listening to another Make-A-Wish promotion directly on the heels of our final push through the snow and cold to Minnesota. I listened for about five more minutes and then I slammed the receiver down in anger and resignation.

Steve walked over to me from his nearby booth. He knew that I was hot and it was time for him to just let me vent.

"I'm speechless. I really am…speechless. After everything that we have talked about with each other, with Dick with John…and in our face is this other promotion. Why didn't they simply do that at another time or on another day! I swear to God that nobody gets it. Maybe *we* don't get it. But I am beyond exasperated. I'm suddenly really tired. I just need to hold my head in my hands for a few minutes and not move or think."

Steve sat in the grass next to me and did not say one word. Several minutes passed.

"I really liked what you said, Steve. You did a great job with your part. I got a little wordy towards the end but you cut to the quick and focused on the kids and their families. It was heartrending and true. I was and am really proud of you."

"Thanks buddy. You too, though. You broke it all down really clearly and simply. You always do such a great job, 'Mr. FM-radio-guy.'"

The pay phone rang. It was somebody from Make-A-Wish calling us back with a weekly update and call feedback. I was too disappointed with the world to take it. Steve already knew that and stood up and picked up the receiver.

"Hey Joe. What's up?"

It was Joe Coppersmith, another Make-A-Wish Board member. John must have been out of town and Joe was taking his place. Joe was always congenial and engaging. I could tell from Steve's responses that Joe was reassuring him that our call went well. Finally, Steve offered the phone to me.

"I'm not in the mood," I whispered.

"Joe wants to talk to you."

I reluctantly took the receiver.

"Hey Joe. What's going on?"

"Great job today, Kenny. As I was telling Steve, the phones are ringing off the hook. They still are."

"Pledges on our behalf?"

"Heck, yes. The response has been great."

"Well, that makes us feel good. As you know we really thought this plea through and changed the strategy about every two days. I was just perturbed that they promoted another event immediately, and I mean immediately following our once-in-a-lifetime appeal. Promoted at any other time, fantastic for everybody. I just thought that we were all on the same page for a focused final push with only three weeks to go.

Joe and I talked for quite awhile. He understood our frustration and our exhaustion but better explained that there was a lot going on back home with multiple promotions for Make-A-Wish.

"Steve and I would love nothing better than Make-A-Wish generating thousands and thousands of dollars without our help. We simply believe that if there was ever a time to focus everybody's efforts and get the most out of the remaining weeks out here, now is obviously the time. Let's blow this out! Let's get all of Minnesota and the media involved."

We eventually hung up amicably. Joe seemed to be enthused and fired up by my ideas but I was no longer sure if I was making sense to anybody. There was nothing more that I could do in my attempts to influence Make-A-Wish. We were all doing what we thought was best. Steve and I would bicycle back to Minnesota and engage all of the media and centers of influence that we could on our own. I needed an attitude change. I slowly shifted my mood from being angry and perturbed to accepting things as they were.

I had been on the phone way too long. I found Steve in the gas station talking with three or four guys about our trip. We said good-bye to everybody and headed back to our bikes, formulating a plan to stop at a nearby Dunkin' Donuts a block away before getting back on the road. We were straddling our bicycles preparing to pedal when someone in the gas station called back out to us.

"Hey guys! We called the local television station several minutes ago and a reporter and a cameraman just arrived. Can you guys come back in and spare a few moments?"

Television. That got our attention. We could spare a few minutes.

"Hey guys! How are you? I'm Pamela Hess and this is my cameraman Peter. We want to do a taped interview with you here and get some footage of you bicycling down the road for a segment on our six o'clock news tonight. You game?"

We were momentarily in a city of about 60,000 people, a rarity for us to be in a city of that size, but because of their population they had a television station. We jumped at the chance to tell our story to a larger audience. It was a heartening pick-me-up.

Pamela was an extraordinary interviewer and we all enjoyed creating the raw footage for later editing. It was soon time to really get going.

"Have you guys had a good meal lately?"

"Well, we've stocked up here at the service station for some food on the run."

"I have something more substantial in mind."

Pamela left us to make some phone calls. She rejoined Steve and me and told us that she had paid for two lunches at a little restaurant called Casey Jones Village up the road in the direction that she knew we were going. We were greatly appreciative and flattered.

"The only catch is that we are going to videotape you as you bike away and then I want to get some more footage of you eating at the restaurant. Deal?"

Steve and I happily complied. Over the next few days as we bicycled the remaining miles of Tennessee, we discovered the power of television. It became almost impossible to pay for a meal, as it seemed that everybody had seen us on TV. One afternoon when we stopped for lunch at a café, a young man gathered with his prayer group slipped us ten dollars for our lunch. As we went to the cashier, she told us that our bill had already been paid by a dad and his young son sitting in the corner, two people that we had never even met!

We were now "regional" celebrities and folks talking about Make-A-Wish and granting special wishes for children were everywhere.

CHAPTER 55
TEMPS COOL DOWN, MEDIA HEATS UP & OUR FIRST ROTARY

"They are grinding out their average of 60 miles a day with a larger realization of the enormous diversity, breadth and fundamental good will of this country."
~ **Jim Klobuchar of the Minneapolis Star and Tribune**

OUR PACE GOT SLOWER AND SLOWER THE FURTHER NORTH we climbed. It seemed like a miracle that we had encountered so little snow this far into winter. The subfreezing temperatures reminded us though that it was indeed winter.

I longed for my hockey skates as we passed many frozen lakes without a trace of snow on them. This was an unusual winter. The last time that I remembered skating across a lake was when I was just a little kid with strap on double blade skates.

The frigid weather did not sap our spirit but it sure sapped our strength. Whenever we would stop for a meal, the moment that we got inside the heat would radiate from our wind burned faces, seeming to carry all of our energy out with it. Many times, whether it was breakfast, lunch or supper I found it very hard to even stay awake.

We bicycled north into Kentucky and then into Illinois. Illinois was a huge, huge milestone for us. It signaled that we were back in the Midwest and almost home. The west, southwest, northeast, east, south...the majority of the country was behind us and we were now in our own backyard.

We bicycled into Murphysboro, Illinois and spent our final two days off of our bikes with a friend. Bill Atkinson and Ken had known each other from college and from a business that they had created several years ago. They had not seen each other in years but they had stayed connected in their souls. That was obvious within minutes of observing their reunion.

I had been anxious to meet Bill. I had a picture in my mind of what he would look like based on the letters that he sent to Ken along our route. With every letter he sent Ken, he would also send some photos of "macho baldies" and "wimps with hair" that he had cut from magazines. Bill was the only man in the world that I knew that was looking forward to baldness. Ken was just the opposite of Bill and he had evidently shared with Bill the fact that he was getting thinner on top.

Bill would write Ken about how anxious he was to get rid of all of his useless hair and write longingly about the day when he would finally have a clean head and his wife could run her fingers over his skin.

I was expecting to meet a nearly bald man. What I met was Murphysboro's version of Grizzly Adams. Bill's head and bearded face were almost all hair!

"...AND TO THE REPUBLIC FOR WHICH IT STANDS, ONE NATION under God, indivisible, with liberty and justice for all."

As I sat down to finish my hot bowl of beef stew, I tried to remember when the last time was that I had recited the "Pledge of Allegiance." I glanced over to a smiling Steve. We were the program tonight at Bill's local Rotary Club meeting. This was going to be our first speaking engagement together. We were excited.

This was our second and final day with Bill and his beautiful and pregnant wife, Johna. Bill and I had connected at a Catholic retreat on campus several years ago and had bonded almost instantly. Years later I had moved back to the area to create a business with Bill where we offered interpersonal relationship seminars and classes to the college students at nearby Southern Illinois University. This was the school where he and I had met as students. Our business failed but our friendship flourished. That was the better deal! Bill was one of the better listeners that I had ever met (after my mom). He was a special friend and I was privileged to be the best man at his wedding a few years earlier. We didn't see each other that often anymore, but as great friends do, we always picked up right where we left off.

"Please give a warm southern Illinois welcome, to our two special guests tonight, Steve Anderson and former SIU grad, Ken Rogers."

I led off the presentation, informally telling our story. We only had about 25 minutes including a Q & A session. We could have shared stories for hours. Steve took over after about ten minutes and brought out our "visual aids", our maps of the trip. It was soon opened up for questions and the hands were everywhere!

"What was one of the most pleasurable experiences that either of you had on the trip so far?"

Steve immediately grabbed the microphone.

"That one's easy for me. I was in the middle of the desert of Nevada when this pretty girl pulled over to take a turn driving the car, then she hiked up her skirt and literally mooned me!"

They roared and I mean roared with laughter. I had been eating dinner with Jim, a Baptist pastor, and I meekly looked over to see what his reaction had been as a man of the cloth.

Tears were streaming down his cheeks as he too tried to catch his breath.

Later that night back at Bill's, we all relaxed as Johna made us some extraordinary homemade egg rolls and Bill completed my caloric consumption for the day by making me a great big bowl of hot-buttered popcorn. I was in heaven.

We shut it down at about 2 AM as I had promised Dale, a Rotary member, that I would do a radio interview with him at around 8 AM. The road was also calling and tomorrow we would be again heading north.

"TIME TO RISE AND SHINE ADVENTURE GUYS!" IT WAS 6:45 AM and I was not ready for Bill's chipper greeting nor for the day to begin. Steve jumped into the shower first. Minutes later the phone rang.

"Ken, you ready?"

I was still groggy, dazed and not quite fully conscious nor removed from my dreams.

"Sure, Dale. Let's do this."

My instincts were taking over. I was not even awake and I thought that I had another good hour before my call in radio interview was to start. I was wrong.

"We won't be live but I'm going to tape this thing and then put it on the air in about a half hour."

Before I knew what was happening, brain cobwebs everywhere, I realized that he was asking me real questions and that the tape was rolling. I literally shook my head in an effort to fully wake up and to get in the game...*now!*

Thankfully I had lived this story and told it many times to media outlets around the country and so I was able to pull off the first part of the interview without anyone suspecting that I was still partially asleep.

"We were talking last night that the same bicycles that you guys have been riding have held up for the whole 10,000 miles basically."

"We have bicycled on bikes more than anyone would usually ever do in a lifetime. The bicycles have gone through some changes. We've gone through ten or eleven tires, thirty flats, eight spokes, I went through a bicycle seat and a bicycle frame, but basically we have the same bicycles that we started off with. We've been real fortunate."

"Well, I know you're just about to get packed up and leave and I want you to keep your mittens on because cold weather is coming. If you can get to the state line before the cold front gets in there I think you'll be in good shape."

"I think we're running out of time, Dale. The cold weather is inevitable."

We wrapped things up and Dale wished us well and thanked me for taking the time.

"Ken, you should be in radio broadcasting!"

Coming from a talented man in the business for many years, I thanked him for the generous compliment. If he only knew how I sounded later in the day!

I joined Steve and Bill for a glorious and rare breakfast buffet of dry cereal. I had some Cheerios, Rice Crispies, Shredded Wheat, Raisin Bran and a bowl of Corn Flakes. I was enjoying carbohydrate euphoria.

The rest of the morning was a whirl of productive activities as we prepared to get back on the road. Bill took the notes that Steve and I had created and hammered out on his typewriter our fundraising brochure, titled "We Need Your Help!" With a photo of Steve and me on the road and about 200 words telling our story and making a case for a $20,000 pledge drive, we had a one-page brochure that we made 150 copies of and started mailing. Steve's fiancée Lori wanted 50 copies, friends Nealy and Holly and Deb and Jeff wanted another 80 copies between them. We then mailed single copies to a few of our closest buddies who had already promised to help us out.

Steve also called a couple of Minnesota radio stations without much success. Then something fun and spontaneous happened.

"Why don't you call the governor's office?" Bill asked Steve.

"What?"

"Why don't you call the governor of Illinois?"

"Now?"

"Now."

"And tell him what?"

"Tell him to meet you at the Minnesota border on February 5th! Tell him that Ken grew up in Illinois and graduated high school and college here. Tell him that there will be all kinds of media coverage there. Their egos love that stuff!"

Within a solitary minute, a crazed monster was created. Steve went nuts.

Steve called the governor of Illinois, the governor of Minnesota, the mayor of Minneapolis, the mayor of St. Paul, radio stations and television stations. If someone in the mayor's office in one city showed some interest, he would tell them that the mayor of another city had already committed. He was on fire! Then I got into the act. Steve's courage was contagious!

"Everybody else is coming!" I heard myself saying.

The response was overwhelmingly positive, exciting and hopeful.

Taking matters into our own hands, we believed that we might just pull out our $20,000 goal after all.

As we left Murphysboro, I finally broke down, spent $21 and bought myself a pair of warm boots. They were guaranteed to take me down to ten degrees below zero. The rubber boots over the sneakers just weren't making it in this sub-freezing weather anymore.

As uncomfortable as I was getting because of the cold, I couldn't help but marvel at the extremes in temperatures that we had endured the past six months. I remembered back when we were riding through Kansas on that 106-degree day. The water in my bottle got too hot to even drink. These days it was freezing up before I got a chance to drink it!

CHAPTER 56
SIX MONTHS, 9,600 MILES & GROUNDED FOR THE FIRST TIME

"All of our dreams can come true, if we have the courage to pursue them."
~ Walt Disney

MY BRAT WAS BROILED AND HOT, MY BEER FROSTED AND cold. I was in midwestern heaven. Two hours earlier we had bicycled into Nashville, Illinois, a town of about 3,000. A comfortable and friendly community, many people of Polish and German descent, I took note as to why I felt so at ease this evening. My fifty-cent beer in front of me helped my mood, as it was mighty gentle on my pocketbook, but I also knew something about this town and so many others in this part of the country.

This little town had a main street, a police station, fire station, banks, taverns, a Catholic church, a Methodist church, a convenience store that sold bags of popcorn, a café called, "Jim and Dottie's" and lots of friendly people talking about the cold weather. This was typical of so many of the towns and small cities that I had grown up in, around or traveled through in my life. Even my descendents were either Polish or German.

Steve and I were in our own backyard and almost home.

GRUNTING, GROANING AND USING MY ONE AND ONLY SPARE shoestring, I tied a square knot "securing" the muffler back to the car's frame.

"God bless you young man. You've been our guardian angel!"

I waved as the elderly couple slowly drove away in their old Ford Fairlane. I had bicycled up to their stranded car several moments earlier, as they finally realized that their muffler had been dragging possibly for miles, still connected to the exhaust piping. I had promised them that I would somehow get it off the road and tie it to their car chassis. Between the three of us, all we had was my extra pair of shoelaces. Somehow, someway, I made it work.

Steve caught up to me as they drove away.

"I am just about out of time," I told Steve. "When I contacted KROC in Rochester at Bill's, he told me to call him by 3:30 PM today. It's like 3:10 now and I need a phone. Let's get after it."

Seven miles and 25 minutes later, I found a pay phone.

"Hey, Kenny, Roger O'Day. Glad you got in. We are actually in a newsbreak. If you can hang in for about five minutes, I'll put you on the air."

Perfect. When I set up this phone call days ago, I had no idea what to hope for or what would happen. I couldn't ask for more than the opportunity than to be live on the air. Five minutes blew by.

"We have Rochester native Ken Rogers on the air. He and his buddy Steve Anderson have been bicycling around the country for the past half-year. Today they are somewhere in Illinois. What in the heck are you guys doing out there?"

I proceeded to tell our story. Minutes later, I heard magical words from Roger.

"Well, what can we do for you guys? How can we help? I guess bottom line, how can we get involved down here in Rochester, Minnesota?"

I gave him the Make-A-Wish address and phone number.

"We are going to make this fly down here in Rochester. I love what you guys are doing. Hey, is your buddy Steve around?"

"You bet.'

Steve wrapped up the call. After he hung up, Steve and I high-fived each other. We were taking some control of the fundraising of our own dream. This was exhilarating.

Incredibly pumped, Steve then called a Duluth radio station that he had previously contacted but missed the decision-maker. The news director answered the phone and recorded her call with Steve. She promised him that she would at a minimum create a PSA, a public service announcement, for the station and get the word out and our contact information telling how people could pledge and get involved. She too was very excited.

This was invigorating and eye opening. Our enthusiasm was tempered by the fact that we were quickly discovering how few people in our own state had ever heard of what we were doing. They were excited to get involved! We should have been doing this months ago. For Steve and I, so much of this trip revolved around our own personal survival and getting to the end. We now realized the stunning fund-raising potential of our adventure.

It was, however, a time to celebrate what we were doing right, not to be disheartened over our missed opportunities.

EXACTLY SIX MONTHS AGO TODAY, KEN AND I JUMPED ON our bicycle seats and pedaled west out of St. Paul and then Minneapolis. Tonight was our 185th night on the road and we had just entered the town of Greenville, Illinois, about 50 miles east of St. Louis on Interstate 70. Greenville was the home of Greenville College, a small Christian liberal arts college with about 800 students.

The campus looked like the resort ghost towns of the east coast last November. Apparently the school had a 4-1-4 schedule, first semester, January off, second semester, and we were walking our bikes towards the housing area in the middle of January. There was not a single student in sight. We finally walked up to a woman with a bucket full of cleaning supplies.

She was in her late 50s, the housekeeper with all the power today. We politely introduced ourselves.

"My name is Mrs. B. I've been here for about 40 years, as a student and now a janitor. I can get you guys set up for five bucks apiece for the night as guests. What do you want to do?"

Steve looked like he was about to say something. I cut him off.

"We are bicycling all 48 states in an effort to raise money for kids."

"What kids?" she asked.

I told her our story in detail. Tonight I did not want to spend any money.

"I lost a daughter twelve years ago to an incurable disease. She was only eleven. It was a neurological disorder. Tonight, your stay is on me."

We sorrowfully thanked her for her generosity. I had no idea that my story was going to hit that close to home.

"If I explain you guys to my boss correctly, maybe he will let all of us slide!"

She was cute and endearing. People who have suffered tragic losses always seemed to be so gentle and sensitive.

She gave us keys to a three-bedroom suite! We walked to town and got some Braunschweiger (liverwurst), a big bag of Doritos, a box of Club crackers, two bottled waters and a bag of Oreos. Not exactly a healthy supper but it was easy, satisfying and actually pretty darn tasty!

We relaxed, did our traditional workout of pushups and sit-ups, got some more phone calls of Minnesota media contacts and blissfully went to sleep.

WE WERE ANXIOUS TO GET GOING THIS MORNING. WE HAD traveled exactly 9,600 miles. As near as we could figure, we had about 650 miles to go. We also knew that we had been beyond lucky not to have encountered much snow yet, but we couldn't help but feel that we were due to be dumped on somewhere between here and home.

We just wanted to put on as many dry pavement miles as we could before the snow came.

The second that I stepped outside I realized that we must not have even opened our shades this morning. As I stared at the ground, it was obvious that it had snowed overnight.

"Piece of cake," Ken confidently stated as he walked up behind me. "We've been through more snow than this before."

It was true. Back in Pennsylvania we had ridden through almost four inches of snow. Here it looked like about only two inches had fallen overnight. We fully intended to bicycle today, until we walked our bikes out on the street. Every time that we tried to get on our bikes, they would slip out from underneath us.

Under the measly two inches of snow was a sheet of glare ice.

We hated the thought of wasting a day not riding since we were getting so close to home. We had never missed a day since we had left over six months ago because of weather. For the first time, we had no choice.

We were quite literally stranded.

In a deserted and dry town, with no TV, Ken and I hammered out an incredibly productive day back at our free suite. We talked to Joe Coppersmith of Make-A-Wish and got up to speed on their marketing efforts. Joe was trying to get a commitment for some exclusive coverage from the Minneapolis Star and Tribune for our story. If that fell through, the Board was planning on blitzing media all over the state. They were wonderfully making a great effort on our behalf! KSTP station manager Bob Oakes informed us that he had secured legendary Jason Davis of the "On the Road" series. Jason was committed to taping us on the road in Hudson, Wisconsin on February 4th. We both called several radio stations and Ken contacted the producers of the national television show, *Real People*, and submitted a four-page written proposal and immediately mailed it!

By days' end we were mentally fatigued for a change and chomping at the bit to get some miles on tomorrow. As we listened to the weather forecast that did not sound very promising, I had to write a big, fat goose egg, a disappointing "ZERO" for the day's mileage.

CHAPTER 57
KEN REPAIRS FOUR FLAT TIRES IN WET SNOW IN TWO HOURS!

"The harder the conflict, the more glorious the triumph." ~ Thomas Paine

STEVE LOOKED OUT THE WINDOW. WITHOUT SAYING A SINGLE word he started to pack his bicycle for the second morning in a row. I followed his lead. There was nothing to discuss. It was time to bicycle north regardless of what the weather was going to throw at us.

After a great breakfast we walked our bikes to the street. It was a gloomy and damp 33 degrees, with a bone-chilling breeze out of the west. A couple of inches still lay on the ground but fortunately the ice below it had melted.

We straddled our bikes and inched forward. It was slippery, treacherous, snowing and intermittently raining. As we ever so slowly pedaled down Main Street and towards the country, the road surface gradually improved.

We were moving again.

For the next four hours we tracked northward in the sloppy snow and cold. It was a tough grind but it was great to be slogging out some pretty good miles. I finally leaned down to check my odometer attached to my front wheel. "36.8 miles." We were about halfway to our destination city of Greenfield, Illinois, a town we had to make today or risk freezing, starving and camping in a snowy field. Then I saw something I had feared for a month.

"Damn it!" I screamed.

My front tire was rubbing on the ground. I had a flat! This was our first flat tire in the most inclement weather conditions of this entire trip. The snow was still steady and wet and the wind was growing bitter. Steve had been ahead of me and was now completely out of sight. Hoping that he wouldn't worry about me, I tipped my bicycle upside down on the snowy shoulder and with freezing, wet and reddened bare hands, changed my inner tube.

I bicycled to the next town of Carlinville, where I met up with Steve.

"Where've you been?"

"Flat tire!"

"Oh, no! I bet you were angry. What a day for that to happen! Well, we have always feared what would happen if we had bike problems in the wintertime. Now we know. You okay?"

"It was a pain in the butt but I made it. I'm just mad at myself for holding us up. It's getting late and we need to get to Greenfield."

Steve climbed back on his bike and we continued our day's journey. I was right behind him, when not more than ten feet further, I looked down and my front tire was about to go flat again! Only this time, I saw five or six air bubbles. I had six damn holes in my tire!!

"STEVE...STOP!"

He turned and looked at me bewildered.

"It's flat again!"

Steve biked back to me and saw the final puffs of air leave my tire in several places. He was as confused as I was. To compound the problem, with each tick of the clock we were jeopardizing a shot at our destination city where we might find a warm place to stay and some food.

"Ken, let's head across the street to that Laundromat. We can quickly dry some of our wet outer clothes and you can fix whatever is going on inside where it's dry and warm and you have some good light."

It was a great plan. Steve threw all of our outer garments in the warm dryers and I looked at my tire. It was a sieve, full of at least five and maybe six holes. Exasperated, I completely threw the inner tube in the trash. I put on my only spare in my saddlebag and Steve gave me a spare of his. Now we each had the bare minimum; the two on our bikes and a single spare apiece.

The wet snow continued its relentless shower on us as we headed out of town. Our dry clothes were quickly getting wet but they really reenergized us for a few miles. About an hour and ten miles later, with Steve about 300 yards ahead of me, I slowed to a stop.

My front tire was flat.

I screamed in Steve's direction through the blanket of snow and cradled my head in my arms on my handlebars. I could not believe that this was happening to me. I was furious. I was beat. To make matters worse, I felt incredibly guilty about being the one holding us up when we needed to get to the next town.

Thankfully Steve heard my initial scream and circled back. I changed the inner tube. My hands were painfully cold and raw. I pumped it back to 90 pounds of pressure.

Then, with Steve holding my bicycle, the tire went flat for the fourth time today. *I screamed bloody murder to the heavens!* I was beyond furious! I now replaced my entire rubber tire with an almost bare extra that I had held onto in my saddlebag and used Steve's only spare inner tube.

Steve did not say a word. It was not possible for me to be more frustrated and maddened and infuriated than at that very moment changing another tire and an inner tube in the freezing wet snow as darkness was falling.

My fourth tire changed in the wet snow in just less than two hours!

By day's end we were 75 miles closer to home, but we voted this our new "worst day of the trip." Twenty-five miles out of Greenville, in the small town of Worden, the snow and rain turned into a miserable drizzle. Despite pedaling down primarily back roads all day, there was a lot of traffic. The wind was never favorable. But the worst part of this day was that Ken got four flat tires!

With every flat tire, I could see the lines of frustration etched deeper into his face. We had both learned from similar situations that the best thing for the person not having trouble to do was to stand close by in case needed and to not say a word unless asked a question. It was painful to stand silently on the shoulder of the road as Ken knelt in the slushy snow and patched up a flat tire with wet snow falling all around.

In Carlinville we went to a Laundromat to run our clothes through the dryer. While there, Ken was telling some guy about his misfortunes of the day. The man told Ken that he was probably getting flat tires from the cinders the highway department puts on the roads during icy conditions. It was good to know the cause of all the flats, but there was nothing we could do except pedal on those roads.

The last 20 miles of the day were trouble free, but it started snowing pretty heavily. The last two miles we bicycled, we were the only living things on the road. The snow fell silently in huge flakes, completely muffling any sound our tires might make on the pavement. The moon and the stars were blocked from our view by the clouds that were dropping snow on us and there were no street lights and yet it was strangely a very bright night.

I followed Ken's lone tire tracks and tried to savor the serenity of the moment. Today was like riding through a very cold Hell, and these final miles pedaling in the peaceful, calm snow with the road all to ourselves was our r eward for surviving it.

WELCOME TO GREENFIELD. What a beautiful and welcoming sign. It had been a ferocious 75 miles with lots of strange adversity thrown our way today. As we hit the city limits in darkness, I saw light still coming from a building on the left side of the road that Steve and I desperately needed.

"Buddy! Let's check to see if they're still open."

It was a Western Auto, hopeful home of bicycle patches. One more flat would knock Steve and me off the road and into a hitchhiking mode.

"Hey guys! What can we do for you this evening?"

"Do you have any patches to repair a bicycle tire?"

"Sure do. What in the heck are you guys doing bicycling this time of year?"

I was really not in the mood to share our story. However, he had such a warm, genuinely interested and engaging way about him that I took the time to tell our story.

"Where are you guys staying tonight?"

"I don't know. Do you have any suggestions? Any place warm with a floor works for us." He had unexpectedly given me our perfect setup question.

"How about a motel?"

"We're actually raising money for kids and we don't have money to do that kind of stuff."

He handed me some rubber patches and a repair kit.

"Wouldn't you guys really like to stay in a motel with warm beds and a color TV?" He was grinning mysteriously.

"Sounds great. Can't do it."

"We'll work something out," he replied undeterred.

He proceeded to call his pastor who apparently had one of those church alliance projects that pooled money for transients and families in need. I could hear his side of the telephone conversation and I knew that we really were not interested. He then turned to me with an offer.

I listened and then politely replied, "As much as we appreciate your efforts, we really don't need any money..."

He abruptly cut me off. "I know that you don't need money but we're offering. I'm part of the congregation too. I've kicked in and we want to do this."

He made one more phone call and then came back to us. "You're all set up," he said with the biggest, warmest smile.

Steve and I humbly accepted.

As I went to hand him a ten-dollar bill to pay for my patches and repair kit, he pushed my hand away, winked and smiled. "The name's Russell."

Later as Steve and I chowed down some convenience store food in our motel room, I thanked him for his patience with me today. We also agreed that tonight's motel room was incredibly sweet and renewing after our brutal day. Then Steve brought up a great point.

"Last night stuck in our luxurious 3-room suite for the second night in a row because we could not bike on the ice, was actually stressful and definitely not enjoyable. Tonight, after battling a tough 75 miles in the elements, being here is joyful. That must be why vacations are so well deserved and appreciated after you've busted your butt for months. Great day today, buddy."

Unfortunately, we were overly exhausted and sore and consequently we slept horribly.

CHAPTER 58
CHANDLERVILLE, IL– OUR 2nd TIME THROUGH 87 DAYS LATER!

"Don't be dismayed at goodbyes. A farewell is necessary before you can meet again. And meeting again…is certain for those who are friends." ~ Richard Bach

NEWSPAPER REPORTERS CONTINUED TO WRITE ABOUT US. Occasionally we had opportunities to read the articles they had written. The word "heroes" had been used more than once. I never felt like a hero. I was just somebody living out one of my dreams of adventure. I always maintained that the real heroes were the people behind the scenes at Make-A-Wish. People like John Rubel, Joe Coppersmith, Kermath and Mary Beth Ward, Tom Reid, Karla Blomberg, Don Lee, and over 200 volunteers. Many of them were married and with full-time jobs and yet they found time in their busy lives to help some kids and families in need, free of charge.

In my book they were the real heroes.

However, in this little town, Ken and I were literally treated like heroes. On October 28 of last year, we had passed through a little town called, Chandlerville, Illinois on our way to Maine. We had actually spent the night there as well. The mayor had put us up at the town's community center.

It was 87 days later on the 23rd of January.

Our original route for biking through all 48 states looked like a big wiggly circle of the United States. Our route had changed considerably since then, especially as we headed to Maine before Florida, and now our route was like a huge wiggly figure eight! Chandlerville, Illinois is where the big figure eight crossed.

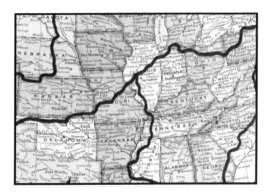

It was another tough day of bicycling, compounded by the fact that Ken had two more flat tires today. That was six in less than two days! It was a gloomy, cloudy and depressing day of bicycling. Ken said to me that he had "mental nausea." I was wishing that we were home.

However, the closer that we got to Chandlerville, the more excited we became. We wondered what the response of the townspeople would be or if they would even remember us.

As we approached the restaurant where we had eaten last year in Chandlerville, The Hitching Post, I had a strong intuition that neither of us would be paying for our dinner tonight!

The Hitching Post looked exactly the same as I had remembered. Its facade made it look like it could have been part of Marshal Dillon's in Dodge City. It looked even more authentic as we hitched up Betty and Acabar to the rail out front.

As we started to enter the restaurant, I remembered back in August we had met a motorcycle rider at the Craters of the Moon State Park in Idaho and actually shared a campsite with him. Twenty-four days later we were climbing our way out of the Boulder Dam lower basin on our way to Kingman, Arizona when we saw him again on his motorcycle. I remember him saying, "Wow, I can't believe that I saw you two again and I really cannot believe that you are still bicycling!" As we opened the door to the Hitching Post, I was expecting a similar response. We were not disappointed. Jackie, the owner of the restaurant, was behind the counter and was the first to recognize us.

"Are you guys the bike riders?"

"Yes we are! Your chili was so good the last time that we were here that we had to stop back for some more," Ken quipped.

The excitement that showed in her face was more than I had expected.

"You mean that you've been riding ever since we saw you last fall? I thought about you guys for a long while but I believed that you would have been home by now!"

"We've put on another 4,500 miles and 24 states since we saw you last, but obviously we are not home quite yet," Ken answered.

"I don't believe this! I cannot believe you guys are still riding, and now in this weather! I've got to call the mayor. He's going to want to see you two!"

She dialed the mayor at home and I overheard her conversation.

"Hello Mayor? This is Jackie down at the Hitching Post. You will never believe who's here right now! Remember those two guys who came through here on their bikes last October? They say that they have ridden 4,500 miles since then and now they're on their way back to Minnesota and they are here in front of me right now!"

She got off the phone and told us that the mayor was on his way. Then she made a call to the reporter, Chad, who wrote an article on us our first time through. I finally discovered that Chad was her nephew!

It was a festive night for us and for most of the people in the café. Our coffee, hot chocolate and slabs of pie were "on the house," and we were interrupted constantly by a barrage of questions that we did not mind answering tonight at all.

We proudly showed the people our two maps of the country. One of the maps showed the route we had taken in the last three months and on the other map I crossed out and numbered the states as we eliminated them. Illinois had been our 19th state when we pedaled through the first time. Now the only states remaining were Wisconsin, Iowa and Minnesota.

The mayor and his wife, Faye, showed up shortly after Jackie called them. It was a real kick to see them again. After Chad took pictures of Ken and me with the mayor and his wife, Faye told us that we looked a lot worse our second time through!

Men stop in Chandlerville on way across United States

Minnesota men return to Chandlerville near end of their 10,000-mile odyssey

I didn't need to see any photos to know that Ken's beard had kept growing another three or four inches and that my hair had gotten grayer. Plus the constant exposure to the sun, wind and cold seemed to have etched a few more lines and a dark brown tone to our skin. I felt as healthy as I could ever remember but I did agree that I looked worse than I did three months ago.

A reporter named Dorothy came over from the newspaper and did another story on us before we left the restaurant. Her questions were sharp and intuitive. I had come to realize on this trip that the more seasoned the reporter, the better the questions and the eventual story. It was a fun interview and one that I looked forward to reading after she mailed us a copy back home.

The mayor told us that the community center was again ours for the night. He was "the mayor" last time we were in town. Tonight he introduced himself to us as "Wayne." The uniqueness of crossing this community at our figure eight had bonded all of us to each other in a very unique and special way. This was the only town in the entire trip that we would ever visit twice.

As we headed out the door of the restaurant, the reporter Dorothy asked me, "Do you guys need anything for the night, like a portable color TV?"

"That would be awesome!"

It was a thoughtful and greatly-appreciated offer.

Mayor Wayne drove over to the community center and was turning on the lights as we biked up to the door. Dorothy drove up at the same time with our luxury color TV and two lawn chairs to watch it on! We were starting to feel like kings when the mayor then asked, "Do you guys need any clothes washed?"

"As a matter of fact…"

"I've got the keys to the Laundromat and another key to the change machine full of quarters. It's two blocks from here and I'll unlock it now for you."

After opening the Laundromat for us, Wayne made a final, incredibly generous offer.

"You know you still have about 500 miles left to go. You say the word and I'll load your bikes into the back of my pickup and I'll drive you the rest of the way home."

We graciously declined. I wondered if he or anyone else could understand how driven we were to complete this trip on our bicycles no matter what kind of weather we encountered. I was also blown away that he was prepared to drive 1,000 miles if it would help us out!

We washed clothes, cleaned up our bikes and relaxed with a little TV before taking our pick of long hardwood tables on which to sleep.

We both slept horribly. How I longed for my own bed again.

The next morning the mayor topped off his hospitality by buying us breakfast. He also made one more offer of a free ride in his truck before we left. It was funny and endearing how serious he was!

It was 15 degrees when we left Chandlerville. There was virtually no wind and the roads were clear of snow and ice. By our new winter standards it was a wonderful day for a bike ride.

As close as we could figure, we did indeed have almost exactly 500 miles left to go. We rode for 20 miles before we stopped to warm our toes and spoke to each other for the first time since Chandlerville. Ken's thoughts, as so often happened, mirrored mine.

"People like that are why I'm going to miss this trip so much."

"My thoughts exactly," I answered.

"Obviously the bad people in the world get all the press because you sure don't read about people like Mayor Wayne very often."

My thoughts and Ken's were with the people of Chandlerville for the rest of the day, and it was a very, very, very long day.

It was pitch black. The sun had set over two hours ago. Steve and I were as exhausted as we had ever been on this trip. A car passed me. He then pulled over to the shoulder in front of us. My heart started pumping as he turned on his police lights, lighting up the woods in red, blue and yellow hues.

"Good evening gentlemen."

He was stern but at first glance didn't seem angry.

"Good evening officer. What's up?"

"We've had a few complaints from motorists that have seen you guys out here after dark with no lights. They were concerned about hitting you."

"I'm sorry, sir. We're trying to get to a town of a couple of thousand people so that we can get some food and shelter and we ran out of daylight. We're raising money for kids. You'll never know how much we want to end this day too."

Steve sounded contrite, sincere and exhausted.

"Well guys, I just wanted to check on you and to remind you to wear as much reflective clothing as you can. I could see you from the back but not from the front. You are in range of Kewanee, which should work out for you. Be careful and good luck to both of you."

As he pulled away, my adrenaline and heart rate slowed back down and I could feel my exhaustion returning. We still had a ways to go. Forty-five minutes later, I saw car lights coming from both directions. I headed for the ditch in an effort to get completely off the road. Working my brakes, I looked up to see Steve ten feet in front of me, completely stopped! I squeezed both sets of brakes as hard as I could. Then I hit Steve's bike.

"Damn it!" Steve ripped his head around towards me terrorized.

"Man, I am so sorry! I looked up and there you were. I didn't have enough room to stop. You okay?"

Steve was still a little angry and a lot scared. In the dark of winter, it was almost impossible to hear our bikes moving. Sounds were muffled in the snow and cold. I had really shaken him up. This day had to end soon.

"I'm okay. Let's get to this dang town before we die out here."

After three full hours in the darkness we pedaled into Kewanee, Illinois. My odometer read 92.0 miles. It was 8:30 PM. We had been bicycling for 11 hours.

Inhaling hamburgers at a McDonald's, no place yet secured to sleep, Steve looked like he wanted to say something.

"Let's never do that again."

I weakly nodded my head. I was too exhausted to talk.

CHAPTER 59
FRIGID WINTER BICYCLING THROUGH 10,000 MILES

"Time for the weather report. It's cold out folks. Bone crushing cold. The kind of cold which will wrench the spirit out of a young man, or forge it into steel." ~ Diane Frolov

OUR ENTHUSIASM WAS GROWING WITH EVERY MILE THAT WE got closer to home. The thought of riding back into Minnesota from the opposite direction from which we left over six months ago had at times been almost a fantasy. But now we could smell the finish line.

We were trying to charge for home but the weather and road conditions were frustrating our efforts. In many of the small towns we biked through, we were reminded by temperature displays on banks just how cold it was. Every time I thought to look I would see temperatures of 5, 6 and 7 degrees lit up. Adding a wind chill factor or a bicycle ride down a hill and I'm sure that quite often we were pedaling in below-zero temperatures.

 I rode with virtually none of my skin exposed on some of those frigid days. I would wear a ski mask with just a slit for my eyes and over that I had the hood from my parka tied securely under my chin. When I put my sunglasses on, there was no part of me exposed at all.

Ken on the other hand braved the cold with just a stocking cap. His beard was so long by now that it probably provided his face with all the warmth that it needed. Any time we took a hot chocolate and toe-warming break, Ken spent half the time thawing out the icicles that hung from his beard.

"STEVE, PULL OVER AND LAY YOUR BIKE DOWN. SOMEWHERE on this last stretch of road we did it!"

He knew exactly what I was talking about. I was incredibly bummed to discover earlier in the day that my odometer had broken down for the second time in as many weeks. This day I really wanted to watch it turn over. Best as we could determine, somewhere in the last three miles, we had hit mile...**10,000!**

We hugged and danced in the sunshine. I have absolutely no idea what we must have looked like to passing motorists. But the added beauty is that they were *Wisconsin* motorists! We had also hit our 47th state an hour ago. This was a major, major, major, major, major milestone too! We were giddy with pure joy.

The Wisconsin border sign was a beautiful site earlier in the morning. It was a huge, beautiful three-color sign welcoming us to the state famous for cheese and Packer fans. It just as easily could have been two feet high, in black and white and bullet-ridden for all we cared. Holding hands and bicycling past any Wisconsin marker clearly meant that we only had one state left. Now hitting mile 10,000 was fueling our excitement.

"I imagined duct-taping an "X" on the road like we did at mile 1,000 and having stashed a bottle of champagne in my bags for this moment. Not knowing the exact spot kind of screwed that up. But I have an even better idea buddy! Let's celebrate with a brat and beer lunch!"

"Now that sounds a little more macho and a lot more fun!" Steve laughed.

Ten miles later we found a tavern serving a special of deep-fat-fried-smelt and tap beer. That would suffice as a perfect Wisconsin meal. Steve and I never had a beer on this trip before our day was done. Today we made a rare exception and enjoyed a frosty mug of Wisconsin brew with our fish. It was the perfect treat to celebrate life on the road beyond 10,000 miles and only one state to go.

While we were eating, someone called a local reporter and drove to the tavern and grill and did a story on us. The reporter, John, was enthralled with our adventure and had more provocative questions and interest than many who had interviewed us along the way. After a few photos and as

Steve and I were saddling up to go, he startled us with a final thought.

"I cannot believe that you two have not had more national press! This is a great, great story on so many levels. In fact if you don't mind, a friend of mine owns a chain of small newspapers that cover the Twin Cities metro and I'm going to give him a heads up and see too if he can meet you at the border."

We thanked him profusely. Steve and I were on top of our world.

We ended our spectacular day in Platteville, Wisconsin at the University of Wisconsin – Platteville. We spent the night with the hilarious Stuart Johnston, who generously shared his dorm room with us. He was quite a character who had us laughing so hard we were often crying. I topped an almost perfect day with a bear hug from my special cousin, Linda Rogalinski, my Godfather Uncle Bob's only daughter, who went to college here. I had known and loved my little cousin since she was born, but on campus, I discovered a beautiful adult woman, an intelligent, free spirit who was fun and great to relate to. We enjoyed a long two-hour conversation before I had to get to sleep back at my dorm room. It had been an emotionally wonderful and yet exhausting day.

"WE'LL SEE YOU AT THE BORDER IN EIGHT DAYS, LEE!"

I was wrapping up our weekly KSTP Friday call with Make-A-Wish Board member, Don Lee. We had never talked much, but as with the other Board members, he was a selfless, genuine and encouraging guy. We were looking forward to a hug from him after we crossed into Minnesota next Saturday.

"I can't do it."

"What do you mean, 'you can't do it?'"

I'm on the team that's doing a wish that day. Steve's told you about little Katie Campbell, right?"

"Yeah, he did. The trip and the fundraising have gotten really personal for him since he found out that news. It really sucks. How is she doing?"

"Not well at all. Her wish is for a special birthday party when she turns six on February 24th. There are growing concerns that she's not going to make it to then. We've changed plans and are putting together a party for her on Saturday, February 5th of all days. We've got a magician, all of her friends and family and some special surprises. This is going to be a tough one."

Moments later, as I shared the news with Steve, he was really shaken. He knew Katie wasn't doing well but this downturn in her condition was a shock to him. As perfect and exhilarating as crossing into Wisconsin had been, Don Lee's news was equally devastating.

Make-A-Wish of Minnesota was a very young non-profit organization dealing one-on-one with very emotionally exhausting and heartrending situations. We knew that these were real people, but now one of us knew the family and the little girl personally. When you donate money to wonderful charities like the Red Cross or to the American Lung Association to name only two, it's hard to connect lives that you are affecting with your money. When Steve and I pedaled, we knew that with each revolution of our tires we were bringing dollars and cents to help fund special wishes for little boys and girls like Katie. It was a very emotional day for both of us. The Make-A-Wish Board was also in process of setting up an ice cream and cake reunion for the entire wish recipients to date and with Steve, Lori and me once we got back home. I could only imagine how wonderfully satisfying and humbling an experience that would be.

Steve and I rode most of the rest of the day in silence, deep in our own thoughts.

WINTER BICYCLING CONTINUED TO CHALLENGE US AS WE pedaled towards home. We gave up on taking shortcuts and stayed just on the main roads. As a rule, they were fairly dry but any time that we had to pull off on the shoulder we had to be extra cautious. They were glare ice. The last shortcut we attempted was between Viroqua, Wisconsin and Coon Valley. We estimated we could cut off five miles by taking little County Road B instead of staying on US HWY 14 and reaching Coon Valley by way of Westby. This particular shortcut was only 12 miles but it took us three-and-half-hours! The plows had not gone all the way to the surface and had left a three-inch layer of slush for us to wallow through. We spent most of the time just trying to stay on our bikes. We had to actually push our bicycles up the smallest hills and we had to pedal to get down hills. To add to our aggravation we encountered nine different obnoxious dogs that day trying to chew on our legs. By the time we reached Coon Valley we had only ridden 32 total miles for the day, but we were bushed and stayed there for the night.

IN THE MORNING OF OUR 196TH DAY WE WERE ABOUT TO
leave Galesville, Wisconsin. I was waiting down on the road for Ken who was still up in the motel room making last-minute adjustments on his packs.

I was still thinking about my phone call last night to my friends Craig and Nancy Campbell, Katie's mom and dad. Unfortunately Katie was going to be wish recipient #5 in exactly five days. They were really excited to hear my voice from the road. I eventually asked how they were all doing. They did not have anything encouraging to say except that they could tell that little Katie seemed excited about her upcoming special birthday party. My eyes were wet when I finally hit the pillow.

A car approaching from the east, slowing down noticeably as it got closer interrupted my thoughts. It finally stopped across the road from me. The driver, who looked like a salesman in his late 20s, rolled down the window and asked, "Are you one of the Make-A-Wish guys?"

I felt a rush of adrenalin as I realized that I was close enough to home now that I might be running into people that had actually heard of us.

"I'm one of them!"

"Congratulations! You're almost home. I've listened to you guys on the radio every Friday since you left."

"Well, thanks a lot! You've made my day."

As he started to take off down the road toward what was probably his first sales call of the day, he yelled back to me, "I made a pledge to Make-A-Wish, too!"

"All right!" I yelled back.

When Ken finally came out to meet me on the road he was disappointed at having missed this "stranger" who had been following us for more than half a year. It hit us both that we had been bonding with people that we did not know at all during these many months on the road through our weekly radio call in segments.

It was a great day as we plodded along slowly through Centerville, Bluff Siding, Fountain City, Cochrane and Alma. I was committing this scenery to memory. To our west was the Mississippi River and on the other side we could see our final goal – Minnesota. Yesterday we had gotten our first glimpse of our home state while pedaling just south of La Crosse, Wisconsin.

To the east of us were the Mississippi River bluffs as we biked on the flats below them. I had lived in Minneapolis for 12 years. During those years I had vacationed many times on Lake Superior's legendary north shore and had fished many of the lakes in Northern Minnesota. I had experienced all of the beauty Minneapolis had to offer and I had driven through western and southern Minnesota's farm country many times. However I had never seen this part of the country before and it was only three hours from the Twin Cities by car. I knew that I would be back here during summers with Lori to spend weekends exploring little towns and climbing a bluff or two.

Just north of Alma the snow started falling in large flakes. We had ridden in the rain on 24 different days on this trip. Our attitude on riding in the rain was unanimous; we hated it! However both Ken and I genuinely enjoyed bicycling in the snow. Snow was a beautiful sight to see and I think it made us feel like rugged adventurers. Prior to this trip I had never ridden a bike in the snow and I personally did not know of even one person who ever had either.

Ken had been riding a little ways ahead of me most of the morning. As I bicycled closer to him I heard him singing a tune that sounded like "Walking in a Winter Wonderland." When I finally caught up to him, I realized that the tune was right but he had changed the words to "Biking in a Winter Wonderland." I joined in. Neither one of us remembered any words to the original verses in the song and so we did the "da, da, dada" thing until we hit the chorus. It was a fun, stupid and spontaneous moment as we laughed, sang and talked about the day together with the snow now pouring down.

"This sure beats working for a living!" I said.

"Yeah, the pay isn't as good but it sure is more fun."

"Let's say that you're back at Starr and you pick up 3M as a new account and their first order is for 300 desks and secretarial chairs. Would you say that riding side-by-side with your buddy in the snow is more satisfying?"

"No contest. You're only talking about a $3,000 commission."

"Okay, you're in Maui sipping something with a little umbrella in it on the beach, surrounded by beautiful, bikini-clad women. Would you still rather be here?"

This time he was laughing and taking a little longer with an answer.

"Still here, buddy."

"Then let's say you're in the Louisiana Superdome watching the Vikings beating the Dallas Cowboys for the Super Bowl. It's in the fourth quarter, Vikes up by three touchdowns, the clock is winding down to..."

"Now you've gone too far. You're biking in the snow by yourself."

"I knew I'd lose you on that one!"

For as much time as we had spent together the past year we certainly had our share of deep conversations. But I would still say that the majority of our dialogues were not very serious at all. We continued to love to make each other laugh with either verbal stupidity or visual humor. That was one of the big reasons we got along so well. We both laughed and found humor in the same things.

The snow was now coming down at a blinding rate and building up on the road. Being a dry snow it was still fairly easy to bicycle through. If it got any worse we believed that the cars and trucks might not be able to see us very well. Lord knows that the last thing they would expect to see on the road in a snowstorm would be a couple of bicycle riders.

We stopped briefly in the little town of Nelson to look at our map.

"Pepin is just six miles further with a population of about 900. We should be able to find lodging there. I think it's our only real choice. You game?"

Ken smiled and nodded.

"Even in this snowstorm if we bear down and charge through it we should get there in about a half an hour. See you in Pepin."

Three miles later I was not sure that we made the right choice. The snow was now coming down in what looked like a solid blanket. Ken was pedaling right behind me when I heard him yell at me, "Wouldn't it be something to make it this close to home and then get flattened by a truck in a blinding snowstorm?"

I put my head down, did not look back and pedaled like a madman to Pepin with Ken right on my tail.

CHAPTER 60
MAJOR BLIZZARD SNOWS US IN AT THE PEPIN HOTEL

"When you get into a tight place and everything goes against you until it seems that you cannot hang on for a minute longer, never give up then, for that is just the place and time that the tide will turn." ~ Harriet Beecher Stowe

"TWO BEDS FOR TWO PEOPLE WILL BE $15."

Now that was music to our ears. We were safe, about to be warm and our total out of pocket for lodging at the Pepin Hotel was incredibly reasonable. Gutting out 52 miles in heavy snow also meant that tomorrow's bicycling goal of River Falls would be a very doable 40 miles. That was a comforting thought as we rolled our bikes into our warm and cozy hotel room, complete with two big brass beds and a color TV.

Hungry and tired, we headed down to the hotel lobby to get a feel for our options. It was a quaint little hotel on the east shore of beautiful Lake

Pepin, a lake that actually is a 15-mile-long bulge in the Mississippi River. Half of the main floor was a little tavern with a U-shaped bar and the other half was a restaurant. Upstairs were six rooms, which were normally rented out to railroad workers when they had a layover in town or to boaters in the summertime that docked their boats at the nearby Pepin Marina when they were too tired to drive home. We were very thankful that we even got one of the six rooms without a reservation.

Someone suggested that we could grab some awesome burgers with onions about a block away and so we did before retiring to our color television for the night. We were both exhausted from our snowy adventure and excited about pedaling closer tomorrow to Hudson, Wisconsin, a border town that we had been dreaming about for over six months. Once we got to Hudson we could finally relax. We easily drifted to sleep in our incredibly comfy beds with goose down comforters as it softly snowed outside of our window.

THE FIRST THING I DID WHEN WE WOKE UP WAS TO LOOK OUT the window.

"How does it look?" Ken sleepily asked.

"White."

"How white?"

"White as milk."

Quickly running out of patience with me, Ken asked louder, "How DEEP is the white, Mr. Weatherman?"

"Eight feet!"

"Anderson, if you don't give me a straight answer right now I am going to throw you out that window and I'll see how deep it is by how far your feet are sticking out of the snow!"

Ken always had a way of getting me to come to the point by threatening bodily harm. Chuckling at his latest outburst, I finally gave him a straight answer.

"I really don't know, but it looks deep."

We didn't bother to check any further or to turn on any weather reports. No matter how deep it was, we had to ride. We had made firm arrangements for almost a month now that we would cross the border at 10 AM Saturday, February 5th and meet the press, the media, KSTP followers, local politicians who might show, friends and family on the Minnesota side. It was now Wednesday morning, meaning that we had only three more days to bicycle those 51 miles. There was a time on this trip when we could have bicycled that mileage in half a day with one leg tied behind our back, but good biking conditions were almost nonexistent these days.

Depending on the weather and the road conditions, it could take us all of the three remaining days to make it to our border crossing.

Today we would have to pedal through it.

We packed up our bikes, dressed for battle in our now daily regimen of layered clothing and headed down to breakfast at the hotel. I glanced out the hotel door and grimaced as I readily saw that the snow was really coming down hard.

All eyes in the lobby and restaurant seemed to be focused on us.

"Good luck, guys. I don't know what you can realistically handle but the schools are closed in about a 50-mile radius. It's been snowing all night."

I smiled weakly at the well-intentioned middle-aged man eating his breakfast.

We ate in silence, psyching up for what could be a very tough day.

We slowly walked our bicycles to the street. The snow was swirling all around us. Both of us having grown up in the Midwest, we knew deep in our hearts what this was on this day.

It was clearly called a blizzard.

"What do you think?" I asked Steve the question, but I honestly didn't even know what I thought yet.

"I really don't know. I want to go, but...give me a percentage. Out of 100%, what's your number for wanting to bicycle out of here and attempt River Falls?"

"Boy, that's a great way to put it. I'd say, right now, yes is at about 45%."

"I think that I'm about a 40% yes. I really believe that we need a little bit more information to work with. I'm up for a good challenge today but..."

"...not for risking life and limb." I finished Steve's sentence.

We went back inside and attempted to ask people who may have driven outside of town already this morning.

After consulting with several people including calling the Wisconsin highway department for road conditions, we concluded together that it was...a day to hunker down in Pepin!

"Let's tell the front desk that we're staying one more night." The pressure was now gone and a weight was lifted off of both of us.

"Good morning Carol. Good morning Joanne. Steve and I have decided that..."

"We're already ahead of you! Several minutes ago when we saw you two discussing something out there with your bikes standing in about four inches of snow, we called the owners, Ralph and Mary Wallin, and they told me that they are picking up the tab for another night. If you want to stay, and we hope that you do in this blizzard, you can check back into your same room and it's free!"

"Wow!" After all of these months of generosity and hospitality, Steve and I were still humbled to the point that our cheeks blushed when unexpected and kind offers like this were extended to us.

"Please thank them for us. That's great and really, really appreciated."

"They'll be by later. Ralph actually is the bartender in the bar from 5 PM to close. They're both great people and involved in a lot of fundraising and cancer benefits. They've heard about you and I know they're proud of what you guys have accomplished and that you both are here in their hotel."

Unbelievable.

Later back in our room as we started to get out of all of our layered clothing, Steve stopped me with a very fun idea.

"While we're still all packed up, let's go bicycle and play in the snow and take a bunch of photos!"

"That is perfect. Perfect!" I was giddy.

The morning had us bicycling in town, taking some incredible photos and getting that stuck-in-town and cooped-up feeling out of our system. We also imagined what the roads in the country must have looked like as the snow continued to billow around us. We knew intuitively that we had made the right decision.

All afternoon we stayed in our rooms and made phone calls to the local media as well as following up with national contacts that we had initiated awhile back with the *Today Show* and *20/20*. Local television and radio sounded promising, with many at a minimum taking our information and promising to broadcast our border crossing and drive for pledges in public service announcements. Our national contacts again seemed to be elusive and slipping away; the *Today Show* producer telling me that they needed a three-to-five-week written proposal to get anything started with them.

After about three hours working the phone, Steve and I were exhausted. We were down to the wire and we had given it all that we had. I wished that I had been better informed and prepared with national exposure, but that was behind us.

At exactly 5 PM we went down to the little tavern on the main floor to meet the hotel owner and thank him for his hospitality.

Ralph was a big man with a warm smile and a hearty handshake. He was genuinely excited to meet us and bowled over by our achievements.

As he slid two beers our way, Steve reached for his pocket.

"It's on me, boys; my pleasure. I also have one of the best pizzas that you will ever taste ready for the oven when you say the word."

The rest of the evening was spent telling stories about our many adventures to the locals like Buck Hovde, a wonderful and engaging character and to our bartender and host Ralph. We played pool, savored the scrumptious food and discovered that our money apparently was no good at the Pepin Hotel. We relished an incredibly fun evening of hospitality and friendship.

My prayers as I again lay in my brass bed were for the snowplows and sanding trucks to be working as we slept. It had been a great time but the clock was continuing to count down to Saturday at 10 AM.

THE WIND CHILL FACTOR WAS 24 DEGREES BELOW ZERO. FOR the third day in a row, we were shattering bicycling weather records. The past two days, pedaling to and then being stuck in Pepin, we experienced the heaviest snowfall of the entire trip, shutting down our bicycling because of the weather for only the second time. Today, pedaling towards River Falls, we were enduring the most savagely bitter temperatures of the winter.

The wind was blowing directly at us, brutally out of the north. Steve was miserable. He was completely wrapped up for the extreme of winter biking except for a small area on his face. His sinuses were acting up; he was getting windburn and sleepy being surrounded by so many layers of clothing. He told me that he did not feel well and that he was ornery.

Every single mile was a battle today.

I was not doing much better in the stiff wind. The wind not only tried to rip the skin off of our faces, it also blew the snow out of the fields and across the highways. It was a draining and exhausting day as we battled and pedaled for 41 miles trying to keep warm and to stay on the road.

When I hit the city limits of River Falls, I looked back for Steve. Several minutes later he bicycled up to me with a huge smile. Being ornery and miserable all day, I was more than anxious to see why he was smiling unusually broadly.

"I just ran into two people who have been listening to us on KSTP since we left! The woman was walking and screamed out, 'There's one of the guys from Make-A-Wish!' She hugged me and her husband congratulated me. What a needed boost for me today!"

We biked to a Best Western and Steve marched to the front desk and immediately told the front desk our story. Although in a motel chain of this size we were not going to be dealing with an owner, caretakers Don and Ruby offered us a $30 room for only $22 and kept two free breakfasts at Country Kitchen across the street. They then asked to see our maps. They were really interested in our story. As we went to take our keys from them, they put them back on the wall and gave us another set of keys for a huge double room for the same price.

"Good luck you guys."

It really hit me for the first time later that night as we relaxed in our room. We were staying in a motel that was only 11 miles from Hudson, Wisconsin. We were bicycling back into Minnesota in a day and a half. This was really going to happen and soon!

I did not sleep well at all. With butterflies and excitement filling me up, I felt like I did as a young child trying to sleep on Christmas Eve.

We would be home in less than two days.

CHAPTER 61
FINAL ACABAR BREAKDOWN ON DAY #200

"Begin with the end in mind." ~ **Stephen Covey**

9:30 AM, FRIDAY, FEBRUARY 4TH, DAY #200 OF OUR ADVENTURE. The sun was shining, the temperature seven degrees and I was smiling as Steve took a photo of the "HUDSON 11 MILES" road sign. We had already done two interviews and we still had our last 11 AM Friday call to KSTP to do on the road. Our day of bicycling would be over by noon.

We had made it.

We jumped back on our bicycles and Steve slowly pulled ahead. About five minutes later, my bike started acting and feeling strange. I stopped, got off of Acabar and took a good hard look.

Damn it.

My metal derailleur had snapped like a fractured bone protruding out of the skin. It was definitely broken and my bike, unridable. Steve had bicycled out of sight. I took a deep breath and realized that I was not that upset. Nothing could dampen my spirits today. I just had to figure out how to manage the next couple of hours.

I put a plan together. Step #1, write a note for Steve and flag down a motorist heading north. A blue Chevy Impala pulled over to the shoulder of the road.

"Hey, thanks for stopping. I've got a buddy bicycling a few miles up the road on his way to Hudson. I have a bike problem that I need to fix back in River Falls. If you could just give him this note from me, that would be great. His name is Steve Anderson. I really, really appreciate this."

Step #2, hitchhike a ride in a truck or a van back to a bike shop in River Falls. I actually saw one in town that morning as I was heading out of town. I walked my bike over to the other side of the road, set it upside down and stuck out my thumb.

"WE'LL NOW GO TO KEN AND STEVE. GENTLEMEN?"

"Hi Dick!"

"Hey Dick!"

"Good morning guys. Steve, I'll begin with you. Where are you?"

"I'm in Hudson, Wisconsin right now. I just got here about a half hour ago, and for the first time on my trip I'm separated from my buddy."

"Are you divorced?"

Steve laughed.

"It's not that serious, Dick. Ken had mechanical problems."

"Kenny, what happened?"

"About ten miles out of Hudson my bicycle broke. Steve was about a mile ahead of me and I couldn't flag him down so I had to hitchhike back to River Falls. I'm at the Peddler Village Bicycle Shop getting some major repairs done so that I can get those 12 more miles to Hudson out of the way."

"How long do you think it will be before you rejoin your partner?"

"About another hour and a half."

"So you'll make it by tonight?"

"Oh heck yes. No problem. We gave ourselves a lot of time this week, Dick, but we didn't think that we would have to use it all. But the weather, as you well know, has been hellacious."

"What do you mean it's 'hellacious?' It's seven degrees above zero with a wind chill of one below. It's hot!"

"That's a little less than ideal biking conditions," Steve chimed in from Hudson.

"Gentlemen, how many miles will it have been by the time the both of you are in Hudson?"

"Hudson should give us 10,260 miles."

"Tell us a little more about the plans for tomorrow as you complete your trip."

"I'll handle this, Ken, for a minute..."

"Steve, I'm amazed by your assertiveness. You used to be so shy."

"I guess this trip has been a character builder in many, many ways and that's one way I've changed, I don't know." He was laughing and obviously smiling through his words. We were so excited that we could hardly contain ourselves.

"But, tomorrow morning we're going to be crossing the bridge from Hudson into Minnesota, which may be a problem. I was stopped for the first time by the Wisconsin Highway Patrol today and given a warning. If I get caught one more time on the freeway I will get a ticket tomorrow. So I have to make it across the bridge quickly! We'll be doing that at ten o'clock in the morning and hopefully everybody will be meeting us on the Minnesota side. From there, after we've said our hellos and kissed and hugged everybody, we'll ride to KSTP studios where we started last July."

"And you will be here at a reception at 1 PM."

"That is correct."

"Does it seem somewhat anticlimactic at this point?"

"Boy, I'm just numb. I really am. It's not computing yet. We've biked for so long that it's just part of our lives and hard to believe that we've gone 10,000 miles. It's just something that we've done every day, breaking it down into bits of 70 miles a day or so. I guess I'm excited. It's just like being a little kid before Christmas. I can hardly wait for the presents to be opened. So I'm excited but it's just not registering quite yet."

"Kenny, I'll ask both of you the question sometime next week, both personally and on the air, but I'll ask both of you right now. What will you be doing on Monday morning?"

I couldn't help but laugh out loud on the air.

"Well, Steve and I keep telling everybody across the country that we are going to be local celebrities one day and unemployed bums the next. We are, as Steve said, so excited about tomorrow. In fact it hit us last night; the adrenaline started pumping and we didn't sleep really well. We're just going to enjoy it all on Saturday and Sunday and Monday we will have to be making the transition back into the work-a-day world. We don't have any real set, sure plans right now but it's going to be another major challenge to get our lives back in order. For instance before I left I sold my car and all of my furniture. So it's going to be a matter of starting all over again in the Cities."

"Does it seem somewhat surrealistic from the time that you left this particular studio over six months ago when I interviewed you outside the building and now you are almost here again?"

Steve very naturally took the lead back.

"Yeah, that's about the best word that you can pick. It's 'surrealistic.' It is just unreal. You try to recapture those thoughts that you thought back in July. I remember when we were just out of town and Ken and I took a break under a shade tree. It was a hot day and we were numb that day wondering 'what have we done?' We have all these states and miles ahead of us and now…we're practically done. I wish that I could recapture those exact feelings that we had when we started just to compare the difference."

"Kenny, you've still got the 12 miles to go before you join Steve, but I'm wondering in your view what is the worst memory and the fondest memory?"

I hated questions like that when I've had no time to prepare a well-thought-out answer. It's a great question but the kind I don't do well with when put on the spot and asked in this case, to immediately review over six months of experiences in a split second. Dick's audience deserved my best shot.

"That's difficult. The worst memory…well, Steve and I almost agree that we had one particular really, really difficult day where every single element was against us. We didn't feel good that day, it was rainy and windy and we were trying to get to a town 67 miles away with no towns in between. It was a real frustrating, maddening day. We've had some really tough days when we didn't feel like getting on a bicycle and bicycling. That, when I think over the trip, has been the most difficult element of this trip, the relentlessness of knowing that you *always* have someplace else to go seven days a week. Even when you take a break, have lunch, regardless of whether it's raining, snowing, 105 degrees or whatever, you have to get back on that bicycle and continue down the road to complete the task at hand."

"The fondest memory has been the people that we have met along the way, of which there have been so many. After a long, weary day where we are sick of bicycling, sick of talking about it, sick of everything, some kind person who doesn't know us and sees these beards and ravaged bodies and all of a sudden says, 'Come on in and I'll share my family, my food, my home, my warmth, my friendship'; there have been a multitude of those throughout this trip that have made this whole adventure the memorable experience for us that it has been."

"Steve, if you've changed in any way in six months and 10,000 miles, what would you say the biggest change has been?"

"My legs. They're pretty strong."

Dick didn't laugh but I roared. I thought that it was funny as heck after my long-winded and deep answer that Steve came back with a five-word quip that was actually pretty darn true. Of course, Steve continued.

"Before I started the trip, I really wasn't looking for any self-revelations of any type, trying to improve my character or anything about me. I was basically setting out to do something that I had never done before and to hopefully raise some money for Make-A-Wish. I guess, Dick, I probably won't know how I've changed until maybe a few days after the trip's over or something. I will tell you that it is a character builder. It makes you feel that you're pretty invincible and that you can do anything you want to if you want to do it bad enough and if you have a good enough reason to do it. Our reason has been Make-A-Wish. It's been the driving force; it really has. I'd personally like to think that Ken and I both would have continued the trip regardless of whether Make-A-Wish was involved or not but it's taken the element out that, 'Hey, I can quit any time I want.' We've never thought that all along because we've been committed to this and I think that when you have a reason like Make-A-Wish to do it for, it makes it a lot easier."

Now it was Dick's turn at levity.

"Do you remember the tarantula that Ken put his shirt over?"

"*That* was my worst experience of the trip, Dick!"

We were all three laughing over the airways from our three different locations.

"Gentlemen at ten o'clock in the morning you will be at the border and we hope that everybody will come out to meet you."

"Dick, are you going to be out there on a bicycle with us?" I interrupted.

"Not on a bicycle, no, I mean one of us has to keep the sanity tomorrow, right?"

"It's going to be a pretty crazy day, you're right."

"I hope that I will be at the reception tomorrow. I candidly did not know about the reception until about five minutes ago."

"Oh geez, well you better be there, Dick. You're going to get a big bear hug from both of us."

I was honestly starting to bum with the thought that Dick might not be there for our homecoming. He was always a part of our mission, but after seven months he was now a part of us too.

"I'd look forward to those hugs except that I hate beards."

"Well, I've got a long, ugly one, Dick. You can hardly see my face but it keeps me warm. The other thing I want to let everybody know is that we are going to be in the St. Paul Winter Carnival Torchlight Parade tomorrow night. So if anyone is unable to see us at the border or along our route back into town, please look for us at the parade in one of the first five or ten floats, as I understand it. We would really, truly love to see people who have been supporting us and with Steve and me in thoughts along the way. That would really enhance the day even more."

"Well Ken let me do it the following way. For you, be safe for the next 12 miles once the bike finally gets fixed. Enjoy the evening wherever you two are located and we will see everybody tomorrow at the border and then here at KSTP studios for the one o'clock reception.

"Finally, on behalf of Make-A-Wish, and particularly the children of Make-A-Wish, all one can say is 'Thank you.' I look forward to having you on the program. We'll do an hour together. We'll set that up later and see everybody tomorrow. Enjoy, guys."

I set down the phone at the Peddler Village Bike Shop. Then it hit me. When Dick asked me what we would be doing on Monday morning, he had given me a hole big enough to drive a truck through to say on the air to thousands and thousands of people, "We will both need a JOB!" I laughed thinking about what kind of a response we might have actually gotten.

Suddenly, an unfamiliar man briskly came around the corner and extended his hand.

"I'm sorry to intrude, but I've been following you guys since last July. I live in town here and when you said over the air exactly where you were for the call, I had to drive down here and meet you. Hope you don't mind. Just wanted you to know how inspiring you and Steve have been to me and my family and how thankful we are for what you guys did for the kids. Needless to say, having followed you these past months, we know that it sure as hell wasn't easy."

I warmly and humbly shook his hand. I have never thought, even the day before completing our 10,000-mile adventure, of Steve or me as anyone more special than anybody else. I had to admit, however, that the fact that we had inspired or encouraged anybody was very, very satisfying.

"She's ready to go!"

I admired the shiny, new derailleur installed on my back bicycle wheel.

"What's the damage?"

"Parts, including a brand-new derailleur and chain total $34. Labor…free."

"Come on now," I blushed. "You've been working on this for a good hour!"

"Consider it my small contribution to the kids of Make-A-Wish."

Before I left, I asked the young man that had worked on my bike, Dan Fahs, the actual owner of the bike shop, where I could find a cheap stocking cap in town.

"Take one of these."

He showed me a wall where he had several warm, cozy stocking caps priced at eleven dollars apiece. I looked at him quizzically.

"Yes, I mean *take* one of these. Stay warm, be safe and I'll be listening and watching the news tomorrow."

The bicycle ride to Hudson was the most enjoyable and satisfying stretch of road that I could remember. The sun was shining, Steve was waiting at the Hudson House with a room already paid for by Make-A-Wish and all I had to do was pedal for about an hour and my workday was over.

When I finally bicycled up to the "HUDSON POP 5,434" road sign, I stopped, took a photo, made an audio recording, pounded on and hugged the sign and deliberately took in the moment with all of my senses. I had seen this little green and white road sign a thousand times in my daydreaming climbing mountains, enduring the desert and slicing through headwinds that blasted both heat and bitter cold. Now I was here. I could not explain this particular almost crazed moment to another human being other than Steve who would understand my euphoria.

It would have been a fun-shared moment. It was kind of funny and perfectly appropriate that we missed celebrating this milestone together because I broke something on my bike. I couldn't remember Steve having so much as a broken spoke on this entire trip! His FUJI AMERICA bicycle should eventually be enshrined!

I walked my bicycle into the lobby of the Hudson House Motel.

"Hello! I'm looking for Steve Anderson. What room is he staying in?"

"He's in room number 171."

"How do I get there?"

"Should I call him first?"

"I'm staying with him. I'm the other half."

She laughed nervously. To me, a guy walking a loaded-down bike through the lobby with a beard to his knees would obviously…be nice, Ken, I reminded myself. Maybe she was just protecting our privacy. That would be a good thing.

"By the way, congratulations!"

"Thank you." I immediately regretted my initial poor opinion of her.

I opened the door to room 171 to a relaxed and giddy Steve. It was fun for us to compare notes over the past few hours. Everything now seemed to be happening at an almost warped speed.

I discovered that Steve had already received two offers from "strangers" to pay for our room, had gotten the bartender in the lounge and a businessman sitting at the bar to make a pledge for Make-A-Wish, had a newspaper reporter from the Hudson local paper coming over in about an hour and although we were sort of sequestered at an "undisclosed location," our phone kept ringing off the hook. Well-wishers were trying to drive over to see us. We told everybody that we would see them tomorrow.

Steve and I finally left the room and sat in the Jacuzzi, updating our audio log and enjoying the final moments of this six-and-a-half-month trip reminiscing together. We both knew that tomorrow we would be going our separate ways and our lives would be heading in different directions.

We relaxed, had a leisurely supper and relived several trip memories, both exhilarating and painful.

We tried unsuccessfully to get a good night's sleep.

CHAPTER 62
STATE POLICE ESCORT US TO A TRIUMPHANT HOMECOMING

"Now this is not the end. It is not even the beginning of the end. But it is, perhaps, the end of the beginning." ~ **Winston Churchill**

I WOKE UP AFTER TOSSING AND TURNING MOST OF THE NIGHT. The electricity was definitely in the air as I grabbed my audio tape recorder. I imitated the legendary Ray Scott of Twins, Vikings and Packers fame, as I talked into the microphone.

"Day #201, Saturday, February 5, 8:07:44 AM. We are now under two hours. You are hearing the remaining sounds of Steve, in the shower. I am combing my hair and waiting for the Wisconsin State Highway Patrol to call me about a possible police escort in this morning. It's all systems go now! The day we've been shooting for, for a long, long, long time is finally here."

I showered, dressed and packed up my bike. I am not sure if I had ever been a combination of this nervous and excited in my life. Eventually I reached for my tape recorder again to document the moment.

"It is now 9:40:25. We're getting close now."

I was definitely too nervous to do any more structured "record keeping." It would soon be time to turn the tape recorder on, let it record whatever was happening and for me and Steve to simply get caught up in the moment. I took a final photo of Steve's watch.

Zipping up my last pannier, I looked over to Steve. He was always ready to go before I was and so I smiled to myself wondering why this day should be any different. He flashed a huge smile and spoke first.

"You ready to do this, buddy?"

We both knew that we were probably experiencing our last alone moment of the trip and definitely the final minute of any kind of serenity and calm. Once Steve opened that motel door that led to the lobby it was all going to instantly change.

I walked Acabar the few feet over to Betty and Steve and extended my hand.

"I'm as ready as I will ever be. Just want you to know how proud I am of you."

This had all the earmarks of a sentimental and possibly mushy moment. Steve and I were always clear about our deep and growing friendship and for a couple of guys, we articulated that love to each other really well. Intuitively we knew now was not the time. There really was nothing else to say. Plus, our emotions were raw and our nerves off the chart. It was simply time to go.

"I'm darn proud of you too, Ken. Let's go finish this thing."

With a firm handshake and a more determined look than relief or joy, Steve opened the door. We were still in Wisconsin and not in Minnesota. It was indeed time for us to pedal the highway and finish what we had started.

The decibel level in the lobby was escalating as we hit it. Reporters, Make-A-Wish Board members and the Wisconsin State Highway Patrol were the first to grab our attention.

"Kermath, how you doing buddy?"

He bear-hugged me and then Steve. Make-A-Wish founding Board member Kermath Ward was a wonderful man and a joy to see.

"Great to have you guys back!"

"Believe me, it's great to be back!"

"When you said you grew a beard, Ken, you were serious!"

"Yeah, I shaved my face the day before we left and haven't touched it since."

"Well, you both look great. Seriously, you look great."

"Can I take anything for you?"

"Thanks, but Ken and I are going to bicycle the rest of the way with what we started with."

The clock was marching forward. The lobby started to spill out into the parking lot. In a flash moment, a Wisconsin Highway Patrol officer walked up to Steve and started to explain how the bridge crossing was going to be negotiated. Today's crossing between states was going to be tricky and dangerous because we would be pedaling on the interstate. We were very thankful that they were going to assist us instead of ticketing us! As I attempted to reach Steve and the officer and get filled in on the critical instructions on our imminent crossing, Mary Beth Ward, Kermath's wife and fellow Board member, came out of a small crowd and literally grabbed me. I loved her the moment I had met her over a year ago.

"Mary Beth you're a lot littler now! It's great to see you!"

She was about five months pregnant when we left and now she had a little baby.

"You look beautiful! You're great!"

I don't believe that I had ever been called "beautiful" in my life but it sounded great. Mary Beth was normally effervescent but now she was so excited that she was lighting up the entire parking lot.

"Has it been wonderful?"

"It's been a lot of things. We just want to be home now."

"Oh you look so good and you're so tan!"

"We call it terminal tan. I think it's just 'weathered' now. I don't know if it's because of sunshine anymore."

"You probably never looked better," Kermath chimed in.

It was time to go.

"We love you guys!" a female voice yelled.

Steve and I bicycled out to the road and got lined up with the state patrol car. He would be in back of us instead of escorting us, lights flashing, keeping us safe and alerting cars at 65 mph to avoid us on this dangerous bridge.

"Let's do it. That's it. Big border."

Steve nodded back to me in agreement.

"Let's take it slow and together," I added.

We started to pedal, side by side with the squad car lights flashing in back of us.

"We must have been gone a long time, Steve. They said we look good!" He enjoyed that one. We were about six feet from each other and picking up speed and adrenaline.

"Oh, buddy. This is kind of big! Wheels are turning!"

My audio recorder was on, picking up my every word and sound from the road. Cars were flying by us on the right, many of them honking congratulations. I started humming the theme from the movie Rocky. It was exactly 10:05 AM.

Three more highway patrol cars passed us. Suddenly it seemed like law enforcement was everywhere. I looked back at the flashing lights of the car that was escorting us. It was a dramatic, once-in-a-lifetime moment in time.

"Steve, look in back of you!" I screamed to him over the noise of the traffic.

"Aghhh! This is incredible!" Steve yelled back.

Steve was obviously as in the moment as I was. Words seemed useless in trying to describe anything.

"Geezzzz!"

"We're doing it buddy!" Steve screamed. "We're doing it!"

The next sound my recorder picked up was an unintelligible "yelp" of joy from me.

"That's Minnesota over there, huh?"

"Yup."

Unfortunately this was going to be a fuzzy border. The other side of the bridge was definitely Minnesota soil. However, there were no clear markings or border sign yet and because of the narrow shoulders and high speed traffic, no people were in sight. We kept pumping our legs. The horns of passing cars continued to beep and "thumbs up" from windows were flashed our way.

"So many times I've thought of this," I reminded Steve.

Our hearts beating wildly, the bridge behind us and we seemed to now be in Minnesota but nobody was in sight.

"I guess we just keep biking."

Pumping my pedals with my head down watching the road for glass or debris, I suddenly heard a smattering of clapping and voices. I looked up to see several people for the first time, shouting encouragement and congratulations.

"Way to go guys!"

I looked intently at the bundled-up well-wishers for a familiar face. I did not know these people. I shifted to a smaller gear and bore down as we climbed a hill.

"There's a big group waiting for you after the hill."

It was the highway patrol escort's loudspeaker in back of us. It was the first time that they had used it today.

"A real big group up there!"

I laughed at how information was being communicated to us and transferred by somebody. This was nuts.

"Did you see the 'Welcome to Minnesota' sign, Ken?"

"No!" I said disgustedly. "Back there by the people?"

"Yup."

"Darn it! Never saw it. I was searching those folks for a familiar face."

We kept grinding up the hill. Several minutes later the crest was finally only a hundred yards away.

"Is there a Minnesota sign up there, you think?"

As I asked Steve the question, we were just cresting the top and we immediately heard the hoop and hollers. Then we saw them.

"Let's hold hands!"

We held hands and screamed back at the crowd. Pandemonium immediately ensued.

As I let go of Steve's hand, I started to focus in on the sea of smiling and cheering faces.

"There's little Nealy!"

As we slowed to a stop, friends and family immediately swarmed our bikes. I lost Steve in the crush and got hugged and kissed by more people in the next three minutes than I had in literally a year. There were banners everywhere. My best buds Brad, Pack and Foge were holding my favorite,

Jeanne Palmer, Pack's wife hugged me first. Then Holly, Nealy, Deb and Jeff, our buddy Tom McNally…and oh my God, there was my boss, Fred Starr Ryan!

Fred had taken my quitting at Starr Office Services poorly. He really liked me and he was "old school," in a good way. You don't quit a good job, much less in *his* company where we were all family, as the most recent Salesman of the Year, in a recession, to bicycle around the country. But there he was, miles from his home on the west side of Minneapolis, shivering his butt off at 10:15 AM on a Saturday.

"Ken, I never believed that you would make it. I honestly didn't. But you did. And I am here at the border with a check for $100 for Make-A-Wish."

It was another in a series of unbelievable moments.

"Hi Ken, I'm Steve's sister, Jeanne. Welcome home. Thanks for taking care of my brother. Good luck the rest of the way."

"Thanks. We're almost done. Then everything's all over."

We hugged. Steve's whole family, mom and dad, sisters and brothers and their families seemed to be there. People I had never seen before in my life were congratulating me.

Somebody thankfully grabbed my camera and starting taking pictures. There were cameras shooting everywhere.

I finally caught up with my best buds, lying back in the weeds as they so wonderfully did, as all the hoopla surrounded us.

"Hi Brad! That was a great sign." We hugged and hugged.

"Good to see you! Really good to see you! Too long."

"Too long! Agreed. What in the hell is that?"

I was sure that Brad was about to give me guff about my new look, the Amish-farmer-look with a ten-inch beard. But somebody else grabbed me. I would see him later in the day and long into the night as we celebrated our homecoming.

"Which one's Kenny and which one's Steve?"

Little kids were everywhere trying to figure out what all the excitement was about.

"I'm Kenny and that's Steve over there."

"I get them mixed up," one of the kids said.

Some adult shouted, "I can't recognize them anymore anyway!"

Our appearances *had* changed. I had also lost about 23 pounds.

"Packer, Foge!" Good hugs from good buds. I would see them later too.

"Kari! Hey sweetie! Jamie, Josh! Do you remember this bearded guy?"

Kari was Brad's wife, a precious friend of mine in her own right. Their children were bundled up in the cold, Jamie, four-years-old and Joshua only two. I loved those two little ones as if they were my own. I am sure that they were confused and only wanted to be somewhere warm. Their kisses were sweet on my cold cheeks.

"Knobs! Patty! I can't believe that you're here!"

"How are you? Look at this!" My beard mesmerized Patty Knoblauch. I had had no feedback for months on my facial hair. It was obvious by today's comments that my 6 ½-month-beard was making an impression.

"That's a good looking beard, there!" Knobs, Patty's husband added.
Every time I turned around it was another wonderful friend helping celebrate an incredible day.

"Are you Ken Anderson or Steve Rogers?"

The small crowd gathered around this handsome and charismatic man laughed.

"I'm Steve's dad."

"Great to finally meet you! Steve got to meet my whole family and I finally get to meet you guys."

"We heard you on a tape you made us."

"Oh, good. I forgot about that."

"Guten Tag, Ken!"

It was John Priyatel, a fellow salesman and good friend from Starr. This was completely overwhelming. I was spending less than seven seconds with someone when another cherished soul would reach out and grab me.

"Don!"

Another fond Starr employee, Don Nash was there with his wife Karen and two little boys. The hugs were wonderful.

"Michael!"

"Good to be here, really good to be here."

I heard his words muffled by our hug. Mike Newman and I had been college friends for over a decade. I was living in his house the weeks before we left.

Out of nowhere stepped Foge.

"Welcome home, roomie. Love you."

"I love you too, bud. Thanks for making today happen."

Foge was one of my favorite people in the whole wide world. I had lived with him in college and almost up until I left on this trip and I hoped that we would bunk together again. Being around Ron was effortless. I was pumped that he was here.

I turned to my left and saw Steve hugging his great friends, Ken and Vi Lewis. Ken was in his 50s, a mentor of Steve, a colorful character and a bicycling inspiration. I had met them briefly before we took off on our trip. Ken and Vi had biked several Iron Man events, a single day event where you pedal 100 miles. That's a brutal day; I don't care how avid a bicyclist one is. He was one of the few bicyclists that I knew and he was over 20 years older than us. As Ken worked through the crowd to get to me, within earshot he turned to no one in particular and proudly stated,

"What these guys did was almost impossible!"

Seconds later Ken was directly in front of me, firmly shook my hand and looked me squarely in the eyes.

"Bottom line, you guys did what you said you were going to do. You guys are winners. I mean it. You guys are winners."

I got chills.

"Time to get going. We got to keep moving!" someone yelled.

"I'm sick of that!" I yelled in mock anger. "There's always someplace else to go!"

A little girl's voice rang out over the din noise of the crowd asking her parents the question,

"Where are they going now?"

A voice that I did not recognize, told the girl,

"They're going home. They're going home."

Pedaling back to the exact spot where we started

The St. Paul Winter Carnival Torchlight Parade

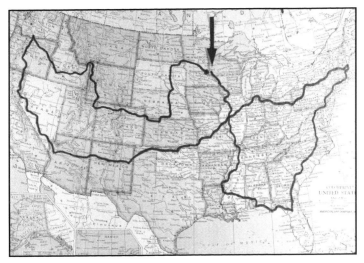

48 States covering 10,288 miles in 201 Days

EPILOGUE
ABOUT THREE MONTHS LATER

"For afterwards a man finds pleasure in his pains, when he has suffered long and wandered long." ~ **Homer**

I CRINGED. FOR THE THIRD TIME IN A ROW, THE VERTICAL SLIDE dissolved into a horizontally shot slide. What were we thinking? We obviously weren't thinking of fading images when we shot slides on our bicycling trip. I hoped that nobody would notice it as much as I did when we finally made this presentation to a real audience.

Now what in the heck was that? I turned off the two slide projectors and listened intently. SMACK. I relaxed and smiled. Only one person on the face of the earth would be doing that. I looked out the screen window of my second floor apartment over the landlord's house and into the backyard below.

"Hey you! Knock it off! It's one thing when you throw a rock and hit my screen. It's another when you hit the window! You want to get me kicked out of here?"

"Took you awhile. I'll be right up!"

I opened the door to Steve Anderson.

Steve was infamous for never doing a traditional knock on my door. Instead, he would find small pebbles and throw them at my screen until I finally noticed his smiling face. It was his signature, "Are you home?"

"Hey buddy!"

It had been over three days since I had seen him last and a handshake wasn't going to cut it. We hugged like brothers.

"You ready to get your butt kicked in tennis or are you going to whine and tell me that we have to work on our slide show? We spent about 20 hours on this last week and I'll see you again Saturday to work on the winter stuff."

"For starters if those clouds out there that smell like rain are any clue, I will not be able to kick *your* butt this afternoon, Bjorn. Secondly, I want to show you the 'I Want to Live' close with those new slides of the kids you shot at Nokomis added to the Make-A-Wish wish kids from our ice cream social last month. Other than our darn slides not being consistently horizontal, it is powerful. I got goose bumps a few minutes ago when I dissolved them with the music."

"Still can't believe that it never even entered our mind to shoot photos with the camera from the same position."

"Well, seriously, who knew? As a photographer you fill the frame. As someone trying to dissolve slides into one another, it's a different deal. You and I know as much about creating a slide show as we did about bicycling the country!"

"You thirsty? I've got lemonade, water or spoiled milk."

"Pass."

The sound of rain started to pelt my roof. It was really coming down.

"I hate you and your forecasting, Ken!"

Steve and I talked about our new places, Lori, job opportunities and life in general. We had been home for three months and yet it was still an adjustment. Steve and Lori were incredibly happy to be reunited after a half-year separation. I had been on a couple of dates, but nothing was happening at the moment in that arena. I missed being in a loving relationship with a special woman and sharing all of this with her, but at the same time I was busy trying to figure out where I now fit in the world. With Steve and Lori at least, she had been a part of this since the beginning.

Our playful, newsy banter suddenly got serious.

"We knew this would be hard Ken, but it really is tough."

"How do you mean?"

We had gone down this road before since we'd been back, but it felt like he wanted to say something else.

"Well, we've talked about the astronaut thing, adjusting to life and enduring a letdown after the excitement of a significant challenge achieved. I don't know exactly what it is. Something's missing besides the excitement and purpose."

"You and Lori okay?"

"We're doing great. We have so much fun together and, not to rub it in, but she went through this with us in her own way. I can't imagine how lonely you must feel some days."

"Thanks. I do miss you and I certainly wish that I had had a 'Lori' in my life before we took off, or even now. I'm proud of what we accomplished and it certainly would be cool to share this with somebody prettier than you. But, I'm okay. I'm just not pumped up about anything at the moment. Honestly? One of the hardest things I'm dealing with, besides my body craving physical activity and exercise, is simply being indoors. It continues to really drive me crazy."

"Isn't that the truth?"

We vigorously shook hands. I was blessed to have at least one human being who had experienced the last year with me who understood my thoughts.

The rain was softening. Out of nowhere, I had an idea.

"You trust me?"

"Duh." That meant an unequivocal yes.

I proceeded to pull up the screen window in my dining room. Outside of the window, was my very gently sloping roof over the downstairs' porch. I crawled out the window and into the rain.

Without a word, Steve followed me onto the roof.

For about five minutes, we sat in the now softly falling rain, getting soaked and taking in the smells of the buds on the trees and lilacs and the wet rain itself. Finally, Steve spoke.

"This does feel right, doesn't it?"

I looked over at his drenched hair and the water running down his happy, smiling cheeks.

"Yes it does, buddy."

Quietly and without warning, a thought filtered through to both of us. It was not a melodramatic moment, but it was as pure and clear as the water falling from the sky.

"You know…"

Steve stopped me in mid-sentence. "I know."

"Even the slides were not shot correctly." I added. "I'd hate to waste that learning experience and not be able to get it right a second time."

There it was; out in the open.

"You know what this means, don't you?"

We were in another zone.

"Yup."

We looked at each other.

"Someday, somehow, someway, we have to do this adventure thing again. No promises today. But someday."

Looking comically ridiculous as the rain continued to drench us completely, we together extended our arms towards each other.

We shook hands.

And it was good.

THE END

"….and so there ain't nothing more to write about, and I am rotten glad of it, because if I'd a knowed what a trouble it was to make a book, I wouldn't a tackled it and I ain't going to no more. But I reckon I got to light out for the territory ahead of the rest, because Aunt Sally she's going to adopt me and civilize me and I can't stand it. I been there before."   - Mark Twain

LIFE LESSONS LEARNED PEDALING 10,288 MILES AND REFLECTED ON 33 YEARS LATER

When I ended our adventure at the Minnesota border during the first printing of this book, I felt like I left the reader who had traveled with us for about a year, out in the snow and cold. I then added an epilogue. That still left me wanting to leave you with more.   So I finished the book with some frequently asked questions, the corresponding answers and about five or so appendixes. I was now satisfied and so would be my readers, or so I thought.

Something was nagging at me as the positive reviews came in. I still felt as if I had not said everything that was in my heart. Then a reader who loved the book but felt disappointed with the ending had the courage to write and tell me why he finished the book immensely inspired, but unsatisfied. He wanted me to wrap up all of the valuable lessons that we learned along our monumental journey and state them so that he and others could use them in their every day lives. It all clicked.

With that as a backdrop, let me share the top dozen or so lessons, strategies, principles or insights that have made a huge impact for me over this past quarter century plus. There were many more than a dozen, but this list is a great place to start.   Life "lessons" sounds a little condescending, and I don't intend to be. I would actually prefer the word "insights," but the alliteration is so perfect with that "life lesson" combo platter. These insights for me are time-tested and not always executed well or consistently in my life today. They are for you to consider, expand on and discuss, keeping what may work for you and throwing out the rest if they do not resonate with you. We will also check in with Steve and close this final chapter with his top three life-changing perspectives as well.

In no particular order:

LIFE LESSON #1   Clarity = Courage when taking action on your dreams and goals.

"You, my friend, are a victim of disorganized thinking." ~ the Wizard of Oz to the
Cowardly Lion immediately before bestowing him with his Medal of Courage

Steve and I, with the release of our book after all of these years, are once again hearing about how "courageous" we were to have made our journey. We have never accepted that well-meaning compliment very well. Over the years, I have simply come to terms that we were both crystal clear about what we were endeavoring to do. Clarity and focus with my goals, dreams, mission in life, has created courage for me as I have moved towards them. It is one of the biggest life lessons that I learned while pedaling through four seasons over 10,000 miles to achieve my predetermined goals. I have honestly lost my way at times in life, as exemplified by taking twenty-five years to write this book. When I take the time to reflect on my gifts, talents and joys, and then focus on how to best use them in life, my specific plans and goals for achievement bring out my courage.

LIFE LESSON #2   Solitude is a gift from our Creator. Seek to create more in your life.

Smart phones. Ipods. Blackberrys. Radio. Television. Texting. MP3 players. Video games. Laptops. I haven't even begun to identify the necessary human interactions of daily living like caring for the people in our lives and trying to stay calm when our children whine or scream or our spouse needs to vent or the boss needs that report by noon. It is called the noise of the 21st century. And I believe that it is revving up the stress in our lives to dangerous levels. When Steve and I headed out west on the back roads of America, we experienced decompression and peace and gentleness like we had never known. What we accidentally discovered is how much quiet and solitude blesses, calms and restores you. Since I don't have a desire or an empty spot in my schedule today to hit the road for another 10,000 miles (and I'm guessing that you don't either) I need to try to create more solitude in my days. Getting up and NOT turning on the radio first thing in the morning, reading a daily meditation book for a few minutes in complete silence, walking the dog in a nearby woods versus down a busy street every once in awhile. You can figure this out for you too. As a man of prayer, I believe that at least 50% of prayer is listening. If the radio is blasting a recap of last night's ball game, I hardly can complain that my prayers for answers are never coming. I now seek opportunities to create solitude, with again varying degrees of success. I am always more focused, calmer, grateful, renewed and gentler with loved ones and my associates when I do.

LIFE LESSON #3   Deeply value the power of your associations.

"You're a hell of a singer and a powerful man, but you surround yourself with people who demand so little of you." ~ Kenny Rogers

I am not exactly sure when I first heard the above lyric in a song called "Sweet Music Man" by my namesake Kenny Rogers, but it has always stuck with me and lived to the fullest while pedaling across America. You are who you hang with. The music you listen to, the television you watch, the books that you read and the people closest to you will affect all areas of your life. So be aware. Better yet, be vigilant. Pedaling across America for seven months allowed me to be with a like-minded individual who passionately and intimately shared my goals and values, joys and pain. That was huge. But besides my relationship with Steve, we were also partnering with the Make-A-Wish Board of directors and volunteers with a shared purpose and vision of making life a little bit gentler for children and families in crisis. We were aligned with KSTP staff including not only Dick Pomerantz but also his producers behind the scenes, substitute hosts, program managers and others helping us get the word out. The people that we met across America befriended us, assisted us, protected us and encouraged our mission and our safety. Today integrating into society, the workplace and complex families, purposely surrounding yourself with only people who share your values and goals is literally impossible. But you can be aware, as I do today, to limit some relationships, expand others and change viewing and listening habits. I try to surround myself with doers, dreamers, encouragers and positive people. I am also very aware of this principle in the lives of my children and teach them about choices. Far from perfect with this again, it worked almost perfectly 33 years ago on our journey and continues to be the benchmark that I aspire to each and every day.

LIFE LESSON #4 Create a <u>why</u> outside of yourself to carry you through.

Discovering Make-A-Wish of Minnesota was the defining moment of our trip before we pedaled a single mile. It was an intuitive inquiry and decision by me, fueled in part because I needed to make more of a difference in my world. It ended up being a perfect fit that was so gratifying in so many ways. What I learned through all of this is the incredible power of finding a reason outside of myself and my desires to motivate me and keep me on track during the inevitable challenging times that accompany any goal or dream, big or small. Steve and I never allowed ourselves to think that we would not achieve our goal of bicycling all 48 states. Failure was not an option. That is what we believed. We always knew that we could never let down the kids, the families, the people who had pledged their hard-earned dollars, the Make-A-Wish Board and volunteers and even the people we were meeting across America who were inspired by our mission and were praying for and encouraging us every mile of the way. We were being held accountable. Discovering an inspiring cause beyond our desire for adventure made all the difference.

LIFE LESSON #5   Reclaim the outdoors.

All things outdoors dominated my childhood memories growing up in the 60s. Baseball, kick the can, hide-and-go-seek, bicycling to the lake to fish, cops and robbers, cowboys and Indians, catching butterflies, flying kites, ice skating and on and on and on. I don't remember much television, and playing indoors was for rainy days and blizzards. But as I grew older things slowly changed. Priorities shifted to girls, sports, work, homework and driving a car. Outdoors became more of a place I spent time in on my way to somewhere else. As a young professional, I worked hard and played hard but even more of my time was spent indoors. When Steve and I jumped on our bicycles, I didn't even own a sleeping bag. The next seven months we spent almost all of our moments outside.

Outside. Weather. Aromas that overwhelmed us. The warmth of the sun, the refreshing cool rains, the bite of a cool breeze in the mountains. And did I mention the smells? My newfound lesson in all of this was the following. Create more moments, days, weekends, vacations, time by myself, time with my family and friends…out of doors. I am fortunate to live in a small midwestern town where I can still have a campfire in my backyard 365 days a year. When I hold my children in my arms roasting marshmallows and competing in a little contest to see who can count the most stars, I am the happiest man on earth. This is a gift that you can give to anybody, your children or somebody else's children. Let's all turn off the video games, television set, computers, cell phones and get back outside. Together let's at least make an attempt to do so more often.

LIFE LESSON #6 Persevere until you finish what you started.

"Never, never, never, never give up." ~ **Winston Churchill**

There are hundreds of quotes and scores of books written about the power of persevering. My own brother Tom, who visited us in the fall of 2008, made a statement from his heart that I immediately wrote down. *"I don't know anybody who is relentless who has failed." ~* **Tom Rogers** He is absolutely correct of course. Sometimes words and speeches inspire, motivate and encourage us. Sometimes we simply have to live the lesson.

Pedaling for 10,288 miles over seven months proved to me the benefits and confidence gained when you persevere to the end on something that you said you were going to do and then do it. One revolution of my tire at a time got me home. That confidence has stayed with and buoyed both Steve and me for over 30 years. The mindset and pedaling experience was also critical in helping me overcome my insecurity and fears about finally writing this book after starting it over two decades ago. I now can again say that I finished what I started. It is an overwhelming feeling of accomplishment, achievement and confidence that I once again "took it to the house." I am now continuing to benefit from this life lesson on working on my garage, my disorganized office and my next book. The applications in my life have the potential to be everywhere.

LIFE LESSON #7 The secret we discovered and lived before "The "Secret." Be what you want to receive.

The past several years have seen the monumental explosion and several million copies sold of a movie created by Rhonda Byrne called simply, "The Secret." I hope that I don't offend anybody when I say that I have never seen it and have no time nor desire to at this point. Rhonda has defined "The Secret" as the law of attraction, which is the principle that "like attracts like." In my life experience and on our journey across America, this was no "secret."

As the reviews pour in our book, many, many people remark to me via email and more often in person, how wonderful the people across America were to Steve and me. I could not agree more. I have even had a few people remark with astonishment and some disbelief that people actually took us into their homes. I was "accused" by one reader that I must have been embellishing some of my stories. (Not true.)

Here is the lesson that I did not learn pedaling across America, but was deeply affirmed and reemphasized to both of us. Who you are, what you project, the way you treat people, will all come back to you. People were indeed wonderful to us, almost without exception. But guess what? Steve and I were polite, appreciative, kind, authentic, vulnerable and trustworthy with all of them. We lived by the golden rule and very practically treated everyone that we met the way that we wanted to be treated. And very significantly, that is also the way we treated each other. It wasn't a game or a strategy. That is simply who Steve and I were, always have been and will continue to be. We trust people. We try our best not to judge people. We give folks the benefit of the doubt. We are thoughtful, personable, humble and engaging guys. And those are the kinds of people we met in almost every state of the union, regardless of color, sex, religion, age or occupation.

People challenge me today and declare that our trip took place 30 years ago and that if we left today, things and people's reactions would be radically different. "There are more drugs and crazies out there now!" I am told. Maybe it's the idealist and optimist in me, but I honestly don't believe that is true. I'm betting that pedaling the back roads of America tomorrow (with my arthritic knees and replaced right hip, and probably taking a few more months) I would meet the idealists and optimists of the country. It still is a pretty wonderful world out there.

And that is no secret to Steve and me.

LIFE LESSON #8 Get moving. Today.

I will make this life lesson, as critically important as it is, short and to the point. ALL OF US NEED TO GET MOVING! Get moving as in our bodies! Get off the couch, turn off the television and go take a walk, a bike ride, a jog, a trip to the health club for 30 minutes, mow the lawn, chop some wood, play hide-and-seek with the kids at the park (or with each other as Steve and I did!) but move our bodies. The older we get, the more we seem to go from vehicle to home to vehicle to work to vehicle to the grocery store, etc. Bicycling from sun up to sun down for seven months will NOT fit into most people's schedules. I get that. But at now 63-years-old I am so sold on the benefits of getting back in shape, losing those extra pounds, feeling invigorated again in all areas of my life. Our ability and huge window of time to get in such superior shape on our journey was a wonderful, wonderful gift and byproduct of our adventure. This is a tough lesson for me today with my aging bone-on-bone knees, young family and busy lifestyle but one I will not quit on. Join me in finding something that you enjoy and consistently do it. Our health and the quality of our lives depend on it.

LIFE LESSON #9 Together we can - The power of a diverse community.

This was one of the more significant lessons that I learned while engaged in this mission of ours. I will always remember the many newsprint media interviewing us as our miles pedaled grew to become eye-popping numbers for their readers. Again, Steve and I were given accolades for making this journey happen and for the money that we were "single-handedly" raising for sick children and their families. Nothing could have been further from the truth.

Although Steve and I were getting the press and congratulations on an almost daily basis during the second half of our trip, original Make-A-Wish Board members Kermath Ward was back in Minnesota volunteering his time addressing boards of companies looking for more funds and public relations and Karla Blomberg was interviewing potential Make-A-Wish children and their families in their homes. Board members, close to 200 Make-A-Wish volunteers, Chairman John Rubel doing talk shows spreading the word, Dick Pomerantz keeping the mission in front of his listeners, thousands of dollars pledged by hard-working Minnesota men and women, friends and family praying for us, "strangers" across America feeding and housing us. Steve and I? We were only a part of a community of selfless strength, heart and resolve coming from all parts of the county from all kinds of people from all walks of life. The lesson in all of this? Once you commit to a worthy cause, project or goal, people will come out of the woodwork to help you accomplish your objective. I need to keep in mind that as an independent business owner I have resources and alliances and people more than willing to help me with the drop of a hat. We rarely accomplish great things in a vacuum. People want to believe in purposeful projects, people and dreams. Tap into it. Share your dreams, your plans and your goals. Enjoy the miracle of enthusiastic support and encouragement.

LIFE LESSON #10 Create dreams big enough to discover your greatness

In 1967, I set a passionate goal to make my high school freshman football team. As a fourteen-year-old clumsy and uncoordinated sports dweeb, my goal was not to start or even to do well, but to simply make the team. Back in those days I am not sure if they cut anybody, but I stuck out the incredibly physically demanding practices and made that squad. That was the first of many goals that I set and eventually achieved as a young man. I understood the power of achieving a difficult and challenging dream or goal. The power came from digging down deep and discovering resources and a mental, emotional, physical and spiritual toughness that I did not know that I had in me.

Years later at the age of 28 when Steve and I shook hands on bicycling all 48 states, I intuitively knew that I was in way over my head. This decision and ultimately all the things that I needed to do to survive this monumental challenge forced me to summon every skill, personal relationship insight and strength that I had developed inside up to that time. Seven months after we weakly bicycled west from St. Paul in the summer sunshine, we triumphantly pedaled back into a frozen Minnesota victorious.

What I learned in that process is that I did not know how capable I was. I had no idea how far I could push myself in every area of my life. What I really discovered is that we are all so much more talented than we believe that we are. In the ensuing months I made a decision to never be fearful of dreaming huge dreams or pursuing seemingly outlandish goals. Big dreams and big goals bring out the best that our Creator instilled in us. No matter how long it takes me to achieve the dreams and whispers of my heart, I will not be afraid and I will always believe that if I have the dream or goal, that I also have everything I need to accomplish it already within me, along with my unfolding community.

LIFE LESSON #11 Commit, get started and watch the miracle unfold.

As I said at the outset, these "lessons" or insights are in no particular order. But this one is a real winner and one I exemplified to the point of ridicule and embarrassing humor. Once Steve and I shook hands to take on this adventure, the world seemed to speed up. Everything was happening at once. As you know from reading the book, I bought my bicycle about one week before we were to leave. I never physically trained. I could not change or repair a flat tire on the day that we left. I rode out of town under the watchful eyes of television cameras representing the 14th largest media market in the United States with dirty clothes in my backpacks and a sincere prayer that I not fall off of my bike at least until they turned off the cameras. My point in all of this? YOU DON'T HAVE TO HAVE ALL THE ANSWERS OR EXPERIENCE BEFORE YOU DO SOMETHING SIGNIFICANT! JUST GET STARTED! This does not mean that you want to purposefully be reckless or dangerous or stupid and/or unprepared for no reason. It simply means that you don't have to have all of your ducks in a row before you start or do anything. Had I been in better shape, better prepared, bike repair trained, it all would have of course helped. However not having any of those skills did not stop me. Don't let not being 100% ready, prepared, unafraid or unsettled ever stop you from taking action on your dreams or goals.

LIFE LESSON #12   Seeking success makes me stressful, while seeking significance makes me joyful.

"The place God calls you to is the place where your deep gladness and the world's deep hunger meet." ~ Frederick Buechner

When I first sat down with Steve, and I vented my frustration with work at Starr Office Services, I realized that I was not doing what God had created me to do. Over the years I have come to love the above quote.   If you are not a very spiritual person, it still makes sense that making a living doing something you love and the world needs would be incredibly fulfilling. That is really what I mean by doing something significant, or meaningful or purposeful. Seeking success is emphatically different than seeking significance. When I realized that I was only chasing income to take care of my basic financial needs versus using my unique God-given talents to make a difference in people's lives, the lights went on.   That is why for years I have told audiences around the country that my bicycling America for Make-A-Wish wasn't particularly courageous or noble. It was simply what I was supposed to do and consequently loved doing.   It involved all of my talents, skills and passions…working out, the outdoors, adventure, camping, meeting new people, freedom, raising funds and awareness for a very worthy cause, working with the media (My BA degree was in Radio, Television and Photography), journaling at night and taking photos during the day preparing for one day inspiring and encouraging people with my writing and multi-media shows…I was doing what I was designed to do and I was joyful and peaceful. It was emphatically worth the time to figure that all out.

Have you ever bought a dozen donuts or ears of corn? The "good guys" always throw in one more just to make sure they have delivered value. So, here we go:

THE BAKERS DOZEN/CORN STAND EXTRA LIFE LESSON

When you work at work and play at play, it really is sweet both places.

One of my mentors, the late, great Jim Rohn, told the story of the executive working at his office wishing that he was at the beach with his family. He finally goes to the beach with his family and spends his time thinking about things he should be doing at the office. Or closer to home for me, as my mom always says, "Wherever you are, be there!"

This principle really hit home as we pedaled the country. I remember some of our savage climbs inching up mountains out west, perspiration dripping everywhere, quadriceps burning, and our lungs gasping until we finally reached the top. Then we quickly discovered that we always got to "blow" down the other side of the mountain, breeze whipping and cooling our damp bodies, effortlessly flying down into a cool valley. We worked and then we played.

Many days in all parts of the country were challenging with weather, sweltering heat, devastating cold, white-knuckle traffic battling 18-wheelers blowing by literally inches from our fragile and vulnerable bicycles. But at night we camped under the stars, made new friends, enjoyed wonderful meals some nights (not always!) and after a really hard or wet or cold day, treated ourselves to a motel room. Those were some sweet nights well deserved.

To this day, I love to work hard and focused during the day and enjoy my evenings with family and sometimes with my friends. My down time, my family time is always the most fun, relaxed and "sweet" when I know that I have put in a good, solid day. Work at work and play at play. It's the only way to go.

I called Steve and he enthusiastically responded with a few ideas that have really worked for him over these many years. Let's see what he wants to share with you.

STEVES THREE LESSONS

I sit here under blue bird sunny skies at my home Lake Vermilion writing these thoughts. Life is good.

The story of our bicycle trip is over 33 years old, and as Ken and I thought when we first started writing it, the story remains timeless.

Lesson # 1 FIRST RULE OF THE ROAD "THE TIRED OR HUNGRY MAN IS ALWAYS THE BOSS."

This simple rule Ken and I had adopted early on in our bicycle trip has been invaluable in helping maintain marital harmony in my 29-year marriage to Lori.

We have changed it slightly. "The tired or hungry spouse, or the one who has to go to the bathroom is always the boss."

If we're at a party and one of us is ready to leave, we leave.
If we're on a trip and one of us has a bladder that is ready to burst, we stop.

This is a simple, easy, and considerate rule. I know that a lot of people have a challenge with this. But I highly recommend this to any couple. It works.

Lesson # 2 WE ARE ALL INSIGNIFICANT – AND THAT IS GOOD!

By this I certainly don't mean we are insignificant in God's eyes. The feeling that I am significant to Him gives me great comfort every day.

My insignificance to my fellow man is what I'm talking about. All those nights Ken and I spent under the stars out west, all the traffic that blew by us out east, and all the miles of desert we saw stretched out in an endless ribbon before us made me feel so small and unnoticed, but I absolutely loved it.

I think that a lot of us have struggled with trying to "make our mark" on this world. I probably even thought making my mark was important at some time in my life. Not anymore!

My insignificance in the over all scheme of everything in the universe totally takes the pressure off. Sure, I still worry about things, but when I can take a moment and recapture this perspective of insignificance, nothing seems to be that big of a deal.

Lesson # 3 YOUTH IS GOOD. ENJOY IT.

I have had the great fortune in the last 25 years to meet and befriend many young men and women in their early to mid twenties. They are facing the same issue I was at their age. "What do I do with the rest of my life?" I never have an answer for that but I have told every one of them to be aware that they are young. Enjoy it. They will eventually figure the rest out.

Well that is really, finally it from Steve and me. Thank you for hanging in here throughout our entire journey. On some level we are connected now, although I may never know your name. But as I close, what are you going to do now with all of this new information?

Instead of putting this book back on the shelf, I really hope and pray that you consider doing something even more special in your life. I hope that our journey inspires and encourages you to reconsider a dream that you let go of years ago. Maybe you have always thought of doing a walk for breast cancer or a bike ride for MS. My sister Mary and her husband Mark just got back from Haiti having helped the victims of recent hurricanes. Maybe there is a neighbor down the street who is alone and would simply love you to stop by with some homemade goodies. My wife Robin shared three plates of her homemade chocolate chip cookies with widowed and hurting neighbors yesterday.   The fact that it took me 25 years to finish my book maybe has inspired you to finish that Afghan that you started five years ago. The possibilities are endless.

Consider doing something significant or that you have procrastinated on for way too long and then email Steve and me at www.pedalingonpurpose.com and we promise to send you words of encouragement and eventual congratulations.

May our book be a new beginning for you.

Steve closes out with his final thoughts…

My last thoughts:

Almost on a daily basis something comes up that reminds me of our excellent adventure. Any time news happens in any state (except Hawaii and Alaska) I wonder if I was in that town or how close to that town I was. Any time I fly somewhere in this country I look down and know that I will at some point be flying directly over a place where I was a tiny speck on a stretch of road 30 years ago.

That little bike trip I took with my best buddy Ken is a big part of who I am today. It has given me confidence that anything is achievable. I know that when I die, it won't be long before memory of me fades away. I don't care. No worries here.

Mel Gibson said while portraying William Wallace in the movie Brave Heart, "All men must die. But not all men have lived."

Well, I've lived. And so has Ken.

TRIBUTE TO KATIE CAMPBELL

Katie and her brother Christopher
The fall before she was diagnosed with cancer

"Thank you for saving your story and for sharing Katie's inspiration in your story. We all want to know that our lives have meaning and purpose. You shared an important part of your lives with us and let your readers know that Katie's little life also had a purpose.

I read your book-cover to cover-on this 25th anniversary of your return and of Katie's wish for a 6th birthday party. Your book will be a gift to all of our family and friends.

Thank you for caring and thank you for your friendship."

~ Craig and Nancy Campbell
Parents of Katie, February 24, 1977 – February 15, 1983

Let's continue to honor precious Katie's legacy, as we reach out to courageous children like her with life-threatening medical conditions and their families, with our hearts, prayers, time and treasure.

FREQUENTLY ASKED QUESTIONS

After hundreds of question and answer sessions immediately following our multi-media presentation on our bicycling adventure, I have a pretty good handle on what people are curious about. Now that the book is out, I am getting even more. I am going to answer six questions here and then you can go to my website at www.pedalingonpurpose.com for several more questions and answers that I believe you will find fascinating, educational or at least fun. Let's start with the number one question that is always asked.

ARE YOU AND STEVE STILL GOOD FRIENDS?

Steve and I have maintained a very close and special friendship over the past 34 years. We've been told that our time on the road could be compared to going to war and doing foxhole time together. I have too much respect for our military to agree completely with that analogy, but by surviving adversity side-by-side, we have indeed bonded in a very unique and lifelong way.

For the first 11 years upon returning from our 48-state pedaling adventure, we lived within about a half-mile from each other and saw each other most every week. I was honored to be the best man at his wedding with Lori, and he is now the Godfather of my only daughter Amanda. Although he and Lori now live over a five-hour drive from me and we don't see each other as much as we once did, we are still child-like and pumped whenever we get the chance to be together.

AFTER SHAKING HANDS ON YOUR ROOF, DID YOU AND STEVE EVER DO ANOTHER ADVENTURE TOGETHER?

I'm glad that you asked! As a matter of fact, we did. In 1994, Steve and I attempted to be the first to ever negotiate a man-powered watercraft UP the entire length of the Mississippi River. We actually hydrocycled on HYDROBIKES; a bicycle frame constructed on two pontoons that drove a propeller instead of wheels. It turned into a very dangerous and life-threatening trip and one that we did not complete our goals. We did, however, Steve at age 42 and me at 41, pedal over 1,000 miles up the Mississippi under enormous stress and odds. That book is scheduled to be released in July 2017. You can stay posted about how and when to order by going to my website at www.pedalingonpurpose.com

We are now in the very early planning stages for our third and probably final adventure, tentatively scheduled for around 2020. We will both be in our late 60s, proving once again that being a "couch potato" is a choice that you do not have to make at any age!

WHERE IS STEVE NOW AND WHAT IS HE DOING?

Steve achieved another one of his life-long ambitions by moving to northern Minnesota where he and Lori bought a beautiful home out in the country near Lake Vermilion. He is continuing a long and distinguished career in sales; currently working for a company called Street Smart Rental and has his own business selling Hydro-Bikes on the Internet. Hydro bikes were the unbelievable machines that propelled us up the mighty Mississippi River on our second adventure in 1994. Steve and Lori celebrated their 29th wedding anniversary late last year in 2016.

Steve can be reached at funwatercraft@yahoo.com

WHERE IS KEN NOW AND WHAT IS HE DOING?

I live in a little town just north of Rochester, Minnesota with my wife Robin, sixteen-year-old daughter Amanda and thirteen-year-old Andrew (making a baby at 50-years-old as I did is an "adventure" all of its own!). We also have a 29-year-old soon to be married son, David, who returned from his deployment with the Army National Guard of Minnesota overseas in Kuwait. We remain very proud of him. After a very "circuitous" career path in sales, speaking and business ownership, I am now devoting all of my time to writing, creating information products, fundraising and speaking engagements around the world.

I can be reached at kcrcourage@aol.com

HOW MUCH MONEY DID YOU EVENTUALLY RAISE FOR MAKE-A-WISH WITH YOUR PEDALING OF ALL 48 STATES?

After all of the concern, eventual focus, sometime frustration and overwhelming desire to "finish strong," I honestly do not know what the final collected pledge total was! My best guess is that the number was between $20,000 and $25,000. All I know for sure is that in retrospect, everybody connected with Make-A-Wish, especially the Board members and all of the many selfless volunteers, did all that they possibly could do to contribute to a successful bicycling fundraiser. We all followed our hearts and tried to do the right thing. We learned on the fly and would certainly do an even better job with pledges and publicity if we had the opportunity to turn back the clock and do it all over again. I will always be proud of everybody who was involved those first days, especially Dick Pomerantz who "rallied the troops" and got this all off the ground, and then the management and support staff at KSTP-AM radio who all contributed to making those first wishes come true for some very special children and their families.

WHAT HAPPENED AFTER YOU CROSSED THE BORDER? I FELT SORT OF DISCONNECTED AND NOT READY TO PUT YOUR BOOK DOWN.

I did not mean to leave you literally and figuratively out in the snow and cold after following us for about a year and a half and almost seven months on the road. Sorry about that.

The Minnesota border crossing was in fact the crowning moment of the trip, and everything else felt anticlimactic. Steve and I bicycled another 25 miles or so over the next two hours back to the KSTP studios in St. Paul. It was a nondescript final stretch drive, as we both bicycled in relative silence, basking in the sensory overload of the border reception. We eventually pedaled back to the exact spot from the east that we had pedaled west from seven months ago. That was an emotional moment that we thankfully shared by ourselves. In the back of the KSTP building they had the traditional ribbon ceremony that we bicycled through and ripped for the local television network coverage, as scores of well wishers, family and friends cheered wildly. The best part was a bear hug from our beloved Dick Pomerantz. I loved that man. The rest of the day was a surreal fog of radio and television interviews, celebration with friends and riding in the torchlight parade over the streets of St. Paul.

We ended the night with a gathering of our closest friends, simply enjoying the security of being together again.

The hardest part of our entire trip was waking up Monday as I say in earlier interviews, as "unemployed bums." The language that I used was obviously accurate, but the reality was much more terse and challenging. The world awoke on Monday and went back to work and we awoke and were literally lost. I could write another book on this reality alone. The best thing that we eventually did was to set a new major goal for a second trip someday, which really helped us through the expected but huge emotional and mental letdown.

TRIP NUMBERS AND FUN STATISTICS
DOCUMENTED BY "STATS" ANDERSON

902 The number of towns that Steve and I bicycled through.

107 The hottest temperature that we endured

80 The largest number of towns we bicycled through in one state, Illinois

42 Total flat tires between us

25 The number of pounds that Ken lost on the trip

24 The number of days it rained on us bicycling

14 The number of pounds that Steve lost on the trip

11 The number of our tires that either **wore out** or eventually exploded

10 Total number of broken spokes between us (*NOTE: Ken had all 10!)

8 Days in a row that we did not bathe – a trip record

5 The number of Make-A-Wish wishes granted through the day we returned

4 Snowstorms or blizzards that we bicycled through

2 Number of bicycle frames Ken used to get back home

-24 The coldest temperature that we bicycled in and through

UNOFFICIAL TRIP NUMBERS

1,284,305 Rough estimate of squished animals we saw over 10,288 miles

6,000 Average number of calories we burned daily

703 Number of Big Macs Steve estimated we ate. Seems high to me!

THE 902 TOWNS THAT WE PEDALED THROUGH
LISTED AT WWW.PEDALINGONPURPOSE.COM

My greatest respect and admiration goes out to "Stats" Anderson, who unbeknownst to me for several years compiled all 902 towns while we were bicycling the country! I don't know how nor when in the heck he did it!

In preparing this list, I have spent many, *many* painstaking hours checking Steve's notes for errors of any kind. I have had to refer to atlases, state maps, google searches and satellite map technology only to discover that Steve was accurate about 99.2% of the time 28 years ago! This particular document was a true labor of love from both of us that I hope you enjoy.

MINNESOTA

Rockford
Buffalo
Aberdeen
Maple Lake
Annandale
South Haven
Watkins
Eden Valley
Paynesville
Regal
Georgeville
Belgrade
Brooten

Partial listing. Full list at www.pedalingonpurpose.com

If you enjoyed this book, check out my website for lots of fascinating and fun information. There are colored slides from the trip, inspiring quotations, updates on my speaking engagements, new books and multi-media projects and most importantly, coming soon, opportunities to network and share with like-minded folks trying to make a difference in their communities. I would also love your feedback and to have the opportunity to encourage each other as we continue to journey together. **Let's inspire one another!**

THE FASCINATING HISTORY AND PHENOMENAL GROWTH OF MAKE-A-WISH AND HOW YOU CAN CONTRIBUTE

The Make-A-Wish Foundation® traces its beginning to one little boy's wish in April of 1980. All of his life, 7-year-old Christopher James Greicius (pronounced "gracious") of Phoenix, Arizona dreamed of becoming a police officer. He often drove around his neighborhood on a battery-powered three-wheel motorcycle writing tickets and putting them on unsuspecting cars!

Chris was being treated for leukemia when U.S. Customs Officer Tommy Austin befriended Chris and his mom, Linda Bergendahl-Pauling. With Chris's health sadly deteriorating, he planned a day to lift his spirits.

On April 29, 1980, Austin and a caring group of Arizona DPS personnel took Chris on a helicopter tour of Phoenix and then flew him to headquarters for a tour. He sat on a patrol motorcycle, "drove" a police car while on an officer's lap and was given a Smoky Bear hat and a badge. Finally Chris was given a certificate and sworn in as the first honorary DPS patrolman in Arizona history. It was an incredible day for everybody involved.

What happened then was another sequence of events that transpired more by chance than by design. Sergeant Schmidt, Officer Ron Cox and others, realizing that there had never been an honorary DPS patrolman before, contacted John's Uniforms and the owner and two seamstresses agreed to work through the night on a custom-tailored DPS uniform for Chris. The officers presented it to Chris on May 1st, along with a motorcycle "proficiency test" to earn his wings to pin on his new uniform. Needless to say he passed the test with flying colors on his battery-operated motorcycle.

Two days later Chris passed away, but not before seeing his dream come true and experiencing the hope and profound joy that came from receiving his life-long wish of becoming a police officer.

Chris was buried in Kewanee, Illinois and Arizona Department of Public Safety spokesman Sergeant Allan Schmidt committed two Arizona officers to make the trip to Illinois to say goodbye to Chris, Scott Dahl and Frank Shankwitz.

It was obvious to everyone who surrounded Chris and his mom Linda during those final days how much the special wish unfolding serendipitously appeared to take away the pain and anguish from both mom and son and replaced them with some relief and light-hearted moments. If this unplanned wish had brought this much joy to Chris and his mom, maybe they could do this for other children. By January 1981, the Greicious Make-A-Wish Memorial, founded by Linda Bergandahl-Pauling, Frank Shankwitz and Scott Stahl received its tax-exempt status as a non-profit organization and began fundraising in earnest. The non-profit memorial later became the Make-A-Wish Foundation®.

On February 4th, 1982, the Dick Pomerantz Show on KSTP-AM in St. Paul called Sergeant Schmidt and aired the show that I heard sitting in my car after a sales call. It forever changed my life along with thousands of others. At that time, Chris Greicius and only nine other wishes had ever been granted. Five months later, immediately following Linda Bergendahl-Pauling telephoning encouragement to all of us in Minnesota on the air, Steve and I, Dick Pomerantz and the Chairperson of Make-A-Wish John Rubel were sitting in KSTP's studios raising approximately $4,000 for the first wishes through listener's pledges. **MINNESOTA WAS THE SECOND MAKE-A-WISH CHAPTER IN THE WORLD**, thanks to Dick Pomerantz's passionate plea within seconds of Sergeant Schmidt's' phone call and his spearheading efforts in the ensuing months. Men and women like Bruce Furu, John Rubel, Kermath and Mary Beth Ward and many others called in those first two days as I did and got this slowly moving forward. I recently read a copy of the original volunteer list that called in to Dick's show. I saw the name, Tom Reid, former North Star professional hockey player, and a sweet older woman who stated, "I have no money and I have no time to volunteer. But I can pray!" Remarkable. It indeed took all of us to make this work.

Steve and I bicycled back into Minnesota on February 5th, the same day that Minnesota's fifth wish was being granted to precious little Katie.

Today, 30 years later, the Make-A-Wish Foundation ® of Minnesota has granted over 3,000 special wishes, averaging about 200 wishes a year. As an international organization, the Make-A-Wish Foundation® has granted over 233,000 wishes as of this writing in the winter of 2013, **now averaging a special wish every 38 minutes!** They have over 66 chapters in the United States and they are in more than 30 countries on five continents, easily the largest wish granting organization in the world.

"It's been over 30 years since my son Chris received his wish, and I am still amazed and inspired how one little boy's dream to be a policeman has touched the lives of so many people."

~ **Linda Bergandahl-Pauling, mom of Chris Greicius**

If you would like to contribute your time or money to the Make-A-Wish Foundation® of Minnesota go to: www.minnesota.wish.org/contribute.html or to find your local chapter anywhere else in the world go to: www.wish.org/help/donate

If you purchase **Pedaling on Purpose** from me or from my website at www.pedalingonpurpose.com I will donate a percentage of my profits from the purchase price to the Make-A-Wish Foundation®, and whenever possible I will donate the money to the chapter nearest to where you live.

Although there are many, many worthwhile groups in the world that need your money, I cannot think of a more worthwhile organization to donate your time or your money. Almost 80 cents of every single dollar goes directly to granting the special wish. Inasmuch as we all continue to pray for cures that help our precious children, unfortunately the need today is endless for finding and helping children with life threatening medical conditions and their often emotionally and financially devastated families.

To order more copies of <u>Pedaling on Purpose</u>, to inquire about discounts on multiple copies for fundraising or group events or to contact Ken Rogers to ask about his speaking availability, please go to:

www.pedalingonpurpose.com

You can also go to the website to post a comment, view colored slides from the trip, ask questions and to get connected with other like-minded people. A free newsletter will also be available in January 2017.

Ken Rogers, adventurer, entrepreneur, speaker and author has the unique perspective of 38 years in sales, management and business ownership, as well as completing two extraordinary record-breaking journeys. A decade after their unprecedented bicycling adventure, Ken and Steve pedaled on a Hydrobike over 1,000 miles upstream against the powerful and life-threatening Mississippi River. Over the years he has presented keynotes, programs and workshops to non-profit organizations, national associations, companies, universities, schools, churches and other diverse audiences. He currently resides in Pine Island, Minnesota with his beautiful wife and precious two young children. He continues to write and speaks all over America.

Ken can be reached by calling 507-202-7054 or emailing him at kcrcourage@aol.com

"I expected to read a book about a bicycle trip-even an adventure. And it was that! But what I encountered was an incredible story of a friendship, and of personal accomplishment. Two "blood brothers" with a purpose greater than themselves, just regular guys that give hope to ALL of us regular guys out here. I laughed, I cried, I felt your moments of fear and triumph as if I was stowed in a sidecar with you. Your readers feel the scorching desert heat, the bone chilling cold of Wisconsin and best of all get a glimpse into the soul and the character of this great country. Thanks for the ride guys! ~ **Paul "Pigeye" Jackson**

"I was absolutely captivated by your book and adventure! Once I started reading I found it very difficult to put down. Thank you for such a motivating story. Miracles are possible and a good adventure is never out of reach." ~ **Lorri Rennie**

"What a fantastic, inspiring book! In these days of corporate greed, shady politics, economic unease, shallow pop-stars and lousy newscasts, it was heartening to read about two seemingly average guys, doing something heroic and altruistic. A hero is someone who is admired for their achievements and qualities. They fit that description perfectly. Now time to dust off my 25-year-old TREK bicycle, do a couple of stretches and hit the road..." ~ **Jon Klinkenborg**

"Congratulations on a best seller. I have not read a book that has moved me this much in many years. I felt like I was with you on this trip. You are truly a gifted writer! To make a person feel so many emotions; I loved it...The first night I read until I was halfway through the trip. I knew that I would have to put it away for a while or not sleep until I finished it and my family would not eat. So now I am done and as with any great book I wish it would not end. I can't wait for your next book! Thanks for the ride. ~ **Shirley Peterson**

"I really enjoyed your book. There's a reason that stories about cross-country travel are a tradition in American literature – there's just something compelling about the promise of the open road. I have to say that my favorite sections of your book are those in which you and Steve have doubts about finishing the trip you started together. Conflict is the essence of great drama, and seeing whether or not a friendship can survive such a long and arduous trek is the emotional heart of this story. It's what keeps the reader reading. Again, thanks for your very compelling book." ~ **Nick Stanton**

"Kenny, your book is amazing. I could just imagine myself right there with you, but not nearly as strong as you ☺. Whenever I find myself in a tough situation where I just don't think that I can do it, I always think of you and Steve and it just inspires me and uplifts me. Your book is so wonderful and encouraging that I hope everybody gets a chance to read it." ~ **Jennifer Hauschulz**

"In addition to gaining a better understanding of the logistical and physical side of riding 10,000 miles, the book offers accounts of people, situations and challenges that transcend the trip mission itself. You provide important life lessons, which are particularly relevant today. I know that was your intent all along and you succeeded in every way. More than a good book, a great story…" ~ **Rick Palmer**

"Let me tell you that I'm not a real avid reader and usually pick a book that isn't quite as thick but as I began to read, I knew that I would easily get through this one. This book is unbelievable! As I was reading, the laughter (and I mean bellowing) just kept coming. Then, as I turned the page, the tears would start welling in my eyes and a feeling of "this should be a movie" kept coming to me. I can't seem to put the book down for long." ~ **Patty Knoblauch**

"I loved this book! What a great book to read to get outside of yourself. Ken has an easy, understated and humorous way of storytelling. It was easy to feel the obstacles, disappointments, and also the joys and triumphs that Ken has so aptly described. I read this book for a couple of months right before bed. It always put a smile on my face and gave me peace even if I had a bad day. The whole undertaking was such a big goal with such little chance of success. To carry through with such a dream which then became a goal was inspiring. Ken and Steve showed how taking each day at a time can make daily struggles tolerable and that sometimes what looks like struggles can be seen as opportunities. The physical struggles were many and were well described. It was the mental and emotional struggles that were for me, more interesting. This book was inspiring and celebrates life and what is good in people. Thanks, Ken for getting it down on paper." ~ **Jeff Millen**

"Wow. I have to say your book was one of the most inspiring books I've read in quite a while. The humor and sense of wondering what's going to happen next made it nearly impossible to put down…I know that I am a better person because of your influence." ~ **Scott Miller**

"Once I started reading your book, it was difficult to put down...I came away impressed with the adventure/mission, but more importantly your telling of it. There is an honesty to your voice that is compelling and attractive. You have done something really good here. But most impressive for me, is your having done it after all this time. You had every opportunity to self-recriminate and bemoan the lost opportunity, but you invested the time to make sure this story could outlive your own life. Well done! Thanks for blessing me with the book." ~**Thomas James**

"I couldn't put the book down and read the whole thing in two nights. What a great story." ~ **Bob Deiley**

"I received Pedaling on Purpose in the mail today and at page 248 I am going to call it a night. It is a very easy read. Ken your writing style just flows like you were sitting right here telling the story and Steve's added insight on the trip completes the story. You both take the reader along for the ride...just finished the book and GREAT JOB! Thank you for sharing your adventure." ~ **Ron F.**

"I must say Ken and Steve that in my 'heart of hearts' your book is a winner. I laughed, cried and thoroughly enjoyed every minute of my marathon reading experience. I couldn't put it down! I will be sharing it with my two adventurous, twenty-something sons, friends, relatives, book club members, colleagues, coffee friends, neighbors, church friends, the cashier at the grocery store, the mailman...and anyone else who wants to enjoy an incredible tale of adventure and commitment to a cause. Thanks!" ~ **Mary Jo Schimelpfenig**

"This is a wonderful book celebrating an accomplishment that most people just think about doing or say that someday they will accomplish...but these two put financial reward, love and family on hold for the rest of us to benefit. They have impressed me not only as friends, but also as adventurists and as human beings. They left behind goals, dreams, and aspirations for the future generations, to really participate in life and do something that will better the world for being here like they have. God bless them and their families." ~ **Tom McNamara**

"Incredible book. Very inspiring. Your book was passed on to me by... who bought it at your book signing at Lake Vermilion. He said that I would really enjoy it and he was right. I can't even imagine the hardships and thrills you guys must have experienced along the way. Congratulations! Your book has really got me thinking." ~ **Jeff Swenson**

"Your book was great. It took me awhile to find the time to read it, but once I started I couldn't stop. I was amazed at how well written it was and how you could just draw someone into the story. Through the whole book I felt like I was right there enjoying the adventures with you guys. I think it was wonderfully written and one of the best books I have ever read. Can't wait for the next one!" ~ **Nicole Weiss**

"Each and every comment others have entered about this thrilling story accurately describes my own sentiment. Kenny and Steve fulfilled their dream of biking the 48 states, and it was kicked in gear by a reason, Make-A-Wish. Pedaling on Purpose is a thrilling, heartwarming, inspirational and adventurous story! With each page I turned, I kept seeing their story in movie form." ~ **Vivian**

"God is giving us wonderful messages through you and Steve. What an inspiring book; one of the best I have ever read. It is a great book for all ages and I encourage all to please share it with the young and old alike. Thank you both for giving encouragement to all of us. Heaven knows our world is a bit tough right now and by reading your book it renewed me and my mother, Dorothy. Her faith in people, purpose and God were restored and renewed...Simply, reading your story felt good."
~ **Alan Myers**

"I finished your book a couple of days ago and it was GREAT!!!!! You did an excellent job of compiling both of your stories together and kept it a page-turner. Of course, every day for you guys was a page-turner!
~ **Jeanne Gearhart**

"I finally had a chance to read your book, cover to cover, and what a great book. I was drawn in as the story went on, and what an amazing journey it was that you described. You are a gifted storyteller and I loved the various stories about people, situations, challenges and successes. I was so impressed by your destiny, that this book was a launching point to larger things...I intend to buy...copies so I can share it with my staff and drive a discussion/conversation around the key points of the book." ~ **Ken V.**

"I honestly felt like I was with you guys when I was reading the book. I sometimes complain when I have to change a flat tire! That must have been awful dealing with bike problems...The Make-A-Wish kids were very lucky to have the two of you working for them...God bless you for this and for how wonderfully you treat people..." ~ **John Priyatel**

"Just finished your book...you two had a ride together! The drama of the drudge of day-in, day-out jumping on those little metal horses of yours, mixed in with the twists and turns, the fantastic people and places you encountered, and of course the joy of keeping each other smiling- was a great read! Your Odyssey was truly fun to witness through these pages. Congrats to you both! And especially to you Ken: I do know a thing or two about how hard it is to write a book and not only did you complete the task, but you made it heartwarming, inspiring and readable on every page. Gentle winds..." ~ **Tom McNally**

"I deliberately read a little each day, not wanting to end this one too quickly...What strikes me most was your commitment in bicycling for such long hours to reach 'unreachable' goals almost every day, regardless of some pretty fearsome conditions. Your great friendship with Steve, which developed into a precious comradeship (we in Australia would call that Mateship) was enviable, and your commitment to Make-A-Wish inspirational. I think the great attitude and response you encountered from most of the people along the way had to be due mainly to your trust in God's favor, whose blessing on your trip was so obvious. How people yearn to encounter people like you, hopefully prompting a lifted vision: 'Wow, maybe I could do something that could make a difference too.'" ~ **Barbara Ridyard**

"An incredibly exciting account of an amazing journey by two exceptional men for a most worthy cause." ~ **Kent Allen**

"...I just couldn't put your book down. By Chapter Six I only read with a box of tissue as it tugged at my heartstrings. Thanks to Make-A-Wish we met the Campbell family in 1983. Katie and Amy were diagnosed at almost the same time with brain tumors at the same age. Katie was wish #5 and Amy was wish #7. I am not too good at putting thought into words but what you and Steve did for Make-A-Wish was no less than miraculous. Amy's wish was so fun for our family at such a stressful time in our lives with a critically-ill child, a toddler and a newborn baby. Today Amy is 31 years old, happy...she doesn't remember much about the surgery and treatment, but she sure remembers every part of her wish. I savored every paragraph and enjoyed reading about every mile of your ride. ~ **With Much gratitude, Mary Lilyquist"**

"It was very inspirational and motivating to see how God worked in your lives and all the lives you and Steve touched along the ride through the 48 states." ~ **Paul Zilka**

Unsolicited **Pedaling on Purpose** Reviews
From "regular folks" posted on my website:

"A wonderfully-inspiring book. I tip my hat to two unselfish young men whose unbelievable accomplishment not only satisfied their own quest for adventure, but in doing so, made a huge contribution to the then fledging "Make-A-Wish Foundation" that has continued to flourish to be a huge success today. Also their warm and personal encounters along the way with Americans everywhere, have rekindled my pride in America." ~ **Bob Bruno**

"What a great book and great accomplishment! I hadn't read a book for pleasure in many years, only business related material. When I started your book, I couldn't put it down. I finished it in one weekend. It was thrilling, exciting, inspirational and challenging…Can't wait for the next one." ~ **Fred Majerus**

"I was captivated with the book, a truly wonderful story, told with such feeling. I laughed, cried and felt part of the adventure. Tears of joy fell from my eyes as you returned to Minnesota, as if I was standing on the crest of that hill celebrating your arrival 25 years ago today."
~ **Gale Hendrickson**

"Your book was amazing. I stopped reading <u>One Minute Millionaire</u> and just read your book. I enjoyed every bit of it! What an amazing thing to have done and I can't wait to hear what you do at 60. I was very inspired by the people you met and how you grew during your journey. I thought it was well written, with lots of great anecdotes and humor.
~ **Karen Robertson, Australia**

"Your stories restored my faith in the heart and soul of the USA and its people." ~ **Denny Stoterau**

"My wife read it first…then when she finished and told me it was really, really good. I started reading it and had a hard time putting it down. I haven't read a complete book for over 20 years…I read the whole book in about three sittings. It was most enjoyable to read and brought out a lot of emotions. ~ **Ted and Sharon Jacobson**

"This book is easy to read but hard to put down. After reading this book it will be hard to imagine life without miracles." ~ **Barry**